THE MAKING OF A MISSILE CRISIS:
OCTOBER 1962

Other Books by Herbert S. Dinerstein

Fifty Years of Soviet Foreign Policy

Intervention against Communism

War and the Soviet Union

Communism and the Russian Peasant

THE MAKING
OF A MISSILE CRISIS:
OCTOBER 1962

HERBERT S. DINERSTEIN

THE JOHNS HOPKINS UNIVERSITY PRESS
BALTIMORE AND LONDON

The Johns Hopkins University Press, Baltimore, Maryland 21218
The Johns Hopkins Press Ltd., London

Originally published, 1976

Johns Hopkins paperback edition, 1978

Library of Congress Catalog Card Number 75–36943
ISBN 0–8018–1788–9 (hardcover)
ISBN 0–8018–2146–0 (paperback)

Library of Congress Cataloging in Publication data will be found on the last printed
page of this book.

To my wife, Rita

 **CONTENTS**

O what a tangled web we weave
To guard the myths that we believe.

 **PREFACE**

Originally I planned to bring up to date and expand to book length my article *Soviet Policy in Latin America* published in *The American Political Science Review* in March 1967. Very soon it appeared that the formative period of Soviet policy in Latin America offered more interest to the investigator than the later years in which the Soviet authorities applied the lessons they had learned from 1954 to 1962. It also appeared that an understanding of Soviet policy required a better knowledge than I possessed of the new theaters in which the Soviet authorities elected to act, and it became necessary to examine the events in Guatemala in 1954 and the events in Cuba after 1958. Thus, while reducing the years covered, the scope of the study was broadened and it became a study of international relations rather than a study of Soviet policy alone.

The space devoted to the different problems is not proportionate to their intrinsic importance. The extensive literature on American policy permitted brief, and perhaps brisk, treatment of that subject. The materials available for the study of Soviet behavior are quite different in nature. They yield a satisfactory record of Soviet actions but very little about the political process in the Soviet Union. However, they do permit the reconstruction of the development of Soviet beliefs about the international situation in general and about the situation in Latin America in particular. Sometimes it is possible to indicate the differing views held on these subjects by Soviet officials and to see that Soviet statesmen, like others, are plagued by doubts and divided in counsel. These glimpses of the stuff of Soviet politics, rare and tantalizing as they are, furnish a useful corrective to the image that Soviet leaders like to put forward and thirst to believe, namely, that Marxism-Leninism provides a complete explanation of politics and that good Marxists can always agree on the correct course at any juncture.

In the period covered by this book the Soviet, North American, and Latin American actors had quite different appreciations of the political events in which they all participated. These appreciations often owed more to preconceptions than to reality, and the theme of this essay is the slow and partial victory of reality over stubborn faith.

Because this is a study of changing political beliefs, I have drawn as much as possible on contemporary materials. *The New York Times, Pravda,* and *Noticias de Hoy* are preferred to the works of interpretation and the memoirs written after the events precisely because of their immediacy. I have found that the reporters of *The New York Times* presented an accurate picture of the views held in Washington and that the Soviet and Cuban press did the same for Moscow and Havana. This does not diminish the debt I owe to the extensive secondary literature on the subject, which has furnished me with the questions to address to the source material. I have not made a practice of listing the occasions on which I have differed with points in the extant secondary literature because it would be tedious for the reader and because in many cases the views are ones I myself held at an earlier stage of my investigation.

I am responsible for the translations except where I have given credit to others. In this edition the text of the book, except for the correction of some typographical errors, remains unaltered. However, I have added as Appendix 3 the full text of Khrushchev's letter of 26 October 1962 to Kennedy. At the time of the first printing I did not know that it had been published in the *Department of State Bulletin* for 9 November 1973. A statement of its effect on the argument of the book is appended

The Tinker Foundation has supported me very handsomely during the period of intensive work on the manuscript. My colleagues at the Johns Hopkins School of Advanced International Studies relieved me of my teaching duties for a sabbatical year and furnished me with a most useful criticism of chapter 6 in a faculty seminar.

Piero Gleijeses generously shared his special insights on the events in Guatemala. Eric Willenz has read the whole manuscript and this time has again made available his vast knowledge of the international communist movement. My colleagues share the credit for this work; but of course, I am responsible for its failings.

I must acknowledge my debt to the staff of the Library of Congress, strapped by limited funds and harried by importunate readers, who have helped me in my search for materials with complete efficiency and unfailing courtesy. Miss Linda Carlson of the SAIS library has been resourceful and imaginative in locating research materials. Michael White performed invaluable editorial assistance and checked the references. René Harris typed the manuscript.

THE MAKING OF A MISSILE CRISIS: OCTOBER 1962

 **1. THE GUATEMALAN CRISIS**

On 17 March 1954, the U.S. Department of State announced that an important shipment of arms from behind the iron curtain had reached Guatemala, whose government had been infiltrated by communists. The security of the United States was in danger. On 22 October 1962, President Kennedy announced that the presence of Soviet ballistic missiles in Cuba constituted a threat to the peace of the world that the United States could not tolerate. This book will examine the connection between these two events, starting with an examination of politics in Guatemala in 1954 and concluding with an analysis of divergent Soviet strategies in the missile crisis of 1962. Emphasis will be placed on the different ways in which the major actors perceived the main events of this period. Only by reconstructing how the various actors understood the situation at each stage of its development can we understand their actions.

For John Foster Dulles, the activities of the left-leaning president of Guatemala, Jacobo Arbenz now supported by Soviet military aid, represented an instance of communist expansion that had to be and—what was probably decisive—could be scotched. For the Soviet leaders, or some of them, the survival of a reformist Central American government over which native communist leaders exerted considerable influence meant that American power was being undermined in its strategic rear at a time when it was too dangerous for the Soviet Union to make a direct assault. For the noncommunist left in Latin America, whose own experience had convinced it that communists were sometimes useful allies who could be exploited and then discarded, the events in Guatemala demonstrated that the cold war had again made the United States an enemy of Latin American national self-assertion.

The overthrow of the Arbenz regime led the Soviet Union, the United States, and the Latin American communists to much the same conclusion: the United States could dominate political developments in Latin America as a whole and particularly in the Caribbean. Hence the Soviet Union lost interest in Latin America, and the communists of that continent were confirmed in their belief that a passive strategy of waiting was the best.

Four years later neither the Russians, the Americans, nor the Cuban communists believed that Fidel Castro was a serious contender for power until shortly before he assumed it. During the first year of his regime, Castro continued Fulgencio Batista's policy of nonrecognition of the USSR, and the Soviet Union, for its part, confined itself to verbal support of the new Cuba. Castro soon revealed himself to be more radical than the Cuban communists, and as he moved leftward he lost the middle-class supporters who had been the mainstay of his movement and replaced them with individual communists. This produced fears in Cuba and in the United States that Castro had been a secret communist or that he was converting to that cause. The Soviet Union maintained its distance from Castro until the U–2 fiasco of May 1960. Up to that point, the Soviet leaders had hoped that they could wring concessions from President Eisenhower on the German and other questions and had accordingly refrained from embroiling themselves in the Cuban-American dispute, which was becoming increasingly bitter.

Feeling that they had little prospect of persuading the United States to acquiesce in their purposes, the Soviet leaders shifted to a policy of thwarting the United States wherever they could find a suitable instrument. In the second half of 1960 the most promising candidates for such use were Patrice Lumumba in the Congo, Souvanna Phouma in Laos, and Castro in Cuba. The first effort miscarried, but the second two bore early fruit. Now Khrushchev began to employ the menacing rhetoric about missiles, which had thus far failed to move the Americans on the Berlin question, to support the Cuban regime. In July 1960 he stated that an American invasion of Cuba *could* bring in its train a world war in which nuclear weapons would be employed, and at the end of October he practically said that the Soviet Union *would* employ nuclear weapons to protect Cuba.

In the United States, as the electoral contest between Richard M. Nixon and John F. Kennedy reached its climax, the two contenders competed in expressions of revulsion for the progress of communism in Cuba and determination to do something about it. Khrushchev's missile threats were largely ignored by those to whom they were addressed, but Castro, at least publicly, set great store upon them. On 16 April 1961 Kennedy executed the plan contrived by his predecessor for the overthrow of Castro by Cuban exiles. Before Kennedy finally rejected a proposal for direct American military participation in the venture, Khrushchev repeated his promise to offer Castro "all necessary aid." Thenceforward Khrushchev professed, and probably believed, that the USSR provided an effective nuclear shield for Cuba's independence.

Even before the Bay of Pigs invasion Castro had espoused his own brand of Marxism, according to which middle-class leaders like himself were to lead the peasants to revolution all over Latin America, with the proletariat and their communist parties playing only a minor role. With surprisingly little demur the Soviet leaders accepted this radical revision of their version of Marxism. Now a noncommunist leader could execute a successful national revolution and transform it into a socialist revolution by an act of personal conversion. Heady vistas of a new cycle of the establishment of socialist states were opening up.

The Soviet leaders said, and believed, that the United States was in retreat all over the world. In response, the Kennedy administration in the fall of 1961 asserted that the United States still enjoyed a preponderance of nuclear power, leading the Soviet Union to consider the military advantages that Cuba's location offered. At the beginning of 1962 Khrushchev and the Soviet government formally asserted that they had as much right to overseas bases as the United States and claimed that they possessed the power to enforce that right. This claim was largely ignored by the United States. In the early part of 1962 the Soviet Union and Cuba agreed to locate Soviet medium and intermediate range missiles in Cuba —a measure that would have gone far to compensate for the Soviet inferiority in delivery vehicles for nuclear weapons. Khrushchev and Castro believed that if the United States had been deterred from a direct effort to overthrow Castro in April 1961 by the threat of the employment of Soviet nuclear power, the actual presence of such force on Cuban soil would guarantee U.S. passivity. Kennedy, on the other hand, believed that the presence of missiles in Cuba would constitute a radical shift in the balance of power and that, consequently, he had no choice but to seek their removal at some, or even considerable, risk.

Mutual misperception had brought the great powers to the point of confrontation. In the last chapter of this book the argument is advanced that some elements of the Soviet polity, notably the military, felt that the Soviet conception was sound and that if the Soviet Union stood its ground, the United States would yield. Khrushchev, when he realized that he had deceived himself about Kennedy's beliefs, pushed for retreat and carried the day. The divergent Soviet strategies are analyzed in detail in the light of all that had happened until then. As always, the indispensable tool in the analysis of texts is their context, and therefore the bulk of this book is devoted to establishing the context of the events of October 1962.

THE GUATEMALAN SCENE

The beginnings were commonplace—a change of regime in a Central American state. On 1 July 1944 a popular revolution unseated the dictator Jorge Ubico, who handed over the reins of government to a triumvirate. Events did not follow the usual pattern—the assumption of dictatorial power by a general. Instead, Juan José Arévalo, an exile who had been a university professor in Argentina, became president in the wake of an unsuccessful army attempt to overthrow the new provisional government. Some of the military, notably Arbenz, the man who was to succeed Arévalo, supported him. The Guatemalan revolution of 1944–45 was a pseudo-revolution in that the basic political forces in the country did not change. Parts of the army acquiesced in the reforms as long as they were not too radical.[1] Like many Latin Americans of his generation, Arévalo knew what he wanted but not how to get it. He wanted freedom, economic progress, and above all, independence from foreign domination, i.e., from the United States. He believed that all Latin America and especially Guatemala had been subjected to shameful foreign domination. His views are readily available in a best-selling polemic against the United States published after the overthrow of the Arbenz regime.[2]

The depth of Arévalo's hatred for North American domination is expressed in the following passage: "Servility sometimes arises from sexual desire, from love of the powerful male, the servile citizen lamenting that he is not a true female in order to give himself and be possessed literally. . . . I have heard of homosexuals who actually have served as Ambassadors in Washington, but I do not know whether they have rendered physical service to the Secretary of State or to a President of that great nation."[3] One should not dismiss this passage as an egregious example of bad taste. It expresses rage at powerlessness and contempt for Latin American politicians who serve what are believed to be North American interests. Often what North Americans view as mutually beneficial cooperation is perceived by Latin Americans as shameful servility. Arévalo, although anti-American, was hardly procommunist. In 1947 he denounced communism as an alien doctrine but as less dangerous than Falangism. He said that "Falangism is not only an anti-democratic but also an insulting doctrine for Latin American countries. . . . Communism as a doctrine is innocuous but communists with political power are a danger in Europe and a shadow over the future of the American continent. . . . We don't have to ask Russia, Czechoslovakia or Chicago how to improve the life of our workers in Malacatlán, Chiquimulilla or in San Jerónimo."[4]

Arévalo moved slowly. Only his successor, Colonel Arbenz, carried out an agrarian reform, and he had no plenitude of power. A faction of the military tried several times to depose him. During Arévalo's presidency Colonel Francisco Javier Arana, an aspirant for the succession, was killed in mysterious circumstances. As is common in states under weak civil authority, the beneficiary of such a murder is automatically charged by his opponents with its instigation. The factual basis for such charges is usually impossible to determine, but the charge of political assassination dramatized the division of the Guatemalan military. Arbenz maintained himeslf in office by keeping the loyalty of part of the military and by beginning to politicize union labor and the peasants.

Arbenz started his land reform in the manner that has become traditional in Latin America—by expropriating the properties of foreigners. (The former dictator, Ubico, established a precedent when he confiscated the large plantations owned by German nationals during World War II.) The Guatemalan government consistently maintained that the land reform law was not specifically directed against the United Fruit Company but was a general law that applied to all, including foreigners. But the United Fruit Company owned large tracts including reserves of uncultivated land—a particular target of the law. (The banana crop was vulnerable to a disease that could only be controlled by abandoning the land for a few years, necessitating the transfer of the crop to another place.) Thus United Fruit felt itself to be the target of the land reform. Arbenz was careful not to confiscate the lands of army officers, and some of them even benefited from the land reform.

Arbenz, like many leaders of backward countries, could call upon only a few educated people to help in the reform program. Prominent in this small group were communists who had recently been permitted to operate as a party. One of them, José Manuel Fortuny, a close personal friend of Arbenz, was in charge of the land reform program and another, Victor Manuel Gutiérrez, was the leader of the confederation of trade union organizations. Consequently, many believed that Arbenz was a communist sympathizer. We shall probably never know what his political philosophy was or if he indeed had a systematic political program. In fact, when subjected to U.S. pressure to get rid of the communists in his government, he stuck to his friends and to his principles. From the North American point of view this demonstrated his sympathies for communism. For the noncommunist left in Latin America it demonstrated what they already believed: that the United States would use its power to unseat governments that sought to effect social reform.

There had been many attempted coups d'état during Arévalo's term of office, and they continued into Arbenz's term. Naturally, Arbenz sought to broaden the base of his political support and could ill afford to dispense with the communists who not only supported his program of agrarian reform but also were willing to work for it. A severe leftist critic of communist mistakes reports that the communists were not personally dishonest. "The leaders of the PGT (The Guatemalan Labor party, i.e., the communists)," he wrote, "did not enrich themselves—a generalization which does not apply to the leaders of other parties. . . ."[5] Given the paucity of able and honest people, Arbenz could not easily have rejected the help of such people even if he had wanted to. The communists did not expect to come to the stage of building socialism for a very long time. On this point their public statements and the internal documents of the communist party are completely consistent.[6] The Guatemalan communists felt, like the Russians and the Chinese, that the best policy at that stage was to enlist the support of the bourgeoisie against the more backward land owners. In the struggle to accomplish "the task of the democratic revolution," opposition at home and abroad was expected. But neither the Guatemalan nor the Soviet communists, who occasionally voiced their views, believed for a moment that socialism was being established in Guatemala. The more sanguine may have hoped that the bourgeois revolution could be quickly completed and the next stage readied. If there were such views, no records, not even private ones, have been left.[7]

THE LATIN AMERICAN VIEW OF U.S. CHARGES AGAINST GUATEMALA

The Latin American left, which comprises all political groupings opposed to military dictatorship, including political figures with a rather moderate program of social reform, made up its mind about the events in Guatemala on the basis of much less information than is now available. It was convinced that the Guatemalan land reform was a genuine democratic land reform, and it dismissed or ignored the charge that President Arbenz was a tool of the communists. Many Latin American countries had had experience with their own communist parties, and in every case they had turned out to be easy to dominate and even to exploit. Therefore, little credence was given to the notion that these weak forces were in a position to take over a government that rested, in the last analysis, on the military.

The files of the Mexican magazine *Humanismo* serve to document the view of the noncommunist left. The contributors to this magazine and its editor after July 1954, Raúl Roa—then an anticommunist and later the Cuban foreign minister—were representative of Latin American exiles opposed to dictatorship and the United States. It is noteworthy that this magazine always carried paid advertisements from the Mexican government oil company, so that the views of the magazine reflected the views of at least some high officials in the Mexican government. The magazine reported at the end of 1953 that the American capitalists were advising right-wing groups in Guatemala to organize and stop the advance of communism but that the real purpose of the Americans was to frustrate social justice. When in the summer of 1953 the State Department complained about the confiscation of the property of the United Fruit Company, *Humanismo* concluded that "the North American government has returned to the times of direct intervention and to colonialism in its relations with Latin American states." In December a writer in the magazine characterized anticommunism as a pretext for opposing all kinds of reforms and argued that there were only four communist deputies out of the fifty-four members of the Guatemalan Parliament. The author asked rhetorically whether the White House believed that it could win the sympathy of the Hispano-American people and the battle against Red fanaticism by relying on the most irresponsible enemies of the dignity of man in Latin America. Didn't Washington understand that by underwriting the insatiable greed of Wall Street and its discredited Latin American allies it was only sowing the seeds of a bitter fruit that would turn all Latin America against the United States?[8] These predictions that the U.S. government was about to abandon the Good Neighbor policy were promptly confirmed, and the prophets naturally believed that they could appraise U.S. intentions quickly and accurately.

The Guatemalan government announced at the end of January 1954 that it had discovered a plot to overthrow it. Offering photostatic copies of correspondence, the government revealed that Castillo Armas, an opponent in exile, had written to the son of the Nicaraguan dictator, General Luis Somoza, that the government of the North had encouraged him to overthrow Arbenz. Armas claimed that the Guatemalan government was moving toward communism and that the Honduran and Salvadoran governments and their friends in Santo Domingo and Venezuela were inclined to help them. Two days later the U.S. Department of State denied the existence of such a plan. The accusation, of course, caused a sensation in Latin America, and when several months later troops crossed the borders with air support as outlined in the revelations of 29 January 1954, the credibility of the U.S. government reached zero.

In the midst of these charges and countercharges the Tenth Inter-American Conference of the Organization of American States (OAS) was convened in Caracas, Venezuela, at the behest of the United States. The United States insisted on putting the question of "the intervention of international communism in the American Republics" on the agenda. The North Americans contended that communism was a menace to all of Latin America. The Guatemalan foreign minister, Guillermo Toriello, rejected this charge, arguing that his government had made the first genuine reforms in Latin American history—the best method for countering communism. For its troubles it had been rewarded with the label "communist." Every national movement and every attempt to assert independence was classified as communist, as was every antiimperialist or antimonopolist action. Those who call democracy "communist" destroy democracy, Toriello said. Guatemala had been subjected to an economic boycott. This tiny republic was called the bridgehead of communism and was charged with being a menace to the security of the whole continent. Toriello went on to argue that the international policy of any country was its own affair and to put it on the agenda of the OAS was an unequivocal act of intervention. He attacked the United States directly and said publicly what was in so many Latin American minds and what had appeared in so many Latin American newspapers, namely, that the United States was going through a stage of antidemocratic obscurantism in the form of

McCarthyism and that the U.S. resolution before the OAS on Guatemalan communism reflected this obsession.[9]

Although only Guatemala voted against the resolution, and Mexico and Argentina abstained, the general impression was that the United States had suffered a severe defeat. In the past the United States had not met with much opposition at OAS meetings, and the feeling was widespread that many delegates voted with the United States because of threats of economic reprisal. At any rate, the Caracas conference posed the question sharply. The United States contended that communism was a danger in Guatemala. The Guatemalans denied it, accusing the United States of using communism as a pretext for interventionism. It may be noted parenthetically that political victories of this sort are very expensive. Latin Americans who sympathize with David defying Goliath and who then, for reasons of prudence, have to vote with Goliath, are often filled with deep feelings of shame and disgust at their own powerlessness, which is readily converted into hatred for the United States.

THE U.S. APPRAISAL OF THE GUATEMALAN CRISIS

The U.S. view of the situation in Guatemala differed widely from the Latin American view. One must recall the atmosphere of 1954 to appreciate the pressures on President Eisenhower and Secretary of State Dulles. The Republican party had scored some points with the electorate by charging that the Democratic party was soft on communism and had negligently, if not treasonably, permitted it to expand. Employing such arguments in the electoral campaign, the Republican party gave hostages to Senator Joseph McCarthy, who had elected himself the main proponent of such charges and whose political career had battened on intemperate and inaccurate accusations. The victory of the Republican party, far from reassuring Senator McCarthy, made him even more reckless, and he seemed to be on the point of accusing his own party of treason. Eisenhower and Dulles did not oppose this uncomfortable and dangerous ally directly, but allowed him to destroy himself by his own excesses. But the Republican administration was careful to present a public image of staunch anticommunism—a posture that did no violence to its private convictions.

At the very time that the crisis in Guatemala was coming to a climax, the Eisenhower administration, after painful consideration, decided not to substitute its armies for the French armies that had been defeated in Indochina by a nationalist coalition led by the Communist party of Indochina. Within the Eisenhower administration there was deep division as to whether or not the United States should intervene in Indochina with large forces, and the decision not to do so was made over the opposition of the chairman of the joint chiefs of staff, Admiral Radford, Secretary of

State Dulles, and Vice-President Nixon. Eisenhower skillfully managed the situation so that the veto seemed to come from the British and the Democratic leadership in the Senate, then in the hands of Lyndon B. Johnson. Eisenhower was of course not procommunist, but he was a man of prudence and caution. His own military experience and that of many generals with whom he had served argued that large-scale involvement of American troops on the mainland of Asia would fail and that the United States could not turn the French failure into victory. But Guatemala was close to the United States, tiny and feeble. Indirect methods and pressures might well succeed. Given the menace of McCarthy and the bitter reverse in Indochina, it is no wonder that the opportunity to nip Guatemalan communism in the bud was seized upon.

In the panicky atmosphere of the fifties, the success of the communists in Czechoslovakia and China was ascribed to the marvelous efficacy of communist intrigue. The devil had special magic denied to the virtuous. For the conventional wisdom that the strong usually prevailed over the weak, a belief in the efficacy of conspiracy was substituted. This belief submerged the obvious facts that communism had triumphed in Petrograd in 1917, in Belgrade in 1945, and in Peking in 1949 because the existing regimes had been smashed in war and that communism had been imposed in the Eastern European states because the Red Army was in occupation.

Many who should have known better were convinced that a handful of communists could seize power in Guatemala simply because they were communists. These simplistic views were accepted as obvious truths, not requiring much examination, by the secretary of state and the president.[10] But the working-level specialists in the State Department understood the situation in terms that, on the whole, meet the test of time. A contemporary estimate argued that the prospects of the Guatemalan communists were poor because the party was so dependent on the good will of the Guatemalan government, particularly of its president, and required at least the neutrality of the Guatemalan armed forces into which the Communist party had made no palpable inroads. The party cadres were green and had absorbed little Marxist doctrine. Furthermore, the noncommunist political groups supporting Arévalo and Arbenz had a large component of opportunism, some of it characterized "by a good deal of uncomprehending lip service to communist slogans and much real concentration on graft and political chicanery. The PGT is in a minority position where failure to manipulate these anarchical currents to its advantages [sic] might result in its being overcome by them."

As communist assets, the writers of the State Department memorandum noted (1) that Arbenz could not get rid of the communists without emasculating the program to which he had dedicated himself; (2) that the opposition to the communists was not organized; and (3) that as the agricultural program was implemented, the communists would gain.[11]

President Eisenhower said in a press conference that "to have the Communist dictatorship establish an outpost on this continent to the detriment of all the American nations, of course, would be a terrible thing. . . ."[12] Such expressions of American fear of communism in Central America were dismissed as hypocritical by Latin Americans who had little respect for the communists they knew.

HOW THE SOVIET UNION SAW THE GUATEMALAN SITUATION

In the Soviet Union the strength of foreign communist parties was more realistically assessed than it was in the United States, and therefore the Soviets, too, were inclined to dismiss the American statements of alarm as hypocritical.

The Soviet press began to scout the possibilities of opposition to the United States while retaining its longtime position that the United States would not be thwarted in its basic purposes. One Latin American specialist wrote that although American private investment in Latin America was increasing rapidly, opposition to such investment was growing. Washington, it was argued, installs dictatorial regimes headed by its stooges. "It is enough for any of these dictators to betray the slightest sign of independence for him to be immediately replaced, usually through an engineered *coup d'état* by a more pliable American tool." As we shall see, this view of extensive American power was soon to be modified in the Soviet press. The article concluded by arguing that the United States, in order to offset the antagonism that was increasingly being expressed in Latin America, had clapped the label of "communist" or "communist menace" on every government leader who came out in defense of national independence and had even plotted to overthrow the government of Guatemala—a plot that was scotched in good time.[13]

The same author, writing a month later, in March 1954, noted that the United States had only won a Pyrrhic victory at the Caracas conference because the myth of the solidarity of the American states had been dispelled. He quoted a good deal from the Latin American press to demonstrate that the delegates showed more independence than ever before despite the fact that some of them behaved like lackeys. One of the signs of the growing independence of the Latin Americans was their demand for trade relations with the socialist countries and the creation of stronger working class organizations in alliance with the peasants, who were creating the necessary conditions for the future development of the national liberation movement.[14]

A month later the tone became even more sanguine. Washington had suffered a serious moral and political defeat, and "the opposition put up by the majority of the Latin American countries to the United States on a number of fundamental issues testifies that their political leaders cannot ignore the urge of their peoples for deliverance from the imperialist oppression. The moral and political defeat sustained by the United States at Caracas is therefore an objective reflection of the spread of the national liberation movement in Latin America."[15]

In May of 1954 a book review appeared in *Kommunist,* the organ of the Communist Party of the Soviet Union (CPSU). This journal devotes the bulk of its space to internal matters and ideological questions, and Latin American affairs have always had slight claim on its space. Therefore, a long review condemning a scholarly book on Latin America indicates either that policy has changed as a consequence of a new appraisal of the situation or that policy has changed after a sharp conflict of opinion. The polemical quality of this review favors the second reason in this case. Since one of its authors, A. Sivolobov, was in charge of the secret school for training Latin American communists in the Soviet Union,[16] it seems likely that the article represents the success of the party apparatus in changing an appreciation of the situation made by academic specialists.

M. V. Danilevich, the academic specialist, had written: "If anywhere the U.S. monopolists are met with anything that can even remotely be termed opposition from the governing circles of the Latin American countries, if they believe that the president or the government conducts a pro-American, anti-popular policy with insufficient servility, then their agents carry out a lightning coup."[17] The party journal argued, on the contrary, that the United States was on the defensive, as demonstrated by the Bolivian and Guatemalan land reforms and by the "disaster" of the Caracas conference. "The time has passed when Wall Street, unopposed, inspired and executed coups d'état in Latin America." Now, in the second stage of the general crisis of capitalism, the forces of national opposition had become strong enough to oppose the United States successfully in a number of cases. Recent attempts to overturn the governments in Guatemala, Argentina, and Bolivia had failed because of the opposition of the masses. Danilevich was mistaken in believing that Latin America was a U.S. patrimony; she underestimated the force of the nationalist opposition in Latin America. The communist parties of the area based their struggle on a realistic appraisal of the situation, and their first task was to create a bloc of the working class peasantry, the urban petite bourgeoisie, and the national bourgeoisie. It was not true, as Danilevich argued, that the large bourgeoisie, some of the middle national bourgeoisie, and the wealthy peasants were allied with the pro-imperialist capitalists.

In other words, the situation was ripe for an alliance, including almost all sectors of Latin American society, against the United States. The hapless Danilevich also failed to demonstrate that the communist party, through the working class, was already supporting the peasant by concrete actions. The review ended by charging the Academy of Sciences with unsatisfactory work. Underneath this cloud of standard communist political language, a genuine meaning lurks. A party official views scholarship as a political weapon rather than as an analytic tool. If the goal of the party is to push for a worker-peasant alliance in the pursuit of a national liberationist movement, then the scholar must demonstrate that the peasant is already benefiting from the working class even if the data for that conclusion is scanty. The book review shows that the party officials responsible for the affairs of Latin American communist parties concluded that the United States was on the run in the area and that the time had come to encourage opposition to American interests.[18]

The high level and official nature of the new appraisal was revealed when a prominent party leader wrote a major article for *Pravda* in the same vein. The United States, wrote the vice-chairman of the Supreme Soviet, O. Kuusinen, realizing that opposition to its exploitation was growing, had responded by slandering the USSR. At the Caracas conference, when Dulles tried to bend the Latin American states to his will by raising the threat of the interference of international communism in American affairs, he was greeted by "a very significant silence." But U.S. interference in Latin American affairs predated the very existence of the USSR. Dulles recognized the growth of nationalism in Latin America when he remarked, before the Caracas meeting, that if North Americans were not careful they would read in the newspapers one fine day that the same thing had happened in Latin America as had happened in China in 1949. Dulles's alarm had a genuine foundation. The countries voting for the U.S. resolution against Guatemala at the Caracas conference did so only from fear of U.S. economic sanctions, but on many other issues the United States was defeated.[19]

Since Kuusinen had been responsible for the affairs of the international communist movement for many years, his signature on the article indicated that at the highest level, the CPSU had accepted the optimistic estimate of the party specialists on Latin America and had rejected the more sober outlook of the academic specialists. But the party specialists were indulging in an outburst of euphoria that was to be repeated after the Bay of Pigs, as will be described later in these pages. In 1954, a Central American regime considered unfriendly to the United States could be overthrown in a twinkling. But the euphoria was only slightly premature. Five years later Cuban nationalism was to challenge the power of the United States and meet with success. In Guatemala, for the first time (except for Czechoslovak arms sales to Israel in 1948) since World War II, the Soviet Union made military equipment available to a backward country in conflict with the United States or one of its Western European allies. Stalin did not help Mossadegh in Iran or Nasser in Egypt when the latter first challenged the West. The sale of arms to the Guatemalans was never admitted by the USSR. In later years the Soviet Union would advertise its delivery or sale of arms to countries in conflict with the great powers, convinced that this would enhance Soviet political prestige.

The sale of arms to Guatemala was apparently poorly organized. Captured German World War II equipment, much of it not in working order, was dispatched to Guatemala. What was in working order was otherwise unsuitable: the cannon intended to be moved along German highways were useless in Guatemala.[20] On subsequent occasions the quality of weapons furnished by the Soviet Union was improved and provision was made for training the recipients in their employment.

One can only speculate as to why the Soviet leaders decided to encourage the enemies of the United States in this way at this time. Stalin had been dead for only a few months and a battle for the political leadership of the Soviet Union was underway when the decision to help Guatemala was made. The Soviet leaders were painfully aware that U.S. military power had grown very quickly since the outbreak of the Korean War, putting the Soviet Union in a strategic situation much less favorable than that of 1950. The greatly increased U.S. military budget had improved the regular U.S. forces and the strategic forces in particular. Now, in 1954, the United States could inflict a massive nuclear attack on the Soviet Union within a very short time after the decision to do so had been made. By contrast, in June 1950 a mobilization period of several months or a year would have been required to strike a similar blow. Nuclear weapons were in short supply; the B–47's were not ready, nor were their crews trained. Even though the United States had a nuclear capability in 1950, it had to be mobilized. As in World War II, a considerable time had to elapse between the outbreak of war and the application of the weight of fire power directly to the enemy. Now it was much more dangerous to make miscalculations like the Berlin Blockade or the instigation of the North Korean attack. Indeed, in January 1954, Mr. Dulles warned that this new strategic nuclear force might be used immediately in the event of a fresh aggression like Korea.

Between 1953 and the early sixties, the disparity between U.S. and Soviet strategic forces was at its greatest. The United States seemed to be moving towards the right wing internally, and its secretary of state regularly emitted puffs of anticommunist rhetoric. The Soviet leaders, however, were confident that their relative military position would improve markedly in several years. This appreciation suggested caution and the creation of a better political climate. Indeed, the Soviet Union pursued such a policy in Europe and in its direct relations with the United States. But was such reserve and caution necessary elsewhere? Soviet leaders, like others, modify or abandon long-held assumptions (axiomatic truths) slowly. They were still guided by Lenin's work on imperialism, which argued that the imperial powers derived much of their economic strength from the exploitation of colonies. If decolonization could be accelerated by Soviet verbal encouragement and material assistance, the inevitable crisis of capitalism could be brought somewhat closer. Although this was a long-term strategy and its effects would only be reflected in the international scene gradually, it was the only prudent way to put pressure on the United States, given the unfavorable military balance.

In the political circles of Moscow, optimism fulfilled a special function. In the bitter political struggle taking place between G. M. Malenkov, V. M. Molotov, and N. S. Khrushchev in the latter part of 1953, when the decision to make arms available to Guatemala was probably taken,[21] different views of foreign policy were propounded. The Korean and Indochina wars were quickly brought to an end. But in Europe, the North Atlantic Treaty Organization (NATO) had been transformed into a formidable military force. The Soviet leaders could only look to improving the situation in Europe when the military relationship between the Soviet Union and the United States would have been brought into some balance. In such an atmosphere a low cost, almost risk-free action in the Caribbean was difficult to oppose. Whatever group proposed it could expect to reap political benefits in the internal power struggle by plucking a few of the American eagle's feathers. The opposition could hardly have argued convincingly that it was dangerous for the Soviet Union.

THE CRISIS ERUPTS

The course of the crisis, largely as seen by contemporaries, will be described in the next pages. The documentation for a detailed account of the events is lacking since U.S. and Guatemalan official records are not available. But the following account, incomplete and perhaps even inaccurate in some particulars, represents contemporary understandings of the situation, and these views were the basis of the main assumptions that guided the political actors in 1959 and 1960.

By January 1954, Guatemalan diplomats were reporting plans to employ refugees to attack Guatemala.[22] In April the New York Times reported that the U.S. ambassador in Guatemala, John E. Peurifoy, had submitted a series of recommendations for dealing with the infiltration of acknowledged communists at high official levels and at strategic places in the governmental machinery. The correspondent reported that although the ambassador's recommendations had been kept secret, there was considerable speculation that other Central American countries, fearing communist infiltration from Guatemala, might be prompted to take some sort of multilateral action either under or beyond the Caracas resolution.[23]

Meanwhile, in Guatemala itself, the situation was becoming tense. The government had threatened internal radio stations that were broadcasting anticommunist messages. On 21 April one such station was invaded by an armed band of unknown men who beat up some of the personnel. Somewhat later, the Guatemalan Confederation of Labor complained to the government that a clandestine radio transmitter, presumably operating across the border, had called on the people to rise against the government.

On 17 May the crisis suddenly assumed grave proportions with a State Department announcement that an important shipment of arms from communist-controlled territory had arrived in Guatemala. The State Department was alarmed because the Guatemalan government had been heavily infiltrated with communists. The account went on to say: "There was some puzzlement here [Washington] about the destination of the arms since the Guatemalan Army is generally considered the main restraining force limiting the influence of the Communists." This reassuring reflection was soon to be lost sight of. The *New York Times* then reminded its readers of the fact, repeatedly noted in Latin America, that without a formal embargo, Washington had forbidden shipments of U.S. arms and aircraft to Guatemala.[24] (The account might have added that Washington had also been successful in stopping the shipment of arms from its allies to Guatemala.)

Later the Guatemalans complained that since they had then been denied access to normal sources of arms, they had to seek them behind the iron curtain. Sidney Gruson reported on two occasions that the U.S. outcry against the dangers presented to the continent by the Guatemalan acquisition of arms from the USSR had only attracted support from elements opposed to the government. Guatemala had long been trying to purchase arms in the West to replace its antiquated materiel, so the army was delighted with the acquisition of new weapons, wherever they came from. Arbenz's position had been strengthened as a consequence. Although there was some speculation that the government wanted to use at least part of the arms to equip the workers and farmers as a balance to the army, most of the officers saw no present danger from communism.[25]

On 25 May Secretary of State Dulles pointed out that although the Guatemalans were patriotic and as a whole not communists, the danger was great. Guatemala was the only country that had voted against the Caracas resolution and the only nation to receive a massive shipment of arms from behind the iron curtain. Dulles stated that "the extension of Communist colonialism to this hemisphere would, in the words of the Caracas resolution, endanger the peace of America."[26]

News stories indicated that the arms had apparently been purchased in Czechoslovakia and had been shipped from the Polish port of Stettin.[27] According to reports, the Guatemalans felt that the cause of the crisis was the dispute with the United Fruit Company; they could not believe that the United States was really exercised about communism. Czechoslovakia was close to the Soviet Union, the Guatemalans argued, and Guatemala was close to the United States. The army was overjoyed by the arrival of the arms, and the shipment caused no concern to the officer corps, "upon which, in the long run, the power of President Jacobo Arbenz Guzmán must rest." On 28 May the *New York Times* reported that an unidentified plane had dropped leaflets over Guatemala City. The Guatemalan foreign minister said that if leaflets could be dropped, other things could be dropped, too. The leaflets called upon the people to rise up and overthrow the regime.[28] Most Latin Americans believed that these planes came from the United States and that American pilots flew them.

The Guatemalans refused to believe that the United States was really concerned about communism, although, "without so formally expressing himself, Mr. Peurifoy has let it be known unofficially numerous times that he would prefer to devote his diplomatic energies almost solely to what he considers the greatest obstacle to international understanding, communist infiltration and expansion in Guatemala."[29] A few days later Secretary of State Dulles confirmed the tenor of the newspaper report when he said that if the United Fruit Company "gave a gold piece for every banana," the problem of communist infiltration would still exist.[30] A week later, Dulles called a news conference, charging that the actions taken by the Guatemalan government against those suspected of disloyalty were a communist type of terrorism.[31] On 18 June the Guatemalan foreign minister announced that the battle for Guatemala had started and that invasions across Guatemala's borders had taken place. Eight days later, after what the Guatemalans later described were threats of bombing from U.S. Ambassador Peurifoy, the Guatemalan army asked that Arbenz resign. He did so, turning over the government to a loyal follower who promised that the social reforms made by the revolution would remain. But this loyal associate was soon to be displaced, and Castillo Armas, who had been in exile, returned to assume the reins of power.

Although it cannot be definitively proven that Washington inspired the overthrow of the Guatemalan government, the U.S. government made no secret of its delight with the new arrangement. The Latin Americans, whether pleased or outraged at the change, applying the principle of *cui bono*, assigned responsibility to the United States.

THE LESSONS OF THE CRISIS FOR THE UNITED STATES

The various actors drew differing lessons from these events. The U.S. leadership formed the opinion that it was both feasible and suitable to intervene against the danger of communism. Although U.S. estimates of the danger of a communist takeover varied—from the very sober appraisal of the State Department specialists that such a takeover, if it occurred, would take a long time, to the fear that communist takeover was imminent—the very ease with which the intervention was accomplished and the seemingly small political cost established the conviction that semilegal or clandestine means should be employed to nip communism in the bud in Latin America. While some accepted the intervention as an unpleasant feature of power politics, others embraced it. Dulles and Eisenhower were very clear that they were pleased with the changes in Guatemala. Six years later, during the 1960 U.S. presidential campaign, John Kennedy charged that the Republicans had let Cuba go to the communists. He asked for a more active anti-Castro policy, which Nixon rejected, saying, "We can do what we did with Guatemala. There was a Communist dictator that we inherited from the previous administration. We quarantined Mr. Arbenz. The result was that the Guatemalan people themselves eventually rose up and they threw him out."[32]

Kennedy apparently shared the belief that a small, low-cost, low-risk effort could dispatch Castro as Arbenz had been dispatched. At the level where it was most important, the level of presidential decision making, the Guatemalan affair established the belief that the United States could easily overturn a communist-leaning or a communist government in Latin America. How ready the United States would be to employ this power it believed itself to possess depended of course on the general assessment of the international situation and upon domestic pressures.

THE LESSONS OF THE CRISIS FOR THE USSR

The Soviet and American appraisals of the lessons of Guatemala were similar. Writing in 1954, Soviet journalists pointed out that the United States was prepared to intervene against regimes that were not communist but that seemed to threaten American interests by their excessive independence. The real goal of the Guatemalan revolution, a Soviet specialist wrote in *Kommunist* immediately after the events, was to assure the free development of capitalism and to protect the internal market from the pressure of North American capitalism. The communists in Guatemala united with these elements in a popular front.[33] In the Soviet view such popular fronts could eventually lead to the establishment of a socialist government. Therefore, in a very general way, the United States and the Soviet Union were in agreement that reformist governments in Latin America, which were generally anti-American, could eventually pass over to communism. But U.S. and Soviet opinions differed concerning the pace of this development. For the Soviets the path from a coalition with a bourgeois government to socialism was a long and thorny one, and good tactics dictated that the Communist Party preserve its identity and avoid blame for a failure. The revolution would come, according to the Soviet analysis, after fundamental changes in the class structure had been made so that the Communist party and the proletariat could play a leading role. On the other hand, the United States felt that communist takeovers were the results of small conspiracies and that unless they were stopped early on, one could wake up one morning to find that a country had gone communist.

The Soviet leaders were impressed by U.S. resoluteness. In a contemporary account, a Soviet writer repeated a common charge of the Latin American press that Ambassador Peurifoy, in order to "make it clear that the American Ambassador was the real master of the country," savagely bombed the defenseless Gautemalan towns and warned that the raids would continue unless Arbenz and his government resigned. The United States, the Soviet commentators believed, was prepared to take such drastic measures when efforts to suborn the corrupt Latin American military failed.[34] The few Soviet comments generally supported the decision of the Guatemalan communists not to arm the peasants and workers since the army was permeated by bourgeois elements and the "cowardice and treachery of certain bourgeois circles in Guatemala played a role in the success of the counterrevolution."[35]

Writing six years later, a Soviet analyst retained the idea that Arbenz really had little choice in not fighting. Arbenz ordered the troops not to give battle, believing that to do so would serve as a pretext for intervention.[36] The general Soviet view seemed to be that the nationalistic, anti-American elements in Guatemala were too weak to survive once the United States had determined to eliminate them. The Soviet writers were silent on the tactics of the Guatemalan communists. They simply repeated the standard formula that the leading role of the working class makes possible the victory of the antiimperialist, antifeudal revolution.[37] The failure of this revolution therefore meant that the Communist Party did not have the leading role. The Soviet writers probably concluded that American imperialism in Latin America was still powerful and resolute and that although nationalism could be expected to grow,[38] the estimates printed in *Kommunist* and *Pravda* in mid-1954 were probably a little premature. The Soviet Union then was prepared to support verbally and by the resolutions of the communist parties of Latin America any anti–North American tendencies in Latin America. But until 1959, the occasion for giving military aid to such a regime did not arise, and there is no evidence that the Soviet Union, through the agency of its communist parties, sought to structure a situation in which Guatemala could be replayed.

THE LESSONS OF THE CRISIS FOR THE
LATIN AMERICAN LEFT

The Latin American left understood the situation differently. The events in Guatemala had stirred the continent, and the Latin American press was filled with discussions of the significance of the Guatemalan events. The big issue was whether the Guatemalans should have fought the U.S.–sponsored intervention. Almost all agreed that the failure of the army to support Arbenz, and Arbenz's inability or unwillingness to arm the population, was critical.

Writing a few months after the events, former Guatemalan foreign minister Toriello offered an estimate of the character of Latin American military leadership that retained currency in Latin America until modernizing anti–North American military leaders appeared in the late sixties. Toriello explained that military treason was a common phenomenon in the political life of Latin America. The old-style military leader was poorly educated, his character formed in a bureaucracy where his main occupation was executing profitable deals. For these people the prospect, however remote, of having to take up arms and risk their lives as soldiers, was abhorrent. This military class was horrified by the idea that any political change could deprive them of a soft life. In such states, the military officer is a "docile instrument of internal or external conspiratorial machinations and is spiritually prepared to become a traitor."[39]

Thus, the Latin American left, among them the Cuban exiles in Mexico City, concluded that the regular army could not be relied upon to support a revolution and that the communists were useless or worse. The communists in Guatemala, they felt, were timid and quite passive, and their failure to organize resistance was widely, if not charitably, interpreted as cowardice. A Cuban reporter who had sought asylum in the Mexican embassy, together with the leading officials of the Arbenz government, gives the following account of the behavior of Fortuny, a prominent communist close to Arbenz.[40] A fight had broken out between a Guatemalan and a Spaniard over who should use the toilet first. Fortuny, unaware that order had been restored, began to scream hysterically, "Guatemalans, come over here to me." The Spaniards in the embassy were Loyalists who had fought against Franco and later against the Germans in Africa. They despised Fortuny, and one taunted: "Why didn't you yell, 'Guatemalans to arms! Fight to the last man,' when there were still means and opportunities left to save democracy? Why did you take to flight without telling your comrades who later became victims of the mercenaries?"

The failure of the revolution caused the communist parties and the Soviet Union to revert to their earlier position, namely, that the prospects for Latin American nationalist opposition to the United States were still modest and that the revolution in Latin America lay in the distant future. The Latin American communist parties were confirmed in the conviction that "premature" militancy led to defeat and that waiting was the better part of wisdom. The United States, judging the situation in much the same way, concluded that prophylactic action to stifle potential communist regimes was an effective, low-cost strategy. But the Latin

American left, especially the younger generation, perceived a significant change in the situation. The U.S. Good Neighbor policy had been abandoned; now, in the name of the ideological struggle with communism, the United States had reverted to crude intervention to preserve the profits of U.S. private enterprise. Only the naive or the suborned could assume that the United States of Eisenhower, Dulles, and McCarthy was the United States of F.D.R. and the New Deal. Now it was inevitable that a program for reform would provoke swift intervention and that the native armies would betray the revolutionaries. Reliance on the liberalism of the United States or on liberal forces within the United States was self-delusion. But instead of waiting (like the communists) for the correlation of forces in the United States to change, the noncommunist left, in a phrase that was later to become famous, believed that the duty of a revolutionary was to make a revolution. Whether or not these conclusions were based on a correct understanding of the motives and actions of the chief actors in the Guatemalan affair is unimportant. They became the guiding principles for the successful Cuban revolution five years later.

2. THE CUBAN REVOLUTION: THE BEGINNINGS AND THE FIRST YEAR

Only a short time before Castro entered Havana in January 1959, the Cuban communists and those few Soviet officials who watched Latin American affairs did not expect Castro to win. American officials were not much quicker to realize that the old regime under Batista could not last very much longer, although a growing number of officials felt that Batista should be jettisoned.

Unprepared as the two great powers were for the advent of Castro to power, they were even less prepared for the radicalization of the Cuban revolution and its rapid conversion into a socialist revolution. At the outset, both the Americans and the Soviets expected the Cuban situation to deteriorate, that is, the Americans feared that Castro would go too far to the left and the Russians feared that he would go too far to the right. But the intensity and resonance of these fears was hardly comparable. For the Soviets, it was just another case of a nationalist leader with radical phrases who would probably eventually accommodate the imperialists. For the United States, as the months passed it seemed as if the political counterpart of the sputnik nightmare was at hand; the Russians had finally succeeded in harnessing nationalism to communism, and the communization of Cuba would be the first step in a massive shift of political power on a world basis.

How the Soviet Union and the United States came to understand the situation in Cuba and how they responded is the subject of the remaining chapters of this book. While the United States saw its worst fears realized, the Soviet Union saw come to pass what it had not dared to hope for.

The roots of the Soviet and American misjudgments of the Cuban revolution are to be found among the lessons the leaders of each country had learned in the past. The United States and the Soviet Union had learned somewhat different lessons from the events in Guatemala, and Castro, for his part, interpreted the significance of those events still differently. Leaders in Moscow and in Washington (and for a time the Cuban communists organized in the Partido Socialista Popular, commonly referred to as the PSP) believed that if Castro followed Arbenz's example, he would share his fate.

In the Soviet Union, Khrushchev had replaced Malenkov as the leading political figure, but it was probably the same small group of CPSU and government figures concerned with Latin American affairs that continued to follow events and volunteer advice or respond to queries from the top leadership.

The Soviet leaders had drawn the conclusion that the United States was determined not to permit any radical Latin American regimes to survive, especially if the Communist party played, or might play, a significant role. The communist parties of Latin America were therefore expected to pursue modest goals. The scant attention accorded to Latin American events in the Soviet press reflected a low estimate of the likelihood and utility of radical revolutions in Latin America. We shall return to the changing Soviet understanding of the events in Cuba after we review the events in Cuba and the role of the PSP.

THE PARTIDO SOCIALISTA POPULAR (PSP)

The Cubans, like everyone else in Latin America, had been enormously interested in the Guatemalan events. Fidel Castro had to follow the events from prison; Ernesto "Che" Guevara was actually resident in Guatemala at the time, and Raúl Roa, who was to become the foreign minister of Cuba, was the editor of *Humanismo* in Mexico City. On the basis of their own experience in Cuba, the Cuban communists did not believe it possible to overthrow Batista, and their understanding of the events in Guatemala only reinforced that belief. Before Batista became a dictator he had controlled Cuban politics through puppet governments with the aid of the Cuban communists. Carlos Rafael Rodríguez and Juan Marinello had served as ministers in the first Cuban government controlled by Batista. All over the world communist parties were pursuing the policy of the Popular Front, that is, cooperating on as effective and as official a level as possible with the governments whose policies were anti-Nazi. Cuba, however, was one of the few countries in the world where communists were members of a government.

Other communist parties in Latin America had also come to an understanding with a dictator. Often a weak party with some capacity to organize and manage labor unions would do so in cooperation with the dictator. Since the likelihood of a socialist revolution was deemed small, a mutually advantageous bargain was struck. In return for controlling organized labor, the communist party acquired the right to exist and to build cadres for a better day. The dictator had little to fear from a weak communist party that served to direct the actions of a potentially troublesome part of the population. In most Latin American countries unionized labor is privileged, and as long as its situation is better than that of unorganized labor, it is loath to risk its status by making purely political demands. This was indeed the situation in the 1950s in Cuba.

But in the atmosphere of the cold war Batista found it convenient to discard the communists. Eusebio Mujal, a former communist, took over the management of organized labor. Batista could easily make such a change because organized labor saw in the communists the instrument for gaining economic benefits only, not wider political goals. After the revolution, the PSP admitted that the "spirit of economism" had prevailed among the workers.[1] In communist language economism is the sin of being beguiled by the pursuit of purely economic goals.

Organized labor is rarely an exception to the political rule that men seek their own self-interest before that of others, and the pressure to do so is very great in countries where unemployment is high, as it was in Cuba. Laborers enrolled in unions that enjoyed the protection of the government were in a privileged but precarious position, since others were ready to work if they struck. Organized labor owed its favored position to the dictator and not to the communist party labor bureaucrats who served at the head of the unions at the pleasure of the dictator. Thus Batista could replace the communist leadership with a man of his own choosing without losing any support from organized labor. Discussing the matter retrospectively, the secretary of the PSP admitted that Batista was popular with labor and even with "some backward members of the party."[2] He explained, rather lamely, that labor had failed to realize that Batista and the situation in the country had changed. Of course, he did not say that labor understood that the communists had been Batista's agents or that labor's situation in contrast to that of the PSP had not changed appreciably when Batista got rid of the communists. Later the communists were restored to the leadership of the trade unions by the new dictator, Castro, in opposition to the wishes of the majority of the membership.

To accept the reality that they had no secure political base within organized labor, let alone a mass base, the Cuban communist leadership had also to believe that a socialist revolution was an impossibility unless they were prepared to accept the then-unheard-of proposition that a socialist revolution could be made by a nonsocialist. The PSP accepted the dictum that national liberation movements had to be led by the working class in the form of its vanguard, the communist party. In 1919 and 1920, at the first and second Congresses of the Comintern, Lenin had identified the struggle of colonies for independence as an opportunity for communists to assert leadership. By the middle fifties communist party leadership had become the touchstone for the authenticity of a national movement, or to put it more correctly, the persecution of communists was regarded as evidence that a national liberationist movement was or would soon become an instrument of imperialism. This test was soon to be abandoned, and nationalist leaders only had to be neutral in the cold war to gain and keep Soviet approval and support.

The Cuban communists, thinking in terms of Cuban history, believed that Batista could be overthrown only by a popular uprising, that is, a general strike, and they took the position that a people's uprising was only possible when the working class participated directly and occupied the vanguard of the common front.[3] The necessary conclusion—which the PSP did not draw in so many words—was that a revolution against Batista could not succeed until the Cuban workers accepted the leadership of the communists. The preconditions for revolution were not present, and all attempts to overthrow Batista by force were therefore opportunistic, putschlike, adventuristic, and wrong.

THE YOUNG CASTRO IN THE CUBAN SETTING

Fidel Castro was hardly the man to accept such an analysis of the situation. He probably shared the disdain for communists felt by the Latin American noncommunist left and probably believed with them that the communists in Guatemala had been cowards. Fidel Castro is a difficult figure to understand, despite the thousands of pages that have been written about him. His lengthy and frequent public speeches, often extemporaneous, blur rather than reveal his character. In presenting so many different facets to public view, he creates the puzzle of who the real Castro is. An orderly political and strategic plan cannot be derived from Castro's speeches. Often major policy decisions are taken on the spur of the moment while Castro is speaking. But this impetuousness, this seeming surrender to moods of the moment, is misleading. The verbal pyrotechnics and the sudden assumption of new postures are deceptive. Beneath lie a few simple principles and a strong sense of strategic purpose. Castro's agility and extreme tactical flexibility often cause those who have dealt with him to feel deceived; but Castro has hewed to his deep convictions.

Castro wants to make Cuba a nation and the Cubans a people. This nationalistic aspiration is a common phenomenon, and Castro's father, like the fathers of many other nationalist leaders, served the colonial power. It was to be expected that in a country with a low level of education, the children of the favored would have access to the education that seems to be a requisite for a successful career as a revolutionary.

Castro's father had been a soldier in the Spanish army in 1898 and settled in Cuba after the Spanish failure to frustrate the Cuban revolution for independence.[4] He even worked for the United Fruit Company, that archetype of Yankee imperialism, before he bought his own land and became rich. Castro spent his formative years in an area "dominated by the North American presence. The United Fruit Company's employees had a polo club, swimming pools, shops for U.S. goods . . . the company had its own force of twenty field soldiers, licensed to bear arms."[5] Castro, in revolting against Batista's domination of Cuba, was revolting against the order established by his father's generation.

The indirect rule of the United States over Cuba was perhaps more demoralizing and more resented than Spanish rule. Direct colonial rule is straightforward. The colonial power is fully responsible for the affairs of the colony, justly claims credit for progress, and equally justly is faulted for failure. The native agents share the praise or blame. A semi-colony like Cuba was worse off. Close by, overwhelming U.S. economic and military power meant that Cuban political independence was a facade and that those who insisted on its reality were either hypocritical or naive—and Cubans are certainly not naive. The position was worse than humiliating; it was ambiguous. No U.S. colonial office issued directives, but Cuban leaders felt impelled to be in the good graces of the U.S. ambassador. Since U.S. domination was not admitted, no formal organization for the transmission of U.S. preferences existed. Although the U.S. ambassador to Cuba was regarded as a proconsul, his authority was by no means complete. Batista, for example, in 1932 installed himself as the successor to Gerardo Machado against Ambassador Sumner Welles's wishes.

Sophisticated Cuban politicians knew that the United States would often settle for less than the maximum it had demanded, and that influential persons in Washington could be persuaded to act in favor of one Cuban faction rather than another. But since the United States could exercise effective pressure ranging from reducing the sugar quota—that is, reducing the subsidy to Cuba—to outright military intervention, success in Cuban internal politics often meant gaining or maintaining the favor of Washington.

The United States on the whole wanted domestic order and a favorable climate for investment but had little interest in how this was accomplished. Cuban nationalists could therefore convincingly complain that the United States was only interested in what it could get out of Cuba— that the United States was an exploiter. Although the United States seemed willing to accept harsh and arbitrary conduct by Cuban leaders if its basic purposes were served, it was prepared to abandon support of such leaders if they provoked general protest or rebellion that threatened public order. This was the fate of Machado and Batista. When, at the end of their careers, they could not maintain the public order that justified the harshness of their rule, they lost the U.S. support on which they ultimately depended.

Such an ambiguous relationship with a great power distorts the politics of the dependent country by inhibiting the development of local constituencies. In underdeveloped countries, the tendency is for power to flow from the top rather than from the bottom. The pattern has many variations. Sometimes a new dictator will derive part of his support from the disinherited and will staff his army and police forces with them. For example, Peron appealed to those who did not wear shirts; Duvalier to the blacks with a sense of grievance against the mulattoes, and Trujillo to the mulattoes against the whites; and Batista was very popular with the Cuban Negroes. In some countries this process of introducing even wider strata of the population into the political life of the country modifies the direction of the flow of power, and instead of proceeding only from the top down it begins to move in both directions. However, when it is generally believed that the great foreign power, the Yankees in the Cuban case, in the last analysis decides who rules, the ambitious seek preferment in the court of a petty ruler, who himself must remain in the good graces of his master, the foreigner. Such regimes are neither always nor uniformly oppressive. They derive some of their strength from the contentment, which is different from the consent, of the governed. Batista therefore kept pointing to the prosperity of Cuba in the middle fifties to make the case that Castro's opposition had to be inconsequential.

The psychological costs of the semicolonial relationship are heavy. Although many persons feel autonomous for long periods, there are searing periods of humiliation. The quality of Batista's feeling of ill-use by his patrons, which appears on almost every page of his memoirs, differs very little from Castro's outrage at the effrontery of the North Americans. Sensitivity to affronts to one's self-respect and independence (*dignidad*) is a heritage from Spanish culture, and such affronts are an inescapable feature of the colonial relationship. Impotence in the face of this humiliation produces self-contempt or rage on a much wider scale than is generally realized in North America.

The Cuban political class could always argue that it was unable to make political progress because *they,* that is, the vague North American authorities, economic and political, prevented it. Therefore, the Cuban political leaders had a built-in excuse for their own failures and misdeeds. One of the high costs of Latin American anti–North Americanism is that it provides an excuse for inaction, political ineptitude, and worse. The situation in Cuba was especially bad in this respect. The feelings of self-contempt, inadequacy, and resentment were, of course, most prevalent in the middle classes, whose members read the books and magazines that ventilated these sentiments. The rural population of Cuba had yet to be drawn into the active political process on a large scale. The nature of the Cuban economy, with its dependence on the sugar crop, whose price on the world market had fluctuated wildly in the last several decades, had created a large middle class—large, that is, by Latin American standards—with a relatively high educational level but with long periods of impoverishment during which people had to scramble to maintain the respectability their fathers had earned. Such a resentful class is much better material for a revolutionary leader than a class that simply wants to break out of poverty and need.

In his own person Castro represented this class, with its fierce pride and sense of humiliation. He himself had early cast himself in the role of heroic leader. At times it seemed as if he might follow the pattern of many other Cuban leaders. In clawing for a political purchase in a situation where there were many aspirants and few positions, the tactics and the need to maintain a place might have become an end in itself. But Castro was fiercely ambitious and soon burned his boats behind him. By attacking the garrison at Moncada in 1953 he brought himself to the attention of the Cuban population. The venture was reckless and dangerous, and most of the attackers were killed. Only Batista's clemency saved Castro from execution and secured his liberation from prison and his exile from Cuba a few years later.

While in exile in Mexico, Castro cast about for support in Mexico and the United States, sometimes accepting it from Cuban refugees whose politics he despised. His flexibility in the search for support, his willingness to compromise, and the fuzziness of his ideas convinced many observers that Castro was a complete opportunist. But this estimate overlooks the central core of Castro's ideology: to restore the dignity of the Cubans and to make Cuba a nation. To this end Castro was willing to risk his own life and the lives of others, not faltering when his comrades-in-arms were killed. But the communists, who had an organization to lose, felt that bold, unsuccessful actions were the hallmark of the politically immature. Therefore, Castro and the Cuban communists disagreed on how to topple Batista.

CASTRO BEGINS THE REBELLION

The two conceptions differed fundamentally. Castro's bent was to find his strategy through action. "Engage and then see" could have been his motto. Castro planned for an uprising to coincide with his landing in Cuba in December 1956. The uprising miscarried, but his revolution succeeded nevertheless. The events of the revolution and its implications have been thoroughly analysed elsewhere and only the features relevant to Soviet policies need be examined here. It turned out that Castro was able to survive in the hills of Oriente, and later his augmented guerilla bands were able to move down into the plains and to survive in the face of the ragged opposition of Batista's troops.

The situation in Cuba was totally different from that in Guatemala. Writing in the official Communist newspaper a year after the victory of the revolution, Ignacio Reyes made some trenchant comparisons. The

Guatemalan revolution became radical only slowly; the Cuban revolution became radical with a rush. The Guatemalan revolution proceeded from the city to the countryside; in Cuba it was the other way around. In Guatemala extensive violence and civil war marked only the end of the revolution. In the Cuban revolution armed struggle marked the beginning. In Guatemala the workers furnished the principal and initial support for the revolution, with the peasants entering upon the scene only later. In Cuba, Batista and Mujal had suborned the working class, so the principal base of the revolution had to be the peasantry. The working class played its role only at the end in the strike actions.[6]

The bulk of the middle class had become disgusted with Batista and his military and police supporters. Americans residing in Cuba shared this feeling of revulsion. In late 1956 and January 1957 Batista's police tried to cut Castro off from his middle-class supporters, mostly the sons and daughters of the Cuban middle class, by employing terror against them. The brutalities only served to convert the politically inactive parents into bitter enemies of Batista and finally into sympathizers with or active supporters of Castro.[7] It was a representative of this group, Felipe Pazos, and his son, Javier, who arranged for New York Times reporter Herbert Matthews to visit Castro. The photographic evidence that Castro was indeed alive, contrary to the government's contention, lowered Batista's prestige still further and made Castro a world figure overnight.

While the Cuban middle class and some elements of the U.S. government in Washington were shifting to tentative support of Castro, the PSP was keeping its distance. In their clandestine organ, Respuestas, on 7 December 1956, the PSP put the full blame for the "Cuban tragedy" on the Batista government but also said that "isolated armed uprisings" served to support the existing regime. A week later Respuestas wrote that decisive results could not be expected from terrorism, putschism, or the actions of the armed detachments in the Sierra Maestra. A people's uprising is born from the conviction of the majority, "with the working class being a direct participant and the true vanguard."[8] Furthermore it was necessary to employ peaceful methods until "the experience of the majority convinced them that violence was necessary."[9]

But since the PSP could not take Batista's side in the atmosphere of revulsion against the brutalities of his government, Castro's guerilla struggle was criticized as premature and hence "objectively" of service to the Batista regime. Furthermore, to say that a true revolution had to have the working class in the forefront was to say that a revolution was a revolution only if the PSP led it. And since the PSP admitted that the organized working class had been corrupted by Mujalism, i.e., satisfied with its comparative prosperity in a country of high unemployment, the revolution was a long way off.

In early 1957, the PSP took a position expressing its sympathy with Castro's objectives but criticizing the tactics of his 26th of July Movement. In an open letter written in February and published in June in Havana, the PSP insisted that terror and sabotage only served to give the dictatorship pretexts for its actions. Violence and the burning of sugar cane fields would serve to turn the working class against Castro rather than against Batista. After these seemingly uncompromising strictures, the letter somewhat surprisingly said that the 26th of July Movement "came closest" to the communists' "strategic conception." It then asked for better understanding between the PSP and the 26th of July Movement on the basis of common strategy despite a divergence on tactics.[10]

On 17 March 1957, the PSP rejected futile attacks like the assault on Moncada and the landing of small groups of insurgents on Cuban shores. However noble the intentions of the 26th of July Movement might be, its tactics were mistaken.[11] In February of 1958, almost a year later, the PSP made a "half-turn" and adopted a dual policy, simultaneously supporting "both the armed struggle in the countryside and the unarmed civil struggle in the cities."[12] In March the PSP gave some support to Castro on the ground that he was waging a real guerilla war, relying on the peasant masses.[13] Apparently this turn toward the 26th of July Movement represented the victory of Carlos Rafael Rodríguez and, quite likely, Roca over Aníbal Escalante within the PSP.[14]

Soviet press reports reflected the PSP appraisal. A letter from the PSP in *Pravda* on 14 February said that "our Party, as is known, rejects terror as a method of struggle, considering it ineffective and paralyzing to the will of the masses. We communists have never had any relationship, direct or indirect, with terrorist acts."[15] A week later an article on Cuba appeared that described individual terror as "a product of despair and the erroneous political views of certain bourgeois and petit-bourgeois groups." Yet, the article continued, the country is in flames, a military uprising has taken place in Cienfuegos, and general strikes are breaking out. The strike of August 1957 was premature but now a general strike supported by a broad coalition is the correct method of struggle.[16] The Soviet assessment pointed in two directions: terror was wrong, but it was leading, nevertheless, to a general strike that could topple Batista. Yet only a short time later *Pravda* published a statement signed by the PSP in which Batista's persecutions were mentioned, but the armed struggle in Cuba was not, thus tacitly withdrawing support from Castro's activities.[17]

The three items appearing in *Pravda* after a silence of several years did not offer clear guidance. In a sense, as Thomas, in his *Cuba,* argues convincingly, the decision was forced on the communists. Castro had been identified as a communist for propaganda purposes; Batista's police found it difficult to reach Castro's forces in the hills; why not harry the communists who could be reached? Police ill-treatment in certain provinces forced the communists into the formation of their own guerilla groups, e.g., the Máximo Gómez column led by Félix Torres.[18]

While the PSP was moving slowly and uncertainly toward Castro, the United States had pulled the rug from under Batista, suspending arms shipments on 14 March 1958. On 31 March 1958, in a response to a request for information, the U.S. Department of State informed Representative Porter of Oregon that it had halted a shipment of arms to Cuba "to allow us the opportunity of consulting further the appropriate Cuban officials."[19] Apparently the State Department announcement was just what it was purported to be, a temporizing measure rather than an embargo.[20] But a few days later a report appeared that the United States had indeed imposed an embargo on arms to Cuba in a little noticed action ten days earlier.[21] Whatever the original motives of the arms halt, it became an embargo in fact because anti-Batista sentiment in the administration had become dominant. As two ex-Cuban scholars have written, "United States disapproval simply meant in influential circles on the island that Fulgencio Batista had to go."[22] Since Batista was dependent on the United States for arms and support and since his police and army were dependent on him for their existence it is not surprising that Batista was abandoned by his corrupt henchmen when the mantle of imperial favor was removed from his shoulders. As Batista wrote bitterly in his memoirs: "At the beginning of autumn, 1958, through negligence, through complicity, for financial gain, or through fear or cowardice, Army units frequently surrendered to rebel groups." Others, as Batista angrily recounts, approached the U.S. ambassador with proposals that they be taken on as substitutes for the doomed Batista.[23] The Batistas and the Diems of this world are always bitter when their great power supporters abandon and dismiss them by withdrawing the magic of their approval. They are bitter because most often they have done what was bidden but have become unable to continue playing the role they had been assigned. In Cuba the staunch anticommunist Batista was being abandoned while his successor was still unknown.

Castro would have been objective indeed had he assigned more weight to the withdrawal of American support for Batista than to the fighting of his own men. He believed that the dribble of U.S. support—the replacement of defective equipment sent earlier—continued the old policy under a new facade. In fact it represented the residual opposition of those in the U.S. administration who supported Batista.

Underestimating the significance of the withdrawal of U.S. support from Batista contributed to the legend of the Cuban revolution that was to cost Castro, and especially his close associate Guevara, so dearly in the years to come. Believing firmly that the Cuban revolution was successful because the peasants had been quickly and effectively politicized by the example of a few invaders from the outside, the Cubans believed for many years thereafter that this could be the model for other revolutions. But only in a very few places where guerilla efforts were attempted was the regime discredited as was Batista's, and nowhere did the United States publicly withdraw support.

Until the United States imposed what at least Batista and his supporters believed to be an arms embargo, the PSP could safely continue to applaud Castro's bravery, attack Batista for his policies, and argue in effect that Castro's tactics were misguided. The correct leadership would be furnished by the PSP when the majority of the population formed a united front under PSP guidance. As long as it seemed unlikely that Castro would prevail, to embrace his movement probably meant to share in his defeat. Batista's police left most of the national leaders of the PSP alone. Carlos Rafael Rodríguez and Juan Marinello, both former cabinet ministers, lived practically undisturbed in Havana according to Boris Goldenberg, himself a resident of Havana at that time. Goldenberg states that Batista's police took sharp measures against the terrorist groups, which were largely recruited from middle-class students.[24] Claude Julien, a reporter from *Le Monde,* interviewed Rodríguez in Havana in May 1958. Another French journalist reported that of top PSP leaders only Aníbal Escalante did not live in Havana and that no communists were released from jail after the revolution because none were lodged there.[25]

Association with a revolutionary movement that foundered meant reprisals from the victorious government forces, but failure to support a successful revolution did not necessarily mean exclusion from political leadership. The PSP could not capture a revolution whose tactics it criticized and whose leaders it scorned. In later years, after having served their purpose, the leaders of the PSP were expelled from the communist party that Castro had formed. The only active survivor of the major PSP leaders is Rodríguez, who seemed to have early pressed for support of the 26th of July Movement and who spent some time with Castro in the Sierra Maestra as the representative of the PSP.

The shifting PSP line on a general strike illustrates how the communists sought to preserve a revolutionary image without taking any risks. In 1933 the dictator Machado was overthrown after a general strike that took the PSP by surprise and that they more or less ignored. After the dictator's fall, however, the PSP claimed credit for a role in the strike.[26] It had become conventional Cuban political wisdom that a general strike could unseat a dictator, and Castro counted on a general strike timed to coincide with his landing to topple Batista.[27] Castro's landing in December 1956 was a failure; his forces were reduced to a handful of men, and the general strike was postponed. In the spring of 1958, when Batista's government had been weakened, Castro and his associates again organized a general srtike in the hope that it would then succeed. The PSP gave some verbal support to the strike but managed to avoid involvement.

After the failure of the strike, the anti-Batista groups engaged in mutual recriminations. The noncommunist left was suspicious of communist behavior and a contemporary account argued that, as a general principle in Latin America and in Cuba in particular, the communists preferred dictatorships. The communists sometimes pursued a dual strategy of infiltrating the democratic movements and simultaneously supporting the dictatorship. In Cuba the communists tried to enter the revolutionary movement but were rebuffed.[28] According to one analysis the communists made their assistance in the strike contingent on their control over it—a price that Castro found too high.[29]

Although the circumstances of the strike are still hazy, it seems that Castro, unlike his followers in the plains, wanted the communists to participate, but the Havana 26th of July Movement was able to exclude them. When the strike calls were issued without preparing the strikers, the communists ignored them and later blamed the failure of the strike on its having been called prematurely.[30] Subsequent Soviet accounts put the blame for the failure of the strike on the desire of the 26th of July Movement to monopolize credit, but Castro was not specifically included in this condemnation.[31]

The communist leader Rodríguez discussed the strike soon after its failure with a French journalist in Havana. He hoped that Castro would now be more conciliatory and willing to broaden his political base to include all forces of opposition and even to create a kind of shadow cabinet representative of the various political views. He was even purported to have wanted Castro to tone down his anti-Americanism because it put off some potential members of an anti-Batista coalition. Rodríguez later claimed in a letter to the same journalist that he had been misquoted, that the PSP had supported the strike as much as possible, but that the strike had been inadequately prepared.[32]

The PSP must have been relieved that the anticommunist elements in the 26th of July Movement in the cities of the plain excluded them from the preparation for the strike. If they had been drawn into it in good time, the failure of the strike would have underlined publicly how little influence the PSP had over organized labor. The communist leader Rodríguez saw in the failure of the strike confirmation of his belief in the strength of the Batista regime and the necessity to create a broad coalition, including presumably parts of the army. But in mid-May Castro expressed confidence that Batista could be defeated without his soldiers being offered a share of the power in post-Batista Cuba if they deserted to Castro. A then-sympathetic journalist asked Castro about the criticism that Castro was not winning because he would not consider the transfer of power even temporarily to a military junta. Castro answered: "It is true that if we had accepted the hypothesis of a military junta, the dictatorship of Batista would already have been defeated. But that is not a revolution. The military also put Batista into power. We do not settle anything with the overthrow now of a dictator if within four or five years another is imposed."[33]

Castro may have been whistling in the dark or he may have been prescient, but events were soon to prove him right. In the last week of May, Batista launched his army on its first, and last, offensive against the guerilla forces. The offensive was a fiasco, many officers avoiding battle and others, former classmates of Castro's, changing sides. As in China nine years earlier, power fell away with a rush once the regime that had been abandoned by the United States began to suffer defeats in the field. The servants of the master who had himself been dismissed by his foreign master fled in mounting panic. But even as the rout of Batista's army confirmed Castro's optimism, Rodríguez responded to criticism from a foreigner sympathetic to the revolution, saying that "if there already existed forces in the country capable of overthrowing Batista and putting in an anti-imperialist government, things would be easy. Unfortunately that is not the way it is."[34]

But although the communists did not yet believe in, and were not for a long time to accept, the likelihood of Castro's victory, they negotiated with the anti-Batista forces in order to be playing some political role. They seemed to be following the course that Sacha Volman had described as characteristic of Latin American communists several months earlier.[35] The communist leadership tried to get into the revolutionary movement but did not cross the line into advocating terror—a self-limitation that until then had served to keep the leadership out of jail. The communists began to negotiate an agreement with the other revolutionary forces for common action in the labor field, and at the beginning of July Carlos Rafael Rodríguez went into the Sierra to confer with Raúl and Fidel Castro at the different fronts on which they were fighting. Rodríguez failed to get an agreement on unity of action in which the communists were included. On 20 July in Caracas, Venezuela, the opposition groups, with the exception of the communists and the group of Grau and Márquez Sterling, formed a common front. But the communists were still trying. Rodríguez came down from the mountains to seek agreement on common action within the labor movement, claiming that this was Castro's wish. Again he was rebuffed. Whether Castro's control over other members of the 26th of July Movement was still quite imperfect, or whether he did not push very hard for the inclusion of the communists is not clear; both factors probably contributed to the situation. Right after his return from the mountains with the victorious army in January 1959, Rodríguez said that the Caracas meeting had failed to formalize a unity pact as he had hoped and that some of its signatories had not participated in the strike.[36] Subsequently, both Castro and the communist leaders pretended that they had achieved more unity in the summer of 1958 than they in fact had. In 1960 the secretary of the Cuban Communist party, Blas Roca, explained that the anti-Batista forces had met in Caracas and made an agreement that could not be given final form before Batista fell.[37] In early 1961 Castro glossed over the whole matter by saying, "We met with each other, we understood one another and started to work together."[38]

Even as Batista's collapse became imminent, the communists continued to insist that Batista could not be overthrown until and unless they were included in the united front against him. It is hard to judge whether this insistence represented a belief that formal PSP participation was necessary to overthrow Batista or whether the PSP was simply pleading not to be left out. In November 1958 Blas Roca, the secretary of the PSP, and Juan Marinello, its president, in a letter of greeting to the Congress of the Chilean Communist party said that only a coalition of the opposition could overthrow Batista.[39]

In other words, by November the position taken in the middle of the summer had not changed. At a meeting of the Uruguayan Communist party in August, its long-time leader Rodney Arismendi put the heroic struggle of the Cuban people in the general context of the fall of Latin American dictatorships. He appraised the situation as a contest between those who submitted to the dollar and those who realized the necessity for democratic changes that would bring genuine national independence to Latin American countries. This would contribute to world peace, because international tension would be reduced and peaceful coexistence furthered as Latin American countries ruptured the network of military relations that bound them to the United States.[40]

Arismendi hoped the new military and political strength of the Soviet Union would improve the position of communists in countries within the U.S. sphere of influence. Not only would the United States be afraid to make war on the Soviet Union, but for some unexplained reason, in the new power constellation it would accept the assertion of independence by client states. But as yet, in Cuba as elsewhere in Latin America, those who preferred to continue in client status were locked in struggle with those who wanted to assert independence. The hope that the Soviet Union as a newly minted great military power could limit U.S. options in Latin America flourished until the missile crisis of October 1962.

To return to our account of the late summer and fall of 1958. It was easy to believe that as the power relationship between the United States and the Soviet Union shifted, anti-American nationalism would be the beneficiary. Communist parties found it useful to advertise Soviet support for Latin American nationalism. But such support by itself could hardly cause the ejection of the United States from Latin America. The outcome in each case would depend on the balance of forces within a particular country, and in the long run, within the United States.

As for Cuba, Khrushchev remarked in an interview given in November 1958 to a Brazilian journalist that everybody remembered the tragic fate of Guatemala and talked of the heroic but unequal struggle "of the people of Cuba."[41] Thus Khrushchev was hardly optimistic about a successful anti-Batista revolution. In the long run or even sooner it was expected that Latin American countries would increase their independence and whatever the United States lost would constitute a gain for the Soviet Union and the forces of nationalism all over the world. But one could not predict that Batista would fall in 1959 or any other year.

The Cuban communists of course would have preferred that Batista fall after they had been accepted into the coalition that overthrew him and after they had been given formal assurances of what their role in the new political authority was to be. Perhaps this wish distorted their judgment. But they would have been no better off if they had believed and stated their confidence in Batista's early defeat. They failed to gain admission to the united front against Batista not because their optimism was tempered, but because the other political leaders either hated them bitterly, disliked them, or merely felt that association with them would not further the common cause and might even harm it.

The success of the revolution, unexpected as it probably was, was nevertheless viewed as an opportunity by the communist leaders. The Cuban communists had taken an equivocal stand during Machado's deposition in 1933. But this did not prevent Batista from taking them up and granting them wide influence in the trade union movement. When Batista returned to power for a second time after a coup d'etat in 1952, he precipitated a break with the Soviet Union. But the motive was rather to do the United States a good turn cheaply than to find a pretext to persecute and destroy the communists, for the latter were permitted a semilegal status. Although the Communist party was outlawed, its leaders were not arrested, and they continued to reproduce their weekly newspaper, *Carta Seminal,* and their theoretical monthly, *Fundamentos.* The Cuban communists had gained power and authority not by revolutionary activity but by service to the dictator, and when for reasons of state the dictator disowned the communists, he put them in the doghouse rather than in dungeons. Our information does not permit us to go much beyond stating that the Cuban communists flourished as the dictator's agents, prospering in the sun of his favor and surviving not too uncomfortably in the shadow of his disfavor. With such a history their policy was likely to be passive.

Although we have some evidence of rivalries within the party, most of it has been made available by the victors in later factional battles. Draper suggests that Rodríguez and Escalante were the antagonists.[42] Very probably the Cuban communists argued among themselves about the timing and magnitude of the steps they would take toward Castro, but our information is scanty. The tendency of the PSP to submit to the holder of power—a tendency Castro found despicable when he sought allies against Batista—probably seemed reassuring when he himself was in power. The same persons who served Batista as ministers during the "good" years and lived unmolested in Havana during the "bad" years were given high, but not top, positions under Castro.

THE TRIUMPHANT CASTRO KEEPS THE PSP AT ARMS LENGTH

When Batista was deposed it was not at all certain that Castro would be his automatic successor. An attempt was made to form a military junta to replace Batista; had it been successful, Castro would have been robbed of the fruits of victory. To preclude that possibility, Castro did not rush into Havana on the heels of Batista's departure. He waited a few days while a general strike was in progress. The general strike was not against Batista, who had already fled; it was a warning to the military that a mere game of musical chairs would not be tolerated. Thus the general strike with which Castro and the PSP had believed the revolution would start was the last act.

Despite Castro's triumph, his position was not established beyond any possibility of a coup. As the PSP explained a few days after Castro had arrived in Havana, the government was composed of the petite-bourgeoisie and of the national bourgeoisie, who were antiimperialist, in contrast to the great sugar magnates and banking interests. Although this coalition was anti–United States, it wanted to preserve capitalism at any cost. Since the coalition was supported by elements more liberal than itself, the future was promising. The United States was frustrated in the execution of its last minute plans to intervene in Batista's favor and had retreated to cajolery and vague threats. The time of easy intervention was over, because the situation in Latin America had changed and because of the powerful help of the USSR and China.[43]

The issue of U.S. intervention was a delicate one for the PSP. To convince Castro that the United States was about to invade might have provoked him to jettison the communists. Nevertheless, the PSP insisted on a greater role and on the radicalization of the revolution. They had made the decision, whether deliberate or not, to accept the risk that their greater prominence would feed U.S. anticommunism, produce threats of intervention, and frighten Castro into suppressing them. While supporting the new government, they demanded a formal role in its composition.[44]

The PSP was following the general line of the international communist movement as expressed in its organ, *World Marxist Review,* which had put the Cuban revolution into the general context of the liberation movement in Latin America. Rojas Pinilla had been overthrown in Colombia; Perez Jiménez in Venezuela. Only the proletariat could lead the national liberation struggle since the national bourgeoisie was too divided in its purposes. Indeed, in a number of countries the communist parties were beginning to lead the proletariat.[45]

This was another of the ritual incantations of the international communist movement. Ever since the enunciation of the two-stage theory by Lenin in 1920 it had been dogma that the communist party would join the anticolonial revolutionary forces and ultimately lead them. In the forty years since the theory had been enunciated, only in China and in North Vietnam had the communists emerged as the dominant member of a coalition. In Latin America the communists had difficulties in leading the proletariat, not to speak of bourgeois nationalists. But no matter how difficult the situation, good communists must have faith in the future.

When Castro entered Havana on 8 January 1959 at the head of his guerillas, a coalition government was established following the lines of the Caracas Agreement of 20 July 1958, in which the PSP was not represented. The PSP started to publish its newspaper on the assumption that its activity was legal. Carlos Rafael Rodríguez, who had returned to Havana with Castro, said that the legality of the communist movement was taken for granted in a democracy. "It would have been offensive for Fidel Castro and his comrades to negotiate this point, and we would never have consented to this kind of negotiation."[46] The Soviet Union, on 10 January in the person of K. E. Voroshilov, officially recognized the new government of the Cuban Republic.[47] Cuba did not reciprocate.

Soon after his arrival in Havana, Castro made it clear that he would tolerate the communists. At a lunch in the Rotary Club he reassured the U.S. and Cuban businessmen by saying, "I am not a communist." But the next sentence was a reassurance to the communists. "Whoever is not a sellout or a stooge is accused of being a communist." Whoever believed in democracy, Castro said, could not deprive others of their rights.[48] If the PSP was not being warmly embraced, it was at least being given the hope that it could function openly. Even before Castro's entrance into Havana the PSP had promised support to the revolution and noted "the unusually favorable conditions for the revolution to complete its work."[49]

On 15 January, five days after the event, the Cuban communist newspaper reported in a dispatch from Moscow that Voroshilov, on behalf of the USSR, had recognized the provisional government of Cuba.[50] But the PSP was uncertain about the future. Blas Roca pointed out that the revolution had been made by the right, the center, and the left. The task of the PSP was to work with the center and the left against the right. Structural reforms had to be made, since the economic foundation of imperialism persisted. The PSP wanted to participate equally with other parties in the new tasks. But it was pushing unity too far to retain the Mujalists in the labor unions.[51] The workers did not yet have the right to assemble, and the old leadership still retained their posts. The armed forces of the 26th of July Movement had occupied the trade union meeting places and new appointments to leadership posts were made in rump meetings.[52] When the PSP complained to Castro, a committee in which they did not participate was appointed to lead the Confederation of Trade Unions.[53] The PSP also complained that safe conduct out of the country was permitted "for the miserable imperialist agent Eusebio Mujal."[54] The 26th of July Movement was not inclined to allow the PSP to recapture its position in the trade union movement, and it was to be many months before Castro would reverse that position.

Despite this cavalier treatment, the PSP continued to ask for participation in the government or at least for the exclusion of the more right wing elements. "The PSP is prepared to participate in a revolutionary cabinet that would be ready to consider and to satisfy the necessities of this moment and of the historic process. We want a change in the composition of the cabinet whether or not we are included in it." "We believe that if the Provisional Government is determined to be revolutionary, our inclusion in the cabinet would be highly useful. Indeed, it would be necessary."[55]

Castro was soon to assume the office of prime minister himself and to form the new government the PSP was demanding, but he was to ignore or reject the PSP's bid for participation. Meanwhile, the Soviet Union was beginning to make its judgments of the new situation in Cuba. A Soviet reporter in Cuba, in his first question to Fidel Castro, revealed the salient features of Soviet concern. What guarantee did Castro have that the United States would not invade Cuba as it had invaded Guatemala in 1954? Without reflection, Castro answered: "We have three guarantees. First, the guerilla army; second, the general support of the people in the country; and then, the situation is not the same as in 1954. It has changed in our favor."[56]

The same Soviet reporter in an interview with Guevara was told that the revolution was made mainly by the peasants and that in the rebel army the peasants constituted 50 percent, the workers about 10 percent, and the bourgeoisie the rest. Although the strike was of considerable help, it was basically a peasant revolution.

Marinello, the titular head of the PSP, explained that the 26th of July Movement, the largest mass organization in the country, had neither worked out a strategy for itself nor created much of an organization. Its right wing was larger than its left wing. But numbers were not important since the real power was held by the leftist revolutionaries who commanded the guerillas. The unsatisfactory composition of the government did not tell the whole story. Although Fidel was not in the government, he was the real ruler of Cuba.[57]

Thus, by talking to Castro and Guevara and the president of the PSP, a Soviet reporter in Cuba concluded even before Castro became prime minister that the rebel army, largely peasant in composition but led by intellectuals, exercised effective power in Cuba. Given Soviet experience in Latin America, two outcomes must have seemed likely. Either this government would come to represent the conservative elements in the 26th of July Movement with the consequence that the PSP would work alongside or in uneasy cooperation, or the government would move leftward and the United States would encourage the conservative elements in the 26th of July Movement and others to overthrow Castro. It seems unlikely that the Soviet Union on the basis of its earlier experience would have expected Castro to move leftward, the United States to invade and then quit, and Castro to then convert to communism and subordinate the communist party to his will.

On the contrary, the Soviet press and the international communist press did not hide their doubts about Castro. The major Soviet magazine devoted to international news greeted the victory of the people of Cuba, gave the PSP more credit than it deserved, and concluded by saying that many problems now confronted the people of Cuba. "They can cope with them only given unity of all the democratic and progressive elements."[58] The international communist movement was badly informed about events in Cuba and made its judgments on very general principles. Thus the French communists said that Castro, who had received much support from the United States, had become more conservative since 1956. But, on the other hand, the communists and organized labor had played a large role in the victory and thus for the first time had imparted a social content to a Cuban struggle against a dictator.[59] The president of the Cuban Communist party, in an article dated March 1959 for a Soviet book on Latin America, lamented the fact that

in some cases the officials of the Military Intelligence Service, an organization created by the tyranny especially for political persecution, and the members of the Bureau for the Repression of Communist Activities continue at their former posts. They were ardent adherents of the tyranny who hated the revolution and were imperialist lackeys.

The retention of these elements could lead, although in a different form and to a lesser degree, to a situation similar to the one that existed after the war for independence. Then, many petitioners who after the war went to one or another government office, there met the officials who had served the colonial power or officers who had sided with the Spanish Army and, with weapons in their hands, had campaigned against the independence of Cuba.[60]

Many months were to pass before the Cuban communists and their fellow communists abroad were to believe that Castro had burnt his bridges with the United States and could no longer dispense with their support.

When Castro took the office of prime minister on 16 February 1959, the PSP was disappointed. They were neither included in the new government nor were they permitted to expand their control in the labor unions. In foreign policy, too, Castro continued to hold the Soviet Union at arms length. At the end of January, the foreign minister of the Cuban provisional government, Roberto Agramonte, said that relations with Russia remained unchanged, that is, they were nonexistent.[61] Writing in a Soviet magazine in March, Marinello stressed that Cuba was formally free but economically subordinate, like other Latin American countries. Castro's actions are promising, he wrote, but our path is not strewn with roses. Cuba still does not have normal relations with the Soviet Union, although it has products that the Soviets would be anxious to acquire.[62] By printing these reflections of the president of the PSP in a popular Soviet magazine, the Soviet Union was inviting Cuba to establish relations and holding out the promise that it would buy sugar; but Castro was silent.

Castro evidently feared that if he moved closer to the PSP or to the Soviet Union he would furnish a pretext for foreign intervention in Cuba. Those who called him a communist because he did not attack communists were conspiring to cause foreign intervention in Cuba he said.[63] Khrushchev, in an interview with Latin American journalists, replied to a question about the limited market for Cuban sugar by saying it was not the Soviets fault that neither diplomatic nor commercial relations existed. After all the Soviet Union had been the first nation to recognize the new Cuban regime.[64]

But Castro was not responding to the importunities of the communists. The trade union leader, the mulatto Lazaro Peña, complained that after the triumph of the revolution the workers and not the state should run the unions.[65] But Castro was silent.

Although Castro gave the communists only the right to publish their newspaper, he refused to promote anticommunism. Just as the Cuban right wing and some persons in the United States threatened Castro with a new Guatemala if he went too far, so Castro threatened them with the communists if they went too far. If Castro proscribed the communists, he would have nothing left to threaten with. He was quite aware of the relationship between the communist issue and the possibility of a new Guatemala. The purpose of anticommunism, he said, was to justify an armed attack against Cuba and to combine Cuba's internal and external enemies. But the comparison, he said, with Guatemala was not appropriate. "The situation is very different. I know the men of the Rebel Army, I know the people of Cuba, and it would be a serious mistake to have illusions of this kind. In Guatemala the military were treacherous and fled, but here the soldiers of the Rebel Army are men who know how to die."[66]

Castro was treading very carefully between right and left, and on the eve of his visit to the United States in April, in response to an invitation from U.S. newspaper editors, he did not want to tip his hand. He would not tell his own economic advisors whether or not he would ask for a loan in the United States and forbade them, while there, to raise the subject on their own. He would neither embrace the communists nor disavow them. The Cuban communists were understandably quite nervous. General Maxwell Taylor had said that the Cuban revolution was only the first of a series. Nixon, they wrote, would press Castro to yield to his demands, which were identical with those of the Cuban right-wingers, or be labeled a communist—the prelude to an invasion of Cuba. But Fidel was not a capitulator: the existence of the USSR and the People's Republic of China had altered the situation. The U.S. threat to cut the sugar quota was meaningless since the USSR and China could buy whatever the United States did not, and at any rate, in two to four years Cuba could produce most of its own requirements in food and clothing and even produce export items.[67]

The Soviet press gave little attention to Cuban affairs on the eve of Castro's visit to the United States. In March, a Soviet journal devoted to communist party affairs published excerpts from Roca's report to the February plenum of the PSP. They repeated the PSP contention that the revolution had to go forward or lose mass support and that the United States had not yet given up the idea of intervention.[68] Moscow and the PSP were thereby joining in recommending that Castro radicalize his revolution, but their expectations differed. The PSP, believing that Castro could not stand still but had to move either to the left or the right, accepted the risk of intervention that leftward movement represented. The Soviet leaders, like the Cubans, agreed that Castro had to go forward, but unlike the Cubans, they expected the United States to intervene. *Pravda* reported that the Cuban example heartened the Dominican and Haitian rebels against tyranny. This frightened the United States and caused it to accuse Cuba of aggression.[69] The United States was trying to stop social reform and preserve private property in Cuba. When Castro rejected a coalition with the right, the United States made threats by drawing a comparison with the events in Guatemala.[70]

In the United States Castro was careful to disassociate himself from communism, to which he counterposed humanism. At the National Press Club in Washington, Castro, according to the *New York Times,* said: "We are against all kinds of dictators, whether of a man or of a country, or a class or an oligarchy or by the military. That is why we are against communism."[71]

The editors of the PSP newspaper, upset by these wire service reports, made telephone contact with Castro and obtained the following statement from him: "I also said to the American newspaper editors that Cuba has not denounced its international treaties [*viz.* the Rio Pact] and will observe them." "When I was asked what would happen in a struggle between democracy and communism, I replied: We don't agree with communism, but democracy has many faults. And the people should get something besides theoretical democracy."[72]

For the PSP this improved on the flat statement reported by the *New York Times* that "we are against communism." But on the other hand the organ of the 26th of July Movement emphasized the separation of Castro from communism, quoting a speech made by Castro in New York on 24 April 1959: "Neither bread without liberty, nor liberties without bread; neither dictatorships of man nor of classes; the government of the people without oligarchies; liberty with bread and without terror—that is humanism."[73]

If U.S. officials had read this, they might have been reassured, for Castro was saying that communism cannot bring bread without terror. But the U.S. press did not pick up this remark.

The PSP explained why Castro distanced himself from the communists and the Soviet Union. At the National Press Club in Washington, Castro stated that Cuba had not received any aid from the Soviet Union or any other nation, "and we have not asked for it."[74] Roca was asked in a television interview if he believed that the Cuban failure to establish diplomatic relations with the USSR reflected an anticommunist line. He said he did not, for many reasons: "First of all, the importance of certain international realities. They [the United States] threaten us here. If they say this [the present situation in Cuba] is communism, imagine what they would say then. I think that there are elements [in Cuba] who are too greatly influenced by these things. . . . The Platt Amendment was abolished in Cuba in 1933, but there are still people who have it in their heads. . . . You know how these ideas survive. There are even people who don't want to believe that orders can be given in Cuba [that we can be masters in our own house], that what must be done now can be done, but they always think they must do what they, far away, say. And they [Cubans] say that they [Americans] will be irritated and that they can be difficult."[75]

But although Roca explained Castro's caution in establishing relations with the Soviet Union as a concession to the right wing, he indicated that at some time Cuba should establish such relations. When asked whether Moscow would invite Castro, he replied that he had not consulted Moscow, "but it would be necessary for Cuba to have relations with Moscow."[76]

Before Castro left the United States his brother, Raúl, suddenly flew to

Houston, Texas, and met him there. There was some speculation that Raúl feared that Castro was surrendering to the United States.[77] But an alternative or supplementary explanation is suggested by the evidence. The reporter of the 26th of July Movement organ denied that Raúl's unplanned trip was caused by differences and implied that the cause was the unauthorized invasion of Panama by some Cuban members of Castro's army.[78]

In a radio message from his plane, which was proceeding to South America, Castro criticized those Cubans who had invaded Panama as irresponsibles who had probably done nothing during the revolution. Panama, he said, is not a tyranny like the Dominican Republic or Nicaragua. These irresponsibles took advantage of the leniency of the police in Cuba and embarassed the government of Cuba when he was abroad, said Castro.[79] Castro was implicitly justifying Cuban support of intervention against tyrannies, but he wanted, at that point at any rate, to avoid irritating the United States. It was Castro's sensitivity to what the United States might do that in turn worried the PSP.

THE PSP INTERNAL DEBATE AND CASTRO'S ATTACK ON THE PARTY

It was revealed later that before and during Castro's visit to the United States an important debate had taken place in the PSP between the exceptionalists and what turned out to be the majority of the PSP. The leader of the exceptionalists, Escalante, argued that Cuba represented a special case, that the revolution could proceed rapidly from one stage to the next. Just what he might have meant will be examined presently. His victorious opponents later characterized these views as "efforts to show that the Cuban revolution negated the Marxist thesis" but they admitted that at the May Plenum of the PSP, which lasted two months, the matter had been seriously considered.[80]

Escalante's position, to judge from a speech he made later in Peking, was that Castro, breaking with Cuban tradition, had become more radical rather than more conservative.[81] In China the bourgeoisie accepted the revolution and were coopted into it; the same might occur in Cuba, which meant that Castro would later yield control to the communists.

The victorious wing of the Cuban PSP, Escalante's opponents, said that the proletariat was not yet the hegemon of the Cuban revolution. As Roca argued, "the problem is how to establish this hegemony. It is not attained by proclaiming it." As late as October he talked of the necessity of attaining leadership of the revolution and winning over the radical petite-bourgeoisie for the proletarian ideology.[82] In other words, the bourgeoisie was still important in Castro's movement; the PSP had yet to attain ideological leadership. The logical conclusion was that the PSP could not push Castro too hard without risking pushing him to the right.

Very soon the PSP had to worry about defending themselves against Castro instead of arguing among themselves how best to manipulate him. But the Soviet observers were either unaware of or unconcerned by Castro's shift to hostility toward the PSP, because the Soviet press carried a long and favorable report on all the positive events in Cuba and ignored the bitter polemics between the PSP and the 26th of July Movement, which are described below. The Soviet journal *New Times* was presumably moved to its high praise by the promulgation of the Agrarian Reform Law. The day on which the law was promulgated, 17 May 1959, would go down as one of the memorable days in Cuban history, the Soviet journal wrote. Ruling groups had not merely been reshuffled, as had so often happened in Latin American politics, but the composition of the social forces ruling Cuba had been radically changed. The PSP had supported Castro and had urged the inclusion of its representatives in the government. The major opposition to the new government came from the United States rather than from inside the country. The United States was trying to use the bogey of revolution to promote intervention, but Cuba's experience showed that the democratic and national liberation forces on the continent were growing irresistibly.[83] Castro, although not to be trusted completely, had moved far enough to the left to merit official Soviet praise. The PSP supported him, although it was not part of the government. The United States might intervene and crush the Cuban revolution, but anti–U.S. nationalism was growing irresistibly. Castro's revolution was more radical than any earlier revolution. Subsequent events demonstrated that the Marxist frame of reference was a useful predictive tool in this case. The far-ranging agrarian law did change the balance of social forces in Cuba; it led almost immediately to a conflict between Castro and some of his middle-class comrades-in-arms, and it contributed greatly to the radicalization of the Cuban revolution.

Whether the Soviet writer praising Castro was aware that the PSP was being harassed by the 26th of July Movement with Castro's approval we do not know. But since a rapprochement quickly followed the quarrel between Castro and the PSP, the Soviet press was spared the task of reconciling its generally favorable attitude toward Castro with Castro's hostility to the Cuban communists. To anticipate the course of events somewhat, it may be remarked that the radical character of the Agrarian Reform Law precipitated the opposition of some prominent members of the armed forces, who broke with Castro, accusing him of falling under communist influence. Castro's immediate response was to style as traitors those who questioned his authority and to accept the long standing communist offer of service in a subordinate capacity. We now return to the struggle of the PSP and the 26th of July Movement in May 1959.

During Castro's stay in Montevideo, where he stopped before returning from Washington, he said that he was opposed to dictatorships of the left as well as the right.[84] As the leadership of the 26th of July Movement of Havana stated, the slogan of the revolution was "Liberty with Bread, Bread without Terror." They were against unity with reactionary oligarchs and minority antidemocratic groups.[85] It seems very likely that Raúl Castro did not share this very negative appraisal of the PSP, for in his 1 May speech he criticized those who gave lip service to unity but actually practiced disunity, specifically, those who raised the banner of anticommunism and made accusations that there were communists in the government and in the leadership of the Rebel Army.[86] According to Felipe Pazos, who was still in the government at that time, Raúl had criticized Castro privately for being anticommunist.[87]

The 26th of July Movement attacked the PSP, reminding them of their collaboration with Batista and accusing them of trying to divide the Oriente rebels who landed in the ship *Granma* from those who fought in the plains and in the cities.[88] The PSP, which had not yet resolved its internal struggle over the nature of the Cuban revolution, then moved to divide the 26th of July Movement—evidently in order to push Castro leftward. Bypassing the leadership of the 26th of July Movement, the PSP signed a unity pact with a local branch of the 26th of July Movement. In a statement that Castro was supposed to have dictated,[89] the organ of the 26th of July Movement exploded in anger, charging that the communists were intriguing with the lower levels of the 26th of July Movement to force an unacceptable communist cast on the humanist revolution.[90]

A few days later Castro made public his association with these views. In a TV interview he stated that strikes were counterrevolutionary and that there were indeed coincidences between communists and counterrevolutionaries.[91] The PSP protested that this attack was totally unjust.[92]

Emboldened by their victories, the anticommunists in the 26th of July Movement won control of the Sugar Workers Congress in an electoral campaign the communists called fraudulent. Said Roca: "We are at a critical moment for the revolution. The declarations of Fidel Castro have been followed by the employment of methods which are brutally antidemocratic in the Sugar Congress and the creation of an atmosphere of provocation and attacks by rightist elements and the elements influenced by all the anticommunist propaganda. The belief that attacking the communists and fighting against unity with them will prevent the imperialists and counterrevolutionaries from attacking the revolution is a false illusion."[93] Roca was stating as plainly as possible that Castro could not hope to appease the interventionists in the United States and their allies in Cuba by breaking with the communists.

If indeed the PSP had tried to improve its position by splitting the 26th of July Movement and moving the revolution leftward it had failed.

Immediately following this effort Casto hit out more sharply at the PSP than he had ever done since his entrance into Havana in January. The plenum of the PSP, which had been wrangling for two months, with the exceptionalists exerting a great deal of influence,[94] now came down definitively on the side of caution. They secured the adoption of the thesis that the revolution was of the kind often defined as bourgeois democratic in colonial countries. The classes that moved the revolution were the peasantry, the working class, the urban petite bourgeoisie, and the national bourgeoisie.

In communist doctrinal formulations, ranking is of the essence, and to list the peasantry first meant that the proletariat was not the hegemon of the revolution. So as to leave no doubts about the relative role of the proletariat and the peasantry, the armed struggle in Cuba between 1956 and 1959 was described as having been the principal form of struggle, while "strikes and workers' actions in the cities played an auxiliary role of support for the armed struggle." The PSP obliquely confessed its own weak influence over the proletariat by contrasting the supposedly principal role of the workers in the overthrow of Machado in 1933 with the situation in 1957 and 1958 when the workers were divided and under the influence of Mujal (that is, Batista).

As always, the PSP had to be careful not to charge its enemies with encouraging U.S. intervention, for the fear of provoking intervention was the best argument for communist passivity. ". . . The imperialist Yankees can no longer readily impose their conditions and their government on Latin America and can no longer intervene militarily and diplomatically in Latin American countries as readily as thirty years ago." But—and here they revealed the depth of their fears—provocateurs at the service of the imperialists recruit unsophisticated or confused people "to liberate other countries"—like the recent invasion of Panama, "with the purpose of creating a situation that would justify the campaigns of alarm and intervention."[95]

The PSP continued[96] to suggest that the Soviet Union and the other socialist countries would purchase Cuban sugar despite the fact that the USSR was a sugar exporter. The USSR was increasing its sugar consumption and besides, it could reduce its production and sell sugar to China in order to provide Cuba with industrial goods, one Cuban writer argued.[97] Such arguments either fell on deaf ears in the Soviet Union or went unnoticed. The chief organ of the CPSU in making a general argument about the forms of pressure employed by the United States against underdeveloped countries noted that the United States had postponed its decision on renewal of the sugar quota (the agreement expired at the end of 1960), explaining that "the U.S. threat not to renew the agreement to import sugar is calculated to put the revolutionary people of Cuba in a difficult position."[98]

No mention was made of the suggestions in the Cuban press and by Cubans in the Soviet press that the Soviet Union purchase the sugar. Presumably, as Khrushchev had explained earlier, it was up to the Cubans to take the next step. The Soviet Union had been the first country to recognize the new regime.[99]

But the Cuban government was not moving in this direction. A Cuban newspaper, *El Mundo*, argued against resuming relations with the USSR so as, said the PSP, to reduce Cuba's resistance to economic pressure. On the contrary, said the PSP, Cuba should widen her markets.[100]

CASTRO MOVES TOWARD THE PSP

Very soon after the buffeting he administered to the PSP, Castro radically changed his attitude toward it. This change of position seems to have been related to the internal crisis precipitated by Castro's Law of Agrarian Reform. In 1957 many middle-class Cubans had begun to sympathize with Castro because Batista was torturing their sons. In 1959 many of these sons began to lose their faith in Castro because he was threatening to impoverish their fathers by confiscating their property. The United States routinely asked for "prompt, adequate, and effective compensation" for the property of its nationals affected by the Agrarian Reform Law. The next day Castro secured the dismissal of the more moderate members of the cabinet. The most important change was the substitution of Raúl Roa for Agramonte as foreign minister. Although Roa had been anticommunist, he had joined the revolution and was, unlike Agramonte, anti–North American.[101]

Soon the first prominent member of the 26th of July Movement defected to the United States. Díaz Lanz, the commander of the Air Force, stated publicly that he was against dictatorship of every kind, especially communist dictatorship. Castro reprimanded him and relieved him of his military duties. Díaz fled Cuba for Miami with his family. Soon thereafter a force invaded the Dominican Republic, a force widely believed to have originated in Cuba. Díaz Lanz in his testimony before the Senate Internal Subcommittee said that he had refused to pilot a plane for the group invading the Dominican Republic.[102] In the United Nations the Cuban representative said that Cuba supported the rebels "who have raised themselves against the satrapy of Trujillo."[103] Eisenhower, in a press conference on 1 July, said that the United States was watching developments in the Caribbean but would depend on the OAS to recommend action. Castro discerned, or professed to discern, a plot in all this. The Díaz resignation was obviously part of a plan to accuse Cuba of being communist, since Trujillo was making the same accusation.[104]

Now that Castro was being attacked by his former comrades-in-arms and by elements in the United States, he dropped his attack on the communists. "I hardly consider it honorable that in order not to be accused of being communists, we begin to campaign against them and have to attack them."[105] Dictators are loath to admit that opposition can have native roots. It is easier to say, and to believe, that opposition is foreign-inspired. For the Soviets in 1968, the dissident views of the Dubcek communists could not be a response to a disastrous party policy; they had to be of West German inspiration. To Castro, opposition to his policies had to be a Yankee plot. If some of his former comrades-in-arms in the 26th of July Movement had allied themselves with the Yankee enemy, the communists whom he had scorned during the last stages of the revolution, and whose demands he had since rejected, would become his allies.

The PSP, now that it was no longer ostracized, continued to press for the sale of Cuban sugar to socialist states. In this campaign the party discovered, or was informed, that it could use the Chinese to move the Russians. The PSP organ reported that Chinese visitors to Cuba had said that it was possible that both countries would soon establish relations. "We [the Chinese] are ready to buy all the sugar that Cuba sells us. When relations with China are established we will be able to sell Cuba machinery, agricultural and industrial equipment, and other things we manufacture."[106]

Castro, for the first time, addressed himself to the subject of establishing diplomatic relations with communist countries. "We understood that it is a right of the peoples to maintain relations with all the other peoples of the world. We have not directed our attention to these problems because we were busy with others."[107]

Consequently both the Cuban communists who had been complaining about Castro's behavior and the Soviet organs that had been silent now joined in praising Castro's resolution and his revolutionary example.[108] Another sign of the PSP-Castro rapprochement was the publication in *Hoy* of a statement by the Dominican communists that the Cuban guerilla struggle was a model.[109]

Possibly in response to the indications that China would buy Cuban sugar, the Soviet Union started to purchase Cuban sugar, but at low prices and in modest quantities. Between 1955 and 1958 under Batista, Cuba had sold over a million tons of sugar to the USSR. In 1959 the USSR bought half a million tons from Castro's Cuba. This was not necessarily the beginning of growing annual purchases, since in 1959 the Soviet Union had experienced a drought that had reduced its sugar beet crop.[110] Yet the PSP claimed that Cuba could sell all its surplus sugar to the socialist countries once it had established economic relations. Probably because of the modest size of the Soviet purchases, the secretary of the PSP hastened to add that Cuba did not want to lose the North American market as long as it could sell sugar there and yet maintain its dignity and independence.[111] Chou En-lai told visiting Cubans that "we can purchase a very large amount of sugar from Cuba if our commercial relations are directly established."[112]

Encouraged by the prospect of help from the socialist camp, the PSP outlined a strategy less optimistic than the exceptionalist theory of Escalante but more optimistic than had seemed possible when Castro was attacking them in May. At the October plenum of the party, Blas Roca dealt with the Cuban problem more realistically than ever before. Cuba was very close to the United States and had to import much of her food and fuel since the population had become accustomed to a standard of living not commensurate with the stage of development of the country. (A curious admission that semicolonialism brought some benefits to the masses!) Some used these undoubted disadvantages to preach defeatism. But they were wrong. The deficit in food and fuel was transitory. The economic reforms would soon bear fruit. But even if the enemies of the revolution denied Cuba food and fuel, Cuba could obtain them from the socialist market. The power of the imperialists was not to be despised even though they had become weaker. The United States could not obtain an OAS resolution against Cuba as it had done against Guatemala in 1954. In Guatemala the treachery of the army had insured the success of the counterrevolution, but in Cuba the army was thoroughly revolutionary.

Roca then proceeded to repeat the standard communist arguments for a decision to move cautiously. The middle classes had not yet exhausted their revolutionary potential, and premature steps toward socialism would drive them to alliance with the imperialists. The Chinese had handled the situation skillfully. The Chinese bourgeoisie had not been frightened off by immediate confiscation of their property; they had cooperated with the communists and had finally submitted to the communists' political will. But in Cuba, the radical sector of the bourgeoisie (i.e., Castro) led the revolution and might adopt socialism if the international situation continued to be favorable and if revolutions like its own succeeded elsewhere in Latin America.[113]

The estimation was sober but not gloomy. The Cuban revolution could survive and become more radical if the United States did not intervene or sponsor intervention; if other countries in Latin America would follow the Cuban example; if Cuba could quickly produce her own necessities; if the socialist countries would render assistance; and if the Cuban bourgeoisie would accept the radicalization of the revolution not only as inevitable but as in their own interest. As we know, only some of these conditions were met, and the revolution survived nevertheless.

The next step in the radicalization of the revolution occurred in connection with another defection from the 26th of July Movement. Hubert Matos, a much acclaimed hero of the revolution, resigned as military governor of Camagüey on 19 October, a few days after Raúl Castro had joined the cabinet as minister of the Armed Forces. Unlike Díaz Lanz, Matos did not flee the country, but claimed loyalty to the revolution, a purer loyalty—by implication—than that of Castro himself. Matos's letter of resignation asked for permission to return home as a civilian, "without having my sons afterwards learn in the street that their father is a traitor or a deserter."[114] But Castro was unmoved. The very fact that Matos was parting company with the revolution honorably and not jumping over to the other side made him more of a threat. Castro came to Camagüey personally to arrest Matos, and on the following day Díaz Lanz flew a B–25 bomber from Florida, dropping leaflets over the city. Some casualties occurred, probably from shells fired at the aircraft by a Cuban frigate. Whether or not the bomber flown by Días Lanz was fitted out to drop bombs was never satisfactorily determined, but the Cubans obviously decided to exploit the incident. A pamphlet entitled *Havana's Pearl Harbor* had a picture of an air battle over Cuba. It was a photomontage of U.S. C–54's over New Jersey in 1947.[115] The inevitable comparisons with Guatemala were made. Roca pointed out that the attacks on Havana did not create panic as they had in Guatemala. The masses carried signs saying they would buy airplanes from the Russians if the British refused to sell them.[116]

But the Soviet press, which noted these events after a long silence on Cuban questions, was much calmer than the leaders of the PSP. The events were put into the context of a U.S. anticommunist campaign against Venezuela and Cuba, since antigovernmental conspiracies had broken almost simultaneously in both countries. In Havana, air raids from American territory not only scattered leaflets but employed machine guns. "This shameless act is more like direct armed intervention than ordinary conspiracy."[117] *Pravda* reported that "still another hornet's nest had been liquidated" in the frustration of the Matos plot. But the United States was still not ready to lay down its arms.[118]

The two Russian journalists who had been in Cuba in 1959 were a little more definite about the intention of the United States to intervene. The attempt to stick the "communist" label on Castro was part of an attempt to initiate intervention against Cuba, wrote one observer.[119] Another observer, in the foreword to a Russian translation of an American communist's booklet on Cuba, wrote that the imperialists, echoing 1954, "manufactured provocations, lies, and slanders with the purpose of preparing for open intervention in Cuba." The *New York Journal-American* on 12 November 1959 even went so far as to say that the Soviet Union was constructing missile bases in Cuba.[120] It would be ironic indeed if the first notion of establishing a missile base in Cuba came from the Soviet reading of the Hearst press.

Having gone through the Guatemalan experience and having mistakenly underestimated the U.S. proclivity to intervene, the Soviet Union was cautious in giving aid to Cuba and sober in its prognostications. Unlike 1954, there were no articles in the authoritative Soviet *Kommunist* in 1959 that sharply criticized Soviet authors who believed that the United States could bring about a coup d'état whenever it pleased. On the contrary, the scanty Soviet coverage of Cuban events reiterated the lessons of Guatemala and the possibility that the United States might seek to unseat the Castro regime either by support of internal reactionary forces or by overt intervention. Furthermore, no arms were provided to Castro, even through an intermediary, as had been the case in Guatemala. The Soviet Union probably had learned the lesson from Guatemala that arms shipments to Castro would, to use Soviet language, provoke U.S. intervention.

The relations between the Soviet Union and the United States had changed greatly since 1954. In the first year of the post-Stalin regime the Soviet Union had not settled on a government, and its foreign policy was conducted by a coalition of many diverse elements. Some wanted reconciliation of a kind with the United States, and others pressed for and obtained the adoption of irritating measures like the provision of arms to Guatemala in 1954 and to Egypt in 1955. But by the end of 1959 the Khrushchev faction was firmly in control, and one of Khrushchev's goals was to reach a limited accommodation with the United States on coexistence. This coexistence had to be limited to parry the Chinese charge that the Soviet Union was neglecting its revolutionary duties. Coexistence had to be compatible with some Soviet political gains—in West Berlin, in the Congo, or in Laos. Presumably the United States would yield now where it had not yielded before—because peace demanded it. But the Soviet Union could not credibly argue that peace was in danger, that is, it could not threaten war unless its military superiority over the United States was unmistakable. The adjustment with the United States would be difficult enough without assuming the burden of defending a Cuban revolution whose leader had so recently fallen out with the communists.

Some sense of disappointment at the restrained Soviet enthusiasm for Cuba comes through in Roca's remarks congratulating the Cubans for not panicking as had the Guatemalans when U.S. planes attacked. Support from the socialist camp was appended almost as an afterthought, and the Soviet Union was listed after China.[121] Apparently the Soviet Union was keeping its distance from Cuba. Mikoian was in Mexico in November attending a Soviet trade fair. He was the highest Soviet official who had ever visited Latin America, and *Revolución* proposed that he extend his journey to Havana.[122] According to Felipe Pazos the Cubans made the offer to Mikoian personally in Mexico City but were put off.[123] But later Mikoian stated that the Cubans had invited him and he had accepted.[124]

In late December it was announced that the Soviet exhibition would move to Havana from Mexico City.[125] One can only speculate on the reasons, but an article by Escalanate that appeared in *Pravda* in the interim is suggestive. Escalante had been traveling in China. This temporary exile was probably the penalty for losing in the factional struggle of April and May within the PSP. But he was returning, after having been removed from the scene, with his views somewhat vindicated. Castro had patched up his quarrel with the PSP; he had started the process of surrendering the trade unions to the communists by severing their connections with ORIT (an international labor organization with ties to the AFL-CIO and openly anticommunist), had publicly raised the question of relations with the Soviet Union and, apparently, had solicited a visit from Mikoian.

Escalante returned from China by way of Moscow and (for the first time) wrote an article for the Soviet press. Escalante would have been obtuse indeed if he had not realized that making speeches in Peking constituted the most effective claim for attention in Moscow. In his *Pravda* article Escalante diverged from the formulas of the October plenum of the PSP.[126] While Roca's report to the plenum said that the radical sector of the petite-bourgeoisie was presently the hegemon of the Cuban revolution, Escalante obscured the issue of who the true leader of the revolution was. While admitting that it was not the working class that led the revolution, he described the proletariat and the peasantry, in that order, as the decisive force in the struggle against tyranny and as now exercising great influence on the course of events. Much had been accomplished in ten months. The frustration of the various conspiracies revealed the weakness of reactionaries who could not present a serious danger to the revolution. The conspirators did not have the slightest chance of shaking the government. After these enthusiastic phrases, the most confident appraisal of Cuba's future yet to appear in the Soviet press, Escalante hedged a bit by saying "it would be dangerous on our part to forget *completely*[127] about the existence of . . . the expansionist plans [of the United States]. But if Cuba is attacked directly or indirectly, she will fight. Cuba has not been and will not be a Guatemala. . . ."

Escalante's main point was repeated in *Izvestiia* a few days later. The Guatemalan scenario could not be repeated despite the strong U.S. desire to do so. The next remarks of the Soviet commentator illustrated the dilemma of the Cuban communists. If they stressed the likelihood of U.S. intervention, Castro would be under pressure to push them aside to save himself from the United States; if they discounted the danger of U.S. intervention, they committed themselves to Castro's survival. For the United States to call a country communist that did not even have diplomatic relations with the Soviet Union, *Izvestiia* said, could only be an excuse to prepare the ground for armed foreign intervention. But the determination of the Cuban leaders, actively supported by their own people and the peoples of Latin America, doomed this effort.[128] The Soviet position was a bit inconsistent. The Soviets refrained from offering assistance on the ground that it was not needed and then chided the Cubans —indirectly, as above—for seeking a promise of assistance when they would not even establish relations with the USSR. Khrushchev, in another interview, again protested that the Soviet Union was not at fault for the inadequate state of relations wih Latin American states.[129] The United States will probably invade Cuba and the attempt will fail; this was the Soviet message, with the clear implication that Soviet assistance would not be needed and would not be forthcoming.

But for the PSP it was unpolitic to predict a U.S. invasion without a Soviet guarantee to help repel it. If the Cuban Communist party could have said that invasion was likely and that the Soviet Union would help Cuba to repel it, they could hope to play an important role in Cuban politics. But to say that invasion was likely and that the Soviet Union would not help was an invitation to Castro to patch up his quarrel with the United States at their expense. The PSP handled the dilemma quite skillfully. They rejected the notion that they said had appeared in the U.S. and (noncommunist) Cuban press that Castro, Moscow, or the PSP wanted to provoke a U.S. invasion. The fundamental question was whether the Cuban revolution would have to cope with the enmity of Washington or whether it could gain U.S. toleration. North America would remain an irreconcilable enemy of the Cuban revolution but would not necessarily attack Cuba directly, (so Castro would gain nothing by sacrificing the PSP was the implication); Washington would resort to direct aggression only as a last resort (so Castro need not make desperate attempts to conciliate the irreconcilable enemy), and the most probable form of aggression would be "armed attack by the native Castillo Armas' under the auspices, protection, and direction of North American imperialism" (in which case the PSP would be a valuable ally).[130]

If Castro accepted this analysis, his best tactic would be to provoke, identify, and eliminate his opposition within the 26th of July Movement. Whether Castro even noted the PSP analysis or whether he consciously worked it out for himself cannot be known, but he acted as if he had done one or the other. For the PSP, a rapprochement between Cuba and the United States would have been a disaster. If that had happened, Castro would have had no need for the PSP. Castro had shown himself to be quite ruthless in discarding even former comrades-in-arms, and the communists hardly qualified as such. As a matter of fact, to anticipate somewhat, when Castro achieved—not friendship with the United States, but the deterrence of the U.S. impulse to intervene in Cuba—he absorbed the PSP into his own party with scant ceremony.

As for the Soviet Union, it could not equate the benefits that were expected to flow from friendship with the United States and the political necessities of the PSP. For Khrushchev, an understanding with Eisenhower meant the recognition of Soviet equality with the greatest power in the world; he hoped this would relieve him of the expensive necessity of trying to match the greatly superior U.S. strategic forces. In fact, on 14 January 1960 Khrushchev proposed an extensive reduction of Soviet forces—a project he was never able to fully effectuate—in anticipation of improved relations with the United States. Khrushchev's own career within the Soviet Union depended on the conversion of the generalities of Camp David enunciated in the autumn into tangible benefits, like savings in the military budget. It was too much to suppose that the needs of Castro, Roca, or Escalante would be allowed to stand in the way of Khrushchev's own political requirements.

3. CUBA AND THE SOVIET UNION EMBRACE

During the year 1959 and especially during its second half the Cuban revolution moved leftward faster than Castro had anticipated and faster than most of the PSP had believed possible. Later Castro argued that he had intended to radicalize the revolution all along but that prudence had dictated concealment of his design.[1] More probably Castro, like most political leaders, was following a strategy based on a few simple goals and adjusting his daily course to tactical necessities. He was more concerned with the image he presented of independence than with the ultimate nature of the Cuban polity. Even firmly entrenched leaders of powerful countries behave in this way. A leader of a weak state, especially one newly emerged from semicolonial status, was more urgently compelled to frame his policy from day to day. If Castro was to remain in power as a charismatic leader who bore the aureole of a bright new day, he could not compromise on the issue of sovereignty and independence. If he yielded, or seemed to yield, on the Cuban right to manage Cuban affairs without interference from the United States, he could not claim to be better than many other Cuban political leaders. It was the feeling of "free-at-last" that constituted Castro's greatest political capital. Cuban independence was so new and shaky that it required reiterated validation. This necessity coincided with very different political necessities in the Soviet Union and in the United States, and the interaction among these was to prove fateful for all three.

In 1959 and 1960 the United States feared, more than ever before or ever since, that the Soviet Union could reach and surpass it. The launching of sputnik in 1957 and the testing of the first Soviet intercontinental ballistic missile had set off a sort of panic in the United States, accompanied by public breast-beating and cries of: "We have been asleep at the switch"—and as the presidential elections approached, that the Republicans had been asleep at the switch. It was even feared that the U.S. economy was stagnant, while the Soviet Gross National Product was bounding forward. Both Republicans and Democrats agreed that communism represented a multiple threat; they differed on where blame lay for the sorry state to which the proud United States had been reduced, and they competed in verbal expressions of repugnance for communism and determination to resist its expansion.

Realizing, with the benefit of hindsight, that the missile gap of 1958–61 was the product of overheated fears; that the Soviet attainment of rough parity in strategic nuclear weapons has not radically shifted the balance of power; that the Soviet economy was headed for the doldrums instead of easy superiority over the United States; and finally, that the major communist states were soon to fall out among themselves, it is difficult to recapture the mood of January 1960. But only if we peel away the layers of hindsight and reveal the assumptions of the time can we understand American policy.

Most American political leaders feared that the Soviet Union was a formidable opponent in the military, economic, and political spheres and that the United States had to hold the line against Soviet expansion while it regained the military and economic superiority it seemed mysteriously to have lost since the end of World War II. Even if the status quo in Europe could be maintained in the face of augmented Soviet strategic power, it was feared that the Soviet Union could shift the balance of world power by winning over to its side the newly independent states of the Third World, like Cuba. American political leaders differed only on priorities and modalities in meeting the threat; they agreed that the threat was mortal. President Eisenhower, having access to U–2 photography and long acquainted with the hyperbole of the armed services in assessing the military strength of putative enemies, was quite relaxed about the Soviet missile threat. His Democratic opponents were prepared to believe that the old general had neglected the national defense out of deference to the views of the millionaires in the cabinet for whom fear of an unbalanced budget blunted concern for keeping American power second to none.

Americans could, and did, differ in April 1954 on the wisdom of employing U.S. troops to win a victory over Vietnamese communists, a victory that had eluded the French. But the argument was over price, not principle. As we have already seen, when the price for scotching the possibility of communism in Guatemala was accounted to be low, hardly a voice was raised in objection. Men of both parties had been divided on the issue of intervention in Indo-China, but intervention in Guatemala a month later was hardly debated. The issue was whether the game was worth the candle; never at issue was the desirability of "stopping communism."

Thus, in 1960, the two presidential candidates were Tweedledum and Tweedledee on the Cuban question. Both strongly supported the restoration of "freedom" to Cuba and competed with each other in expressions of revulsion at the prospect of communism in Cuba. That these sentiments served immediate electoral necessities should not obscure the deep conviction with which they were held. Any American president tempted to temporize and to hope that the passage of time would make Castro's bark seem worse than his bite had to be prepared for extensive opposition from both parties. Thus, duty and partisan advantage dictated prophylactic action in Cuba. This precluded American action that would have created the best of all possible political worlds for Castro and not the worst for the United States. The United States could have tolerated assaults on its property and pride and eschewed economic sanctions and subversion. The reward of restraint might have been a Cuban flirtation with the Soviet Union never consummated in marriage. Castro could have accepted costly gifts from Moscow and yet have continued to receive the benefits of the sugar quota from a United States unwilling to impel him into the arms of what was believed to be an eager suitor. Castro would have preferred to play just this role, and at first Eisenhower tended to be accommodating. But as long as Cuba permitted her old patron to hope while winking at a rival, the Soviet Union, which had its own pride to maintain, proferred only moderate aid. But Eisenhower yielded to pressures to do something about the threat of communism (pressures not confined to the right wing of either party) and the dictates of what was thought to be common prudence. To the Cubans and the Soviets, the United States seemed to move inexorably toward a Guatemala in Cuba.

SOVIET APPRECIATION OF THE SITUATION IN 1960

Events at home and abroad since Stalin's death convinced some Soviet leaders and Khrushchev in particular that the world balance of power was shifting and that the new military strength of the Soviet Union was only the most dramatic feature of this general phenomenon. They were anticipating by ten or fifteen years. Very few Soviet (or Western) leaders realized that the striking Soviet achievements in space technology could not be immediately translated into intercontinental nuclear military weapons and that only a decade of intensive effort and massive expenditure would bring the Soviet Union alongside the United States in nuclear military prowess. During the SALT negotiations in 1971 and 1972, U.S. negotiators realized that very high Soviet civilian officials only learned of the number and nature of their own weapons when Americans introduced the data into the negotiations.[2] In 1961 very few civilian leaders (and probably very few military leaders) realized that Soviet nuclear parity was the music of the future.

To attain his political goals Khrushchev needed to keep secret how modest the Soviet intercontinental missile capability really was. Khrushchev's boasts and threats about the power of Soviet nuclear missiles had served him well until then. In December 1956 France and Great Britain, still militarily and economically dependent on the United States, had no choice, they felt, but to break off their invasion of Egypt when the United States opposed it. But Khrushchev injected himself into the situation and addressed notes to the French and British governments pointing out that in the nuclear age, when the Soviet Union could literally destroy France and Great Britain, it was reckless of them to start a war with Egypt. The still incomplete documentation of this episode suggests that the British and French political leaders responded to the threat of abandonment by the United States rather than to the threat of Soviet missiles, but the threat of abandonment was meaningful to the extent that the British and French feared the power of the USSR. Dulles's threat to his European allies was only credible if they believed that the Soviet Union was dangerous.

Whether or not Khrushchev believed that his stern warning had saved Egypt from the reimposition of colonialism, he acted as if he did, and the Soviet press dutifully reflected that view. Perhaps this "triumph" balanced the fiasco that Khrushchev's policies had produced in Hungary at the end of 1956. At any rate, Khrushchev pursued a consistent campaign of nuclear menace from then until the October 1962 missile crisis. He frequently reminded the leaders and populations of Western European countries that only a small number of H-Bombs—four in one case, six in another—could destroy their countries, so that not one stone would be left standing upon another. In 1958, just when the Taiwan Straits crisis had passed from confrontation to negotiation, Khrushchev announced that Soviet missiles would be employed if China were attacked, thus protecting China from a danger that had already passed.

Khrushchev claimed that in Egypt Soviet nuclear missile strength had saved a newly independent country from the restoration of colonialism, and in the Taiwan Straits crisis, a socialist country from attack by the United States. Khrushchev took political credit for using Soviet military might as an effective shield for weak countries whose social policies had excited the hostility of the United States. After some doubts Castro came to rely on that shield.

But Khrushchev's policy was not simply one of employing missile threats to cause Western European states to prefer the costs of accommodation with the Soviet Union to the risks of protection by the United States. He also wished to cause the United States to swallow the hostility of former colonies like Cuba and perhaps even their transition to communism. Such a world process would slowly erode the economic and political bases of U.S. imperialism and eventually but surely cause the socialist commonwealth of nations to grow. Khrushchev believed such an outcome to be inevitable, and his socialist duty was to speed the day. But since the happy day would come sooner or later, great risks could not be justified merely to bring it closer. Khrushchev, therefore, was unwilling to risk ultimata to the United States in the style of Prussia to Austria in the nineteenth century. Either the government of X accepts the government of Y's terms by a certain date, or the government of Y will declare war. Khrushchev believed and said that nuclear war had to be avoided and that coexistence was a necessity since no conceivable gains could compensate for the costs of a nuclear war. On his own assumptions it would have been an act of madness for the Soviet Union to make war against the United States, because the latter refused to surrender a political position. For that very reason Khrushchev's threats on the Berlin question failed to carry conviction in the last analysis. Berlin was Khrushchev's pressure point, or as he put it with his pungent inelegance, the corn on which he trod. But he did not threaten war; he only threatened that if the United States did not yield, events might get out of hand, and that despite the interests of both great powers and the wishes of their leaders, nuclear war might eventuate. This was very different from the ultimatum or last chance to submit before being attacked. The Americans, who had somberly appraised the consequences of a war fought with nuclear weapons and who doubted their own superiority in missiles, were unsettled by even incomplete threats of war, but the flaw in the strategy of nuclear terror was that the Soviet Union feared war no less than the United States did.

Khrushchev's menacing talk or blackmail was calculated to harass his opponents, to get them to yield on a particular issue in order to "relax tension." The issues he chose often did not admit of any clear-cut judgment of who was right or wrong. The political arrangements for Berlin had been intended to be only temporary, a circumstance advanced as justification for their looseness. A West Berlin basically under NATO control and situated deep in the territory of East Germany was neither sensible nor convenient. Justice was hardly the issue. The two great powers shared in the responsibility for the division of Germany that neither had deliberately intended. The awkward status of Berlin was only part of the larger issue of Germany. Both parties shared a belief in the domino theory and therefore believed that a change in the status of West Berlin was a sure augury of great events. The Berlin question, like the German question, was a question neither of justice nor of international law. Each of the two great powers feared that any compromise on the Berlin issue would break the political will of its German client. Hence, a demand by either party on the other for any change in the status of Berlin was inevitably viewed as the first in a series of changes that would produce a catastrophe.

On the Cuban issue, by contrast, the U.S. position was hard to defend convincingly to any but Americans. The U.S. attempts to revindicate its position in Cuba ran afoul of international law. The United States, while insisting that Cuba was a sovereign state, had treated her like a semi-colony. Now Castro sought to convert the fiction of Cuba's independence into reality and claimed that Cuba could make whatever laws she chose about private property in Cuba and could abrogate or make treaties, including treaties of alliance. Cuba proposed to exercise her sovereign rights in defiance of U.S. wishes. Few countries in Latin America had attempted to do this, and fewer had succeeded. In the late 1930s Mexico had been able to exercise sovereignty over her mineral and oil resources largely because the United States, afraid of Nazi Germany's growing power, was prepared to pay a price for hemispheric solidarity. The U.S. position in the Cuban crisis was awkward, because if Cuba was sovereign, her political ideology and her preferences in commercial and political partners were her own business. The United States felt constrained by convention from insisting on maintaining its preeminent position in Latin America as a matter of natural right. The Soviet Union, however, contended that the revolution of the Third World included Latin America as well as Asia and Africa and believed that the peoples of these countries would look to the Soviet Union as a natural (and powerful) ally against imperialism. On the Cuban issue, the Soviet view ultimately prevailed, for after a series of dramatic ups and downs, the subject of the next chapters, Cuba remained defiant and inviolate. The Soviet Union, in associating itself with the forces of anticolonialism and anti-American nationalism, had picked the winning side.

In 1960 the Soviet leaders, while warning that a "lack of realism" might lead to an unwanted nuclear war, avoided a crisis in which the United States would have to choose between surrender on a political issue or war. The Soviet Union sought U.S. retreat without making specific threats that would risk war or whose abandonment would entail a loss of face. Since December 1958 Khrushchev had made the Berlin issue the first priority of international politics, and in his Camp David visit with Eisenhower he strongly implied that once the Berlin question was settled, the ice of the cold war would be broken and a thaw would set in. Naturally, the Soviet leaders would minimize the chances of a concession on Berlin if they simultaneously pressed hard everywhere else, thereby confirming the U.S. fear that retreat in Berlin meant retreat everywhere. Strident support for Castro while there was still a good chance of a concession on Berlin was therefore, counterproductive. After the U–2 crisis and the Soviet abandonment of early hopes for a settlement on Berlin, Soviet support of Castro increased. Before that change in Soviet policy the PSP and Castro understood the contradiction between coexistence and Soviet support of Cuba, and they feared that their interests would be sacrificed to Soviet hopes for favorable agreements with the United States.

But for the Soviet Union the Cuban issue was not merely an interchangeable pawn. Cuba touched the revolutionary legitimacy of the Soviet Union. At terrible cost Stalin had converted the disaster of the Nazi attack on Russia into an enormous victory, bringing the Soviet

Union out of isolation and making her the leader of a socialist state system united—it then seemed—by a common ideology and purpose. Would new socialist states be added to this system or had it reached its high-water mark? Here Soviet hopes and American fears found common ground. It seemed only logical that the great shift in the military balance —whether it had already taken place or would soon take place—the seemingly superior Soviet economic growth rate, and the epidemic of assertive nationalism in ex-colonial and dependent countries would favor the Soviet Union. Would the United States submit passively to the will of history and surrender, or would it try to preserve its system by force? Stalin had more or less accepted the traditional view that the United States would fight to retain what it had, and therefore he had avoided supporting revolutionary movements far from the center of Soviet power. His encouragement to the North Koreans to unify the country by force was probably based on the assumption that the United States had effectively abandoned South Korea.

But some of Stalin's successors felt that the time for caution had passed. Now the nuclear peril in which the superpowers lived made it possible to establish socialist regimes without the presence of the Red Army. The local bourgeoisie now would not fight back nor would they receive effective backing from the imperialists. The Soviet Union, by supporting nationalist and liberationist movements in underdeveloped countries, would not be reckless. What had been dangerous when the world balance of forces was less favorable was now possible and therefore necessary. If Khrushchev was to continue to represent the balance of political power within the Soviet Union (and exactly what that was continued to be defined in periodic political crises) he had to show that he was moving the country forward on some fronts.

Optimism is obligatory for Soviet leaders. Even if revolution could not come in the aftermath of world wars because a new world war would destroy everything, and even if revolution was unlikely in Western Europe, where capitalism was becoming entrenched, hope had to be held out somewhere. Khrushchev looked to the new world to redress the balance of the old. As in 1919 and 1920, the disappointment in Europe produced hope in the revolutionary potential of the colonies and ex-colonies. The Soviet Union was the leader of a movement that would encompass the world, and the great sacrifices made by the Soviet population could not be justified merely by a more prosperous and comfortable Soviet Union. The sacrifice of the Soviet people had to bring salvation to mankind. And not a few Soviet people felt that the suffering they had endured could only be justified if mankind were saved. Soviet ideologists enunciated rosy expectations for the future. A book published by the Higher Party School of the Central Committee of the Communist Party of the Soviet Union and employed for the instruction of higher party

personnel put the matter in terms that require no ideological translation: "An obvious feature of the present situation is that, on the one
hand, the strength of the socialist system is growing at a more rapid pace
and, on the other hand, the world capitalist system is progressively collapsing; consequently, the revolutionary proletarian movement and the
national liberationist movement have grown colossally. In these conditions the likelihood of the peaceful accession of the proletariat to power
in many countries will increase."[3]

Earlier in the book the author had pointed to the people's democracies
in Eastern Europe as an example of how the peaceful assumption of power by the proletariat would take place. "If in Russia the development of
the socialist revolution from the bourgeois democratic revolution could
not be accomplished without a political overturn, then here [in Central
Europe], insofar as the democratic power of the people headed by the
proletariat was already established in the first phase of the revolutionary process, the development of the socialist revolution from the antiimperialist democratic revolution demanded only the exclusion from the
participation in governmental power of that fraction of the bourgeoisie
that opposed the policy of socialist construction."[4]

To those who believe that communism was brought to Eastern Europe
by the bayonets of the Red Army, the above quoted paragraph has a
strange ring. One must remember, however, that to those who believe
that for all its faults communism is a "good" system and that for all its
virtues capitalism is a "bad" system, the paragraph plays upon different
chords. In the view of the latter the presence of the Red Army accelerated a process that would have occurred somewhat later, and by neutral-
izing the reactionary enemies of the people permitted the progressive
forces to become ascendant earlier. Later, in Cuba, these same persons
were to believe that Soviet missiles served as a shield behind which the
Cuban revolution could come to fruition. The Soviet Union, in their version, was not exporting revolution but making the world safe from counterrevolution.

Communists should be taken at their word when they say that revolution is a good thing, but their long history of compulsive optimism makes
it risky to accept what appears in textbooks for the CPSU Higher Party
School as a sober appraisal of prospects rather than as a ritual reiteration
of the belief that History is the God of the communists. Who can tell
what the football coach who always predicts victory really believes?
Thus, it was almost impossible for the Cuban communists to know what
the Soviet leaders "really" thought would happen in Cuba. The immediate question for the PSP (and the Cuban leaders) was whether improved Soviet-American relations would be a greater or lesser problem
for Cuba. Their past experiences caused most Cuban communists to fear
Soviet-American rapprochement rather than look forward to.it.

The Soviet press did not pose the question in these stark terms, preferring to deal with it indirectly. The most serious Soviet journal devoted to international affairs, which appears in Russian only, made it clear that Cuba was facing a great many difficulties as a result of opposition to revolutionary measures at home and abroad, and it obliquely withheld Soviet support by saying that the future depended on the Cubans and their Latin American friends.[5] An article written for a journal on international affairs that appears in many languages seemed to meet PSP complaints that Cuba was the victim of U.S.–Soviet détente. It offered the assurance that as a consequence of the relaxation of international tension attendant upon Khrushchev's Camp David conversations, the United States had become more responsive to public opinion. Therefore, it said, "the efficacy of 'anticommunism' and the 'cold war' as means to oppress the countries of Latin America has diminished. The prospects for establishing normal relations between Latin America and the Soviet Union have improved . . . which opens new economic prospects for the underdeveloped countries of the Western hemisphere."[6] One of the few Soviet journalists with personal expereince in the new Cuba repeated the theme that the Cuban revolution marked a radical departure with the past, that it had aroused the fear and enmity of the United States, which was trying to organize intervention by raising the specter of the red peril. But it was not so easy now to repeat the tragedy of Guatemala. "The path of the Cuban revolution is thorny, but Cuba continues firmly to step forward. The peoples of Cuba believe that only this path will lead them to a new life, to independence, and to freedom."[7] Assessments in *Pravda* were made with full awareness of their implications. Saying that the Cubans believed that their actions *would* lead to independence and freedom meant that Cuban independence and freedom were not yet secure. *Izvestiia*, in a review of the month's news, stressed the positive, contrasting Castro's staunchness with Latin American behavior in the past. Despite U.S. threats, Castro had not yielded.[8]

Meanwhile, the news from Washington, as so often happened, admitted of different predictions about American actions. The Deputy Director of the CIA, in a statement that the Soviets could read in the U.S. press, said that Castro was not a communist and that communists did not regard him as a communist or even as procommunist. Nevertheless, General Charles P. Cabell believed that communists were delighted with Castro and pleased that he delegated authority in important matters to procommunists or persons susceptible to communist exploitation.[9]

Although Soviet analysts would not have used such language, they could have agreed with the assessment. But the real question was not whether Castro was a communist, but whether the United States would take preventive action. A news report from Washington suggested that, at least for the time being, Washington was far from taking extreme measures. Eisenhower rejected direct intervention and the breaking of diplomatic relations for fear of making Castro a martyr. Collective economic and political action against Cuba was considered, but unless firm proof could be advanced that Cuba was in danger of being taken over by the communists, Latin American countries would oppose such action. Bringing Batista back by means of a U.S.–supported counterrevolution would place on the United States the onus of having restored a dictatorship. The policy finally adopted was one of restraint and aloofness. The United States would defend its rights and its own political principles, at the same time holding out hope to Cuban elements who were becoming alarmed by the excesses of the Castro regime.[10] According to this perception the United States hoped that Castro's regime would either become more moderate or would founder because of the resistance its radical policies evoked. This might be called the McCawber principle of international politics. All conceivable alternatives seemed too costly or repugnant, and inaction left room for something "to turn up." Given such a U.S. policy, the Soviet Union could safely continue to support Castro verbally, to raise the level of its sugar purchases, and to take credit for Castro's successes. But the Soviet Union was not yet sufficiently committed to Cuba to suffer much political loss if Castro took a turn to the right or was overthrown by his internal opposition.

MIKOIAN VISITS CUBA

Sometime after December 1959 the Soviet Union decided that Mikoian should visit Cuba at the beginning of February, and this may have encouraged the PSP.[11] A New Year's Day editorial in the Cuban communist newspaper said that expeditionary forces were being prepared in Florida and Santo Domingo but that South America and the socialist camp extended their strong hand in support of Cuba.[12] Another article said that Cuba was better off than Guatemala had been because the cold war had begun to thaw.[13]

In a new edition of a book on PSP policy, the party secretary showed how trade with the socialist countries could influence political developments within Cuba. Trade with the Soviet Union at stable prices and low interest loans would constitute a substitute for private investment and would presumably reduce the power of the enemies of the revolution who wanted to destroy the left and capitulate to imperialism.[14]

Somewhat later an editorial in *Hoy* showed how uncertain and worried the Cuban leaders were. China came before the Soviet Union on the list of states offering solidarity to Cuba; hostile U.S. actions were the subject of bitter complaints. Yet somewhat inconsistently, the PSP supported the spirit of Camp David, that is, peaceful coexistence and respect for small nations, adding that "to defend our sovereignty and maintain our national integrity . . . will be our contribution to the cause of world peace."[15] Thus, on the one hand, the PSP leaders said that the Cuban revolution could move leftward if Soviet economic support replaced capitalist investment, but they warned that Camp David and U.S.–Soviet Union rapprochement did not relieve Cuba of the necessity to prepare to repel a U.S. attack. Mikoian's public statements in Cuba, as we shall see, tried both to dispel suspicions that the Soviet Union placed good relations with the United States above the defense of Cuba and also to justify Soviet caution by pointing to Castro's reluctance to pursue a policy really independent of the United States.

Escalante's statements at this time reflected differences within the PSP on the issue of the radicalization of the Cuban revolution. Escalante explained how in China, which he had just visited, the capitalists were cooperating in the development of a socialist society, and he said that this was more or less what was being done in Cuba. In Cuba, too, the owners of large estates were being compensated.[16] The implication seemed to be that Cuba would build a socialist revolution because the Cuban bourgeoisie would capitulate.

In a speech to a PSP study group in Havana, Escalante described how rapidly the Cuban revolution had moved. "There is a difference from night to day between the government that was formed on 2 January [1959] and the present government" [1960]. Agramonte, the former foreign minister, filled his ministry "with fossils and former servants of the tyranny . . . and even now, after his fall, they survive in the ministry. . . ." But now one can hope, he added, that Cuba would carry out the goals set by Castro in his 23 March 1959 speech. Escalante repeated these goals, one of which was the establishment of diplomatic relations with all states. His listeners presumably knew that relations with the Soviet Union had not yet been reestablished. Escalante then talked of the necessity for industrializing the country and admitted that "some believe all this is utopian, impossible. There are always skeptics, those who yesterday did not believe in the victory over the tyranny . . . those who thought there could be no agrarian reform here. . . . Others profess to believe in a policy of independence and national development, but they criticize what they call 'overrapid steps.' "[17]

On 4 February 1960 Mikoian arrived in Cuba, and on 13 February he signed a commercial convention with Cuba and an agreement to greatly increase sugar purchases. The Soviet press presented his activities as being in the sphere of state-to-state relations, and the intention of spreading revolutions of the national-democratic or socialist kind was specifically denied. The victories of socialism in the last fifteen years had occurred, said Mikoian, where internal situations had developed to that point. Only ignoramuses slandered the accomplishments of these countries by charging that revolution was imposed on them from without.

How could revolution in an enormous country like China have occurred if the situation had not become ripe for it? The Soviet Union had furnished an impetus to revolution by its example because ideas knew no state boundaries. The Cuban revolution depended on indigenous social and economic conditions and on its own leadership.[18]

But Mikoian was avoiding the issue that had been raised in the United States and, as we shall presently see, in the Cuban press. When he argued that the Soviet Union could not cause a revolution in so large a political entity as China, no one but the most committed believer in the jujitsu effect of international conspiracy would have disagreed. But Mikoian's restriction of the role of the USSR to the force of example could not automatically be applied to the creation of the socialist states of Bulgaria or Rumania, for example. The issue was not whether the Soviet Union had fostered Castro's revolution, but whether it could protect that revolution once it had occurred, and this issue Mikoian tried to avoid while he was in Cuba.

On the day after Mikoian's arrival in Cuba, the PSP organ *Hoy* addressed the issue directly, stating that the shift in the international balance of power permitted Cuba to pursue an independent policy toward the United States. *La Calle*, an opposition paper still being published, argued that such a view came from abroad [i.e., the USSR] and that *Hoy*'s claim that international solidarity protected Cuba was unfounded. In other words, Soviet support did not permit Cuba to defy the United States with impunity. The PSP, *La Calle* charged, opposed negotiations with the United States. That was a lie, *Hoy* complained. The PSP favored negotiation, but not capitulation. *Hoy* warned that Cuban policy could not be identical with Soviet policy. "What the heads of a major world military power can do without prejudicing their position in negotiations, the representatives of a small country, whose physical forces in relation to its negotiating partner are too weak for self-defense, cannot permit themselves. Not to understand this is to commit the gravest sin of ignorance. What in Khrushchev and the USSR is a disposition to be pacific and benevolent, in us would be dangerous precipitateness."[19]

The communist newspaper pointed out how much more understanding and generous the Chinese were. In a television report on his trip to China, Escalante explained that the suffering of the Chinese and their revolutionary experience allowed them "to understand our position more easily [than whom?]. . . . The Chinese people understand our difficulties perfectly . . . I have the absolute certainty that the revolutionary government of China stands ready to purchase the products that the revolutionary government [of Cuba] can sell."[20] In an editorial the communist newspaper thanked the People's Republic of China and the Soviet Union, in that order, for support. Even a novice in the communist system of communications would recognize it as a snub to the Soviet Union; the next sentence was even more pointed, since it did not mention the Soviet Union but subsumed it under other socialist countries. "In recent days the press has published the statements of solidarity with Cuba issued [on the occasion of the first anniversay of the Cuban Revolution] in China, Czechoslovakia, Hungary, Rumania, and other socialist countries."[21]

These strictures were seemingly directed to Mikoian. It is perhaps significant that the Soviet report of Mikoian's first speech in Cuba did not mention the PSP at all and that although Castro, Guevara, Juan Marinello, and Carlos Rafael Rodríguez met Mikoian at the airport, the two major leaders of the PSP, Blas Roca and Aníbal Escalante, did not.[22]

In an interview with Cuban *Radio Rebelde* Mikoian indicated that Soviet economic aid to Cuba would be modest and was very guarded about the Soviet defense of Cuba against aggression. When asked about the aid the USSR was willing to give to underdeveloped countries, Mikoian said that his country never refused an outstretched hand. "When our proposal for complete and general disarmament is accepted, we will find a way for aid on a much larger scale to the underdeveloped countries." In other words, large-scale aid to Cuba was a long way off. When Mikoian was asked about Soviet policy toward threats of economic or military aggression to countries defending their independence, he replied: "More than once the Soviet Union has opposed every kind of aggression; it respects the national sovereignty of all the small peoples. The USSR has always fought against any kind of aggression, direct or indirect, military or economic, and will always support those who fight for their national sovereignty and defend it."[23]

When the titular head of the PSP was asked shortly afterwards, "What will Russia do if the United States attacks Cuba? Will they remain with folded arms or will they defend us?" he said: "I can't answer that question. It should be put to the government in Moscow. But what we can say because of the evidence of the facts is that the USSR would offer us timely and efficacious solidarity. In any case, I believe that it would be very difficult for such an attack to occur . . . because the demonstration of firmness and combativeness given by the Cuban people makes them [the United States] realize what they will find if they decide on force."[24]

Marinello also added that he thought it would be a good idea to establish diplomatic relations with the Soviet Union. But the joint communiqué, signed on 13 February, stated only that both governments would discuss at a convenient time the question of the restoration of diplomatic relations. The Soviet economic commitment for the purchase of sugar was substantial but hardly a replacement for U.S. purchases. The USSR undertook to buy 425,000 tons of sugar from the 1960 harvest and a million tons annually in the course of the next four years. The Soviet Union also extended a credit of $100,000 at 2.5 percent per annum for the purchase of machinery and other materials for the period 1961–64 and also offered technical assistance in the construction of factories in Cuba. The communiqué ended with an expression of hope that the coming summit meeting would significantly reduce international tension.[25]

In a press conference, Mikoian pointed to the differences between the two parties and expressed his irritation at the Cuban failure to resume diplomatic relations. He made it clear that it was the Cubans who were holding back on the resumption of diplomatic relations, which had been broken by Batista in 1952. "When the opportune and convenient moment for the Cuban government comes, she will establish diplomatic relations with us . . . we are not in a hurry, and it must be said that the issue is not mutual recognition: we officially recognize the revolutionary government of Cuba."[26]

But leaving aside the Cuban problem, Mikoian went on to say, the Soviet Union did not need recognition. Mikoian recounted that an official of an unnamed American state that did not have relations with the USSR had asked him about the Soviet attitude toward mutual recognition. Mikoian had answered that the Soviet Union did not need relations with any state. It was enough that the people recognized it. After the Russian revolution, many states had intervened in the Soviet Union and refused it recognition, but the Soviet Union had prevailed. Mikoian could not comprehend the actions of states that refused to recognize the Soviet Union when only they suffered as a consequence. "Indeed, they [viz., the leaders of these states] are nothing but ignorant, and the ignorant do not have the right to lead countries. I don't think they will remain at their posts very long."[27]

Mikoian had introduced this diatribe by leaving the Cuban question aside, but his strictures applied directly to Cuba. He was reflecting Khrushchev's annoyance with countries that refused to recognize the USSR, but what was more, he was saying that their leaders were ignorant; in effect, he was saying that any country afraid to recognize the Soviet Union had not yet achieved genuine independence and that the leaders of such countries neither deserved nor could expect to remain in power very long.

Mikoian was pressed on the question of the price that the USSR had agreed to pay for Cuban sugar. A hostile questioner asked why the Soviet Union could not pay as much for sugar as the United States. Mikoian replied: "I don't know what relations you have with the United States. I don't know the history of how the prices that they pay you were established, but we are guided by a fundamental principle of world commerce, to buy and sell at world prices with all countries."

Mikoian obviously knew what the relations between Cuba and the United States were, and his profession of ignorance was a tactful way of saying that Cuba received a U.S. subsidy and was therefore dependent on the United States. When he was pushed further and told that the world price for sugar was 3 cents while the United States paid 5.10 cents, he abandoned tact for bluntness: "I don't want to get into your relations with the United States and I don't want to employ their practices as a model for our relations. We believe that the principle guiding us is much more correct: to trade with all countries at world prices, because if we make exceptions there will never be an end to them and people will think: what is the motive? And I don't believe they [exceptions to world prices] are included only for the benefit of small peoples."

When he was pressed again, Mikoian said he did not want to deal with that problem, because "you have special relations [with the United States], right? Certainly they were formed historically, and furthermore, there are many people who say that we want to cripple your relations with the United States, even though that is an out-and-out lie. How can we, who want to improve our relations with the United States, want to cripple your relations with them?"

Mikoian seemed to be answering questions that had been put in another place. Obviously the Soviet Union was not paying less for Cuban sugar as a friendly contribution to good Cuban-American relations. But Mikoian was making clear that there was a relationship between improved U.S.–Cuban and improved U.S.–Soviet relations, or to put it another way, he was saying that the aggravation of U.S.–Cuban relations would damage the prospects for an improvement in U.S.–Soviet relations.

Nothing could better illustrate the contradictions in the triangular relationship between the United States, Cuba, and the Soviet Union. If the only Soviet interest was in improved relations with the United States, she could simply ignore Cuba and not risk bearing the onus for worsened Cuban–U.S. relations. But the Soviet Union was pursuing two goals simultaneously: to improve relations with the United States on the basis of some U.S. concessions and to enlarge Soviet prestige by supporting Cuba in her assertion of independence against the United States. Theoretically, the two goals were compatible if the United States, recognizing that the power balance had shifted, was ready to retreat on every front. But in practice, as the events about to be described will demonstrate, Soviet tactics were based on a more complex assumption. In the long run, the Soviet leaders seemed to believe, the United States would retreat on every front, but as a matter of practical politics, it would be easier to get one concession at a time out of the United States. Later, when hope of a summit meeting was dashed, Soviet support of Cuba was greatly increased.

But during Mikoian's visit, the Soviets and the Cubans were approaching each other gingerly. Castro was unwilling to make a conclusive break with the United States, because the Soviet Union was not offering equivalent economic support and the value of her political support was an unknown quantity. Mikoian was somewhat caustic about Cuba's unwillingness to even establish diplomatic relations with the Soviet Union, but he had little ground for complaint since he himself had made it clear that the Soviet Union did not want a crisis with the United States on Cuba's account. The Soviet Union did not want Cuba as a client at a time when it hoped to squeeze a concession out of the United States; Castro still acted as if he could maintain a posture of intransigent independence and retain some U.S. economic support. A glimpse of the tensions in the Cuban-Soviet relationship is afforded by the course of the negotiations on the Soviet purchase of Cuban sugar.

The Soviet Union, we know from Mikoian's account, had insisted on world prices for the sugar purchase; whether the Cubans asked for more we do not know. But there was disagreement on the Soviet right to resell the sugar it purchased from Cuba. The million tons of sugar a year to be purchased by the Soviet Union represented only a fraction of the Cuban crop. The reduction of the U.S. quota and the threat to reduce it even further, or to abolish it, made the Soviet commitment to take a million tons a year very welcome. The Cuban practice had been to sell the portion of the crop remaining beyond the U.S. quota at world market prices. The resale of the Cuban sugar bought by the Soviet Union would presumably depress the world market price for sugar and reduce the returns the Cubans could expect for the sugar they had to dispose of on the world market after meeting their commitments to the United States and the Soviet Union. The Cubans therefore wanted a clause in the contract binding the Soviet Union not to re-export the Cuban sugar. Castro revealed that the Soviet negotiators agreed only reluctantly to include such a clause in the contract. The Soviet negotiators felt their word was sufficient. One wonders why Castro insisted on the clause if he "sincerely believed the Soviets" and why the Soviets argued against the clause if they had no desire to retain their option to resell.[28]

CASTRO AND THE PSP FACE HARD CHOICES

Since Castro had received no assurances of full economic support from the Soviet Union, he tried to avoid a complete break with the United States. While complaining bitterly about the bombing and burning of Cuban sugar fields by planes coming from the United States, Castro denied that Cuba had bought planes from the Soviet Union or that Cuba had set up a rocket base in the Camagüey area. Castro also expressed his willingness to negotiate outstanding issues with the United States, but such negotiation was contingent on an agreement to abstain from any unilateral acts that might damage the Cuban economy, that is, cancellation of the sugar quota. The United States refused, saying it had to remain free in the exercise of its sovereignty. Meanwhile, officials of the U.S. government shared their worst fears with James Reston of the *New*

York Times. How could Washington oppose a Soviet-Cuban pact for mutual security, when the United States had such pacts with Iran and Turkey? Could Washington tolerate such a situation? There was no evidence to suggest that such a situation would arise, but no one was prepared to dismiss the possibility.[29] As was so often the case, Washington's fears were to become Mocow's hopes.

At the beginning of March 1960 with the U.S. presidential election nine months in the future, the United States could contrive no better Cuban policy than to hope that Castro would accommodate his country to the political structure preferred by the United States in the Caribbean, and as Castro failed to respond, to step up the economic pressure and permit Cuban refugees to conduct counter-Castro operations. Castro could not have yielded to U.S. demands without losing his militant supporters. But could his internal enemies overthrow him with U.S. encouragement and support?

At this time the plenum of the PSP met for three days and worked out their assessment of the situation and the strategy it dictated. Again the differences within the PSP were revealed. Blas Roca, who represented the dominant faction of the PSP, said that the revolution had become more radical as the opposition within and without the country had become active. The major events had been the agrarian reform, the expulsion of the old-line labor leaders, the severance of relations with ORIT [an anticommunist international labor organization], the organization of a national militia, personnel changes in the government and the 26th of July Movement, the expansion of state ownership, and the establishment of trade relations with the USSR. Roca no longer repeated the earlier formulation that the revolution was a coalition led by the radical bourgeoisie. He now used Castro's phrase that the revolution was of the humble, for the humble, and by the humble. *Humble* does not describe a class in Marxian terminology. Roca made clear that the revolution was not socialist, since the tasks he listed—"the anti-imperialist struggle, the struggle against the semifeudal latifundia, and the struggle against colonialism—were the tasks of a national liberation movement."[30]

For Aníbal Escalante, however, the democratic revolution in Cuba was becoming socialist without the employment of force. Almost a year ago in May, Escalante said, the party plenum had put the Cuban revolution into the class of the democratic bourgeois revolutions of semicolonial and dependent countries. But the Cuban national democratic revolution was taking place in the middle of the twentieth century, when the world had entered the epoch of socialism and when the national and world role of the proletariat had become decisive. The revolutionary struggle had outrun its old limits and the revolution now had a new firmness and driving force. Cuba's task was to attain complete sovereignty and to industrialize. Now that Cuba, for the first time in her history, had a second large market for her sugar in the Soviet Union, she could use the revenue from that market to purchase whatever was required for Cuban industrialization. Cuban private capital could cooperate in a role subordinate to state capital in the industrialization of the country. Cuba had to acquire the means of production, that is, heavy industry, but would begin with light industry based on native resources while simultaneously developing heavy industry. Meanwhile, the petite bourgeoisie as such was passing from the scene as the leader of the revolution. The poorer members of that class were moving toward the proletariat; the richer, toward the bourgeoisie, the large landowners, and the imperialists, thus surrendering the leadership of the revolution to an alliance of workers and peasants. Escalante's listeners knew that according to communist doctrine, the PSP would guide the policy of the worker-peasant alliance.[31]

At many points in the version of Escalante's speech available to us, Escalante cites Fidel Castro as being in agreement with his views. We can interpret this to mean that Castro could be persuaded or was being persuaded to adopt these views. In his speech to the local study group on 20 January cited above, Escalante used the familiar rhetorical device of committing Castro to promises he had made in earlier speeches. Roca, in his speech to the plenum, accused "some comrades," obviously Escalante, of "taking the attitude that the revolution [of Castro] is alien to us and that we should stand aside and not be in its ranks." Those comrades continue to respond to the revolution as if it had not changed. As the formal resolution of the plenum put it: "Because of this basic misunderstanding, some comrades want to resolve the problems that come up in one place or another in opposition to the authorities of the Revolution, instead of resolving them with the authorities of the Revolution."[32]

The majority of the PSP or the victorious faction represented Escalante and his group as too optimistic about the possibility of radicalizing the revolution and as trying to push Castro along or push along without him.

The one issue on which there seemed to be no differences between the victorious faction of the PSP and Escalante was on the likelihood of attack from the United States. At the end of February the PSP view was that the United States was too dependent on Cuban sugar to risk interrupting the supply. At the beginning of March, however, the French freighter *La Coubre*, carrying a cargo of arms, exploded in Havana harbor. Castro immediately charged the United States with responsibility, probably thus contributing to the inflated reputation the Central Intelligence Agency enjoyed for efficiency of operations. Castro immediately began a campaign of accusing the United States of planning to attack Cuba. It was at this very time, 17 March,[33] that the decision to prepare an invasion of Cuba was taken in Washington, and Castro probably learned of it then or soon afterward. The PSP added to the resolutions published on 16 March an item that had not been discussed during the sessions of the last days of February—an appeal to socialist countries for arms, especially aircraft and radar.[34] Obviously, the PSP hoped that increased Cuban dependence on the Soviet Union would strengthen their position. It seems likely that Castro and the PSP had previously ascertained that the Soviet Union would favor their petition, because the arms arrived in Cuba shortly thereafter.

But on the points at issue between the various wings of the PSP, the Soviet Union did not adopt a clear position. A reporter with long Latin American experience transmitted an interview from Venezuela describing Cuba as "an inspiring example" for the national liberationist movement in Latin America,[35] and from Havana he reported that Cuba was "the standard-bearer of the national liberationist movement of the Latin American peoples."[36] But on the other hand, a party leader charged with relations with foreign communist parties, Boris Ponomarev, described Cuba as a country that had valiantly won its independence and had destroyed the old state apparatus. Generalizing, he said that now it was possible for countries to achieve independence in cooperation with national communist parties. Those who persecuted the communists played the game of the colonizers. The reward for cooperation with the communists was an accelerated transition to socialism. Ponomarev wrote that given "the conditions of existence of the world socialist system, the countries that are liberating themselves can skip the tortured path of capitalism. The decisive condition for this is a democratic course in internal and external politics."[37]

A democratic course in external politics meant good relations with the Soviet Union, and a democratic course in domestic politics meant permitting the communist party a role in political life. The transitional state between precapitalism and socialism guided by a charismatic noncommunist leader in cooperation with a communist party was soon to be described as national democratic, but as yet Cuba had not reached that state. In the first of May slogans for 1960, the greetings to each socialist country were followed by individual greetings to the peoples of India, Indonesia, Burma, Ceylon, Cambodia, and Afghanistan. Following the Arab peoples and the peoples of Africa came the peoples of Latin America, who were struggling against imperialism and for the establishment of independence and sovereignty.[38] If the Soviet party officials who ranked revolutionary movements knew of Escalante's views, they failed to accept them. As tension between Cuba and the United States continued to mount, the PSP emphasized the decisive role of the Soviet Union in establishing Cuban independence. If the Cuban-American contest was viewed only in the narrow framework of an economically weak Cuba close to the United States, the outcome would be clear, wrote Roca. "But if we consider the reality of the world as it is, if we understand that the imperialists can no longer do what they like despite their geographical proximity and that today the powerful socialist camp headed by the Soviet Union, with such inexhaustible forces as those of the People's

Republic of China, is a brake and a warning to those who want to show us the big stick . . . Cuba does not have to resign herself to dying heroically, and we have every possibility of winning."[39]

How the United States would behave was not yet clear. According to the *New York Times,* Ambassador Philip Bonsal was urging patience in Cuban relations, while Ambassador Robert Hill urged a tough line. When both appeared before the Senate Foreign Relations Committee, the counsel of moderation carried the day and Bonsal returned to Cuba.[40] At the end of March, Luis Conte Agüero praised his "old friend" Castro in a speech before the Lion's Club but warned him that the PSP wanted to make the Cuban revolution socialist. Conte Agüero argued that the Soviets were supporting Castro in order to provoke an American invasion of Cuba—so that the United States could have its Hungary. When Conte Agüero finally went to the United States in exile, Castro explained the whole incident as another example of official U.S. support of counterrevolution.[41] The U.S. Secretary of State, Christian Herter, confessed in a press conference that relations with Cuba had not improved with Ambassador Bonsal's return, since "those [in Cuba] who express concern about communist influence are now being accused of being antirevolution and anti-Castro, and this is an obvious effort to stop any anticommunist criticism that might arise within the country itself."[42] Herter and Ponomarev were in agreement, although they were probably unaware of it. Both felt that Castro's cooperation with the communists would move him leftward, but only Herter voiced the fear that this would deepen the U.S.–Cuban estrangement.

During the latter part of April, Castro personally led a clean up of guerilla, or counterrevolutionary, forces—the epithet chosen depending on one's sympathies—in the Sierra Maestra. According to the longtime resident correspondent of the *New York Times,* R. Hart Phillips, Castro used five thousand troops in this exercise, expecting that an invasion from the Dominican Republic might be coordinated with an uprising in Cuba.[43] The *New York Times* devoted much more space to the movement against Castro in April 1960 than it had devoted to Castro's own movement in October and November 1958, just two months before he actually took power. Castro feared that if a force opposed to him gained a foothold, the United States would quickly recognize it as the new government. Very soon, however, the Soviet Union was to offer Castro support in a dramatic fashion. Not surprisingly, this came after the crisis produced by the U–2 flight of 1 May 1960.

THE U–2 FIASCO HELPS CASTRO

The U–2 flight represented the first serious setback to Khrushchev's program of menace and cajolery to wring concessions from the United

States. The crisis produced by the flight had not been planned, nor had its consequences been foreseen by either side. But this unanticipated event forced each side to formulate and then reveal its true position. One feature of Soviet policy emerged in greater clarity. Khrushchev had to seem to be making progress if not on one front, then on another. If Eisenhower would not surrender on Berlin, the Soviet Union would play more publicly and more forcibly the role of the defender of Cuban independence.

For several years before 1 May 1960—the day the U–2 piloted by Gary Powers was shot down by a Soviet surface-to-air missile—the United States had been conducting reconnaissance flights over the Soviet Union. The aircraft were specially designed to fly above the ceiling of Soviet fighter aircraft and Soviet surface-to-air missiles. The photographs taken by these aircraft provided varied information, but of particular importance at that time, information on the construction of missile sites. The missiles of the early sixties, since they used liquid fuel and were very large and heavy, required roads from railhead to launch pad, and in a country as meagerly provided with roads as the Soviet Union, these access routes to the launching sites were easily identifiable on photographs. The Soviet leaders knew that these flights were occurring; they furnished the impetus for the development of the missiles that were eventually able to shoot the U–2s down. How was the Soviet Union able to pretend that it had the lead in intercontinental missiles, and how could its claims cause concern in the United States if the program of U–2 flights was known on both sides? Although this question is somewhat removed from the main subject of this study, the question of the weapons balance and mutual perceptions of that balance is sufficiently germane to warrant a digression.

The U–2 flights apparently did not furnish a *completely* reliable basis for estimating the number of intercontinental missile sites in the Soviet Union. Cloud cover, long arctic nights, and restrictions on the number and timing of flights accounted for some unphotographed areas and left other areas unphotographed for months. Later earth satellite photography left no room for doubt, but photographs taken from aircraft left some uncertainties. If it was assumed that in some time periods and in some places, the Soviet Union had built and then camouflaged missiles, and if all uncertainties were resolved in the same direction, a case could be made for the existence of hidden Soviet ICBMs. The U–2 program was a secret known to very few Americans, and thus few persons knew what the estimates were based on. Within the U.S. government itself, not all the authorities concerned with the problem resolved the uncertainties in the same way. Actually, the CIA offered estimates rather close to the true state of affairs, and the service most interested in having the wherewithal to counter the Soviet forces, the Air Force, offered the highest estimates.

The issue was confused and confusing because the estimates that were the subject of public discussion were estimates of future Soviet capabilities. Thus, misjudgments of Soviet plans to invest in missile force expansion compounded the error inherent in accepting very high estimates of current Soviet missile deployment.

In the Soviet Union, the number of persons privy to the figures of missile deployment was, if anything, even smaller than in the United States, although literally thousands of persons had to know that hostile aircraft were entering Soviet air space because standing orders to deal with intruders had to be disseminated to servicemen of all ranks all over the Soviet Union if intruding planes were to be identified and downed. In fact, later in the crisis Khrushchev took personal credit for the order to destroy the American aircraft. The very few people in the Soviet Union who knew how many ICBMs the country possessed may have wondered why the United States did not officially challenge Khrushchev's inflated claims of missile strength. Perhaps they did not realize how good the quality of U–2 photographs was and believed that somehow the Americans had been deceived.

In any case, Khrushchev elected to exploit the incident to further his campaign of wringing concessions from the United States only to cause the collapse of a summit meeting where he had hoped to formalize his victory. Khrushchev, in announcing that the U–2 had been shot down, concealed the survival of the pilot and trapped the United States and President Eisenhower into lying about the purpose of the U–2 mission. Khrushchev then triumphantly and rather good naturedly produced the pilot, invited Eisenhower to disclaim responsibility, place the onus on subordinates, and come to the summit meeting in Paris to discuss the Berlin question. In those simpler times a president who lied in public was something of a rarity, and Eisenhower did not relish the role. Instead of accepting Khrushchev's invitation to foist the blame on a subordinate, Eisenhower told the truth, that he had authorized the flights. But the reason offered for the flights was more wounding than the flights themselves. Espionage among great powers had long been accepted, but convention dictated that governments disowned their spies and that the disavowals not be too closely scrutinized. But Eisenhower said that the flights were necessary for the security of the United States, giving it the right to conduct them. To claim the right to conduct espionage in another country without any concern about the retaliation that might be expected meant that the United States did not respect Soviet sovereignty and, by implication, would continue the flights as long as it deemed them necessary. The United States was treating the Soviet Union like an inferior.

Khrushchev, who had hoped to take advantage of a discomfitted Eisenhower at the negotiating table, was himself held up to ridicule. He tried directly and through intermediaries to persuade Eisenhower to apologize.

But Khrushchev had to satisfy himself with refusing to meet Eisenhower. The emptiness of his threats was revealed in a speech he made in East Berlin on his way back from Paris. There he told the East Germans that the Berlin question would be settled when a new president took office in the United States in January of the next year. Evidently Soviet missile rattling did not mean that the Soviet Union was prepared to take unilateral action in West Berlin, confident that the United States would be afraid to respond. The Soviet aim was to frighten the United States into yielding a political position by raising the possibility of unilateral Soviet action. In 1960, Soviet talk about the possibility of a crisis developing into a nuclear war against everyone's interest and desire could not cause the United States to yield a position. But could missile diplomacy inhibit the United States from initiating action against a country over which the Soviet Union had spread its nuclear umbrella—Cuba? The events of the next year did not yield an unequivocal answer, and the dubiety of that answer goes some distance in explaining the Soviet calculations in installing missiles in Cuba in the autumn of 1962.

On 8 May 1960, between the downing of the U–2 on 1 May and the collapse of the summit conference in Paris, formal diplomatic relations between Cuba and the Soviet Union were established. The joint communiqué explained that in a sense relations had been established when the Soviet Union recognized the Revolutionary Government of Cuba in January 1959 and that Mikoian's visit had served as a ratification. The joint communiqué of 8 May, therefore, formalized the reestablishment of relations.[44]

A Soviet journal devoted to foreign affairs and widely disseminated abroad said, in commenting on the reestablishment of Soviet-Cuban relations, that Cubans regarded this as "another manifestation of solidarity" and that Cuba had "the sympathy and support of all freedom-loving nations."[45]

Raúl Castro's appraisal of the significance of mutual recognition of Cuba went, as usual, much further. Cuba was in a better position than Guatemala had been, he said, since "aggression against Cuba constitutes a most serious problem, a continental problem, and I would say even a world problem."[46]

At a press conference in Paris, Khrushchev praised the Cuban struggle for independence against U.S. imperialism and expressed the conviction that other Latin American countries would follow Cuba's example,[47] but he offered nothing specific in the way of support. In Washington, unnamed State Department officials furnished evidence of the growing power of the Cuban communists. Since all the revolutionary groups had been absorbed into the 26th of July Movement, the PSP remained the only party in Cuba. Although not in the government, it played a major role in giving intellectual guidance to Guevara and Raúl Castro. Although Carlos

Rafael Rodríguez had refused government positions, he gave advice on economic matters. This information purportedly came from a Chilean communist who had visited Cuba in February and March 1960.[48]

THE CUBAN DEBATE OVER DEVELOPMENT

Guevara and Rodríguez argued that Cuba had to industrialize and that it was folly to rely on assistance from capitalist countries for that purpose. Castro had made a speech in which he urged industrialization as a requirement for independence and quite realistically said that the workers would have to provide the wherewithal. It had been easy, Castro said, to lead the workers in the past, when one simply asked for more money.[49] But to say this would be demagogic; instead, one had to explain to the workers why they had to contribute more instead of receiving more. Castro was rediscovering what the leaders of the Soviet Union had already learned. To bring socialism to an underdeveloped or a semideveloped country—and it is perhaps correct to style the Russia of 1917 and the Cuba of 1960 as semideveloped—capital has to be accumulated. In Marx's original vision, the capitalists drove the workers to accumulate capital. The revolutionaries were to have the more congenial task of redistributing the production of factories that earlier generations had sacrificed to build. The question of whether socialists or capitalists accumulate capital at lower social cost aside, there could be no doubt that the Cuban leadership could only offer pie tomorrow and sacrifice today.

Commenting on Castro's speech, Rodríguez said that "everything cannot be done at once. . . . We cannot undertake at the same speed industrialization, public works, health, education . . . and day nurseries. . . . If we want to do everything at once, we will not succeed in the fundamental task, that is, to transform the economy. As long as Cuba does not industrialize itself, as long as it does not augment its agriculture, it will not be able to have all the hospitals or housing it needs. . . ."[50] Save and invest today, consume tomorrow, was the message. Rodríguez rejected the alternative of borrowing capital from the imperialists, because sooner or later the bill would have to be paid, and the economy would decline again. One might question Rodríguez's economics, but not his politics. British capital had played a large role in the industrialization of the United States, and the much wealthier United States that repaid the debt hardly noticed it. But Rodríguez was probably correct if he assumed that the United States would only have been willing to play the role of capital supplier to Cuba if its leaders were replaced, or if those leaders announced their attachment to free enterprise as the U.S. Congress understood it. To accept U.S. financial support on American terms would have meant for Castro, and very probably for his supporters, to compromise independence. Few politicians are willing to relinquish power because they shrink from asking others to make sacrifices.

Guevara made the same points in a radio lecture, and the publication of his remarks in a Soviet magazine indicated Soviet approval of the policy. Until Cuba achieves economic independence, Che said, her political independence will not be secure. Cuban agrarian reform was to furnish the basis for industrialization. Critics have argued, Guevara went on, that Cuba cannot exist without a market for its sugar. But the same things were said when Lázaro Cárdenas expropriated the oil companies in Mexico twenty years ago. Cuba has already broken the monopoly of U.S. trade, and her new trade agreement with the Soviet Union, said Guevara, was an agreement between equals.[51]

But apparently some elements of the PSP and the Soviet leadership did not believe that Cuba was ready to move rapidly toward industrialization and socialism. In an article written for a French communist journal, Juan Marinello, the titular head of the PSP, said that the urban petite bourgeoisie was still the directing class of the revolution and that political power was still in the hands of the petite bourgeoisie and certain strata of the national bourgeoisie. Marinello agreed that these groups were behaving better and that in each political crisis the less reliable elements were eliminated, but his analysis was a far cry from the up-beat appraisal of Escalante quoted above.[52] A full-dress Soviet appraisal of the Cuban situation characterized the Cuban government as a coalition of workers and peasants with the left wing of the bourgeoisie playing the leading role.[53] Yet the revolutionaries were becoming more revolutionary as the counterrevolution showed its hand. During the trial of Hubert Matos, Castro had refused to expel the communists, who he said were "comrades who we know won't betray us . . . comrades who we know are revolutionaries not for one day but revolutionaries to the end."[54]

But while the Soviet analysts did not accept the most extreme Cuban views of the radicalization of Cuba, they did judge the United States to be weaker than most Cubans even hoped. "The victory of the Cuban people has not left a stone standing of the arguments about the omnipotence of U.S. imperialism in Latin America or of the theory of 'geographic fatalism.' "[55] The Soviet Union thus encouraged the Cubans to persist in their independent course and to continue to reject accommodation with the United States.

Meanwhile the United States was increasing pressure on Cuba. At the end of June the Cuban government assumed control of the Texas Company oil refinery when it refused to refine Soviet oil, and soon afterwards Castro seized all the U.S.–owned refineries. The U.S. Congress responded by giving the president authority to reduce the sugar quota, and on 6 July President Eisenhower reduced the quota for 1960 by 95 percent.[56]

The PSP took the news soberly. In an economic war the masses must be prepared to suffer shortages and even hunger for months and perhaps for years. But the hope was expressed that other Latin American countries and also the socialist countries could provide the major part of the goods denied by the imperialists.[57] On 7 July the PSP organ pointed out that the cut in the quota could be reversed, whereas nationalization could not.[58] Castro accused the imperialists of trying to threaten Cuba with hunger, but he said nothing of help from other nations.[59] Castro also dealt with the possibility that the United States might move from economic aggression to military aggression, but he predicted victory because the Cuban people were prepared to fight or die.[60] Escalante went one step further. After saying that if the Cubans could beat the Spaniards in 1898, now, with an army ten times greater, they could beat the American Marines. Moreover, the Cubans could now count on the socialist camp, "which not only buys our sugar and sends us oil, but is prepared to do much more for the glorious cause of the independence and progress of our dear country."[61]

KHRUSHCHEV TALKS OF PROTECTING CUBA
WITH MISSILES

Cuban morale was probably boosted by Khrushchev's acceptance of an invitation to visit Cuba soon,[62] and the Cubans were encouraged to take a firm line toward the United States by Khrushchev's interview with Nuñez Jiménez on 3 June in which the political employment of nuclear missiles in Cuba's defense was first mentioned. The first published reports of the interview recounted that Khrushchev was contemptuous of U.S. charges that missile bases were being installed in Cuba. Khrushchev commented that "the Soviet Union does not need bases for missiles in Cuba, for it is enough to press a button here to launch missiles to any part of the world." Khrushchev then disavowed any intention to use that power because the Soviet Union was a country that loved peace and would not abuse its missile superiority over the other nations of the world.[63] After Khrushchev had claimed on 9 July that Soviet missiles could reach the United States directly from the Soviet Union and had warned the United States against intervening in Cuba (to be discussed below), Nuñez Jiménez revealed what Khrushchev had privately told the Cuban delegation about Soviet intentions. On 15 July, Nuñez Jiménez told a television audience that Khrushchev had informed a group of Cubans in a private interview that the USSR would defend the Cuban revolution. Khrushchev had said that the USSR did not need bases for its missiles in Cuba because it had sufficient range to reach the United States from the Soviet Union. When Khrushchev made public his undertaking to the Cubans, they were pleased, said Nuñez Jiménez, but he did not indicate whether they were pleased because the public commitment came as a surprise or because Khrushchev had made good on his promise to make the private commitment public.[64]

Nuñez Jiménez added that his good impression of Khrushchev had been confirmed by Khrushchev's subsequent actions, thereby indicating either that Khrushchev had not promised to make a public statement linking the Cuban question and missiles, or that he did what he had promised.

In an interview in Paris on 8 July, a day before Khrushchev's public pledge, Nuñez Jiménez again spoke of the Soviet capacity to hit U.S. targets from Soviet bases but omitted Khrushchev's statement that the Soviet Union would not use its missile superiority against other countries. Referring to charges that Soviet bases had been or were being installed in Cuba, he said that "this invention proves the ignorance of certain North American journalists. Anyone knows that if Khrushchev pushes a button in the Kremlin all the Soviet missiles can fly to any place on earth. It would be idiotic for the Soviets to spend money on something useless, and on the other hand, Cuba would not allow it."[65]

In another version of the same interview (apparently the report was based on notes rather than a stenographic report), Nuñez Jiménez was quoted as saying that "if Mr. Khrushchev wants to, by pressing a button he can, without bases, make missiles fall near to the target in any part of the world. The Soviet Union does not need bases near Cuba. The imperialists always consider their actions."[66]

Although Nuñez Jiménez did not commit the Soviet Union to defend Cuban independence with its missiles, the implication was unmistakable. Why else should Cubans repeat to the world Khrushchev's boasts about Soviet superiority in missiles?

In Washington the New York Times military specialist, Hanson W. Baldwin, reported that some American military men, but not the majority, had visions of Cuba serving as a base for Soviet missiles, aircraft, or submarines, but felt that such bases would be easy to destroy and hard to defend.[67] The New York Times Havana correspondent reported a conversation between the Cuban President, Osvaldo Dorticós, and José Miró Cardona, who sought asylum in the Argentine Embassy soon after the conversation. Cardona had complained that the purge of the judiciary that was to follow a purge of the university professors was totalitarian. To which Dorticós was supposed to have said: "And if Cuba wants it, we shall say that yes we are Communists. And what of it?"[68]

Soviet commentaries did not even scout the possibility that Cuba might become a socialist state in the near future but continued to repeat that Cuba was an example of a national liberation movement that had enlisted the support of its communist party.[69] And in a public interview with an Indian journalist, Castro never even hinted at the possibility that

Cuba might choose socialism, although he praised Soviet generosity. The Soviet Union, he said, had loaned Cuba 100 million dollars, while the United States had deprived her of the credits she had in American banks. The Russians supplied oil at reasonable prices; American companies in Cuba refused to refine oil. If the Americans were unable to get some Latin American nations to stifle the Cuban revolution, they planned to do it themselves, resorting "to that old American bugaboo about saving the Americans from the communist peril and protecting 'their' hemisphere from being swallowed up by the Russians or the Chinese."[70]

Speaking to a schoolteachers' convention, Khrushchev reviewed U.S. policy toward Cuba. Since the U–2 crisis his language about the United States and about Eisenhower had become less restrained. The United States was obviously plotting "insidious criminal steps" against the Cuban people and had announced an end to the purchase of Cuban sugar. But the time when the United States could dictate its will was past. Now the Soviet Union was raising its voice and extending a helping hand to the Cuban people. The peoples of the socialist countries would help their brothers, the Cubans, to foil the U.S. economic blockade. "We will do everything possible to support Cuba and her courageous people. . . ." And then Khrushchev proceeded to connect Soviet support of Cuba with Soviet nuclear strength. He said:

It must not be forgotten that now the United States is not so inaccessibly distant from the Soviet Union as in the past. Figuratively (*obrazno*) speaking, Soviet artillerymen, in case of need, can with their missile fire support the Cuban people if the aggressive forces of the Pentagon dare begin intervention against Cuba. And let those in the Pentagon not forget that as recent tests have shown, we have missiles capable of striking accurately in a preset square at a distance of 13,000 km. That is, if you like, a warning to those who would like to settle international issues by force and not by reason.[71]

The statement represented the official position of the Soviet government and was not an off-the-cuff remark or an extemporaneous addition to a prepared speech such as Khrushchev sometimes permitted himself. On the same day that Khrushchev made his speech, the Cuban ambassador-designate to the Soviet Union, Faure Chomón, was granted the facilities of Soviet television to welcome Khrushchev's statement as that of a friend.[72] The Soviet press gave extensive space to the world reaction to the speech and reprinted items that emphasized the minatory aspect of the statement.

The statement followed the pattern of earlier Soviet missile-rattling statements. Khrushchev himself characterized it as a warning, which is defined in the *Oxford English Dictionary* as a deterrent counsel, cautionary advice against imprudent or vicious action or neglect of duty. While

Khrushchev liked to call his little homilies on missiles and the nuclear age warnings, his opponents often preferred to call them threats. The radical sense of threat is given by the *OED* as "pressure applied to the will by declaration of the harm that will follow noncompliance. It is thus indirect compulsion." These definitions, although helpful, do not exhaust the question of warnings and threats in the traffic between opponents. There is a wide range, from "If you continue to behave aggressively, you will rue the consequences" to "If you put armed U.S. units on Cuban soil, the Soviet Union will immediately launch ICBMs against U.S. targets."

One might generalize that if a power of greatly superior strength threatens a weak power it is not necessary to lend the threat force by specifying the sanctions. "A word to the weak is sufficient" might be the motto. Thus, for example, traditionally in U.S.–Cuban relations, polite expressions of U.S. preference often sufficed to secure compliance. By contrast, a weak power threatening a stronger power lends force to its threat by specificity. Thus, during World War II, it was made clear to Germany that Switzerland, if invaded, could and would blow up the subalpine train tunnels that carried goods and troops between Germany and Italy and that the Swiss army had the numbers, armament, and training to hold up a given number of German divisions for a certain time period.

Khrushchev's warning, or threat, followed neither of these examples. It asserted the vulnerability of the United States to Soviet missiles armed with nuclear warheads located in the Soviet Union. The statement did not say that these *would* be employed against the United States, but that they *could* be, and the U.S. action that could precipitate a Soviet response was defined as the beginning of intervention against Cuba. Apparently the dispatch of aircraft to bomb Cuba was below the threshold of the beginning of invasion, because such actions had already occurred according to the Cubans and the Soviet Union. But it was not really necessary to indicate what the threshold opening into great power hostilities would be, since Khrushchev's statement did not promise the employment of ballistic missiles if the threshold were crossed but simply stated a capability to employ such weapons. The statement lacked the essential element of a warning or threat, the declaration of the harm to follow noncompliance.

Perhaps the term *menace* best characterizes Khrushchev's statement, since the *OED* defines *menace* as a declaration of hostile intent or a probable evil or catastrophe. The term *missile rattling*, employed by journalists, caught the meaning very well. Like arms brandishing, missile rattling did not denote an obligation to take specific action in response to another's specified action.

One minor point should perhaps be clarified. Khrushchev's statement fell short of a warning or a threat but not because it failed to define the threshold that had to be crossed before it came into effect. Effective threats and warnings are often deliberately vague about the exact level of the threshold because precision may invite actions beneath the defined threshold. The essential element is the undertaking to harm.

Khrushchev's earlier statements of missile menace, if we may employ that term, were made most notably in the Suez crisis in 1956, in the Taiwan Straits crisis in 1958, and repeatedly, after the ultimatum that was not an ultimatum on Berlin in December 1958. These statements can be divided into two categories. The Suez and Taiwan statements of menace were made after the crisis had passed. In the case of Suez, the Soviet statements menacing Great Britain and France were made after the very effective American threat to terminate the Anglo-American and Anglo-French alliance, so the Soviet words came after the British and the French had been compelled to break off their action. In the Taiwan Straits crisis the Soviet reconfirmation of its alliance obligations to China was made after the United States and China had agreed to resume talks in Warsaw. *Brutum fulmen,* lightning without force, could characterize this kind of menace. The Soviets who entered the fray when it was already over and without taking any risks tried to earn a reputation for facing down a powerful foe. And as a matter of fact, Soviet writers and political figures claimed credit for "saving" Egypt and China.

The missile rattling on the Berlin question was of a different kind. The Soviet Union characterized the status of West Berlin as an abnormality, an anomaly that had to be eliminated. The so-called ultimatum of December 1958 threatened the conclusion of a Soviet–East German treaty within six months if the West did not negotiate some satisfactory adjustment. If the Western powers remained adamant, then presumably the German Democratic Republic could, possessing a preponderance of local military strength, make a *fait accompli* or a series of *faits accomplis* in Berlin that the Western powers would have to accept unless they were willing to risk the consequences of expanding the conflict into an arena where they possessed commensurate forces, a risk that would presumably involve the employment of the missiles the Soviet Union was advertising. Many links had to be moved in a long chain before the link attached to nuclear missiles would be moved. Reiteration of the generalized fear of nuclear war, Khrushchev hoped, would get the West to yield some political ground to the Soviet Union. In September 1961, when the eminent Soviet physicist Andrei Sakharov protested the resumption of nuclear testing to Khrushchev, the latter is reported to have said: "Sakharov is a good scientist. But he is trying to teach us politics, and we know politics better than he does. You have to be clever and tough and use blackmail with the imperialists."[73]

The blackmailer whose victims always pay without ever forcing him to make good on his threats begins to believe that threats are efficacious in themselves. In most of Khrushchev's own experience, those in power were not limited by the rule of law, and they enjoyed a well-deserved reputation for ruthlessness, so menace was often adequate to compel compliance. Soviet, or Russian, society, for that matter, was not organized on the principle that individuals had inalienable rights based on law or custom. Most often, one's position in the hierarchy was all that mattered. Khrushchev was slow to learn that other actors on the international scene coming from different backgrounds behaved differently than he did. Eisenhower's affability and penchant for talking as if he was willing to split the difference in a negotiation was misinterpreted as weakness and vulnerability to threat. The notion that an Eisenhower could be affable and talk about compromise as a ritual precedent to a negotiation in which he would yield little or nothing was alien to Khrushchev. A man who yields verbally thereby signals his willingness to yield in fact; when he fails to do so, he is a hypocrite, as Khrushchev claimed Eisenhower was after the U–2 crisis. Khrushchev believed that threats and menace were in themselves effective against weaker opponents, and his antennae, which had served to preserve him in the jungle of Soviet political life and make him king of the beasts there, gave him false signals outside the Soviet Union.

The 9 July missile statement on Cuba entailed the risk of much higher political costs than the other missile menaces. It required a close knowledge of events to realize that in Suez and in the Taiwan Straits Khrushchev had been breathing fire after the dragon was dead. In the Cuban case, however, the precipitating action did not predate the menace; and the action was defined as the beginning of an American invasion of Cuba. If the United States invaded Cuba and the Soviet Union failed to act, the Soviet Union would lose whatever reputation she enjoyed for being the scourge of her enemies and the succor of her friends. Khrushchev's statement did not commit the Soviet Union to launch ballistic missiles against the United States if the United States began intervention against Cuba; it merely linked such an intervention with the reputed power of the Soviet Union to make such a missile attack. But while mere linkage of the American act and the Soviet response did not formally commit the Soviet Union, the Soviet Union and the Cubans, particularly in their reiterations of the statement, tended to collapse the distinction between linkage of the two attacks and the commitment to follow the first attack by a second. In his statement, Khrushchev risked acquiring the reputation for making empty threats.

Eisenhower responded the next day to Khrushchev, warning that the United States would never permit the establishment of a regime dominated by international communism in the Western Hemisphere. Khrushchev's statement promising full support to Castro, he said, showed that the USSR intended that Cuba should serve Soviet purposes. This reflected the effort of outside nations and international communism to intervene in the affairs of the Western Hemisphere. The Rio Treaty, in Eisenhower's reading, barred this, and he announced the determination of the United States to uphold that agreement.[74]

Eisenhower thus countered Khrushchev's support of Cuba's policies in a way that severely limited his courses of action. By invoking the right under the Rio Treaty to intervene in another country to prevent an alien ideology from entering the Western Hemisphere, leaving aside the validity of such an action under international law, Eisenhower committed himself to acting within the Organization of American States. If the United States acted unilaterally she would open herself to the charge of violating the sovereignty of a sister American republic. Thus, until the United States could persuade two-thirds of the members of the OAS, in conformity with its charter, collective action against a member nation was impossible. The United States had to be satisfied with subversive activity, with organizing on its own an invasion from the outside coordinated with an internal uprising. If Eisenhower had been able to get what he wanted, an inter-American force would have suppressed communism in Cuba and the Soviet Union would have had to deal with the whole hemisphere in defending Cuba. But that was not to happen, for the OAS did not yield to U.S. pressure. Once more a great power learned the dangers of treating client states as equals. The empty forms acquired content and in the extreme case limited the freedom of action of the puppetmaster.

Khrushchev greeted Eisenhower's statement as grist to his mill since it advertised the Soviet support of countries struggling for their independence. He interpreted Eisenhower's statement to mean that the United States would try to keep the Cuban people from winning their struggle for full independence. If full independence means the right of a nation to choose its own system of government, Khrushchev was on solid ground. The Cuban people, he said, follow their own course. If the communists are running the country, as is charged, the Cuban revolution would have taken a different course. The Americans believe that if the Soviet Union supports Cuba, the Cuban leaders must be going over to the system of world communism. That is absurd, Khrushchev said. The USSR had helped the Arab countries, and they were not communist. He might have added, but forbore to do so, that Arab countries imprisoned members of the communist party. But in the future, he said, following the current Soviet orthodoxy, the peoples fighting for their independence would have learned in the hard school of combat that the only way to win is to join the communist movement. Cuba was not now following that path, but the United States was teaching her and others to do so.[75] Khrushchev was to be proved right about Cuba and wrong about some other countries.

Almost simultaneously with his missile menace to the United States, Khrushchev sent a message to Castro saying that he had learned that the United States had reduced the sugar quota in response to the Cuban government's justified measures of intervention against the foreign oil companies that were sabotaging the Cuban government. The imperialists had opposed countries seeking independence before, but they were making a mistake if they thought that these countries were alone. The Soviet government was indignant at the action of the U.S. government, and if the Cuban government were to have difficulties in the sale of its sugar, the Soviet Union was ready to buy 700 million more tons of sugar than she had already contracted to buy.[76]

CUBA WELCOMES SOVIET MISSILE SUPPORT

Castro responded to the Soviet menace to the United States and proffer of aid to Cuba from a sickbed. "The Soviet Union in an absolutely spontaneous manner—and it must be emphasized that we had not been counting on Soviet missiles to defend us, we had been counting simply on our own cause, we had been counting on our dignity, on the heroism of our people . . . Nevertheless, in an absolutely spontaneous manner, the government of the Soviet Union issued a declaration saying that aggression against Cuba could be the cause for putting into action the weapons of the Soviet Union."[77]

The United States, Castro continued, was the enemy of progress and of the peoples of the world. "There is where one must put the blame for the situation here in Cuba and for the absolutely spontaneous declaration issued by the government of the Soviet Union." Why should the Soviet declaration have been the occasion for blame rather than triumph? Castro's repeated insistence on the spontaneity of the Soviet statement suggested that he feared criticism for having solicited the statement, thereby giving the United States a pretext for attack. "The fact is," said Castro, "that the Soviet Union, in an absolutely spontaneous form has declared its solidarity with Cuba. Is this a reason to attack us? How can it [the United States] invoke as a pretext what is a consequence and not a cause of the aggressive attitude of the United States?"

Castro expressed satisfaction with the statement because it meant that Cuba had strong friends who would stifle the U.S. impulse for aggression. "We have to be satisfied that a government with very considerable military strength expresses its solidarity with, and its support for, Cuba, because that means that our small nation, militarily weak, is not going to have to fight—if we are attacked—completely abandoned to our own economic resources, and the world is not going to witness, in Cuba, an aggression like that against Guatemala or, even worse than in Guatemala, an invasion."

In the late summer of 1962 Castro would dwell on the horrors of nuclear devastation in the United States in the case of a U.S. attack on

Cuba, but in late 1960 Castro was restrained. He confined himself to saying that the U.S. response to the Soviet statement should have been to give public assurances that it would not invade Cuba.

The Cuban communists treated the Soviet statement as a warning to the United States. Their newspaper carried on the front page a picture of a young Soviet soldier with a winged missile in his hand pointed at a gorilla wearing a hat marked Pentagon. The caption beneath the picture was "Hands off Cuba."[78] The same issue carried the text of the message of the PSP thanking Khrushchev and stating the certainty of the fullest support in the event of U.S. aggression. The words "fullest support" implied what the cartoon made explicit: the Soviet Union threatened the United States with missiles.

A few days later the newspaper carried an article that explicitly characterized the Soviet statement as a commitment to use nuclear weapons against the United States.[79] Now the socialist world in the person of Khrushchev was saying that if the United States tried to bring death to Cuba, it would die. The American marines would have to fight the Cuban peasants and militia and also the atomic missiles of the Soviet Union. Now that imperialism had been weakened, a warning to the United States could be issued, before it committed an act of aggression. The Soviet Union, the writer went on to say, not only destroyed the strategy of a local war against Cuba but also offered vital economic support. Moreover, if the United States attained the impossible success it dreamed of and suppressed Cuba by force, it would feel strong enough to try to reestablish imperialism in Asia and Africa "and even the socialist world." Thus, in defending Cuba, the Soviet Union was defending itself.

The organ of the 26th of July Movement, *Revolución*, reported that various associations in Cuba had expressed gratitude to Khrushchev for his warning to the United States.[80] Nuñez Jiménez commented on the Soviet statement from the vantage point of his 3 June interview with Khrushchev, and he conveyed Khrushchev's confidence that his warning would deter the United States. "We were told," said Jiménez, "that the imperialists would not attack Cuba openly, since they know that world opinion would not permit it. At that point in the conversation he [Khrushchev] cited the case of the nationalization of the Suez Canal, in which Russia warned Great Britain that Soviet missile forces could respond with their weapons if aggression against Egypt were perpetrated."[81]

Nuñez Jiménez, in quoting Khrushchev to say Soviet forces "could respond" (instead of "would respond") was accurate in reflecting what I have called the menacing rather than the threatening character of the statements on Suez. Khrushchev was saying and perhaps believing that simply talking about Soviet missile capability and mentioning Soviet disapproval of an imperialist action would serve to break off the action or deter it. Jiménez also said that "the statements of the Soviet Union contributed to spoiling any plan for aggression in armed form against our country" and that the Soviet defense of Cuba "represented a balancing of forces in the struggle . . . since its [the USSR's] great power makes us even in our confrontation with the United States."[82]

Jiménez also echoed Castro's note about the propriety of accepting Soviet aid—"I would say it is immoral for us to reject Soviet aid, since it represents security in the face of aggression against our country"— thereby supplying another piece of evidence that some argued that accepting Soviet aid was a mistake.

The PSP continued to interpret Khrushchev's menace as a warning. An *Hoy* editorial said that "in an action of great significance, the Prime Minister of the Soviet Union, Comrade Nikita Khrushchev, announced that if it were necessary the USSR *would* support Cuba with its atomic missiles if Cuba was a victim of direct intervention by the United States. That warning is an act of the utmost solidarity that could prevent hundreds of thousands of Cubans having to die fighting against a criminal invasion from a modern and powerful army like that of the United States."[83]

On 21 July a cartoon on the front page of *Hoy* depicted the Soviet delegate at the United Nations pointing a missile at the U.S. delegate and saying, "I tell you I mean it." The American delegate falls back in consternation.

When the Soviet statement first reached Cuba, Guevara had said at a public meeting that "Cuba is a glorious island in the middle of the Caribbean defended by the missiles of the greatest power."[84] Guevara also said that "by the force of circumstances we are in a position of greater danger and greater glory; we are practically the arbiters of world peace. . . ." Castro moved some distance toward that position in refuting an attack on the Cuban acceptance of Soviet support. According to Castro, Miguel Angel Quevedo, the editor of *Bohemia,* a Cuban weekly that had opposed Batista, had sought asylum and left Castro a letter of explanation. Quevedo charged that the Cuban revolution had been betrayed to international communism, that the acceptance of Soviet support had been presented as a political tactic but that it was really a diabolical plan to establish communism. Khrushchev's statements and their acceptance in speeches before the presidential palace (by Guevara and Dorticós on 10 July) fully revealed the deceit. It was not necessary to submit to odious Russian vassalage. The revolution had been betrayed.

The reason for Castro's defensiveness and insistence that Khrushchev's statement was spontaneous and unsolicited was now revealed. In a country of Cuba's size and history of dependence, the assistance of great powers surely seemed to compromise independence. Castro tried to counter the charge by saying first that he had no choice and then by suggesting that the spontaneous nature of the Soviet offer meant that no conditions had been exacted from Cuba. "If the country is threatened," said Castro, "by aggression, if it has just been attacked economically . . . and the Soviet Union in an absolutely spontaneous manner issues a declaration saying that it would help if Cuba were attacked, the fact that a country spontaneously made a declaration of support to our imperilled people, the fact that this support was announced publicly, for this gentleman, means that our country has been converted into a vassal of the USSR. That is to say, for this gentleman the right thing for us to do is to fold our arms and, disarmed, to resign ourselves to being invaded."[85]

Castro might well have believed that since the United States would not permit the genuine exercise of Cuban sovereignty, Cuba had to accept Soviet economic and political support. But Quevedo sensed correctly that Cuba would have to pay a political price. Castro was implying that Soviet economic assistance and even a promise of some kind of military support came with no strings attached. Castro had to say this, and he very likely believed it at the time, for the alternative was most unpalatable. To restore relations with the United States to a point where he needed no support from the ideological adversary of the United States, Castro would have had to abandon his social program and cope immediately with the charge that he had sold out to the Yankees. Since the political quid pro quo to the Soviet Union might be avoided altogether or would have to be made sometime in the future, there was no real choice for Castro.

SOVIET TREATMENT OF THE MISSILE STATEMENT

For Khrushchev the statement on Cuba and missiles served internal and external needs. If it deterred the United States from action against Cuba, Khrushchev would earn political credit within the Soviet Union and in the world of international communism. At first, Soviet commentaries and use of the statement in political roundups preserved its menacing character. The tone suggested that the mere reminder that Cuba had a friend in the Soviet Union and that the Soviet Union had intercontinental missiles would serve as a deterrent, and no thought had to be given to the contingency of an American attack. Later, some Soviet formulations shifted from a statement of capacity to help Cuba to a commitment to do so.

From the very beginning, however, the Soviet press republished some foreign statements that the Soviet Union *would* come to the aid of Cuba. Thus, while the Soviet Union was not making an explicit commitment to help Cuba, she was not quarreling with such an interpretation and was sometimes repeating it. For example, in a 12 July 1960 press review of reactions to Khrushchev's statement, an East German newspaper's correct rendering of Khrushchev's meaning was repeated, but the Indian press was quoted as saying that Soviet missiles *would* help Cuba if necessary.[86] Dorticós told a TASS correspondent that the day that Khrushchev "declared that the Soviet Union was prepared to offer support to Cuba was a historic day for the whole world."[87] Technically, this did not go beyond Khrushchev's statement, because Khrushchev had promised to furnish economic support. But this was a mere quibble, because after all the fuss about missiles, a historic day for the whole world could not merely mean sugar purchases. When Valdés Vivó's article in *Hoy* quoted Khrushchev as saying that the Soviet Union *would* support Cuba if she were attacked by the imperialists, *Izvestiia* faithfully reproduced this misinterpretation.[88] Guevara was quoted as saying that Khrushchev's statement "showed that imperialists could not invade Cuba with impunity . . . [for] now the mightiest power in the world, which had weapons capable of wiping colonialism from the face of the earth, is on Cuba's side once and for all."[89]

The Soviet press also obliquely indicated that the present crisis about Cuba might lead to the movement of Cuba into the Soviet camp in a diplomatic sense. A *New York Post* editorial was quoted to the effect that senseless American pressure on Castro would push him further into the embrace of Soviet Russia, which was extending its arms to him.[90] Khrushchev also explicitly stated in a press conference that the Monroe Doctrine was dead, thus taking credit for reducing American power in Latin America. He said, "We believe that the Monroe Doctrine has had its day, has outlived itself and has, so to speak, died a natural death. Now the remains of that doctrine have to be buried, as any dead body is buried, so as not to foul the air with its putrefaction."[91]

A commentary in the organ of the Soviet armed forces, *Red Star*, took the line that the United States had already been deterred from a direct attack on Cuba. "Fearing the just anger of the peoples, the United States has not risked an armed invasion of Cuba" but has used other forms of pressure, especially support of Batista's henchmen and economic pressure. Cuba had not submitted at the beginning of the struggle. Now that she enjoyed the support of the Soviet Union, nothing could sway her from her chosen path. Khrushchev's statement was "a serious warning to the more adventurist forces in the United States, who were demanding direct military intervention against Cuba."[92]

Red Star also carried a TASS report of a conversation with a 26th of July Movement leader, Emilio Aragonés, which committed the Soviet Union to employ missiles in defense of Cuba. "We greeted the statement of the Prime Minister of the USSR that the criminal attack on Cuba being prepared by imperialism would bring Soviet missiles into action . . . it instilled in us the absolute confidence that we would win if they attacked us."[93]

Izvestiia quoted a *New York Times* editorial that argued that the Cuban communists who a year ago had had to exert themselves to get onto Castro's bandwagon were now quite influential. U.S. economic pressure has pushed Cuba toward Russia, which might be forced to do more than she had ever intended for Cuba. Much would depend on Khrushchev's visit to Cuba.[94]

While *Red Star* was publishing articles and dispatches from Cuba saying that the Soviet Union had deterred a direct American attack on Cuba or had assured victory for Cuba if such an attack did occur, *Izvestiia*, edited by Khrushchev's son-in-law Aleksei Adzhubei, was explaining by quoting a *New York Times* editorial—an infrequent practice—that Khrushchev and the Cuban communists had taken advantage of American mistakes to make irreversible gains. Soviet readers learned for the first time that Khrushchev's visit to Cuba was to take place "in the near future" and that much would depend on that visit. While the organ of the Soviet military was stressing the role of Soviet arms in gaining political victories, *Izvestiia* was stressing the political gains made by Khrushchev himself and his statements. When Nuñez Jiménez returned to Cuba, he told a television audience that people in Europe were speculating that Khrushchev might visit Cuba on 26 July—the anniversary of the attack on Moncada—but that at any rate he hoped it would be soon.[95]

We can only speculate as to why Khrushchev did not make the trip to Cuba which he had apparently led the Cubans to believe would take place soon. Political troubles at home and the unwillingness of his enemies to permit him to enjoy a personal triumph are possibilities. *Izvestiia* took the trouble to quote Nelson Rockefeller's speculation that Khrushchev's visit to Cuba could "lead to the conclusion of a pact which would furnish Russia with military bases in Cuba."[96] The reader will probably have noted how early and how often the Soviet press picked up American remarks about a missile base in Cuba. Perhaps Khrushchev or Castro, or both, felt that a visit to Cuba by Khrushchev so soon after his missile statement would incite the warhawks in the United States and furnish a pretext for an invasion.

On 9 July, when Khrushchev was making his missile statement, Raúl Castro, who was in Prague, received instructions to go to Moscow, which was not on his original itinerary. He immediately seized upon the decisive importance of the statement. A reporter asked him about Cuba's exposed position, being only ten minutes away from the United States by air. "I would," he said, "divide the problem in two parts. Before and after the rockets" [i.e., the 9 July statement]. Before, he said, the United States "had begun to speak openly of armed action; now they have to think twice."[97]

Later, back in Cuba, he added that the Khrushchev statement of 9 July came as a surprise and explained that it was not a "warning against intervention here [in Cuba] because there is not going to be any intervention here, although they [the Americans] had previously thought about intervening. . . . In the name of the Cuban government and people we expressed our gratitude for this timely warning, which I personally believe spares us aggression and a river of blood, besides."[98]

The communiqué issued after Raúl Castro's visit conveyed the same meaning as the looser language of the subsequent television interview. According to the communiqué, Raúl Castro thanked Khrushchev for his statement that the Soviet Union "possessed everything for the support of Cuba and her heroic people in the struggle for freedom and national independence" and for the assurance that the socialist states would extend help to Cuba in her just struggle. The communiqué noted the U.S. State Department statement of 14 July that the danger of U.S. attack on Cuba was an illusion. Although world opinion considered this statement an undertaking not to invade Cuba, it was not a guaranty against assaults on Cuban peaceful development and sovereignty. Certain circles in the United States had not given up plans for an armed attack on Cuba. "Therefore all peoples, and above all those of Latin America, should always display the highest vigilance not to permit gangsterlike aggression under any flag or in any form, open or concealed, against the Cuban people." All nations including the Soviet Union would help Cuba break the economic blockade. The socialist countries accepted the responsibility of providing Cuba with all necessary goods on the basis of normal trade. Khrushchev again assured Raúl Castro that the Soviet Union had the wherewithal "to prevent armed American intervention against the Cuban republic."[99] Deterrence, not the grim necessity of nuclear war, was the watchword of the communiqué, and the suggestion was strong that the United States had already "obligated" itself not to intervene against Cuba but had not "guaranteed" it. The difference between obligation and guaranty was not explored.

The joint Cuban-Soviet communiqué differs from independent Cuban appraisals. The Cubans, it will be recalled, had been insisting that the United States could dissipate the international crisis simply by a guaranty that it would not invade Cuba. The abbreviated version of the communiqué that appeared in the Cuban press dropped the phrase about world opinion considering the United States to be obligated not to intervene against Cuba. The awkwardness of distinguishing between an obligation and a guaranty was thereby avoided, and only those parts of the communiqué that talked about the continuing dangers to Cuba were reproduced.[100] The regular practice of the Cuban press had been to print such communiqués verbatim.

Khrushchev seems to have been under some pressure from the Cubans to make his statement more a missile warning than a missile menace. In his congratulatory telegram to Castro on the anniversary of the 26th of

July Movement he said that "if armed intervention is launched against Cuba, then Cuba will be offered the necessary help. I declare to you that the Soviet Union will not play the last role in this cause."[101]

Althought missiles did not appear in this formula, the commitment to Cuba was specific, unlike the 9 July statement which only linked the invasion of Cuba with Soviet missiles without saying that the first would be the occasion for the employment of the second.

Izvestiia continued to present the news as if the necessity for executing the threat would never arise. Secretary of State Herter was reported as saying that the inter-American military force that the United States wanted could probably not be created quickly enough to regulate the Cuban problem. The plan, argued *Izvestiia*, smacked so much of colonialism that the United States could not even recruit servile dictators to do its bidding.[102] *Pravda's* treatment of the same news emphasized the opposite contingency by arguing that armed intervention by the OAS violated international law and constituted armed aggression under the UN Charter. Therefore, "any power would have the right to offer Cuba any help, including the employment of the armed forces, in the struggle against the aggressor."[103]

But Raúl Castro, stopping off in Cairo and Athens before returning to Cuba from the Soviet Union, continued to emphasize that Soviet statements had already deterred the United States from its most aggressive plans. "Imperialism has been forced to retreat temporarily," he said in a speech in Cairo, "until it finds other means to attack us. It retreats before the spontaneous solidarity of all the countries and the great-spirited and valuable aid tendered us by the socialist countries, headed by the Soviet Union."[104] Khrushchev's warning "that the Soviet Union would not be quiet in the event of armed aggression against Cuba reminded the imperialists that the era of aggression had passed." These warnings and the joint communiqué "have had their effect." When a newspaper reporter in Athens asked Raúl Castro about the possibility of American armed intervention in Cuban affairs, he replied that "after N. S. Khrushchev's warning to the United States regarding Cuba, hardly anyone would dare touch the Cuban Republic."[105]

Some Latin Americans, notably Arturo Frondizi of Argentina, publicly criticized the Cubans for accepting Soviet help in the form of Khrushchev's statement, since it put them into the Soviet orbit. Guevara responded that it was stupid to spit at those who wanted to help Cuba, and *Hoy* argued that Khrushchev's declaration did not interfere with the rights of any country in the Americas but shielded Cuba from the United States.[106]

On 7 August 1960 the U.S. Department of State, in a seventy-eight-page memorandum to the OAS, charged that Cuba was now in open league with the Soviet Union and Communist China and had become a typical dictatorship and a base for communist propaganda.[107] Secretary of State Herter indicated at a press conference that he hoped for a change of regime in Cuba. He explained that the United States continued to make protests about illegal Cuban actions because it was very important in international law to establish a record. "Furthermore, no one knows what shift may take place in Cuba. We, of course, hope that the Cuban people themselves, with whom we have nothing but sympathy, will take care of the situation, and eventually our long-standing happy relationship will be restored."[108]

Meanwhile, Raúl Castro had returned to Cuba, and in a speech to the Latin American Youth Congress he gave a further clarification of the Soviet missile statements. He quoted some press comment in the United States that the Soviet warning was conditional. In a sense that was correct.

If there is no aggression, there will be no missiles, but if there is aggression, there will be missiles. There are two kinds of missiles, war missiles and peace missiles. We do not accept the help of war missiles; we accept the help of the disinterested peace missiles. There are two kinds of missiles just as there are two kinds of beards in America, Uncle Sam's beard and Fidel's beard. We are for Fidel's beard.

. . . Those friends on the Continent who are so worried don't have to worry, nor does the OAS have to meet for this reason; whatever they say, if there is no aggression, there will be no missiles. But if there is aggression, there will be missiles and plenty of them. . . .

We want peace and we are for it; we are opposed to a world war, but if Cuba is attacked militarily, it [the United States] will get what it deserves, not from here, but from elsewhere, and those missiles won't fall here, but there.[109]

Pravda carried a representative selection from Raúl Castro's speech that interpreted Khrushchev's July statement as a warning rather than as a menace.[110] In November 1960 Khrushchev was to do the same in his own words. Fidel Castro also accepted the idea that an attack on Cuba would bring a world war by saying that if the Americans tried to extinguish the Cuban revolution, "they would not find a Guatemala but their Waterloo."[111]

The United States at this point stepped up its political campaign against Cuba, apparently in the belief that the Soviet missile statement of July had brought the crisis to a new level of seriousness. Eisenhower hinted in a press conference that if the Cuban government chose communism against the freely expressed will of the people, the United States would take action. But he put the case negatively. When a reporter asked him if the United States would permit a communist-dominated regime in Cuba, Eisenhower replied that if Cuba were in the position of a satellite state, very definite action would be called for, in his view. But if communism were freely established, he did not see how the United States could object or intervene. But the president did not believe that this was going to happen. There was no case in the world where any group of people freely voted to regiment themselves.[112]

Eisenhower, however, begged the question of who would decide whether the Cuban people had freely expressed their will or whether Cuba had become a Soviet satellite by assuming that the United States or the OAS had the power to do so. U.S. officials publicly expressed strong opinions on those subjects and, a few days later at an OAS meeting in San José, Costa Rica, tried to convince others. The under-secretary of state, Douglas Dillon, told the Senate Foreign Relations Committee that Cuba now seemed to be following the communist line, and the secretary of state, Herter, on the eve of his departure for the OAS meeting, stated that the ideals of the peoples of the Western Hemisphere were being gravely threatened and that he was confident that the foreign ministers attending the OAS meeting would find ways to meet the threat of extracontinental intervention.[113] At the conference the United States charged that Cuba had established a training program for agents and guerrillas to spread the communist revolution throughout Latin America, that Cuba was eliminating the last vestiges of religious liberty, and that the Cuban government had established work brigades—a communist device. Latin American diplomats were reported to feel that the U.S. charges were not well documented.[114] However, the Colombian foreign minister, Julio Cesar Turbay Ayala, told the Cubans that their acceptance of the Soviet offer to defend Cuba with missiles had destroyed American sympathy for the Cuban government. He himself would have advised the United States not to cut the sugar quota, but Cuban acceptance of Soviet aid violated the juridical and political norms of the American system.[115] The issue was joined. Castro believed that an independent Cuba had the right to accept assistance from anyone it chose; his opponents felt that that acceptance of help from the Soviet Union violated the norms of the American system. Could an American state accept the support of a socialist state and adopt socialism with impunity? In August 1960, the United States with some Latin American support was saying it could not. But the events of the next few years were to prove the United States mistaken.

At this very time the PSP convened its first party Congress since February 1952. The leader, Blas Roca, gave a long report, which was faithfully summarized in *Pravda,* and Aníbal Escalante gave a report on the party program. The Soviet press ignored Escalante's dissenting opinions; as in the past, Escalante argued that the Cuban revolution could move more rapidly. His proposals were largely dropped from the resolution the party finally adopted.

Roca modified somewhat his earlier appraisal of the nature of the revolution. Although the revolution was still a coalition of several classes including the national bourgeoisie and the urban middle classes, the workers and peasants were listed first and characterized as the motive forces behind it.[116] Its class nature and the methods it employed made it an "advanced popular revolution, but it is not a communist revolution."[117] The shift in the world balance of forces, the waxing of the socialist camp and the waning of the imperialist camp, was a factor of major importance for Cuba permitting it to move rapidly in its social and economic changes. Roca also said, clearly but clumsily, that Castro and his immediate associates were adopting the ideas of the PSP: ". . . the left of the petite bourgeoisie is becoming more and more radical and is completely identified with antiimperialism and is closely united with the proletariat and the peasantry. Its [the left petite bourgeoisie's] most advanced elements fuse with the working class, with its point of view and its program."[118]

The Soviet Union, Roca continued, had been a staunch friend and for the time being had caused the United States to drop its plans to attack, thus saving the Cuban people from a bloody and destructive war. On the evidence that the United States planned to occupy Cuba by force of arms, Khrushchev issued "his well-known and sensational warning that if Cuba were attacked in this way, the Soviet Union would offer all its help including making intercontinental missiles fly to the United States in case of need. . . . Because of its [the warning's] categorical nature, the North American imperialists found themselves obligated to declare that they did not intend to intervene in Cuba."[119] The party's task was to finish the democratic revolution and to prepare for the future.

Escalante, instead of emphasizing the necessity for finishing the democratic phase of the revolution, as Roca had done, chose to stress the possibility of moving rapidly to the socialist phase. He failed to have this possibility included in the final resolutions of the congress. In communist doctrine, only the communist party could lead the socialist phase of the revolution, and by citing China as an example for Cuba, Escalante left no room for doubt.[120] But in that case, Castro would have to step aside or become the leader of the PSP, and there was no precedent for a new convert to communism assuming the leadership of a communist party.

Escalante's projections were dropped from the resolutions of the PSP Congress, either because they were considered to be overoptimistic or out of regard for Castro's sensibilities. Roca also dealt directly with the question of offending Castro by seeming to reach out for more power for the PSP. The PSP, he said, had not tried to expand by enrolling new members because competition with other parties would have hurt the unity of the revolution.[121] What he obviously meant was that while Castro was willing to have PSP cooperation on his terms, he would not tolerate a PSP initiative to grow stronger.

At the same time that Roca was endorsing cooperation and not competition with Castro by eschewing recruitment for the communist party, the events at the San José conference were demonstrating to Castro that Soviet support could not help the United States to rally the rest of Latin America against Cuba. Probably few Latin American leaders had much sympathy for communism, and some had good reason to fear the catalytic effect of clandestine Cuban political activity in their own countries. But the threat of Castroism and of the Soviet Union had to be weighed against the precedent of armed intervention in a Latin American state by the United States alone or by the OAS under U.S. leadership. The Roosevelt Good Neighbor Policy of 1933 had marked the beginning of a new chapter in U.S. relations with Latin America, a period in which the United States denied itself the right to intervene in other countries of the hemisphere. The United States had organized the OAS as an instrument in the cold war against communism and the Soviet Union, but in doing so it gave a hostage to the nations of Latin America. The United States could now intervene unilaterally in a Latin American state only at the cost of damaging the OAS.

In December 1953 the United States had tried and failed to persuade the OAS to condemn Arbenz in Guatemala as a tool of communism, and its subsequent decision to employ indirect means to overthrow his government caused the greatest decline in U.S. prestige in Latin America since World War II. At San José in 1960 the United States had to be satisfied with a watered-down resolution against extracontinental intervention in the hemisphere that did not mention Cuba by name. The OAS could not prevent the "indirect" U.S. intervention in Cuba in April 1961 nor the direct intervention in the Dominican Republic in 1965, but it could withhold its approval. As in 1953, the Soviet Union interpreted the failure of the United States to get what it wanted in the OAS as evidence of the decline of American power in Latin America but it was more cautious than it had been seven years earlier.[122]

THE BACKDROP OF THE CONGO CRISIS

The Soviet Union at this point had been very optimistic about harnessing the forces of the smaller states into anti–U.S. blocs. The events in the Congo were coming to a head at this very time, and a brief account of Soviet miscalculation there will serve to identify some of the mental furniture that the Russians brought to the Cuban problem.[123]

At the beginning of 1960 the Belgian government, frightened by the sudden manifestation of Congolese nationalism and fearful of having to face its Algeria, precipitately decided to give the Congo independence on 1 July 1960. The new authorities found it difficult to maintain the discipline of the Force Publique (the internal police) and to contain the centrifugal forces of the country, particularly Katanga, an area rich in copper. The mistreatment of Belgian nationals by the undisciplined Force Publique became an international cause célèbre with strong racial overtones. UN troops were introduced to restore order, but in the view of the national leader of the Congo the major source of disorder was Katangese separatism. To protect Belgian nationals, Belgian paratroopers were introduced into the country, and some Belgian elements began to consider using these troops to support Katangese separatism in order to save the most valuable Belgian investments. Although this was not Belgian governmental policy, Patrice Lumumba believed that it was, and when he failed to get the support and reassurances he demanded from the United States and from Secretary-General Dag Hammerskjöld of the United Nations, he appealed to the Soviet Union for help. The Soviet Union supported the Congolese position at the United Nations and in addition, in August 1960, offered the Lumumba forces the trucks and planes to bring troops into Katanga that the United Nations had refused.

Although the Soviet logistic support, in the short time that it was available, did not measurably improve the control of the central authorities over Katanga, it seemed to strengthen Lumumba's position within the new state, whose capital was Leopoldville. The UN authorities, employing the forces that had been sent to restore order in the Congo, closed the airports, thus effectively depriving the Soviet transport of an opportunity to help Lumumba. Shortly afterwards Lumumba was deposed, first by Joseph Kasavubu, to be replaced for a time by Joseph Mobutu, and one of the justifications for the change was the danger of a communist-influenced Congo.

Much of the world press and especially the press of the Afro-Asian bloc charged that the United Nations had helped oust Lumumba. It seemed, therefore, as if the Soviet Union was on common ground with the great majority of the members of the UN Assembly. But when the Soviet Union, acting on this assumption, tried to force the resignation of the Secretary-General, Hammerskjöld, it found itself isolated. The Soviet diplomats had failed to recognize, or the Soviet leaders refused to accept, that the African states felt that the preservation of the United Nations was the best way for them to accomplish their objectives: namely, to avoid the precedent of the secession of Katanga (few of the new African states were tribally homogenous, and almost all faced serious centrifugal pressures) and to keep any of the great powers from having dominant influence in any African state. In their view, the hue and cry about Lumumba served to put Hammerskjöld on notice that he must change his policy (as he did), and eventually the Congo survived undivided without any predominant great power influence. The new African states put away the temptation of punishing Hammerskjöld and hewed to the goal of preserving the institution that would best serve their interests. Unlike the Yugoslavs, who discerned the underlying policy of the Afro-Asian bloc, the Soviets judged on the rhetoric of newspaper editorials, and consequently Khrushchev, who had come to represent the USSR at the UN Assembly meeting in September hoping to head a new Afro-Asian–socialist block at the United Nations, returned home empty-handed. The Soviet leaders had a penchant for believing that one swallow meant the spring had come, and their disappointment at the United Nations probably contributed to a more sober estimate of the likelihood of the members of the OAS defying the United States. The Soviet Union relied basically on its economic and military support of Cuba to influence U.S. policy.

Castro, for his part, hurled defiance at the United States and used the Declaration of San José as the occasion for issuing the counter Declaration of Havana. In a speech to a mass meeting, which he termed an Assembly of the People, he opened a discussion on the OAS declaration with the people of Cuba. Castro asked them whether it was right to accept Soviet and Chinese help if the imperialists attacked. The people of Cuba assured him that it was right. Then Castro asked who was to blame for the Cuban revolution, and the crowd shouted: "Yankee imperialism, the Yankees."[124]

The apologetic note about the revolution and Soviet help is striking. Castro could have said that Cubans were proud of the revolution and took all the credit for it themselves. But the tone is clearly "Look what the Yankees have made us do!" The Soviet press printed the full text of the Declaration of Havana,[125] but it did not deal with the question of "blame" in commentaries.

Guevara, speaking a fortnight later, went further than Castro in insisting that Soviet aid had not compromised Cuban independence, saying that "if one day in offering us aid, the Union of Soviet Socialist Republics or the People's government of China makes it a condition that we alienate any of our sovereignty or dignity, at that very moment Cuba would break with any government that felt that way and tried to act that way." The arms that were to be seen as he spoke, he said, had been purchased from Czechoslovakia without any conditions. When the Guatemalan arms became obsolete, and the government bought a handful more, it was attacked. Now, said Guevara, the attack was restrained by the Soviet warning, but the United States rages like "corralled and wounded wild beasts who become ever more dangerous and aggressive."[126]

The Soviet Union, in the person of its most prominent spokesman, N. S. Khrushchev, never withdrew the menace of the 9 July statement and on occasion moved toward presenting it as a warning. But there were occasions when official spokesmen, including Khrushchev himself, discussed the Cuban situation dropping both the menace and warning of the July statement. Gromyko's ironical statement of the U.S. position, cited earlier, quoted Khrushchev as saying that the Soviet Union would help any country fighting for its independence, but Gromyko dropped any mention of missiles.[127] When Khrushchev spoke at the session of the UN General Assembly in New York in September he said that the UN "must do its utmost to avert the intervention threatening Cuba from without. To allow another Guatemala would mean to unloose events whose consequences can hardly be foreseen by anyone today."[128] This formulation did not take anything back, but it omitted threats. We can only speculate that other elements in the leadership were not happy with Khrushchev's latest example of missile rattling and preferred the tone Gromyko had adopted or else that Khrushchev himself wanted to soften his tone. At any rate, Khrushchev still led the applause at the same UN session when Castro chided Admiral Arleigh A. Burke for doubting that Khrushchev would fire his missiles if Cuba were attacked. Castro called it a dangerous miscalculation for Burke to think that in case of attack Cuba would be alone. "But suppose that Mr. Burke, even though he is an admiral, is mistaken."[129]

During October the Cuban press continued to report the suppression of mercenaries and counterrevolutionaries supported by the United States. Castro continued to claim that Khrushchev's warning and Castro's exposure of U.S. plots had caused the United States to drop the idea of a direct attack. At first the United States was impressed with Khrushchev's declaration that the United States would be destroyed, but then the United States began to gamble that an attack could be made and that the Soviet Union would not help. What is dangerous, said Castro, is that the United States could come to believe this. "When we. [the Cubans] brought this problem up in the United Nations, Khrushchev got up and said: 'Yes, they [the Americans] are mistaken.' "[130] But the treatment given to this speech by *Pravda* minimized the Soviet commitment. Castro was only quoted as saying that Cuba had sustained the U.S. attacks because the socialist countries existed and provided materials the United States refused to sell.[131] And in a special message to the Cubans from New York, Khrushchev had only said that the Cubans would win if they were loyal to their government and if they organized, and he told the Cuban people there was no need to assure them that "the peoples of the Soviet Union are on your side . . . not merely today but for the whole duration of your struggle for independence. . . ."[132] Castro, who had not voiced formulas of Soviet commitment as strong as those of his brother Raúl and Guevara, now was employing the standard rhetorical device of committing his ally to his firmest formulations.

In the United States during October the two presidential candidates, Kennedy and Nixon, both made it clear that they thought Cuba was lost and had to be freed. Kennedy talked about a new Soviet satellite only ninety miles from American shores and of the Cuban freedom fighters who had been neglected by the Republican administration. Nixon abjured the idea of an invasion of Cuba and the violation of treaties this would entail but said that the Republicans could do what they had done in Guatemala. "We quarantined Mr. Arbenz. The result was that the Guatemalan people themselves eventually rose up and threw him out. We are quarantining Mr. Castro today."[133]

KHRUSHCHEV CLARIFIES THE MISSILE WARNING

The Soviet response was not long in coming. First, Soviet journalists sounded the alarm; then Khrushchev resolved the ambiguities of the 9 July statement, privately to a group of Cubans and then in published form, and made a specific missile commitment to Cuba. A major Soviet journalist reported that the United States planned to sponsor an invasion of Cuba at the end of October just before the presidential elections. The Americans had taken leave of their senses. Such a provocation would have unforeseen consequences.[134]

News reports and Moscow radio supported the speculation that invasion might be timed to influence the election. Raúl Roa had charged that invasion of Cuba could be expected at any moment, and *Izvestiia* carried the story.[135] One Moscow radio commentator said that the imperialist conspiracy against Cuba was apparently entering its decisive stage, and another commented on an Associated Press report that an attack on Cuba might be expected on the last weekend in October.[136]

It fitted in with the Soviet view of capitalist habits and indeed with Khrushchev's own style to arrange for spectacular foreign news in order to gain domestic political advantage. An invasion of Cuba would supposedly help the Republican Party in the United States win the election and hurt the Soviet Union—particularly Khrushchev, who personified the policy of deterring the United States by menacing words.

If the Soviet Union had merely offered verbal protests to a direct invasion, it would have suffered a severe loss of face. If it had attacked the United States with its still very sketchy intercontinental forces, the USSR would have risked its very existence. It was now too late to rescind the Soviet menace of 9 July, which the Cubans had converted into a warning. The Soviet response was to reiterate and reinforce that statement. The circumstances surrounding the warning suggest that Khrushchev seized upon Cuban desires for reassurance in the face of the clear statements of intention by both candidates for the U.S. presidency and that he gained the approval of his associates in the Soviet government.

The Cubans met the statements of the presidential candidates with understandable anxiety. The headlines in *Hoy* for 23 October read:

YANKEE CANDIDATES REVEAL THEIR PLANS
NIXON: A NEW GUATEMALA
KENNEDY: AN INTERNAL COUP

But this time, said the communist news organ, the imperialists had miscalculated, because they had forgotten about the friends of Cuba, "the possessors of a most extraordinary military force equipped with an invincible military force capable of destroying the band of imperial bandits in a few minutes."[137]

At 11:00 A.M. 22 October 1960 Khrushchev gave an interview to a group of Cuban journalists headed by Carlos Franqui.[138] The Soviet version of the text was released by TASS a week later, but *Revolución* published it a day earlier, on 28 October. Soviet and Cuban news treatment suggested that the Soviet Union had increased its commitment. The general tone was that an American invasion of Cuba would threaten the peace of the world and that the Soviet Union would stand by Cuba.[139]

Carlos Franqui, the editor of *Revolución*, raised the question of the nature of the Soviet commitment to Cuba in his interview with Khrushchev: "The imperialists contend that the statement of the Soviet government concerning the possibility of using rocketry in the event of an armed aggression against Cuba has purely symbolic significance. What do you think about that?"[140] It will be recalled that Castro had said how dangerous it would be if the United States came to believe that the Soviet Union would not respond to an attack on Cuba. Khrushchev replied:

I should like such statements to be really symbolic, as the enemies of the Cuban revolution say. For this purpose it is essential that the imperialists' threat of intervention against Cuba does not resolve into military operations. [This requires that the imperialists' threats not be converted into military operations.] Then there will be no need to test the reality of our statement concerning armed assistance to the Cuban people against aggression. Is this clear?

Franqui rephrased Khrushchev's meaning in the following rather obscure way: "Meanwhile we shall also use this figuratively unless and until they do not attack us." The Spanish text of his rephrasing is clearer: "We know that the declaration can have a figurative meaning only as long as they do not attack us."

Franqui either felt that the translation was obscuring the sense of his remarks or he wanted to make doubly sure, because after Khrushchev responded "That's right" to his rephrasing, he pursued the matter: "I should like you to get me right. It would be fine if the threat did not exist." When Khrushchev replied "yes" Franqui then addressed the other possibility: "If this threat does exist, if this threat is carried out, it seems to me rockets are adequately prepared for this?" And Khrushchev replied, "Unquestionably. You have it right. It would be fine if there were no aggression. We are doing everything not to launch combat rockets because it is human life, the flourishing of life and not the destruction of human beings, that is our supreme concern."

Khrushchev's commitment was not couched in the most direct possible language. He could have said as the *Revolución* headline did: "There will be missiles if there is aggression." Instead he phrased it negatively, denying the contention that he had only spoken symbolically on 9 July and saying that the threat would remain symbolic only if the imperialists did not convert their threats into military actions. The *New York Times* report rendered the key parts of the interview correctly in the body of its account but noted in the lead-in to the story that in Moscow the interview with Franqui was regarded as an effort to exert a moderating influence on Castro.[141] It was possible to conclude from the account that Khrushchev had reduced the force of his 9 July statement. The looseness of the language and the form of the interview leave room for doubt, but on balance it seems clear that an important element had been added to the 9 July statement. An American attack on Cuba and the Soviet missile capability were now not merely juxtaposed, but linked.

The *New York Times* account of Khrushchev's interview with Carlos Franqui seemed to undermine the reassurance that Khrushchev had offered. Franqui's journal, *Revolución,* commented that "the repetition by the Soviet leader that Soviet missiles are ready in the event that North American imperialism is disposed to attack our country militarily has been a terrible thing for the Pentagon aggressors." In desperation, therefore, the AP had transmitted a version of the interview that "tried to make out that Khrushchev had said that the assistance of the Soviet missiles in case Cuba were invaded should be considered as symbolic."[142] They are trying to conceal from the American people, said *Revolución,* that an attack on Cuba could spark a new world war.

Hoy also accused the *New York Times,* in the person of its Moscow correspondent, Seymour Topping, of making propaganda. The text of Topping's account of the Khrushchev interview, it charged, belied its intent, which was to convince the citizens of North America that not the slightest danger existed that Cuba could become the cause of an atomic conflagration.[143] These shrill Cuban cries that the North American news services and the *New York Times* were trying to minimize the significance of Khrushchev's new statement reveal how much hope the Cubans had invested in its efficacy. In a speech to graduating military cadets Castro said that the U.S. attack might come at any time, even after the presidential elections.[144] A Soviet news commentator noted that Khrushchev's warning to Cuba's enemies was most timely, since a U.S. aircraft carrier had arrived at Guantánamo.[145] The United States was preparing to concoct evidence of an attack on Guantánamo as a pretext for an attack on Cuba.[146] The next day President Eisenhower said that the U.S. base at Guantánamo had become more important for the defense of the Western Hemisphere because of the intimate relations between Cuba and the Sino-Soviet bloc and that the United States would take whatever steps were necessary to defend it.[147] The President of Cuba, Dorticós, replied immediately that Cuba would never attack Guantánamo. "We would never," he said, "commit the stupidity of providing the North American Empire with a pretext to invade us. . . ."[148]

The Cubans continued to warn of the possibility of an attack while giving Khrushchev's latest statement credit for reducing its likelihood. Guevara had arrived in Moscow shortly after Khrushchev's interview, and he said that the United States was preparing to execute a plan of aggression against Cuba at the very moment Khrushchev made his well-known warning. This warning, he said, made direct armed intervention more difficult, but anything could be expected from the United States.[149] At the United Nations the Cuban foreign minister, Roa, warned that "the imperialist invasion of Cuba in the present international circumstances [would not be] the end of the Cuban revolution but the prologue to the third world war."[150]

The Khrushchev interview with Franqui was not the subject of editorials in the Soviet press, nor did the Soviet press charge that the *New York Times* and the Associated Press had presented the interview tendentiously. It was the Cubans who reiterated that an American attack on Cuba meant the employment of Soviet missiles—a third world war. But as soon as the American election was over, a Soviet reporter in Havana attributed the following statement to an ordinary Cuban militiaman: "Yes, we will fight if we have to. Our enemies, the imperialists and their stooges, force us to hold a hoe in one hand and a rifle in the other. O.K., we know how to use both of them. Besides, we have good friends whose missiles don't miss. . . . Just think, forty-three years ago Russia was a poor, backward country like ours, and now it's a mighty power that can defend not only itself but others, too."[151]

Whatever the Cuban man-in-the-street might have said, Soviet reporters (like many others) consult with their embassy before filing a story, and in the Soviet Union the dispatch passes through the filter of the newspaper editorial office before it is published. Thus, quite characteristically, the i's were dotted and the t's crossed on Khrushchev's statement after the danger point of the U.S. election was passed.

The head of the Cuban communists claimed that Khrushchev's declaration had "paralyzed open military intervention,"[152] and Guevara in Moscow told the reporter of the Uruguayan communist newspaper that "if the United States had not intervened militarily in Cuba, it was because of the Soviet warning."[153]

Now that the immediate danger of invasion seemed to have passed, Castro stressed Cuban determination to fight rather than to rely on Soviet missile support. He argued that the United States would be most likely to invade Cuba if it believed the operation would be a twenty-four-hour affair. Cuba had purchased large quantities of arms and was prepared to fight. Only ". . . without our tenacious and invincible resistance from the first minute, the aid of the missiles of the Soviet Union, of the People's Republic of China, and of the other peoples of the world would not have the opportunity to be effectuated."[154] The Soviet press gave a faithful rendering of most of Castro's thoughts on the subject of the deterrence of American attack but omitted the statement that the Soviet Union would need the time furnished by Cuban resistance to effectuate its missile attack.[155] Castro was qualifying the automaticity of the Soviet attack and seemed to suggest that during the "pause" created by the fighting with conventional arms between the Cubans and the United States the missile threat would be repeated.

Castro seemed to anticipate the doctrine to be enunciated by the Kennedy administration soon after it took office, that an automatic nuclear response to a conventional action was not credible. The Soviet commentary on the excerpts from Castro's speech did say that the danger of aggression against Cuba would diminish as the United States came to understand that a blitzkrieg could not succeed in Cuba. The logic of deterrence was being questioned, as it was to be so often in the future. If Soviet missiles deterred U.S. action against Cuba, what was the relevance of the length of the U.S. operation in Cuba? If the United States was prepared to engage its missiles to defend Berlin, why should the Soviet Union be more deterred if it expected conventional fighting on the Central European front and less deterred if it expected to complete a military action in West Berlin in a short time? In both cases the deterring power balked at binding itself to employ its nuclear weapons if a "small," clearly defined aggression took place. It preferred to say that it or its ally had the wherewithal to contest the attack and that afterward the employment of nuclear weapons could not be ruled out. In both cases, the deterring power hoped that belief in its capability and the anxiety produced by the tone rather than the specificity of its warning would serve to restrain its opponent.

The Soviet press preferred to stress that its warning had forced the United States to abandon its plans. Guevara was quoted as saying in the presence of Khrushchev and Mikoian that Khrushchev had come forward "with a symbolic warning that had stayed the criminal hand of the imperialists."[156]

Meanwhile, there were indications that Cuba might be moving leftward. These were ignored in the Soviet Union and carefully noted in the United States. David Salvador, who had led the fight to expel the pro-Batista elements from the Cuban labor confederation of unions and had earlier resigned as secretary general of the confederation, the CTC (Central de Trabajadores de Cuba), was now expelled from the union after being caught trying to flee the country. He had earlier agreed to the co-option of communists to high posts, and he was now designated a traitor to the working class.[157] The Soviet press did not report this victory of the communists in the Cuban labor movement.

At a labor rally in Havana on the occasion of the anniversary of the Russian Revolution, a labor leader who was not a member of the PSP, José María de Aguilera, predicted that Cuba would become a socialist state: "It is high time to say without fear, without weak knees, without a trembling voice, and with head high that we are marching toward socialism in our country. . . . We cannot be afraid that a socialist regime is being implanted in Cuba. Every Cuban who truly loves his motherland need not fear this, because a socialist regime means the complete eradication of the exploitation of man by man."[158]

Hoy, the organ of the PSP, did not cite this prediction that Cuba would become a socialist state but rather vaguely reported Aguilera as saying that Cubans ought to follow the great example of the Soviet Union.[159] It took very careful reading of the Cuban press to find this paragraph buried under heaps of oratory, and as we shall later see, the PSP was annoyed with the *New York Times* for reporting that Cuba would probably come under the control of the communists.

The journal of the world communist movement, directed by the CPSU, published Blas Roca's views on the recent national congress of the PSP, which had stated that the left radical wing of the petite bourgeoisie exercised hegemony over the revolution. "The Cuban revolution has not yet reached the socialist stage, but neither does it foster the growth of capitalism." The "yet" left the impression that the revolution could become a socialist revolution at some unspecified time in the future, but this followed a paragraph in which the enemies of the revolution were charged with sowing confusion by claiming that the revolution was communist when it was patriotic, democratic, and antiimperialist.[160]

Blas Roca's "yet" in November made the possibility of socialism in Cuba a little more tangible than the resolutions of the Eighth Party Congress of August on which he was reporting. Roca had moved somewhat closer to Escalante. José María de Aguilera, the head of the bank clerks' union, was only a minor figure on the Cuban political scene, hardly the spokesman for the communists.

If anything, the interests of the Soviet Union were furthered by minimizing the likelihood of communism in Cuba and dropping the talk of missiles. Once Kennedy had been elected, Khrushchev hoped to succeed with Kennedy where he had failed with Eisenhower by getting some kind of general agreement after some U.S. concessions. But he could no more meet Kennedy to celebrate such a triumph while U.S. troops were fighting on Cuban soil than he could meet Eisenhower while the latter was claiming the right to conduct reconnaissance flights over Soviet soil.

When the newly arrived Soviet ambassador in Havana, S. M. Kudriavtsev, spoke at the Soviet Embassy in Havana at a reception in honor of the Russian Revolution, he talked only about Soviet support for countries fighting for their independence as Cuba was doing, and he said that nuclear wars should be prevented—unexceptionable sentiments. But Blas Roca, who spoke at the same occasion, repeated Khrushchev's "historic warning."[161]

When Max Frankel of the *New York Times*, reporting from Havana, said that the Soviet Union had been urging prudence and moderation on the Cubans and had told them to "stop rattling Soviet rockets" because Moscow's relations with the United States, especially with the incoming Kennedy administration, were more important than Cuba, the PSP reacted defensively. Frankel's report suggested that the new Soviet ambassador, Sergei M. Kudriavtsev, was urging moderation on Castro and counseling better relations with other Latin American governments. According to Frankel this advice had made some impression on the Cubans, and in recent days Cuban attacks had been aimed specifically at Eisenhower, Kennedy having been subtly dissociated from recent U.S. Cuban policy. In an editorial whose authorship he later claimed, Rodríguez said that Frankel's purpose was obvious: to discredit Khrushchev's warning that the employment of superior American forces against Cuba "would cause the flight of Soviet missiles toward the United States."[162]

In the unsigned editorial Rodríguez argued that the people of the United States, who understood the gravity of Khrushchev's warning, opposed the policy of bringing the world to the brink of nuclear war. Frankel's article in the *New York Times* was a last effort to convince North American opinion that the United States could "continue to go forward with its aggressive plans against the Cuban revolution without causing any further complications with the Soviet Union." On the same day that Frankel filed his story, Rodríguez said, TASS had thrown his castle of words to the ground by in effect saying: "Stop attacking Cuba or you can face the disagreeable visit of Soviet missiles."[163]

In fact the TASS story as reported in *Revolución* supported Frankel's version of Soviet policy more than Rodríguez's.[164] The TASS story said that everyone knew that forces were being readied in Guatemala and Nicaragua for the invasion of Cuba. It added that the U.S. fleet that had just been dispatched to the Caribbean "could not act with impunity as an international policeman since the friends of Cuba would not permit the North American imperialists to strangle Cuba by an economic blockade . . . and these friends would also help her to keep her liberty and independence."

This phrasing is consistent with the Soviet wish to play down the missile threat, and one can understand Rodríguez's frustration at having only this statement to demonstrate his argument that Moscow had not changed its tone. The organ of the 26th of July Movement, *Revolución*, ran the TASS dispatch under the headline "Sensational Moscow Warning: Cuba's friends will not permit her independence to be impugned" and dragged the subject of missiles in by preceding the headline with another headline: "The USSR is the only country in the world that has antimissiles."[165]

Despite his charge that Frankel was trying to mislead U.S. opinion about the danger of nuclear war if the United States invaded Cuba, Rodríguez gave Frankel a long interview. In it he tried to persuade Frankel that in its own self-interest the Soviet Union would have to honor its commitments to Cuba. Frankel's account read: "Rodríguez is an admirer of Premier Khrushchev, whom he has never met, and also of Stalin because of the latter's skill in organizing and industrializing the country at the proper pace. Cuba's leaders and the Communist party here were very surprised by strong statements of support from Moscow last summer, including a qualified threat that the Soviet Union would use its rocket power against the United States to protect Cuba. These pledges from Moscow were not 'emotional phrases' composed on the spur of the moment but a careful and deliberate decision of the top Soviet leadership."[166]

Then Rodríguez was quoted directly as saying that if Cuba were attacked and the Soviet Union failed to act, it would "lose everything, not only in Latin America but in Asia and Africa." Rodríguez also added that he believed an attack likely since it seemed that the moderates in the Democratic Party, like Adlai Stevenson and Chester Bowles, had lost ground within the party. Besides, he had been reading Kennedy's book *Profiles in Courage* and was frightened by the thought that Kennedy might want to prove his courage with military action. On the basis of interviews with others besides Rodríguez, Frankel reported that the Cuban communists were confident that Castro had already accepted most of their ideology and that the PSP had decided to consolidate its position in Cuba on that basis rather than to make an open bid for power. This strategy was adopted only after a bitter struggle within the party—an obvious allusion to Escalante. It was judged that a bid for power at the present time would not only alienate Castro and the Cuban people but would also almost certainly cause the United States to intervene.

Another very well-informed journalist reported that while in Moscow, Guevara, after having approved the ideological formulas adopted by the communist parties assembled there, said that Cuba did not yet have a unified revolutionary party.[167] The prospect of a coalescence of the revolutionary parties was at the bottom of the problem of whether the PSP should conduct a recruitment campaign or not. To do so might well alarm the other Cuban political groups, even Castro himself, and make negotiations for a unified party difficult or impossible. The Cuban communists presumably were aware that Moscow had not insisted on good treatment for Egyptian communists as a condition for its aid to Nasser, and they probably realized that Moscow neither could nor would make good Castro-PSP working relations a condition of its support. However, Castro was finding the PSP cooperation useful, and he may have felt that cordial relations with that party did no harm in his efforts to employ the power of Moscow against the power of Washington.

Whether Moscow was backing away from its missile menace as the PSP and the 26th of July Movement vehemently denied is difficult to say, even with the advantage of hindsight. Khrushchev's interview with Nuñez Jiménez at the end of October was not the subject of a large press campaign as the 9 July statement had been, nor did the first Soviet ambassador to Castro's Cuba mention it publicly.[168] And the Soviet foreign minister did not repeat the declaration when he gave a formal report to the Supreme Soviet at the end of December. But on the other hand the continuing validity of the statements was reaffirmed even though the words were not repeated. Gromyko said that "the position of the Soviet government on Soviet-Cuban political and economic relations has been clearly defined by Comrade N. S. Khrushchev, and it [the position] remains completely in force."[169]

Khrushchev's statement was also reconfirmed in the joint Soviet-Cuban communiqué of 19 December 1960. The communiqué dealt with the many subjects—coexistence, the Havana Declaration, and the admission of China and the Mongolian People's Republic to the United Nations—on which the signatories agreed. The Soviet Union also spelled out the technical assistance it had agreed to offer Cuba in establishing industry and stated that "the most important aspect of assistance was the statement made by Nikita Khrushchev, premier of the Soviet Union, on the readiness of the USSR to render Cuba full support in upholding its independence in the face of aggression."[170]

The foreign correspondents however were still pursuing the symbolic nature of Khrushchev's statement on missiles. Michel Tatu asked Guevara, who had just signed the Soviet-Cuban communiqué for Cuba, about it. Guevara replied that it was clear to the Americans, the Cubans, and the Soviets. "The warning is symbolic if the aggression is symbolic." If the United States sought means of aggression against the socialist countries and the underdeveloped countries, the result would be to push the world to the brink of war and finally to a debacle.[171]

The Soviet position was understandable. The Soviets did not want to jeopardize the chances of getting from the new administration what they had failed to get from the Eisenhower administration—a concession on Berlin and an agreement on the German question. Khrushchev had voiced this hope in so many words in a speech in East Berlin on his way home from the aborted summit meeting in Paris. As has been argued above, the Soviet Union wanted concessions on Berlin from the United

States and the pleasures of the role of staunch supporter of antiimperialism—in the Cuban case, anti–U.S. nationalism. Although Stalin's successors were willing to champion antiimperialist nationalism and wars of national liberation, they were no more ready to risk war for the sake of other states than Stalin had been. Khrushchev believed that he could support nationalist movements with negligible risk of involvement in war. The Soviet statements about support for Cuba did not constitute a formal commitment to go to war with the United States for the sake of Cuba, but they clearly advanced that presumption. The Soviet Union did not have to keep its promises nor was it bound to do what others had presumed it would do. In that sense the Soviet Union was not running the risk of war. But something of its reputation had been invested in the defense of Cuba, and reneging on its commitments or disappointing expectations it had aroused would entail political costs. Khrushchev dealt with that problem by assuming that it would never arise, by assuming that his statements had scotched U.S. plans for invading Cuba.

THE BACKDROP OF THE CRISIS IN LAOS

Khrushchev was learning from events in Laos that involvement in a local situation could pay dividends. Although the situation in Southeast Asia was very different—and it is rather meaningless to draw parallels between Souvanna Phouma and Castro—the drama was unfolding at the same time, and the Soviet leaders (like the American) had a penchant for believing that their major opponent pursued a single, consistent policy everywhere in the world. An excursion into Laotian affairs is necessary to make the point that the Soviet leaders felt that an aggressive policy could, in their terms, frustrate the forces of counterrevolution supported by the United States.[172]

The Laotian state was the weakest of the successor states of French Indo-China established by the Geneva agreement of 1954. The economic base was weak and the political leadership inexperienced, so that even a tiny, inexperienced, and unsophisticated communist guerrilla force in the north and the east of the country could demand a role in a coalition government and/or control part of the territory. Although Laos itself was of little importance, supplies from North Vietnam to South Vietnam passed through its eastern part, which became an object of contention during periods when the guerrillas in South Vietnam were receiving supplies and personnel from the north.

The very small Laotian political elite was in agreement on a fundamental goal—avoidance of domination by the Vietnamese whether northern or southern—but divided on the best method of achieving it. At the far left, the Pathet Lao hoped that a program of active cooperation with the North Vietnamese would permit them to be a junior partner with a significant measure of autonomy—at any rate, a greater measure than they expected Laos to enjoy as a member of the U.S.–South Vietnamese–Thai axis. Those on the far right hoped that a program of active cooperation with the South Vietnamese, Thailand, and the United States would permit them to be a junior partner with a significant measure of autonomy—at any rate more than they expected Laos to enjoy as a member of the Pathet Lao–North Vietnamese–Chinese axis. In the center, Souvanna Phouma tried to carry out the purposes of the Geneva agreement of 1954 —neutrality—but saw this as possible only if he accepted the Pathet Lao's control of part of the territory or else its participation in a coalition government. The communist states saw greater advantages in that kind of neutrality than did the United States and South Vietnam. If the North Vietnamese could have relatively secure communications to South Vietnam, they were prepared to accept, at least for the time being, a secondary role for the Pathet Lao in the Laotian state. The Chinese were primarily interested in keeping the level of U.S. involvement on the mainland of Asia low, and that consideration took precedence over the potential for changing the political regime in South Vietnam or Laos. In any case, Chinese policy, following well-established precedent, preferred several successor states to a greater Indo-China including Laos and Cambodia. The Soviet Union had little intrinsic interest in South East Asia but had a very great interest in disproving the Chinese accusations that it was willing to let the United States do anything as long as nuclear coexistence was safeguarded.

The United States, on the other hand, felt that a coalition government in Laos would rapidly lead to communism and exerted its influence (largely financial) to force Souvanna Phouma from office in the spring of 1958. In violation of the Geneva agreements, the United States assigned its military personnel to improve the supply system of the Royal Laotian Army and provided training for some of its personnel in the United States. After a long series of complex maneuvers a young neutralist officer, Kong Le, in August 1960 carried out a coup d'état and secured the reappointment of Souvanna Phouma as premier. The Thai government, by closing the ferry to the Laotian capital, Ventiane, effectively deprived it of oil supplies and also provided Phoumi, the pro–U.S. general, with artillery.

Souvanna Phouma pleaded with the United States for help to preserve his position and, when refused, established relations with the Soviet Union on 11 October, having announced his intention to do so on 30 September. He also resumed talks with the Pathet Lao for a coalition government. Unlike what occurred in Cuba, in Laos recognition of the Soviet government preceded Soviet aid. On 13 October, the Soviet ambassador arrived in Ventiane and offered Souvanna Phouma aid.

The American ambassador, J. Graham Parsons, tried to pursue a policy of giving aid both to Souvanna Phouma and his opponents so as to prevent the former from becoming completely dependent on the Soviet Union. But he was overruled by Washington, which by 10 November had taken the decision to get Souvana Phouma out of office. On 3 or 4 December Soviet food and oil began to arrive by a Soviet airlift operation, the largest Soviet air operation since World War II. It was almost too late, because General Phoumi, employing his monopoly of artillery, was able to occupy the capital, Ventiane, from which Souvanna Phouma fled to Cambodia. Soviet Ambassador Alexander Abramov followed him to Phnom Penh and encouraged him to continue the struggle by promises to provide material and political support. Soviet aid and parachute drops enabled Kong Le to reach the Plain of Jars, where Soviet air aid and overland supplies from North Vietnam helped him to maintain his small army. Kong Le's success forced the United States to international negotiation in 1961.

By the end of 1960 the Soviet Union had learned from the Laotian imbroglio that it could stiffen the resistance of a weak government pursuing an antiimperialist or anti–U.S. policy. It supplied the neutralist Laotians with oil when they were cut off; it balanced the advantage Phoumi enjoyed in artillery by delivering its own. The Soviet Union could thwart U.S. purposes in the Third World by competing with the United States on its own terms. It could support its political leaders and its generals. It was by no means foreordained that the United States would always have its way. Now the Soviet Union was a global power and could sometimes prevail, as the United States had been accustomed to do, in remote areas of the world.

But once Soviet support to Laos or Cuba had been tendered (whatever it may have meant) it could not be withdrawn without embarrassment. Withdrawing support from Cuba or Laos would have been very different from never having offered it. Now Soviet prestige would be involved. Great powers rarely sacrifice reputation simply because they have reevaluated the possible cost of a commitment. Greater dangers or costs are required to justify a retreat.

Thus, if some Soviet leaders thought that supporting Cuba and Laos minimized the chance of getting concessions on Berlin from the new administration or of creating the possibility of loss of face if the United States invaded Cuba with impunity, the only realistic option was to soft-pedal the rhetoric. A good illustration of this is the way in which the Soviet and Cuban press treated a statement made by Guevara in the presence of Mikoian and several Soviet marshalls.

In the Soviet version, Guevara described the Cuban position thus: "On the one side the American navy, air force, and infantry threaten us. On the other side there has been extended to us the hand of friendship of the Soviet Union, which like an invisible armor protects us from our enemies. I can say now that Cuba will never be brought to her knees."[173] In the Cuban version, Guevara "recalled the aid from the Soviet people and the Soviet government and said that 'we know that Cuba today is unfortunately a neuralgic factor in the peace of the world. We do not like the situation nor do we like the imperialist point of view of playing with fire. We know what a conflict at this time could mean, but avoiding it is not solely in our hands. The forces that support Cuba and those of the socialist camp, he emphasized, are the forces on which we count for the imperialists not to commit the error of attacking us.' "[174]

The tone of the two versions is, of course, quite different. In the Soviet version Cuba is protected by Soviet friendship and nothing is said of war, nuclear or otherwise. In the Cuban version the United States has been put on warning, and the choice of war and peace is unfortunately in its hands. Such word juggling would not have avoided serious political losses for Moscow had the United States overthrown the Castro regime. However, if the United States never attempted to overthrow the Castro regime the Soviet Union could take the credit as it had in Egypt and the Taiwan Straits for preventing an attack that failed to materialize.

What the Kennedy administration might do could be left to the future. The immediate question was whether the Eisenhower administration would seek to unseat Castro before its term of office expired. At the end of November the Soviet press began to report that the CIA had made preparations to mount an attack against Cuba from Guatemala and Nicaragua and that only the signal from the north was necessary.[175]

Soon the Soviet press was able to cite the dispatches by Richard Dudman of the St. Louis Post-Dispatch on the preparations for an invasion of Cuba from Guatemala,[176] and one Soviet account predicted that the United States would provide air and sea cover for mercenaries then concentrated in Florida, Louisiana, and Central America.[177] The problem of intelligence assessment for the Cubans and the Russians was not easy. The reports in the U.S. press about preparations for an invasion only confirmed what they probably already knew. To train hundreds of Cubans at bases in the United States and in Guatemala for an invasion of Cuba in complete secrecy was impossible. Some of the Cubans being trained may have been Castro agents from the beginning; others may have had second thoughts after beginning training; and still others may have been vulnerable to pressure because of fears for the safety of relatives and friends still in Cuba. But although Cuba and the Soviet Union knew that men were being trained to invade Cuba, they did not know if and when the plan would be carried out. Extended mobilization was difficult for the Cubans to maintain.

The Cubans pursued a simple strategy in handling the situation. They gave maximum publicity to U.S. plans to invade, which provoked reiteration of the Soviet statements to help Cuba and presumably created pressure within the United States against the effectuation of these plans, hopefully from the leaders of the new administration waiting in the wings to take over power. In Cuba the militia was only partially mobilized, and production continued.

Castro continued to reiterate that the United States could not hope for a victory over a "week-end" because the Cubans were prepared to fight.[178] Castro on New Year's Eve and Khrushchev a day later referred to news reports that missile bases were being established in Cuba to attack the United States. Khrushchev dismissed these reports contemptuously, saying that missiles based in the Soviet Union could reach any point on the earth's surface and warned that plots against popular governments could "place the world on the brink of war." But, "we hope that there are enough people with common sense in the United States not to permit the accomplishment of these aggressive plans. . . ."[179] The Cuban ambassador to the Soviet Union took his cue from Khrushchev's statement and said in the presence of Khrushchev, Kozlov, Kosygin, Mikoian, Marshall Budennyi, and the minister of war, Marshall Malinovskii, that Cuba would not be abandoned to fight alone as Republican Spain had been. This time war would lead the imperialists to disaster.[180] Speaking in Havana on the same day, Castro said that the administration about to take office in Washington could not avoid responsibility for an invasion, and he expressed the hope that the new administration would change its policy so as not to plunge the world into an "apocalyptic holocaust." He also requested the United States to reduce the personnel in the Havana Embassy to eleven, since most of them, he said, were engaged in conspiring with the counterrevolutionaries.[181] Two days later the United States broke off relations with Cuba on the grounds that it could not maintain an embassy with such a small staff. The Soviet press played the news as a cliffhanger, reporting that the Eisenhower administration, in its last days, had wanted to intervene in Cuba and that the Cuban people were encouraged by Khrushchev's statement that "they could always count on the solidarity and support of the Soviet people."[182]

The Soviet press continued to characterize the crisis as the possible beginning of a world war. One commentary by *Izvestiia's* diplomatic correspondent called upon all peace-loving governments to put pressure on the Eisenhower administration to prevent aggression and "to remove the threat from Cuba and not to permit a flame to flare in the Caribbean pregnant with serious consequences for the peace of the whole world." Observer in *Pravda* warned that now one could not count on keeping local wars isolated and that world peace was in danger. He found some solace in the report that the Democratic Party was "expressing dissatisfaction with the irresponsible actions of the Eisenhower government."[183]

The talk of invasion was calculated to deter an attack by mobilizing sentiment against it. Guevara's answer to a question at a press conference about the break in relations with the United States illustrated this aspect: "Well, the papers are full of invasion talk. We must be very cautious. We accused them of preparing to attack us. All this led to no further news of attack. I think we should be very vigilant and careful, but not exaggerate. We have everyone ready for war—hundreds of thousands of men."[184] And a little later in the interview Guevara said that although they were expecting an attack at any moment, they were ready to sell three million tons of sugar to the United States at a reasonable price. Thus, the Cubans still hoped that relations with the United States could be improved with the new administration. Castro said that as soon as Kennedy took office, the United States would have to decide whether to continue operating the training camps or to disband them and renounce its former policy. Cuba would welcome a change in U.S. policy but was prepared to fight if this was not forthcoming.[185]

A *Pravda* commentator noted that "never in the history of the United States has a change of administration been awaited with such impatience." The counterrevolutionaries within Cuba were unable to overthrow the Cuban government, as the U.S. press had admitted. The reverses that the aggressive American policy had met in Cuba and elsewhere could not fail to "show the new American administration that it is high time to open a new page in the foreign policy of the United States."[186]

The Soviet leaders agreed that the policy of the new U.S. administration was the most important factor in making a judgment about Cuba's future. But the Soviet leadership, which published divergent Cuban views on the question in the middle of January 1961, differed on what Cuban internal policy should be. Juan Marinello, the titular head of the PSP, advanced one view in *Kommunist,* and Escalante advanced another in *Partiinaia zhizn'.*[187] Essentially, Marinello repeated the line taken in the Eighth Party Congress of the PSP of August 1960, and Escalante repeated his more sanguine expectations. While Marinello said that the Cuban government "was acquiring an ever more clearly defined anti-imperialist tendency,"[188] Escalante stated that his country had "definitively departed from the imperialist camp. A free and independent Cuba is a republic headed by a government accountable only to its own people."[189] While Marinello said that important changes had taken place in Cuba's economy and that the workers and peasants had moved into the forefront,[190] Escalante, reviewing the same changes, concluded that the Cuban revolution was "on the threshhold of a new higher and progressive social stage."[191] If there was any doubt that Escalante meant socialism he dispelled it by saying that the Cuban revolution was based on the only genuine revolutionary ideology—Marxism-Leninism.[192]

The appearance in different Soviet journals of these very different estimates of the stage reached by the Cuban revolution reflected the differing appraisals of the Soviet leaders. As yet there was no necessity to resolve the differences, but the actions of the Kennedy administration were soon to force a quick resolution of them.

4. CUBA COMES TO SOCIALISM

Fidel Castro had to decide whether the new Kennedy administration would continue to support his enemies inside and outside of Cuba and whether it would support a landing on Cuban shores. The detailed and accurate information published in the Cuban and Soviet press on which the judgment was made seemed to derive from the Cuban refugees in the United States and from the forces in Guatemala being readied for the invasion.

Kennedy's inaugural address, in Castro's judgment, furnished only "a slight hope" that Eisenhower's policy would be abandoned and the people of the world freed from fear of the abyss that yawned before them.[1] Speaking a little later, Che Guevara, unlike Castro, gave the Soviet Union full credit for Cuba's safety thus far. He said "it is well known that the Soviet Union and all the socialist countries [are] prepared to make war to defend our sovereignty and a tacit agreement [has been] established between our peoples." He also said that the Soviet Union had stopped Eisenhower from playing "his last desperate card." "Winning without war, the best part of humanity won with us."[2] To the Latin tag, "Let him who desires peace, prepare for war," Guevara was adding the words "and threaten to wage it." The words of Kennedy's inaugural address did not resolve the question of U.S. intentions for Guevara. Kennedy, he said, "made some threats and used now familiar language, but he also spoke . . . of some kind of peaceful coexistence." This furnished some hope of talks but did not provide the slightest justification for the relaxation of vigilance.[3]

Speaking only two days later, at a plenum of the PSP, the leading Cuban communist, Blas Roca, made a somewhat more optimistic analysis of American intentions and dealt obliquely with the fear that Castro would sacrifice the Cuban communists, in return for which Kennedy would abandon Eisenhower's Cuban policy.

Roca dismissed the argument of those who doubted that the Eisenhower administration had planned to invade Cuba. An invasion had indeed been planned; but, significantly, the Soviet Union did not figure in Roca's discussion of how "Eisenhower's criminal plans" had been frustrated. Castro's military mobilization and the solidarity of other Latin

American countries and the Afro-Asian bloc had deterred the United States.[4] Indirectly, however, Roca gave the Soviet Union credit by warning that aggression against Cuba would lead to world war, and his listeners presumably understood that a world war by definition entailed Soviet participation.[5] Why Roca so grudgingly gave credit to the USSR will be examined shortly.

Roca explained at length why U.S. policy might change with the new administration. First, in contrast to companies like United Fruit and Bell Telephone, which exploited Latin America directly, companies on the east coast, who profited from exports, wanted peace. Second, the Eisenhower administration and its policies had been compromised. Third, the Cuban revolution had shown that it was invincible, and fourth, the common concern, since the shift in the balance of power had taken place, was nuclear war. Therefore, some imperialists believed that a modification of policy was necessary to preserve their regime and maintain power over the masses; this is what "Kennedy could have been wanting to say in his inaugural address."[6]

This report to the plenum of the PSP invites attention. Guevara had expressed confidence that Cuba enjoyed Soviet support; Roca's cautious, indirect references to Soviet aid seemed to reflect suspicion. Roca was sanguine about Kennedy, and Guevara was wary. The difference cannot be explained as an idiosyncracy of Guevara's, for Castro was to take the same line a week later in interviews with an Italian communist and a Czech journalist. The clue perhaps lies in Roca's discussion of the Guatemalan intervention in 1954[7]—an almost inevitable feature of any Cuban discussion of probable U.S. behavior. Roca reminded his readers that the United States would have spared Arbenz if he had jettisoned his communist supporters, but Arbenz refused to do so. If indeed Roca feared that Castro would patch up his quarrel with the new American president at the expense of the Cuban communists, his analysis of the current situation demonstrated how unnecessary that sacrifice would be. The United States was deterred because of the shift in the world balance of forces.

Nowhere in this long speech did Roca mention Khrushchev's missile statements. Not Soviet missiles, but internal pressures had pushed the United States to a more moderate policy, he said. Thus, even if the Soviet Union had soft-pedaled its missile statements, as *Hoy* insisted a month ago that it had not, the United States had nevertheless been deterred. To suggest that the PSP feared that Castro and Khrushchev could find common ground in improving relations with the United States at the expense of the Cuban communists is to assume that the PSP was singularly untrusting. But Blas Roca had been in China and had attended the world communist meeting in Moscow in November 1960. He could have heard a great deal about how Moscow was willing to sacrifice the needs of other communist parties to its own. As for the lessons of his own experience: Batista had raised the Cuban communists up and then cast them down. Castro had blown hot and cold and might do so again.

CASTRO EXPLAINS HIS BRAND OF
REVOLUTIONARY MARXISM

Apparently Castro was not sharing his thoughts with the Cuban communists, because at the very moment that Roca was ventilating his fears of abandonment, Castro was preparing to embrace Marxist ideology and for the first time to praise the PSP for its services in the struggle against Batista.

Like so many of his major pronouncements, this one seemed impromptu. Arminio Savioli, the special correspondent of the Italian communist newspaper *L'Unità*, had been promised an interview with Castro on 3 January 1961. He had been waiting for almost a month and had almost given up when, at one in the morning, Castro entered the Caribe night club on the third floor of the Havana Libre hotel. The reporter asked for and received his interview in a quieter room, but with forty persons listening.[8] Asked about the nature of the Cuban revolution, Castro said: "You journalists have a craving to define—to put things into categories. You are damnably dogmatic. We are not dogmatic. Anyhow, you want to write that our revolution is a socialist revolution? Well then, write it . . . Yes, we have not only destroyed a tyranny. We have destroyed the pro-imperialist bourgeois state apparatus, the bureaucracy, the police, the mercenary army."

Castro then mentioned the agrarian reform, the expulsion of some foreign monopolies, and the nationalization of nearly all the industries. "We are fighting," he said, "for the final liquidation of the exploitation of man by man by building a completely new society with a new class content. The Americans and the priests say this is communism. We know very well that it is not, but the word does not frighten us. They can say what they please . . . I am not concerned with 'isms'—however, if such a great conquest of well being, which I see with my own eyes, is communism, then call me communist."

On the eve of the Bay of Pigs invasion in April, Castro was to go further and say that the Cuban revolution was socialist, and in December he was to say that he was a Marxist-Leninist. But the idea had been gathering in his mind, and during the remainder of his late-January interview his rationale was revealed. Cuba was to serve as the model for revolution in Latin America, stimulating revolution without exporting it. The United States would be unable to stop it, so Castro did not have to worry about the labels pinned on him. He offered a theory of Latin American revolution that differed from the standard communist theory of nationalist revolution in that it deprecated the role of the national bourgeoisie. His interlocutor asked if the national bourgeoisie still had a role in Latin American revolutions. Castro replied: "I do not think so and I never did. It is true that there are groups of industrial bourgeoisie that are hostile, even very hostile, to imperialism because they are competitors. But these groups hate the workers even more for class reasons. Between U.S. monopolies and the national bourgeoisie there can be momentary friction, skirmishes, but not true and real struggles. There is no historical irreconcilability. The 'national bourgeoisie' here [in Latin America] is satisfied, cowardly, ever ready to make concessions to imperialism, which in the end, keeps it alive and furnishes it with arms and aid to defend itself against revolutions."

Castro said that the national bourgeoisie was not the leader of the revolution, explaining his own role as an exception that proved the rule. When asked who had the historical task of leading the revolution, he replied: "The industrial and the agricultural proletariat, the peasants, the petite bourgeoisie, and above all the intellectual bourgeoisie. I don't want to promote sectarianism. I don't deny that strata of the national bourgeoisie could support, partially and temporarily, some revolutionary actions. I admit that some children of the bourgeoisie could enter the ranks of the people, participate in the revolution, and even lead as thinking individuals armed with revolutionary theory. (I myself, after all, am the son of a large landowner.) [But] I am reasoning in class terms. From the national bourgeoisie as a class nothing good is to be expected any more."[9]

Castro was here revealing a judgment that was to separate him from orthodox Marxists for many years. According to orthodox Marxism, the first revolution in a colonial or semicolonial country is the national revolution against the foreign imperialists and their allies in the colonial country. This is a broad coalition, which moves gradually leftward as the imperialists are being expelled and more rapidly thereafter. After Batista had fled, the Cuban communists insisted that Castro headed just such a coalition. In viewing Castro's assumption of power as a victory of the middle class, the orthodox communists and the Cuban emigrés were in basic agreement. The Cuban emigrés lamented that they, the middle class, had made the revolution against Batista but that Castro had stolen it from them. The Marxist version was that the middle class revolution was moving to the left. Castro's position was that both the emigrés and the orthodox Marxists were wrong. The workers and peasants—and in most Latin American countries the latter far outnumber the former—make the revolution, Castro said, led by a thinking individual armed with revolutionary theory whose class origins are of no intrinsic importance.

One could quarrel with Castro's judgment that the middle class (national bourgeoisie in the new terminology that Castro was affecting) was of no importance in Batista's defeat, but there is little doubt that it had been whisked off the stage much sooner than the Cuban communists, save Escalante, had expected. But the point at issue was the first part of the revolution, its antiimperialist phase, and Castro was saying that the peasants and the workers (who ranged from a tiny to a substantial minority in Latin America), led by a person like himself, could make a revolution while the middle classes looked on.

This left very little scope for the self-appointed leaders of the proletariat, the communists, who had played a minor enough role in the Cuban revolution and who, in Castro's view, were to play a minor role in other Latin American revolutions. The envelope of Marxist terminology notwithstanding, the conception was Latin American. The somnolent masses were to be energized by the spellbinding orator and fearless *guerillero* and to follow him to triumph. Simón Bolívar was the model, not Lenin, who never wore a soldier's uniform, nor Stalin, who donned a marshall's uniform only a generation after the revolution had succeeded. It is no accident that *Hoy* ignored, or virtually ignored, the interview. The editors understood its significance.[10]

Castro's enemies and his friends would have agreed that the Cuban revolution had made radical social changes. In two years it had already gone further than the Mexican or the Bolivian revolution—the two most important social revolutions in Latin America to that date. And in this interview Castro was making claim to a third role beyond charismatic orator and general—the role of social engineer. "I was shaped," he told his Italian interlocutor, "by the books of Marx and Lenin before the attack on Moncada in 1953."[11]

The abrupt adoption of socialism was also within the Latin American tradition. Latin American nationalism was almost necessarily anti–North American. Who else was there to be against? Most Latin American social reformers in the thirties had conceived of reform in association with the United States and had thus espoused democratic ideas. A smaller group that should not be overlooked, believing that true national self-determination—or dignity, to use their word—could only be achieved against the United States, adopted the ideology of the enemy of their enemy and became corporatists, fascists, Falangists, nazis, and even communists. They were not very good democrats, fascists, or communists. The foreignness of their ideology was evidence of their own backwardness. Foreigners owned their industries, the wives and daughters of the rich wore Parisian gowns, and the revolutionaries imported recipes for glory. The borrowed ideological garments did not fit very well, but they did not greatly hamper their wearers' movements. Castro was driven to make Cuba respected in the world, and the events of the last two years had confirmed him in his belief that it could only be done in opposition to the United States.[12] Cuba, therefore, could not fly the banner of free enterprise; it had to fly the banner of socialism.

The rapidity of Castro's conversion to socialism does not mean that Castro was particularly cynical or that his conversion was superficial. Castro did not share his critics' values. In some Western European countries and their cultural offshoots, a good society protects the rights of the individual against the whole, rights being conceived of as personal liberties and the control of one's property. In the Soviet Union and other socialist countries, the good society protects its members against the selfishness of the remnants of the former ruling classes and of individuals. But for the majority of the world's population these are not the true choices, and Castro was one of the majority.

For Castro, the dignity of the individual and of the nation of which he was a member was the primary good. In the Spanish tradition, the hallmark of dignity was the respect of others for one's position or rank. Respect for Cuba and Cubans was in short supply in Castro's formative years, and many Cubans accepted the poor opinion of the world as an inevitable consequence of their size and closeness to the United States. But Castro burned with a fierce pride. In the Cuba he grew up in he could not enjoy the position of the son of a somebody (the origin of *hidalgo*) because he had been born out of wedlock. He could only be respected for what he became, and Cuba could only be respected if she became what she had not been.

For such a man, and for those who shared his feelings about themselves and their country, ideology was an instrument of self-assertion and national assertion. The switch to socialism was a means to an end. For the Americans, who already had power, someone else who sacrificed "principle" for power was a scoundrel. But Castro was too audacious and defiant to be only a scoundrel; he had to be a man who had sold his soul to the devil, and the devil of the mid-twentieth century was communism.

It would be a mistake to believe that Castro's self-conversion to communism is insignificant because in his view it served only as a means to a greater end. For Henry IV, Paris was worth a mass. Henry IV of France was not particularly cynical in sixteenth century terms; for him, as for Henry VIII of England, religious questions played second fiddle to dynastic questions. Yet France has remained Catholic and England Protestant long after dynastic questions have ceased to concern anyone in Europe and long after the variety of Western Christianity favored by the state has made much difference in international life. Cuba similarly may remain socialist long after anyone remembers that Cuba suffered a crisis of national identity and after the official ideology of a state ceases to be a factor of major importance.

Once Castro had decided that he was going to be some kind of socialist, having dismissed as dogmatism a precise definition of the term, it became necessary to change his public appraisal of the Cuban communists. Castro dropped his former contempt for them as cowards and simply stated that whereas he had been politically inexperienced, the PSP had always been right in proclaiming the necessity for radical change. "In the beginning the communists had no confidence in me, in us rebels. The mistrust was . . . completely correct since we, despite our reading of Marx, were full of petit-bourgeois prejudices." Although the rebels had been fervent in their wish to destroy tyranny and privilege, their ideas had been unclear. But now, said Castro, they worked well with the communists, who had shed so much blood and displayed such heroism.[13]

Castro had moved so far left because he had decided that since the breach with the United States could not be repaired, and the Soviet Union would protect him against invasion, he had everything to gain by taking the offensive inside and outside Cuba. He announced his resolve to counter the United States in the rest of Latin America, saying that if the United States could promote counterrevolution, Cuba, in legitimate self-defense, could promote revolution. The United States could not claim the right to act against Cuba without expecting Cuba to act in her own defense.[14] Castro told a Czech journalist that Cuban help and the example of its success would lead to successful revolutions. Cuba's experience had shown that an army of the Batista type that had never fought a war could be destroyed by the people. A situation similar to what obtained in Cuba "exists in some other countries and above all in some Latin American countries." Although the governments of many Latin American nations were willing to do the bidding of the United States, popular opposition limited what they could do.[15]

Castro repeated much the same arguments in an interview with an American reporter, adding, however, that Cuba was prepared to reduce tension in the hemisphere if the United States would accept Cuba's close ties to the socialist states. Otherwise, Cuba considered it legitimate to promote revolution in Latin America in its own defense. The threat was directed only at those countries that were conspiring to overthrow the Cuban government. Although Castro would not name them, he specifically excluded Brazil and Mexico. He stated that he was completely convinced of the superiority of the socialist system over the capitalist and that the introduction of socialist reforms had produced great improvements in Cuban industry and agriculture.[16]

Castro was hardly extending an olive branch to the United States, and the answer was not long in coming. A State Department spokesman said that the basic concern of the United States was "with communist domination in this hemisphere," which could not be the subject of bilateral negotiation with Cuba.[17]

Castro seemed to believe that the United States would not attack Cuba even if other countries in Latin America followed her example. He told the L'Unità reporter: "No the Americans will not attack us. In any case, imperialism is dying. It has the choice between suicide and natural death.

If it attacks, it's suicide, a sure and rapid end. If it doesn't attack, it can hope to live a little longer."[18]

The credit for Cuba's safety belonged to the Soviet Union, Castro told a Czech reporter. "The solidarity and help extended by the socialist countries in this situation have played a decisive role in the final victory of our people. If the socialist camp and its policy did not exist, we would have paid very dearly for our revolutionary laws. Imperialism could have physically liquidated our population, which was resolved not to renounce the conquests of the revolution under any circumstances."[19]

Khrushchev backed up Castro's line in an interview with Ecuadorans visiting Moscow, but the Soviet press failed to print it, pursuing what seemed to be a deliberate policy since Kennedy's election of avoiding direct missile threats. Said Khrushchev: "The United States wants to strangle the Cuban republic, but I doubt that they will resort to direct aggression because aggression would be a service to revolution in all Latin America and even in the United States. . . . I wouldn't like to mention our missiles and our armed forces, but the enemies of Cuba do take them into account. It's very dangerous to put a fire out with gasoline."[20]

Although the Soviet press did not carry this latest version of Khrushchev's missile menace, it printed the Cuban version of the dangers facing that country. The Cuban foreign minister, Raúl Roa, had addressed a note to those Latin American countries that maintained diplomatic relations with Cuba, stating that despite Cuba's readiness to enter discussions with the United States on a basis of equality, Kennedy had revived the cold war. ". . . Armed intervention, direct or indirect, open or masked, will inevitably bring in its train an enormous international conflict with incalculable consequences." U.S. planners contemplated the overthrow of the Cuban government from within, but if that failed, they planned indirect aggression covered by a declaration of war from Guatemala, Peru, or Nicaragua. A bridgehead would be established, and a provisional government created that would then ask for direct military assistance from the OAS, which would play the same role that the United Nations had played in the Congo.[21]

The Soviet press also carried an interview with Castro after he had just returned to Havana from a successful clean up of U.S. supported insurgents in the Escambray. Castro felt the insurgents could be handled easily, adding that the prospects for revolution in the rest of Latin America were even better than they had been in Cuba.[22] The next day, in a public speech, he charged that the CIA supported the counterrevolutionaries in Cuba but expended their lives uselessly. Why did they not invade with the thousands of men they had trained and armed rather than permit them to be exterminated in bands of forty or fifty? They already had more and better arms than Castro's own guerilla forces had until the very end.[23] The counterrevolutionaries were bandits, said Castro, and their lives were being squandered by the CIA, which kept delaying the invasion. But the invasion was coming. Retalhuieu in Guatemala had been converted to a U.S. base; the mercenary army of at least 4,000 was in the last stage of preparation. The Guatemalan communists warned that the action could involve Guatemala in an international war.[24]

As the preparations for the invasion were going forward, with a great deal of fanfare, President Kennedy unveiled the Alliance for Progress on 13 March. Castro and the Cubans dismissed it as rhetoric and reiterated their determination to fight and their confidence in victory. The emphasis was on their own resources, but the solidarity of the Latin American people and the socialist countries was mentioned.[25]

Support from the socialist countries was not the dominant note, however. In a long speech on 25 March in which he attacked Cuba's enemies and the preparations for invasion, Castro devoted only one line to the subject. "If imperialism begins to play with local wars, imperialism may be faced with continental war if not more than that—its total destruction."[26] *Pravda's* short account carried the sentence but dropped the last clause about total destruction.[27] But despite the omission of this phrase, *Pravda* was faithful to the tone of the speech. Although Castro had mentioned the possibility of fighting "the Marines," it said, he had emphasized a Cuban refugee effort to set up a puppet government on Cuban territory. Such a government could not last more than twenty-four hours. Cuba was better armed than the defenders of freedom in the Congo or in Laos or even in Republican Spain. Thus, while mentioning the possibility of direct U.S. military intervention and a world war in passing, he had emphasized Cuba's ability to deal with her enemies on her own. Guevara, too, had spoken of great friends with powerful weapons but had insisted that "Cuba's victory is not in Soviet missiles, not in the solidarity of the socialist world, not in the solidarity of the whole world. Cuba's victory is in the spirit and the sacrifice of its people. The revolution will win if every last one of us is prepared to die."[28]

The unspoken assumption in Castro's and Guevara's speeches was that Soviet threats had already deterred the United States from direct invasion and that a Cuba armed with socialist weapons and imbued with revolutionary fervor could win on her own against an invasion by Cuban emigrés. The publication of the so-called United States White Book on Cuba was interpreted by the Soviet and Cuban press as a call for an uprising and a justification for the impending invasion.[29] The text of the White Book supported that conclusion. It said that Cuba was already a Soviet satellite and already supporting revolution all over the continent. The United States called on the Castro regime to sever its links with the international communist movement. "If this call is unheeded, we are confident that the Cuban people, with their passion for liberty, will continue to strive for a free Cuba."[30]

Three days later Tad Szulc reported that an army of five to six thousand men had been training in the United States and in Central America with the purpose of liberating Cuba.[31] The Soviet press carried an account of a *New York Times* interview with Cuban Foreign Minister Raúl Roa that described the preparations for the invasion quite accurately and predicted the course of events correctly with one exception. Roa said that despite air support from Florida and Guatemala, the counterrevolutionary forces would not be able to hold the bridgehead, and the U.S. Marines would have to come to their aid.[32] But, said *Pravda* three days later, quoting a story in the *New York Post*, Kennedy's advisors are divided on the question of support for an invasion.[33]

In the middle of April the Soviet Union put the first man into space. A Cuban commentator saw a special significance in this event for Cuba. This feat proved that Khrushchev had not been bragging when he spoke of using missiles if necessary to defend Cuba against aggression. But no one could feel anything but horror at the thought of a nuclear war, no matter how just the cause that provoked it. Nonetheless, the dispatch of a Soviet man into space showed how far behind the United States was in the missile race, and this deprived the Pentagon of much of the influence that until then had permitted it to prevail in the cold war. This was a strategic defeat for the United States. Now the American policy of defending colonialism in Latin America by threats of force would not work, and Cuba would be victorious.[34]

THE BAY OF PIGS

On the eve of the Bay of Pigs invasion, *Kommunist*, the journal of the Community Party of the Soviet Union, published an authoritative article on Cuba's future and on the prospects for revolution in all Latin America.[35] The author, Rodney Arismendi, had long been the leader of the Uruguayan communist party and a faithful follower of Moscow's lead. The Cuban revolution in his view was still antiimperialist but had already outstripped the Mexican and Bolivian revolutions, which had stopped in mid-course. Cuba "had created the material preconditions for the transition to more progressive forms of the social structure," i.e., to socialism.[36]

Cuba's very smallness and her proximity to the United States demonstrated what a profound change had taken place in the balance of forces. The colonial system of imperialism was collapsing, and the socialist system and the Soviet Union now represented the decisive factor in international relations. "If that were not so, then despite the heroism of its people, Cuba would have been converted into an island of ruins over which rivers of blood would have flowed."[37]

The lesson was clear. Now even very small countries were shielded by the Soviet Union, and if their peoples were steadfast, imperialism would be forced to abandon its plans of aggression and counterrevolutionary wars.[38] But there was a fly in the ointment. In a thinly veiled way, Arismendi was warning that Castro might deprive the communist parties of Latin America of their true role. Echoing the pronouncements of the Cuban PSP during Batista's last years, he said that the only solution for Latin America was the antiimperialist revolution that made democratic reforms. "Such changes in Latin America are possible only if the proletariat, as the leading force, determines the depth and course of the revolution."[39] Like the PSP in 1959, he was saying that if the communist party does not lead a revolution, it is not a revolution.

Arismendi put Castro and any future Castros in their proper world-historical framework in a general discussion of the contemporary petite urban bourgeoisie. This group had always been a wavering element. Now, as a result of the changed balance of forces in the world, this stratum had been adopting more radical positions.[40] "A confirmation of this is the passage of prominent cultural figures to Marxist positions."[41] Apparently Arismendi was referring to Castro's espousal of Marxist points of view the month before. But he warned that these strata sometimes put forward extreme positions, and their theoreticians tried to subordinate the proletariat—that is, the communist party—to their goals. Nevertheless, these strata represented an important factor in the revolutions of Latin America, and the duty of the communists was to unite all the people and demonstrate the superiority of Marxism-Leninism in the theoretical field.[42] The Castros, Arismendi seemed to be saying, sometimes got off on the wrong foot, and the communists had the knowledge and the duty to set them straight.

One of the errors of petit-bourgeois extremism was to view the Cuban revolution as a recipe for any dish. "It would be a mistake to think that the clocks are striking the same hour all over the continent. Such a view could bring us to schematism, to the 'infantile disease' of leftism that characteristically skips over the stages prescribed by the laws of development."[43] At the very same time, Castro was saying that the prospects for revolution were even better in the rest of Latin America than they had been in Cuba.[44] Arismendi did not know, of course, that Castro was to go beyond the adoption of Marxist positions and declare himself a Marxist before the year was out and later assume the leadership of the PSP after he had fused it with the 26th of July Movement and the Directorio Revolucionario, first purging the PSP of the leaders he found inconvenient. The old-line communist parties of Latin America, while themselves welcoming the demonstrated decline of U.S. power in Latin America, were uncomfortable with Castro because they wanted to lead the Latin American revolutions. In March 1961 the leaders of the CPSU, by giving them space in *Kommunist* to expound that view, associated themselves with it. If any Soviet communists believed that a Castro victory in hand was worth two Latin American communist victories in the bush, their views were not printed at this tme. But after Castro's victory in repulsing the counterrevolutionaries supported by the United States at the Bay of Pigs, the Soviet communists were to accept him in greater measure.

Early in the morning of 15 April, B–26 aircraft bombed several Cuban cities. The next morning Castro spoke at a ceremony for those killed. He interpreted the air strikes to mean that invasion was imminent, and he put the country on a state of alert. He accused the United States of a Pearl Harbor attack against Cuba. What the United States found unforgiveable, said Castro, was that Cuba had effected a socialist revolution under its very nose. He concluded his speech by saying: "Long live the working class. Long live the peasants. Long live the humble. Long live the socialist revolution. Long live free Cuba. Fatherland or Death. We will conquer."[45]

In its account of the speech the Soviet press gave a slightly variant text using the word socialist three times: "The imperialists, stated Castro, don't want to forgive the Cubans for their readiness to sacrifice and for their revolutionary tenacity. They cannot forgive us for making a socialist revolution under the very nose of the United States and for being ready to defend that socialist revolution. The Cuban revolution is a democratic, socialist revolution, of the oppressed, by the oppressed, and for the oppressed, in defense of which we are prepared to give our lives."[46]

The story was filed from Havana on 17 April, a day after the speech had been made, and was printed in the Soviet press on 18 April. Yet on 17 April the Soviet press carried the rebuttal of the Soviet ambassador to the United Nations, V. A. Zorin, to Adlai Stevenson's claim that the United States was not involved in the bombing. Thus, the Soviet press printed the follow-up to the bombing story a day before it printed the account of the bombing and Castro's use of the word socialism.[47] It seems very likely that press officials had to consult with party leaders before reproducing Castro's statement that the revolution was socialist. By the time this statement appeared in the Soviet press, fighting was raging in Cuba. The invasion had begun very early on Sunday, 18 April, and at 4:00 P.M.[48] the same day Moscow radio announced the news. On 18 April a Soviet government statement on the invasion and a message to Kennedy from Khrushchev was delivered to the American Embassy in Moscow. It could have been prepared the day it was delivered, but more likely it was prepared the day before. But even if it had been prepared at the latest possible time, sometime on the 18th of April, it was still written before the extent of U.S. support for the invasion was known. It was only after midnight on 18 April, that is, during the first hour of 19 April, that Kennedy rejected a proposal to land a company of U.S. Marines on the Cuban beach and settled on a restricted naval air mission for the dawn of 19 April.[49] The time sequence is important because the Soviet notes have one significance if they were written after the invasion had been abandoned and another if U.S. plans were still unclear. Although Khrushchev may have anticipated that the invasion attempt would be aborted, there was no way for him to have been certain when he sent his warning to the United States.

The note of the Soviet government charged that on 17 April interventionists landed in Cuba "under cover supplied by military ships and planes of the United States." The attack was a danger to peace in the Caribbean and in the world. Despite Kennedy's protestations the attack had been prepared in the United States and in states dependent on it. The United States had inspired and organized the bandit attack. The United States feared that other Latin American countries would follow Cuba's example and build an independent life. The note then went on to say, as did Khrushchev's missile statements of July and October of the prior year, that the result could be a nuclear war.

The government of the Soviet Union declares that the Soviet Union, as well as other peace-loving countries, will not abandon the Cuban people in their plight and will give them all the necessary aid and support in their just struggle for Cuba's freedom and independence. . . . Interference in Cuba's internal affairs . . . must cease immediately.

The Soviet government hopes that the United States realizes that aggression against Cuba conflicts with the interests of the American people and is capable of placing the peaceful lives of the population of the United States itself in jeopardy.[50]

Khrushchev's letter to Kennedy said much the same thing in somewhat stronger language.

It is not yet too late to prevent what may be irreparable. The U.S. government can still prevent the flames of war that have been lit by the interventionists in Cuba from growing into a conflagration that it will be impossible to extinguish. I earnestly appeal to you, Mr. President, to call a halt to the aggression against the Republic of Cuba. Military technology and the world political situation are such today that any so-called little war can give rise to a chain reaction in all parts of the globe.

As for the Soviet Union, let there be no misunderstanding of our position: We will give the Cuban people and their government every assistance necessary to repulse the armed attack on Cuba.[51]

Khrushchev concluded by saying that the considerations he was laying before the American government were prompted solely by a concern for preventing steps which might "lead the world to a military catastrophe."[52] This was the boldest Soviet move to date. It was not a threat to intervene after the crisis was over, as had been the case in the Suez crisis and the Taiwan Straits crisis. Nor was it a threat to intervene if the United States should attack at some time in the future. It was a promise made to offer "all necessary aid" to Cuba *while* an American supported invasion of Cuba was in progress. If Kennedy had yielded to the importunities of some of his military advisors, and introduced American troops, the Soviet Union could have retreated to UN condemnation of U.S. actions, perhaps rallying more of the Afro-Asian bloc to its side than it had been able to do during the Congo crisis. In the absence of a Soviet undertaking to furnish Cuba "all necessary aid," a general condemnation of the United States led by the Soviet Union would have represented a political victory. But once the Soviet Union had promised aid, the Soviet Union would have suffered a severe loss of face if it failed to oppose an American invasion of Cuba.

Kennedy's response to the Soviet note on the same day he received it seemed to justify Khrushchev's gamble. Kennedy repeated his statement that the United States did not intend to intervene in Cuba and then warned that if there was any military intervention from outside the hemisphere, the United States would honor is obligations to the states signatory to the Rio Treaty.[53] By saying that he still did not intend to intervene in Cuba, Kennedy abandoned the Cuban emigrés at the Bay of Pigs to their fate, thus yielding to the Soviet demand. But the reply tried to seem defiant by threatening a response to Soviet intervention in defense of Cuba—a threat that the Soviet warning had made contingent on the continuation of the invasion.

One might judge, as I do, that Kennedy broke off the invasion when he realized that U.S. soldiers would have to fight Cubans for an indeterminate time in order to unseat Castro. But that interpretation depends on a retrospective reading of Kennedy's mind and the information supplied by his associates after his death. It was just as logical to suppose that fear of involvement with the Soviet Union caused Kennedy to quit.

Small wonder that Khrushchev was confirmed in his belief that the menace of nuclear war was enough so that it was unnecessary to plan for the contingency that the United States would face down a Soviet threat. It was to Khrushchev's political advantage, internally and externally, to pretend, or to believe, that his verbal bolts of lightning stopped malefactors in their tracks and to feign ignorance or fail to notice that his missile rattling on the Cuban question, in contrast to the missile rattling on the Berlin issue, had provoked little concern or even attention in the United States. Kennedy, in the judgment of most American scholars, abandoned the Cuban venture for a reason Khrushchev could not fathom, although he was to behave in almost the same way himself during the Cuban missile crisis of October 1962. Kennedy had not prepared plans against the contingency that the sponsored invasion would fail. It had worked in Guatemala in 1954; why should it not work in Cuba in 1961? Kennedy had to choose between cutting his losses or fighting a war of uncertain duration in Cuba, a war that would have been highly unpopular in the

United States not to speak of Latin America. The memory of the political damage the Democratic administration had suffered as a consequence of the Korean War was fresh in the minds of the Democrats, who had regained the presidency by the narrowest of margins.

But for Khrushchev, who was engaged in what turned out to be a losing battle to reduce the size and cost of the Soviet military establishment, it was convenient to believe and to insist that talk about Soviet missiles (to be manufactured tomorrow) could win political victories over the United States today.

On 19 April, the day after Khrushchev and Kennedy had exchanged letters, a Soviet journalist reported from New York that the American expectation of beating Cuba in a lightning stroke had miscarried and that the United States had failed to anticipate the Soviet offer of aid to Cuba. Khrushchev's warning to Washington showed that the gamble on isolating Cuba had failed.[54] Thus, the Soviet warning of 18 April stopped the invasion of Cuba because it forced the United States to realize that it had been proceeding on false assumptions. By saying that the United States had failed to anticipate the Soviet offer of aid to Cuba, the Soviet writer was implying either that the offer had not been made until 18 April or that it had fallen on deaf ears. It suggested either that there had been no real warnings before 18 April or that they had failed to deter.

In Cuba, the communist newspaper *Hoy* ascribed to the counterrevolutionaries and to an American spokesman the notion that "the Soviet Union could abandon Cuba in the desire to reach a 'global' accord with the United States."[55] Thus a Soviet writer in New York and a Cuban writer in Havana were saying that some people had doubted the validity or the efficacy of the Soviet promise to help Cuba. In the past, as we have seen, the editors of *Hoy* were probably among the doubters. The reasons for doubting that the Soviet Union could make good on its promise were ascribed to a spokesman of imperialism who had stated that the great distance from the Soviet Union to Cuba had made effective assistance difficult.[56] But in fact, *Hoy* explained, coexistence was impossible if small nations were attacked. A few months earlier it had been feared that the Soviet Union would permit herself to make agreements with the United States that a small country could not afford to make. These fears had now been laid to rest.

In Moscow, Cuban Ambassador Faure Chomón predicted victory, thanked the Soviet Union for its great aid, and in an interview with *Komsomolskaia Pravda* declared that a people that has put itself under the flag of the socialist revolution could not be defeated.[57] One wonders whether Chomón meant that the pure in heart had the strength of ten, or whether flying the banner of socialism entitled one to the support of the first among socialist states.

Neither Khrushchev nor Castro referred to the socialist character of the

Cuban revolution in the spate of oratory and self-congratulation that followed the Cuban victory. *Hoy* explained that the Cuban people had demanded that the revolution be called socialist.[58] On 23 April, Castro spoke for five hours about the Cuban victory at the Bay of Pigs giving very little attention to the Soviet Union and not mentioning Khrushchev's letter to Kennedy. He mentioned the Soviet Union last in the list of countries where demonstrations in favor of Cuba had taken place and only indirectly gave the Soviet Union credit for deterring the United States by saying that direct U.S. intervention would have threatened the peace of the world.[59] Castro assigned the bulk of the credit to the heroism of the Cubans and the stupidity of the United States.

For his part, Khrushchev pressed home the advantage furnished by the American fiasco. He claimed rights in the world for the Soviet Union equal to those of the United States. Kennedy had asserted that the United States was obliged to defend the Western Hemisphere against external aggression and from that inferred that a "Soviet base" in Cuba gave the United States the right to attack Cuba. On the subject of a base in Cuba Khrushchev was unequivocal. "We have no bases in Cuba, nor do we intend to establish any." As for foreign bases, continued Khrushchev, the United States had established them in countries bordering on the Soviet Union, and U.S. military leaders had stated openly that these bases were directed against the Soviet Union. "So if you consider yourself entitled to take such measures against Cuba as the U.S. government has been resorting to lately, you must admit that other countries have no lesser grounds for acting in the same way with respect to the states on whose territory preparations are actually being made that constitute a threat to the security of the Soviet Union." But, Khrushchev continued, the Soviet Union did not hold such views. The United States, Khrushchev was saying, considers itself justified in attacking countries that it only claims, without any evidence, are being employed as Soviet bases, and yet it has constructed bases directed against the Soviet Union in many countries.[60] The Soviet Union, said Khrushchev, had done neither one nor the other, nor did it intend to.

Yet, a year later, Soviet missiles were installed in Cuba. Deliberate deception is a possible explanation, but is unlikely on several grounds. First, such cases are extremely rare in Soviet behavior, and when Soviet leaders "practice to deceive" they usually leave themselves legalistic loopholes. (Thus, in October the Soviet Union said no offensive weapons had been introduced into Cuba, using the word "offensive" to characterize the intentions of the possessors of the weapons rather than the weapons themselves.) It seems more likely that after denying that they had any intentions to place a military base in Cuba, some of the Soviet leaders began to wonder why they denied themselves what the United States permitted itself.

In breaking off the invasion Kennedy warned the Soviet Union that American patience was not limitless, probably having something like the establishment of a Soviet base in mind. The Soviet press believed or pretended to interpret this and other statements to mean that the danger of a direct attack on Cuba had not passed,[61] and the Soviet ambassador to the United Nations defined the Soviet obligation to Cuba a shade more precisely. The Soviet Union was ready to come to Cuba's aid in the event of an attack, he said, and the pledge had been given more seriously than the British pledge to Poland that drew the Western allies into World War II. "If the Soviet Union says it will extend assistance, it will extend assistance."[62]

The Soviet press indicated that not only was the American defeat in Cuba a victory for Khrushchev's anti-imperialism but it also represented a victory over the Chinese. The world meeting of the communist parties of the world in November 1960 in Moscow had been the scene of a Soviet-Chinese dispute over the proper communist policy toward the national liberationist struggle. In his speech of 6 January 1961, Khrushchev had restated the Soviet position that had been compromised in November to achieve unity. Now that position had been vindicated. When the invasion started the Chinese, in the person of Chou En-Lai, said that "if only the struggle is persisted in, it is entirely possible to defeat U.S. imperialist armed intervention." Chou assured Castro of the sympathy of the whole world but did not mention the Soviet Union.[63] But promptly after the Soviet government's statement and Khrushchev's letter, an editorial in the leading Chinese newspaper noted the Soviet government statement, passing over Khrushchev's letter, and characterized it as "powerful support for the Cuban people and a warning to U.S. imperialism." But it warned that although victory in the life and death struggle was inevitable, it would be an arduous struggle.[64]

Two days later, in a speech to a visiting Cuban cultural delegation, Chou En-lai expressed gratification that the Cuban people had attained victory in so short a time and gave part of the credit to the "great force of the solidarity of the peoples of the whole world."[65] From the Soviet report of Chinese reaction, the interested reader could conclude that even the Chinese had to recognize the correctness of Soviet policy.

After the Cuban victory at the Bay of Pigs, the Soviet Union was in a position to take stock. The event confirmed that the world balance of force had changed and that the Soviet Union could protect nationalist leaders who wanted to break out of the imperialist system. The November 1960 meeting of the communist parties of the world had concluded that countries could proceed from the national democratic state directly to socialism, bypassing capitalism. But this general proposition was not specifically applied to Cuba. However, as the Kennedy administration seemed to be in retreat and reluctantly accepting the new balance of forces, the Soviet press began to repeat authoritative Cuban statements that Havana was in the process of creating socialism and to report favorably the process of creating an integrated revolutionary party in which the Cuban communists were playing a leading role.

LAOS AGAIN

Like other statesmen, Khrushchev was seized of many problems simultaneously and his judgments about developments in one area of contest influenced his appraisal of the will of his opponents in other areas. The events in Laos showed that Soviet pressure, in this case diplomatic and military support to the Laotian neutralists, forced the United States to retreat. It will be recalled that in the middle of December 1960 the neutralist leader Souvanna Phouma had fled the capital, Ventiane, for Phnom Penh in Cambodia. The new Soviet ambassador to Laos had followed him there, encouraged him to continue the struggle and furnished Souvanna Phouma's man, Kong Le, with sufficient materiel, by a massive air lift and by road from North Vietnam, to consolidate his position in the Plain of Jars. At that point the neutralists could have cut off Ventiane, and by March 1961, chastened by this reverse, the right wing leader, Phoumi, was calling upon Souvanna Phouma in Phnom Penh and talking about an end of all foreign interference in Laos and strict neutrality for that country. The Soviet weapons delivery had shifted the balance of the Laotian see-saw once again. President Kennedy warned the Chinese and Khrushchev in a personal letter delivered by Ambassador Thompson on 9 March that the United States was prepared to intervene in Laos if necessary but preferred a truly neutral Laos supervised by a revived International Control Commission as provided for in the Geneva Agreement of 1954. But no agreements on the restoration of neutrality were possible until the Soviet Union stopped the airlift and a cease fire had been arranged. Khrushchev acted like a rather smug winner. He told Thompson: "Why take risks over Laos? It will fall into our laps like a ripe apple."[66]

Two days afterwards, on 11 March 1961, Kong Le consolidated his position by driving Phoumi's forces from the Plain of Jars and severing the road from Luang Prabang to Ventiane. On 19 March, Dean Rusk asked Gromyko for a cease fire and an end to the airlift but received no encouragement. The United States then began to reduce its terms for an international conference to restore the neutrality of Laos. On 23 March Kennedy made a dramatic public speech on the dangers facing Laos and the world and called for a cease fire, but failed to repeat his demand for an end to the Soviet airlift. The Soviet position then gave very slightly. The Soviet Union was now prepared to move towards stopping the fighting, if the United States did not expand the conflict (and Kennedy had let it be known he would not do so) and if the United States would commit itself to an international conference after the cease fire.

But as was to become clear in the many years before the war in Vietnam ended, the Soviet Union could not dictate to the Pathet Lao and the North Vietnamese. The latter preferred to keep the pressure on Phoumi while an international conference on Laos was in session. On 4 April a Soviet broadcast, which was carried only in the Vietnamese language, reiterated that a cease fire was not a precondition for an international conference, but added that it would create a favorable atmosphere. But this was a nudge rather than an order, because Soviet Ilyushins continued to bring materiel to Kong Le.

Souvanna Phouma then took the initiative. Arriving in Moscow on 16 April, the day of the Bay of Pigs invasion, he visited Khrushchev at the Black Sea and arranged for him to invite his half-brother and leader of the Pathet Lao, Souvannovoung, to Moscow. After consultation with the Chinese, Souvannovoung agreed to a cease fire and an international conference simultaneously because, as he said, his troops and the Laotian people were now in the position of the victor. Hanoi broadcast the cease fire on 2 May 1961. Kennedy later said, "Thank God the Bay of Pigs happened when it did. Otherwise we'd be in Laos by now and that would be a hundred times worse."[67]

It was to be a hundred times worse, but after Kennedy had passed from the scene. The pressures that Kennedy resisted in the aftermath of the Bay of Pigs were to move his successors. The Joint Chiefs of Staff, whom Kennedy blamed for the Bay of Pigs fiasco, were unwilling to promise victory in Laos and Thailand unless they could have 140,000 troops and the right to use tactical nuclear weapons. Kennedy refused but felt the necessity of drawing a firm line in South Vietnam, and on 11 May he authorized the infiltration of sabotage agents into North Vietnam.

Khrushchev could well believe that his missile rattling and his oil and military supplies to Cuba had deterred a direct American attack on that country and that his oil and military supplies to Souvanna Phouma and the Pathet Lao had brought the United States to the conference table after it had insisted that the airlift must first be stopped. The balance of forces had shifted in tiny Laos and in Cuba because the global balance of forces had shifted. Like a good Bolshevik, Khrushchev was putting his shoulder to the wheel of history as it rolled over the defeated enemy. When Khrushchev and Kennedy met at Vienna, Khrushchev was intransigent and, as he revealed after the missile crisis of 1962, the recipient of a statement by Kennedy that he had made a mistake in the Bay of Pigs. Small wonder that in the Soviet Union the press continued to write that the USSR was a reliable shield for the independence of small countries threatened by imperialism.

The growing confidence of the Soviet leader that time was on his side can be traced in the articles that appeared in the Soviet journals in the the months after the Bay of Pigs. B. N. Ponomarev, the head of the International Department of the Central Committee charged with the responsibility for relations with nonruling communist powers and therefore in charge of relations with the PSP, wrote an article on the new concept of the national democratic state.[68] Writing just after the Bay of Pigs, he said that the United States had tried to topple Castro because it feared the example of Cuba and had failed because the colonial system was collapsing as the socialist system was growing in strength. "The world socialist system is a reliable shield for the independence of the liberated nations."[69] In addition, these nations benefited from large-scale Soviet economic aid. Unfortunately, in the majority of the newly free states, the communists still had to work underground.[70] In other words, the Soviet Union served as a shield for states that asserted their independence while keeping communists in jail. "But the idea of the national democratic state was put forward by the communists, again showing that the communists are selfless patriots and most ardent defenders of the national interest."[71] The transition to socialism might take place through the national democratic state. But nothing specific was said about Cuba as a state building socialism.

Somewhat later, Fidel Castro was quoted as saying that the Cuban revolution was moving towards a socialist society and a socialist economic structure and that the revolution should try to win over as many of the middle classes to its side as possible, and build a single party of the Cuban revolution.[72] With the pronouncement that Cuba was on the socialist path, Castro made good relations with the United States impossible. But that did not seem to greatly worry Castro, because an aggressive war against Cuba, he said, could cost tens of millions of North American lives.[73]

Khrushchev continued to back up the Cubans and to reiterate his resolve to protect Cuba. If the United States should engage in new adventures against the Cuban revolution, it would create a situation pregnant with grave consequences above all for the United States itself.[74] Escalante said in a newspaper article that only the strength of the Soviet Union had saved Cuba from the fate of Nicaragua in 1930 or Guatemala in 1954. "Ten years ago the Soviet Union did not have missiles that flew from one side [of the ocean] to the other." Cuba did not mean to export her revolution, but the United States could no longer export the counterrevolution.[75] This meant in Guevara's formulation "that any people that wants to be free can be free."[76]

In the United States the secretary of defense, Robert McNamara, and the chairman of the Joint Chiefs of Staff, Lyman L. Lemnitzer testified before the Senate Foreign Relations Committee that Cuba was receiving large shipments of arms from abroad and infiltrating the rest of Latin America.[77] To meet this threat, the Kennedy administration asked for authorization to equip and train Latin American military forces to fight organized internal subversion.[78] On the anniversary of the attack of Moncada, the Cuban ambassador in Moscow gave a reception attended by high Soviet party and military officials. Mikoian talked in his statement of the Cubans as being "on the path leading to socialism."[79]

The Kennedy administration served domestic political necessities and probably reflected its hopes when it refused to recognize the permanence of Castro's regime. In August the Latin American states met at Punta del Este in Uruguay to establish the Alliance for Progress as a desirable alternative to the Cuban experiment. At the conference, however, the Latin American states praised the principles of the Alliance for Progress but quietly put pressure on Washington to come to terms with Castro.[80] But the U.S. Secretary of the Treasury, Douglas Dillon, said that the United States did not and never would recognize the Castro regime, "because to do so would betray the thousands of patriotic Cubans who are still waiting and struggling for the freedom of their country."[81] At the conference Guevara privately appealed for a modus vivendi to Richard N. Goodwin, Kennedy's special assistant for Latin American affairs and a member of the U.S. delegation to the conference, who later published an account of the conversation.[82]

Guevara somewhat ironically thanked the United States for the Bay of Pigs, which had allowed the Cuban leadership to consolidate most of the major elements of the country behind Fidel Castro. He then said that Cuba's determination to build a socialist state was irreversible. The Cuban people already supported such a course and that support would grow with time. If the United States should invade Cuba again civil war might break out in many Latin American countries, countries that had been greatly influenced by the Cuban revolution. The force of the example of the Cuban revolution was very great.

Guevara was then frank about Cuba's problems. The counterrevolutionaries were still a problem, and the cutoff in trade with the United States caused economic difficulties. Guevara understood that a genuine agreement with the United States was impossible at that stage, but he wanted to propose a formula for a modus vivendi. Cuba could not return the expropriated properties, but it would pay for them. Cuba could also agree not to make any political or military alliances with the East, although that would not affect her natural sympathies. The Cubans were also willing to discuss an agreement limiting the activities of the Cuban revolution in other countries. In Goodwin's words:

Here, almost for the first time, he became cautious and oblique. Clearly he could not affirm that Cuba was promoting revolution in other countries—even though he knew I had access to the facts about such activity—while he was in the presence of the Argentine and Brazilian officials, whose countries, after all, were somewhere on the list. Yet, although he was indirect, Guevara made clear his awareness that any possibility of a modus vivendi would depend on Cuba's willingness to refrain from revolutionary activity in other countries and he was telling me that Cuba was willing to discuss such a prohibition as part of an overall understanding. In return for this package, the United States was to stop any effort to overthrow the Cuban government by force and was to lift the trade embargo. Guevara asserted that there could be no discussion of any formula that would require giving up the type of society to which the revolution was dedicated. I know it will be difficult to discuss these things, he said, but perhaps we can begin by discussing subordinate issues such as airplane thefts. Once such talks begin, more important issues can be brought into the discussion.[83]

The United States failed to pursue the suggestion, Goodwin wrote, because a formal accommodation with Castro might have meant the collapse of the Venezuelan government of Rómulo Betancourt and might have strengthened Castro's appeal elsewhere.[84]

The incident serves to illustrate how potent was the belief in the infectious nature of communism. A curious inconsistency underlay this attitude. If indeed official U.S. recognition of a communist state encouraged emulation, the United States should have contemplated breaking off relations with all the socialist states. It was relations with newly formed socialist states or incipient socialist states that the United States considered to be so dangerous. Apparently, once a socialist state became stable and acquired substantial economic and military power, it no longer represented a danger.

Goodwin's account of his embarassment at newspaper leaks that he was the agent in a secret move to make a deal with Castro illuminates another and perhaps more genuine aspect of the problem. American domestic distaste for the political arrangements in Cuba would become a problem for the Kennedy administration if any accommodation with Castro were made, even one that eliminated an alliance with the Soviet Union and that quietly eschewed subversion in Latin America. The U.S. intransigence, it will be argued later, furnished a pretext or was the reason for the introduction of missiles into Cuba. When dealing with small powers, it seems that great powers permit themselves the indulgence of letting domestic political considerations dominate. If General Motors can believe that what is good for it is good for the country, an incumbent president can easily believe that what is good for his administration is good for the country. When the issues are momentous, or to put it another way, when they involve powers of equal magnitude, U.S. presidents have been willing to ignore public opinion or attempt to mold it. But when the issue involves another small country like Cuba or Vietnam, when no countervailing power seems willing or able to interfere, presidents are more prone to follow public opinion than to question its sensibleness.

The PSP now formally adopted the position that Latin America was in revolutionary ferment. The newspaper *Hoy* printed a communiqué of the communist parties of five Central American states stating that "the avenues of peaceful development have been definitely closed and that no other alternative remains but to attempt to seize power by the road that circumstances impose."[85] A long Soviet summary of the communiqué talked in general terms of the struggle for liberation but passed over the call for violence.[86] Differing Soviet and Cuban assessments of the utility of violence in Latin American revolutions were to be a feature of their relationship for several years thereafter.

Developments in Brazil, the most important of the Latin American countries, served to confirm the Soviet leaders in their sanguine expectations of the decline of U.S. power in the Western Hemisphere. Jânio Quadros, who assumed the office of president of Brazil in January 1961, had visited Cuba and had expressed his sympathy for those developing countries that sought to find a middle course between the Western and Communist paths of development. In many ways he indicated that "he was prepared to follow a less straightforwardly pro-American policy than any Brazilian president since World War II."[87]

The opposition to Quadros, which was substantial, found his "independent" foreign policy, particularly his pro-Cuban gestures, a convenient ground on which to attack him. In August, Quadros resigned suddenly, perhaps hoping that the traditional politicians and the higher military would refuse to accept his resignation because his designated successor, João Goulart, was even more given to leftist gestures. Since Goulart was abroad at the time, some elements schemed to deprive him of the presidency. But because of a division within the military and "a broad base of center opinion anxious to secure the observance of constitutional processes,"[88] Goulart was confirmed as president on probation, and the left mistakenly, but understandably, believed they had foiled the scheme to deprive him of office. The Soviet press followed the crisis,[89] and after the apparent victory of Goulart reported the views of Luís Carlos Prestes, the Brazilian communist leader. The assumption of office by Goulart, in Prestes's opinion, proved once more that the U.S. imperialists could not do as they wished in Latin America. Although the United States opposed Goulart and his policies, the Brazilian bourgeoisie and the majority of the armed forces had supported him.[90] The superficial character of this reassuring analysis was revealed in March 1964, two and a half years later, when Goulart was deposed in a coup d'état; but meanwhile, the Soviet leaders and some American leaders believed that the United States was on the defensive in Latin America.

On Cuba, U.S. policy seemed to face in two directions. A State Department official said it was contrary to American policy to recognize any government of Cuba in exile at that time, since the Swiss could not represent American interests in Cuba if Washington recognized an exile regime. The statement concluded by repeating Kennedy's words that the United States did not intend to abandon Cuba.[91] The secretary of state, Dean Rusk, was asked to comment on a statement by a Cuban exile, José Miro Cardona, that eventually an invasion against Cuba would be launched. Some observers wondered if Cardona had the backing of the United States. Rusk said he imagined that Cardona was speaking for himself, but then said that there was no prospect of peaceful coexistence with Cuba and recalled Kennedy's statement that the Cuban problem was not negotiable.[92] Almost simultaneously Cuba was charging in Havana and at the United Nations that the United States was planning a new invasion of Cuba on a scale larger than the landings of April 1961.[93]

Whether the United States was indeed planning a new invasion of Cuba cannot be known for certain from the documentation available. But Castro's extensive sources among the Cuban exiles would have picked up every wisp of information about plans, real and fancied, for a renewed invasion.* The rebuff of Guevara's approach to Kennedy's advisor, Richard N. Goodwin, together with American statements, made for domestic reasons, that the Cuban problem was not negotiable, reinforced Castro's fears. In any case, Castro had good grounds for procuring more powerful weapons. A better-armed Cuba would serve to dampen American ardor for a new trial by arms.

Khrushchev did not seem to feel that discussion about Castro's possible conversion to communism would alter American purposes, for in September he told Cyrus Sulzberger of the *New York Times*: "As far as we know Castro is not a member of the Communist Party. He is a revolutionary and a patriot of his country. If he were to join the Communist Party, I should welcome him. He would make a fine addition to the ranks of communists. But this is for him to decide. . . ."[94]

The Cuban press, which assiduously picked up every Soviet statement on Cuba and even printed the full text of TASS reports that appeared in abbreviated form in the Soviet press, passed over these statements.[95] Perhaps Castro had not yet decided to announce that he was a Marxist, or he preferred to appear to act without any prompting from Moscow. But Cuban officials continued to say that Cuba was building socialism.

A few days later Cuban President Osvaldo Dorticós was greeted on his

---

* Whatever the plans for a renewed invasion may have been, the CIA attempted for several years afterward to assassinate Castro, according to a U.S. report on intelligence activities issued on 20 November 1975.

arrival at the Moscow airport and in the Kremlin by Brezhnev, who lauded the social progress made by the Cubans, the example it set for the rest of Latin America and "the peoples of many countries of other continents," and reiterated the complete support of the Soviet people for Cuba's just cause. Dorticós responded that the Cubans were trying to make a new socialist society, that having entered on the road to socialism, no force would make them leave it.[96]

THE PSP LOSES ITS IDENTITY AS THE CUBAN REVOLUTION BECOMES SOCIALIST

Later, in the presence of Brezhnev, Dorticós expanded on his optimistic analysis. Many had fallen prey to geographic and economic fatalism, believing that a country so close to the most powerful capitalist country could not carry out such a far-reaching and radical revolution, a revolution that revealed to other Latin American countries what opportunities were open to them. The Soviet Union, Dorticós said, helped Cuba industrialize and gave Cubans encouragement to fight without any compromise of sovereignty and without political conditions. He also warned that new schemes were still being hatched against the Cuban revolution.[97] In a joint Soviet–Cuban communiqué, the signatories enunciated common positions on such issues as coexistence, the Berlin question, Algeria, and the admission of China to the United Nations. The communiqué also stated that Cuba had carried out her revolution on her own and "had freely chosen the path of socialist development."[98] Commentaries in party journals came close to predicting that Cuba's was only the first in a series of socialist revolutions in the Western Hemisphere. The journal of the CPSU carried an article that said that all over the world the newly liberated nations were gravitating toward socialism. The Cuban people, by inscribing socialist slogans on their banners, had shocked Washington. Washington's fears were understandable because the political material in other Latin American countries was no less combustible than it had been in Cuba. The Cuban example showed that a Latin American country could "move from an antiimperialist revolution to a revolution executing socialist tasks." What had been a theoretical possibility had become an actuality.[99]

The role of the Cuban communists now had to be dealt with, since a project for a unified revolutionary party in Cuba had been advanced. It was an awkward question. Soviet approval was implied when Blas Roca's article on plans to amalgamate the Communist party with the 26th of July Movement and the Revolutionary Directorate of 13 March appeared in a Soviet journal. This represented a most radical departure in the practice of communist parties, and the very unobtrusive manner of its acceptance by Soviet party authorities may well have concealed objections or embarassment. Blas Roca's article appeared neither in *Kommunist* nor in *Partiinaia zhizn'*, which had published his and Escalante's articles in January 1961, but in a less important journal devoted to political self-education, *Politicheskoe samoobrazovanie*.[100] Roca wrote that at the present juncture, the unity of the revolutionary forces of Cuba was a matter of life and death, because if the imperialists could exploit a split in the ranks of the revolutionaries, the Cuban revolution could be defeated. He then reviewed the role of the PSP in Cuba since 1952 giving the (erroneous) impression that Castro's attitude toward the PSP had always been as favorable as it had been in recent months.

The various revolutionary parties were fusing on the local level, where leaders were chosen on merit regardless of party affiliation. The Integrated Revolutionary Organization thus created "firmly followed the principles of Marx and Lenin."[101] By the 26th of July 1962 the process of fusion would have been completed and a single Revolutionary Party of the Cuban Socialist Revolution would be promulgated.[102]

The reasons for the radical step of fusion were not really addressed. Roca said that fusion was chosen over the alternative of a united front because of "the proximity of the Yankees."[103] It had long been a tradition of communist parties to preserve their organizational integrity even if they cooperated closely with other parties. (In the case of the close cooperation of the Kuomintang and the Chinese communist party in 1926 and 1927, the results had been fatal for many party members and almost for the party itself.)

The absorption of the PSP was a different matter altogether. The PSP's influence had grown since the seizure of power in January 1959; its members occupied high, if not the highest, positions in the Castro government; it published one of the two main newspapers in Havana. It was being absorbed into a single revolutionary party because of the need for unity in the face of a supposedly heightened danger of aggression from the United States. But recent events supported neither the belief that unity was endangered nor that the danger of invasion had increased. Evidence of friction between the Cuban communists and the 26th of July Movement had virtually disappeared from the press in 1961. The United States was certainly less of a threat after the failure of the Bay of Pigs than before. Thus, the PSP was threatened neither from abroad nor from within Cuba.

Clearly it was Castro who wanted to become the head of the communist party of Cuba, but of a communist party altered and expanded to include all elements loyal or beholden to him. It is easy to see why Castro should have wanted to make an amalgam of all the revolutionary parties and to deprive the communist leaders of whatever independence they enjoyed by having a separate organization. He was not the only nationalist leader of a Third World country to prefer a single party to several.

But for world communism this was a new problem. Communist parties had often adopted a minimal program and cooperated with other parties or with a sympathetic government as a loyal subordinate. In doing so they with few exceptions preserved their identity as an organization. The very notion of the two-stage revolution promulgated by Lenin in 1919 and 1920 at the first and second congresses of the Comintern necessitated the maintenance of the integrity of the party. During a certain stage of the colonial revolution or at a certain point after its conclusion, the alliance of the bourgeoisie and the communists would end, to be followed by a new conflict between the working class, headed by the communists, and the bourgeois nationalists. If the communists had been subsumed into a larger body, how could they make the decision to fight their allies of the day before? In China in the late twenties, when the Chinese communists had gone far in the process of coalescing with the Kuomintang, it was the latter that took the initiative in designating the ally as the enemy.

Whoever in Moscow was responsible for relations with foreign communist parties was silent on the subject (at least in public), and it fell to the Cuban communists to announce, with hardly any explanation, the creation of a new revolutionary organization. Khrushchev himself hinted at the subordination of the PSP in an interview with an American journalist at the beginning of September.[104] He had said that if Castro were to join the communist party, Khrushchev would welcome him, but Castro himself had to make that decision. It was as if the Pope in Rome had said offhandedly that he admired the Archbishop of Canterbury and would welcome him into the Roman Catholic church but that it was up to the archbishop.

Originally, the communist parties of the world were modeled more nearly on the Roman Catholic Church than they were at this time. The Executive Committee of the Communist International, located in Moscow and theoretically international rather than Russian, admitted all aspirants to the Communist International and ejected them if they fell from grace. Within each communist party, including the CPSU, certain procedures were established for the nomination and acceptance of individuals into the party. Recommendations, a period of candidacy, and demonstration of the requisite knowledge of communist doctrine were customary conditions for membership. When Khrushchev said that Castro would be welcomed into the communist party when he elected to join, he was usurping the prerogatives of the PSP and approving from the outside the placement of this newly minted, self-appointed communist at the head of the PSP. No one could have thought that Khrushchev meant that Castro would become a candidate member of the PSP, and after admission become a rank and file member. To return to the analogy with the Catholic church, the Pope, without consulting the Roman Catholics in England, would permit the head of the Anglican church to become the leader of all the English Catholics and the ecclesiastical superior of the bishops, archbishops, and cardinals who had attained those positions after a lifetime of service by his simple announcement that he had become a Catholic.

When Stalin dissolved the Comintern in 1943, no organization existed that could pass on the applications of new parties to be recognized as communists nor to eject communist parties that no longer deserved that designation. Theoretically, a meeting of all the communist parties could perform that function when it was in session.

Not even that formality was required of Cuba. Castro indeed proclaimed himself a communist when he found it convenient, as Khrushchev had invited him to do. His manner of doing so was embarassing, but not insuperably so, to the Soviet Union. On 1 December 1961 Castro, in a public speech, traced his journey to communism. His ideas, he said, had been much the same in 1953 when he assaulted the barracks at Moncada as they were in 1961. His 1953 program had, he said, concealed the full extent of his radicalism because complete revelation would have reduced his mass appeal. But revolutionary as his true beliefs were in 1953, in 1959 he was much more revolutionary. ". . . All the ideas that I have now, I had on the 1st of January [1959]."[105] He modestly added that he had not studied all the history and philosophy of revolution. But he planned, as everyone should, to study it thoroughly. He added, in his view perhaps disarmingly, but scandalously from the viewpoint of a Soviet communist: "A little while ago, looking for some books on capitalism I found what I had studied at one time, and I had read to page 370 in *Das Kapital;* I had arrived at that point. I plan when I have the time to study *Das Kapital* of Karl Marx."

He also confessed that early in his life he had been prejudiced against the communists, viewing them as a burden to any movement and to be kept at arms length. He did not deny that since assuming power he had had differences with the Cuban communists, but upon reflection it turned out that not the communists, but others, had been to blame.

In fact, said Castro, we made a socialist revolution without socialists, because it was impossible to name a communist to even a modest post given the outcry that would have been raised. Good comrades from the 26th of July Movement were assigned to execute socialist measures like the organization of agricultural cooperatives and the nationalization of industry, but they did not carry them out to the end. Now, he said, as the revolutionary forces are being unified and anticommunism is being defeated, it has become much easier to assign duties to PSP members.

The casual acceptance of Castro as a communist and the head of the communists in Cuba was only the latest of many modifications of Marxist doctrine. The Bolsheviks in 1917 had made a revolution without a proletariat, and the bourgeois rule of Russia that had been expected to cover a whole historical period had in fact lasted only nine months. In compressing the period of bourgeois dominance the Cuban revolution was following the Russian pattern. But in Russia, communists had made the socialist revolution. In Cuba, according to Castro, nonsocialists had made the socialist revolution and then, realizing what they had wrought, had assumed the title of socialist promising to continue home study courses in the doctrine of the new faith. It would be easy, perhaps too easy, to say that Soviet leaders only pay lip-service to Marxian doctrine, make their judgments on the basis of traditional great power considerations, and then mechanically adjust the doctrine. Such an analysis would slight the importance of faith in communism as an explanation, justification, and support of the regime in the Soviet Union. In fact, by accepting a radical reduction in the role of communists in creating socialist states, the Soviet leadership was reasserting its faith in the ecumenicism of communism.[106]

Faiths with universalistic pretensions have always modified the original doctrine in order to expand. The proselytizers have always been prone to accept elements of other belief systems to extend the community of the religious. Thus, institutional Christianity has accepted for the greater glory of God the uncircumcised, the veneration of saints, and Mariolatry. Protestantism in part represented the belief that the very essence of the faith had been compromised by some of these accretions. But it would be too much to suppose that Western Christianity, for example, had deliberately diluted the faith to multiply the faithful. Accommodation to, and absorption of, the elements of other faiths had been incremental. The pattern of communist expansion was more or less the same.

Very likely if someone had posed the question in 1960 of whether world communism could survive the self-enrollment of communists, the self-appointment of nationalist leaders as leaders of the communist parties of their countries, and the creation of socialism without communists, the Soviet leaders would have responded in scandalized outrage. But the question was never posed in that stark manner. The question was debated in different terms. In 1956 Khrushchev, shaken by the realization of the destructiveness of nuclear weapons, had promulgated the doctrine that coexistence with capitalism was necessary, but he did not take the logical step of asserting that communism could not survive a nuclear war. In fact, he asserted that a nuclear war would destroy capitalism but that communism would arise like a phoenix from the ashes. But by 1960 Soviet doctrine had acknowledged that neither communism nor capitalism could survive nuclear war. Although Marxian doctrine envisaged the possibility of the transition to communism by peaceful means, as a matter of historical fact every existing communist regime had come to power after the state structure had been shattered in war. (The case of Czechoslovakia might be considered an exception to that rule, and Soviet theoreticians made the most of it.) The Chinese insisted that the Soviet leaders were effectively abandoning the creation of new socialist states by emphasizing the primacy of coexistence and they succeeded in putting the Soviets on the defensive. And indeed, the Soviet leaders had much to be defensive about. The fears of the PSP that they would be sacrificed on the altar of Soviet-American coexistence have already been described. When the Soviet leaders expected what Americans termed concessions or what they termed the belated recognition of the facts of life in the months before the U–2 crisis and the Paris meeting and the few months preceding and following Kennedy's assumption of office, they soft-pedaled their support of Castro and the PSP.

Perhaps because the Soviet leaders feared that quantitative changes could become qualitative, they were sensitive to the charges of the Chinese, their domestic opponents, and perhaps their own Socialist conscience that they were selling the revolution short. Hence the strong impulse to celebrate the victory of communism in the backyard of the strongest imperialist state without close scrutiny of what kind of communism it was. Thus the Soviet leaders almost absent-mindedly accepted the conversion of Castro on terms which a true believer could only have thought scandalous. Khrushchev's opponents were hardly mollified by the realization that Khrushchev's political position within the Soviet Union had been strengthened. Khrushchev, who probably believed that what was good for him was good for the communist party, probably never realized how far Soviet prestige and resources had been committed to Castro.

Although some contemporary foreign analysis emphasized the embarassment that Castro's self-appointment as a communist caused,[107] the Soviet response was reasonably prompt and welcoming. Castro had made his announcement in a speech that started on the night of 1 December and continued into the early hours of the next morning. On 3 December TASS in Havana filed a report on the speech and a version was published in *Pravda* on 5 December 1961.[108]

The *Pravda* summary, like the original, simply said that the creation of a single party of the socialist revolution was necessary for the construction of socialism, without repeating the embarassing statement that socialism in Cuba had been constructed without socialists. Dropping Castro's statement that he would finish *Das Kapital* in the time he could steal away from building socialism, *Pravda* simply said that while still at the university, Castro had acquainted himself with the works of Marx, Engels, and Lenin. It repeated Castro's statement that he was a Marxist-Leninist and would remain one until the last day of his life. The *Pravda* summary concluded with Castro's confession that unitary management of Cuban affairs had been a necessity at one stage but that in the future collective leadership would be the rule. Thus *Pravda* omitted some of the embarassing crudities in Castro's speech but swallowed, as if it were the most natural thing in the world, Castro's decision to become a communist on his own and to assume the leadership of the Cuban communist party after he had obliterated its organizational identity.

In one of the rare commentaries in the Soviet Union on the subject—a comment that appeared in a book rather than in the periodical press—the implication was made that the PSP willed its own absorption. The comment was apparently written before this absorption was complete and seemed to hold out some hope for the PSP's continuation as an independent entity. The alternatives supposedly were the expansion of the PSP or the unity of the revolutionary forces with the retention of a "certain ideological and organizational independence of the working class and its vanguard," i.e., the PSP. The second option was chosen "with great political tactfulness and understanding of the demands inherent in the existing situation." The PSP did not want to compete with other revolutionary organizations in recruitment drives. "The decision was a necessary step to the genuine unity of all the revolutionaries of Cuba who are today fighting together against imperialism and traitors."[109]

Reading between the lines of these apologetic explanations written before Castro's "I am a Marxist-Leninist" speech is not difficult. If the Cuban communists had tried to strengthen their party through recruitment they would have been open to the charge of endangering the unity of the revolutionary forces in the face of internal and external enemies. We do not know whether the initiative came from the Cuban communists or from Castro, but it matters little. The communists had no choice, and there is no evidence that the Soviet Union conducted its relations with Castro in a fashion calculated to enhance the bargaining power of the PSP. Castro's goal was clear from the beginning of 1961. He seized the initiative in his interviews with *L'Unità* and *Rude Pravo*, permitting the Cuban and Soviet communists to follow him or not. And follow him they did.

In April 1961 Castro announced that the Cuban revolution was socialist and after a short delay the Cuban and the Soviet communists repeated Castro's words. In November Khrushchev said that he would welcome Castro if he became a communist, and on the night of 1 December, Castro said he was one. Some observers felt that Castro was foisting himself on the Soviet Union. Castro's manner seemed to challenge the Soviet Union to take him on his own terms or leave him. He seized on a chance meeting in the nightclub of the Havana Libre or on the bombing that preceded the Bay of Pigs invasion. The seemingly impulsive character of these important changes underlined that Castro initiated and the Soviet Union, after a pause, responded. It seemed as if Castro was making large decisions during an interview or on the speaker's platform as he spoke for hours with a handful of notes in front of him. He called the tune and Khrushchev danced. Given Castro's often expressed ambition to make himself and Cuba respected in the world, this must have been highly gratifying.

He was not storming an enemy position but a Soviet leadership desperate to revive the myth of world revolution by accepting this exotic revolutionary into its arms. And like many aging lovers seeking to find youth in the arms of a young admirer, money had to substitute for ardor. A Soviet expert on Latin America said very much the same thing in the stilted language of Soviet political discourse, which the reader is invited to compare with the gloss of the last few sentences.

The experience of Cuba has shown that at the present time more favorable conditions exist for the development of the bourgeois democratic revolution into a socialist revolution. This is a consequence both of the growth of the internal objective and subjective preconditions in each country and the result of the augmentation of the power of the socialist states, which render comprehensive economic and technical assistance to the underdeveloped countries on the path to independent economic and political development.[110]

5. KHRUSHCHEV BRINGS MISSILES TO CUBA

When Castro declared himself once and for all a Marxist-Leninist and proceeded to create a single Marxist-Leninist party under his leadership, the Soviet Union began to establish a military base in Cuba. The movements of Cuba toward communism and of Soviet missiles toward Cuba were almost simultaneous. This chapter will examine the connection between the two events. Although the evidence permits only a general assessment of Soviet purposes, it permits a reconstruction of Soviet motives that is simpler than most.

A brief anticipation of the argument might be helpful at this point. The Soviet Union accepted the evidence of Castro's conversion, or the revelation that he had always cherished Marxism-Leninism in his heart, with remarkably little comment considering the momentous issues it raised about the future of the world's nonruling communist parties. The two-stage theory of revolution in colonial countries was either abandoned or radically modified—we cannot tell which—because Soviet writers simply accepted the change without discussing its significance. Now some or all communist revolutions might be made by a nationalist leader who announced his adherence to communism, assumed leadership of the communist party, filled its ranks with new members, and decided which of its long term leaders were to be retained in secondary positions and which were to be discarded. Gone was the old notion that at a certain stage the communist party, which had been a member of a coalition making a national revolution, was to break with its allies and assume the leadership of a communist revolution, permitting its erstwhile allies to accept subordinate positions in the new political constellation or face proscription. Escalante had interpreted the events in the Chinese revolution in just this way and had expected that Cuba would follow the Chinese example. But in Cuba the communists were forced to accept whatever role Castro cared to assign them.

Communism may have assumed power in Cuba, but the PSP had not. Not surprisingly, the Soviet leaders were ready to abandon the two-stage theory of revolution in underdeveloped countries. Since its promulgation by Lenin at Comintern meetings in 1919 and 1920, most of the colonies had become independent, and only one, North Vietnam, had followed the Leninist recipe. Under the new theory, the leader of the new communist state would not have to be trained as a member of a communist party in opposition to a regime, but would receive on-the-job training as the leader of the ruling party. The Soviet commentaries were vague on just what the character of this Marxist-Leninist party was, but they were clear that it was soon to become a communist party. The old two-stage theory of revolution had been shunted aside; it was not clear whether it had been dropped altogether or whether the Cuban road to socialism now enjoyed coequal status. The subject was simply not discussed. The socialist character of the Cuban revolution was accepted without any systematic accommodation of accepted doctrine to the new phenomenon.

But the circumstances in which the new theory was accepted were reminiscent of the atmosphere forty years earlier. By 1920 Bolshevik hopes for other socialist revolutions in Europe had been dashed by the Soviet defeats in the war with Poland, the collapse of the Bela Kun communist regime in Hungary, and the failures of the left to come to power in Germany. Lenin pointed to the colonies as the Achilles heel of imperialism. The proletariat in the imperialist countries was not yet strong enough or class conscious enough to overthrow the government. But if these governments were to be deprived of the profits from the colonies by their successful revolt, the economic structure of imperialism would be weakened, the funds for the bribery of a labor aristocracy would be unavailable, and the revolutionary movement in the colonies would receive a new impetus. Successful revolutions in the unindustrialized countries would create the conditions for revolution in the industrialized countries. In 1962, in greatly altered circumstances, the Soviet leaders revived Lenin's hopes. Whatever expectations had been placed on revolutionary movements in France, Italy, or West Germany had come to naught. The apogee of the socialist movement in the United States had been reached in 1912 when Eugene V. Debs polled 6 percent of the votes in the presidential election. If the newly independent countries and the formerly dependent countries like Cuba now moved leftward or, even better, moved toward socialism, the imperialist countries, especially the United States, would decline in power, and the socialist camp would gain. The Cuban example would be followed all over Latin America, and Soviet support of Cuba would gain victories over the imperialist states, victories that had eluded the USSR in Europe.

Once the Soviet leaders began to believe in such a happy outcome, they were not inclined to interfere with Castro's disposition of the PSP within the new party structure, nor did they label Castro's aid to revolutionary movements in other Latin American countries as the "export of revolution." The measures for the defense of Cuba were to be continued and augmented in the belief that the United States would continue to be deterred. And what is more, the new feature of Cuban defense, ground-to-ground missiles, promised to improve the strategic position of the Soviet Union.

Neither Khrushchev nor Castro seem to have feared that the emplacement of missiles in Cuba could lead to the danger of nuclear war with the United States. They did anticipate, however, that the United States might again consider invading Cuba as it moved toward socialism (although the evidence seemed to point in the opposite direction). But they believed that the important increment to Soviet strategic strength, appropriately located in Cuba, would deter the American impulse to invade Cuba. The Soviet Union several times reiterated the commitment, first made during the Bay of Pigs invasion, to defend Cuba with nuclear weapons. But the recommitment was in a low key, sometimes taking the form that the well-known warnings to the United States still remained in force, but not dilating on the horrible consequences of nuclear war. The Soviet Union did not withdraw its commitment to risk nuclear war in defense of Cuba, but the tone of its pronouncement was that readiness to go to war was sufficient unto itself.

Castro, however, said in July 1962, as he did not in the months preceding the Bay of Pigs, that Cuba was acquiring the means to inflict millions of casualties on the United States, and with that new strength the last threat to Cuba from the United States had disappeared. Both the Cubans and the Russians believed that augmented military strength meant more, not less, security. They failed to anticipate U.S. readiness to risk nuclear war. Postcrisis analysis has been based on the assumption that Khrushchev was rational, and the lessons of hindsight have crept into the reconstruction of his rationale. Somehow, a rational Khrushchev should have anticipated what happened. The argument of this chapter is that the Soviet Union, or at least Khrushchev, failed to entertain the possibility that the United States might risk war to eliminate ground-to-ground missiles from Cuba. Like so many statesmen before and since, Khrushchev believed that what he wanted to happen would happen. After Khrushchev's dismissal from office, his opponents accused him of pushing hairbrained schemes. Whether or not they criticized the missile scheme as too risky before the fact, we cannot know from the evidence now available.

Before entering upon a detailed narrative of what the evidence reveals about the introduction of missiles into Cuba, the importance of medium- and intermediate-range missiles for the overall Soviet strategic posture might be usefully reviewed, using as our point of departure the postwar history of the Soviet military posture. Nuclear weapons speeded up the process by which the Soviet Union advanced from a second rank continental military power to the second of two world powers, no third existing. The crucial factor in this change was the sudden and unprecedented vulnerability of the United States to the consequences of war, and nuclear war at that, on its own territory.

THE SOVIET STRATEGIC VIEW

At the end of World War II the Soviet Union emerged as a member of the winning coalition. But in the opinion of most statesmen then, and most historians now, the Soviet Union would have suffered defeat in a two-nation war with Germany. In a sense, the Soviet Union was returned to the situation that existed in the aftermath of World War I. Even proceeding under forced draft she could not hope to match or surpass the economic and industrial power—which was equated with military power—of the strongest capitalist state. If the enmity of the capitalist powers was assumed and the possibility accepted that they might sometimes resort to war as Germany had, only one course seemed prudent. The Soviet Union must again seek to industrialize as rapidly as possible and once again seek to avoid war. The prospect of preparing to fight another war a generation or two hence, still lagging far behind in industrial strength, was not inviting, but there was no real alternative. Stalin could hope that once again the imperialist states would be divided among themselves, but he could not count on that.

Although contemplation of the distant future was sobering, the prospect of the near and proximate future was reassuring. The United States had rapidly dismantled its great wartime armies; it was acquiring nuclear weapons and the means to bring them to distant targets very slowly. Clearly, as after World War I, the Soviet Union was to enjoy a breathing space unless internal changes in the United States produced effective pressure for preventive war against the Soviet Union or events in the world arena impelled the United States to rearm. The first possibility never materialized, and despite all the alarms of the cold war, the crucial rearmament of the United States did not begin until after the outbreak of the Korean War.

It seemed that the Soviet Union had some time at its disposal. Accordingly, Stalin reduced his enormous armies and used the resources thus freed to continue the interrupted work of industrializing the Soviet Union. But in his planning for the distant future he exploited the opportunity offered by the invention of nuclear weapons. In the forties and early fifties, the atomic bomb did not hold out the prospect of military parity for the Soviet Union because the United States could deliver these weapons to distant targets and the Soviet Union could not. Even the Soviet possession of a strategic air force comparable to that of the United States would not have overcome this disparity. Since aircraft did not have the range to make round trips between the two states, only staging bases between the two made strategic bombing feasible. Without such bases, only suicide missions could gain access to the opponent's territory. Such missions can be a desperate last resort but not a basic assumption of war planning. The United States, however, had access to bases in Western Europe, the Western Pacific, and the Eastern Mediterranean. These brought the major centers of the Soviet Union within reach of U.S. bombers. By contrast, the Soviet presence in central Germany brought only Western Europe and Great Britain within range.

In an access of prescience or stupidity Stalin decided in 1945 or 1946 to push forward the development of ballistic missiles that could reach the United States. The decision was stupid if one assumed that nuclear weapons would continue to be atomic weapons much too heavy for a missile to carry. And a missile was a most inefficient means for the delivery of high explosives. Following that reasoning, the United States eschewed the development of ballistic missiles and put its developmental efforts into aircraft. But aircraft without bases would offer the Soviet Union only a marginal strategic capability.

Whatever the basis for Stalin's decision to push missile development, it turned out to be brilliant in the end. Since the hydrogen bomb developed in the 1950s weighed very much less than the atomic bomb, missiles could carry it. This technological innovation opened up at one stroke the possibility of a symmetrical strategic relationship between the Soviet Union and the United States. When intercontinental ballistic missiles became organic Soviet weapons, what Khrushchev had been saying since December 1956 would become true. No nation would be safe from devastating damage in a nuclear war. The long and theoretically dangerous situation in which the Soviet Union was vulnerable to nuclear destruction and the United States was not would be behind the Soviet leaders.

Khrushchev had anticipated this development and behaved as if it were already true in his public statements. But by the beginning of 1962 the satellite photography that had replaced the U–2 as an information collection device left no doubt that the Soviet intercontinental capacity was only marginal. As a matter of fact, in the fall of 1961 official spokesmen of the Kennedy administration publicly stated that the imbalance between the two powers was so great that the United States could absorb a surprise attack from the Soviet Union and go on to devastate its attacker. For a variety of reasons, the Soviet Union had not acquired many ballistic missiles of intercontinental range. Its program of missile development had proceeded in orderly fashion extending step-by-step the range of the V–1 and V–2 taken over from Germany. When a weapon reached a satisfactory stage of development it was put into mass production and supplied to Soviet forces in large numbers. These medium- and intermediate-range weapons had been placed in the western Soviet Union and in parts of Eastern Europe and were the basis of Khrushchev's threats that the NATO countries would suffer nuclear destruction in a world war. By the beginning of 1962 the procedures for building launching pads, storing the weapons, and training crews in their employment had become standardized.

It is not necessary to seek elaborate reasons for the Soviet realization that medium- and intermediate-range missiles in Cuba could bring symmetry into the Soviet-American strategic relationship before the Soviet Union acquired adequate numbers of intercontinental ballistic missiles.[1] In every Soviet and American military planning exercise since 1945, nuclear weapons could have been delivered to the Soviet Union from bases between the United States and the Soviet Union and no nuclear weapons could have been delivered to the United States. (This accounts for the enormous Soviet investment in active air defense.) The best that the Soviet Union could hope for was to deter war by holding Europe hostage, in the early postwar period to its conventional weapons and, after the middle fifties, to its nuclear weapons. Since the American impulse to provoke a nuclear war, or even to alter the status quo, was small, the ability to threaten Europe was an adequate deterrent. But the mutual fear of destruction was preferred to reliance on American self-restraint or solicitude for the survival of Western Europe. How vulnerable did the United States have to become for fear of destruction to become mutual and thus provide the Soviet Union for the first time in Russian history with a security based on strategic equality with the strongest putative enemy? This was not an easy question to answer since it depended on so many technological and political uncertainties.

The evidence strongly suggests that on this issue as on most issues involving large resource allocations, the Soviet leadership was divided. On 14 January 1960, Khrushchev outlined his views on Soviet military policy—views for which he was never to find full acceptance. He proposed a very large reduction in the Soviet forces in Europe and a reliance on deterrent strategic forces. The Soviet military and their political allies —or to put it more accurately, Khrushchev's political opponents with the support of the military bureaucracy—were able to frustrate the execution of that scheme. Khrushchev, however, pursued his foreign policy as if the United States and the Soviet Union were already strategically equal, and indeed, as we have seen, many high American officials believed this to be the case until the missile gap estimate was abandoned in the late summer and early fall of 1961.

Missiles in Cuba served many interests in the Soviet Union simultaneously. Khrushchev could acquire deterrent power against the United States directly by having Cuba perform the same function as a base for his missiles that U.S. bases within bomber range of the Soviet Union had performed for the United States since 1948. The scheme had the advantage of using weapons that were in mass production and for which personnel had been trained. The employment of Cuban soil as a base for

Soviet weapons would have advanced the Soviet attainment of nuclear parity by almost a decade. This broad statement requires only slight qualification. A striking force divided between the Soviet Union and Cuba complicated the achievement of complete surprise in a first strike. It made for what technically is called "a ragged attack." Since missiles launched from Cuba might have landed or been detected while missiles launched from the Soviet Union were still in flight, some defensive measures could presumably be taken against the missiles launched from the Soviet Union. But since the flight time from the Soviet Union was only half an hour, the qualification is only of marginal significance. Moreover, while first strike calculations are important in thrashing out nuclear theory, the practical political effect of such calculations on both sides has been to confirm the curbstone judgment that there are no victors in nuclear war. The theoreticians on both sides underestimated the difficulties of designing and procuring a force that would make a first strike seem like anything but madness. The balance of terror was not at all delicate because the chief protagonists were frightened by the outcome of a nuclear war whether it was a "victory" or a "defeat." The antagonists frightened each other into their senses—a rare instance in the history of human folly.

To return to 1962. The military establishments of the Soviet Union and the United States were the product of diverse forces: the growing knowledge of the physical consequences of the employment of nuclear weapons and the theories derived from this realization, the historical tradition of each country, the political interests of particular groups or persons, and as always in human affairs, the leaven of stupidity and ineptitude. Despite the asymmetry of the forces and the confused and conflicting ideas of how to employ them, neither side believed that a first strike could bring a desirable outcome; the Soviet Union because it would suffer much more damage than the United States, and the United States because it could see no goals that would justify the catastrophic damage to the Soviet Union, the slightly reduced damage that the populations of Western Europe would incur, and the difficult-to-calculate-but-still-horrible loss of life in the United States. Since the damage to the United States would only be a fraction of that expected in the Soviet Union, improvements of the same magnitude in each force would have radically altered the balance of forces. Because the Soviet Union had only a rudimentary intercontinental force, an augmentation that would have only fractionally improved U.S. forces would multiply the Soviet striking force and the American casualties to be expected. If the measure of the balance of power was the capacity to create millions of corpses in half an hour, missiles in Cuba would have given the Soviet Union something like instant equality.[2]

Traditionally, an attempt to alter the balance of power by one nation has been considered a justification for countermeasures by its rival. The Anglo-German naval rivalry of the first years of the twentieth century is a classic case. The controversy about the German naval building program, now being continued by historians, illustrates the assumption that governed U.S. behavior in the missile crisis. Supposedly German land power and British naval power constituted a balance of forces that would have been upset if the British acquired a large standing army or the Germans acquired many capital ships. The controversy centers on the German naval estimates. The Germans argued then, and their academic defenders argue now, that they did not intend to procure a large navy. But Great Britain responded, the argument goes, by embracing its traditional rivals France and Russia, to create the Triple Entente and to encircle Germany. This sparked a German naval building program that would not otherwise have taken place. The German case is that the British, by acting on their worst fears, made them come true. The British argue that inflated German ambitions forced them out of the isolation they had cherished for so many years. This old controversy probably cannot be resolved, but the assumption common to both sides in the first years of the century was the basis for U.S. behavior after the middle of the century. The assumption was that a nation has the "right" to prevent another nation from shifting the balance of power.

At the beginning of the century the Germans and the British both accepted that assumption; they quarreled about the British interpretation of German intentions. During the missile crisis the United States and the Soviet Union had diametrically opposed notions about the "right" to alter the balance of the power. The reasons for the differences are instructive. Both the Germans and the British were more the upholders than the opponents of the status quo. Bismarck had unified Germany and made her the strongest power on the Continent. Great Britain was at, or just past, the height of her imperial glory, which depended on her supremacy at sea. In a sense, both nations were victors and, therefore, lovers of peace and defenders of the status quo. They shared a belief in the sacredness of the balance of power. At the time of the missile crisis, the Soviet leaders believed that molecular social processes were changing the balance of power, that the shadows over the imperialist powers would lengthen as the socialist camp assumed its destined place in the sun. Change was natural; the attempt to freeze the status quo was like trying to hold the clock of history back. The existence of nuclear weapons had only changed the modalities of the process, not its essence. Whereas earlier, Soviet attainment of industrial parity would have preceded the attainment of military parity, now it was possible for the latter to come first.

The U.S. leaders, however, feared that a publicized and sudden shift in the balance of military power would undermine confidence in the

United States and that the allies of the United States and the powers that belonged to neither alliance system would rush to accommodate the system whose power was waxing, thus hastening the ebb of power from the system of which the United States was the center. Hindsight is not very helpful in judging the validity of Soviet hopes and U.S. fears. Now that the Soviet Union has gained rough strategic parity with the United States in nuclear weapons, neither Khrushchev's sanguine expectations nor Kennedy's dire fears have been realized. But the equalization of nuclear forces has taken place over more than a decade, and one cannot be certain that a sudden equalization of strategic forces would have not produced sharp political changes. The pursuit of such questions is rarely enlightening. But it is perhaps helpful in understanding the missile crisis to be as precise as possible about Khrushchev's expectations.

Khrushchev believed that U.S. policy was more consistent and had more consequentialness than it indeed had. If the United States and its clients had stayed their hands at the Bay of Pigs, in Laos, and in Brazil in an atmosphere of missile rattling, why should they risk war when presented by concrete evidence of new Soviet nuclear power? In putting missiles into Cuba, the Soviet Union would be doing nothing more than the United States had done in a dozen countries. But Khrushchev failed to realize that Kennedy did not accept a U.S. decline. Kennedy feared that a string of defeats would cause America's allies to abandon her in the conviction that they had been abandoned and that the domestic and international cost of stemming the tide would grow each time that the United States retreated before it. During the missile crisis, Kennedy agreed with his brother Robert that he would be impeached if he did not remove the missiles from Cuba.[3] Some commentators have interpreted his statement as a confession that Kennedy acted only to save his political skin, not admitting the possibility that Kennedy believed, rightly or wrongly, that Soviet missiles in Cuba would have been a disaster for his country and, therefore, for himself, too. This, Khrushchev failed to discern. Soviet political leaders were fond of saying that whoever says a, b, c, must also say z. Kennedy felt that he had already spoken the letters a and b. If he now advanced to c he might indeed have to say z. We shall now proceed to a closer examination of the events of 1962 to see how far a detailed account supports the general picture just sketched.

A SECURE CUBA ESTABLISHES A SINGLE MARXIST PARTY

The Soviet Union did not indicate any misgivings about Castro's formation of a new Marxist-Leninist party; both Cuban and Soviet statesmen and journalists continued to talk about the possibility of American intervention but more in terms of "they will make some attempts and fail" than in terms of a severe trial the Cubans would have to endure. The

Soviets accepted the generally optimistic estimate of the Cubans that Castro's example would be followed throughout much of Latin America.

For example, in a message congratulating Cuba on the anniversary of her revolution, Khrushchev and Brezhnev stated that any new armed attacks against Cuba were doomed to failure and that the Cubans could count on the firm support of the peoples of the USSR in their heroic struggle for independence. The message concluded with a wish for success in the construction of a socialist society.[4] Although Khrushchev did not address Castro's claim of a month before to be a Marxist-Leninist, the acceptance of Cuba as a country moving toward socialism tacitly accepted Castro's self-designation as a party member. Two days later, *Pravda* chose to quote the Cuban ambassador to the Soviet Union as saying that "once a people takes the path of socialism no one can stop it and force it to go backwards." Cuba, he said, had taken the first step "toward a unified party of the socialist revolution, that is, a Marxist-Leninist party of the Cuban revolution."[5]

The Cuban ambassador may not have realized that his history was somewhat erroneous, that Hungary's communist regime established in 1919 lasted less than a year. The failure or the unwillingness of the *Pravda* editors or of any other Soviet commentators to sound a corrective note of caution was consistent with the generally optimistic Soviet outlook on Latin America. A Latin American specialist described current U.S. efforts in Latin America in terms of *opera bouffe* rather than rapacious imperialism. Now James Symington, the senator's son, was employing a guitar in the service of imperialism. In August 1961, while attending a meeting at Punta del Este, he strummed his guitar and sang in Spanish from his balcony a serenade of his own composition entitled "The Alliance for Progress." There was an enormous distance between this kind of singing diplomacy and the routine coups d'état of the past. The old methods were collapsing because imperialism was doomed. American lack of realism was only accelerating the process. The Americans refused to understand that they could not reverse the course of events in Latin America any more than they could in Asia and Africa.[6] The Soviet Union, the Soviet writer seemed to be saying, was moving with the inexorable tide of history; the United States had abandoned the rapine of old-fashioned imperialism for bribery and wheedling. The image was of a harmless tabby begging for indulgence rather than of a wounded beast of prey that could still strike a mortal blow in its last extremity.

Translated into political terms, the opinion was that the United States might try once more to intervene with the mercenaries that it was still training in Guatemala but that it would not attack directly.[7] *Red Star* reported that Raúl Castro had spent a good part of the year in Oriente province, whose terrain provided a good hiding place for the few remaining counterrevolutionaries. The Cubans had to maintain constant vigilance since the United States wanted to restore the old order in Cuba.[8] Sometimes the old theme that an invasion of Cuba could produce a war that threatened millions all over the world reemerged,[9] but it was a minor theme in the chorus of optimism.

Castro conducted a press conference with visiting Latin American journalists and emphasized that revolutions would come in Latin America without world war. Since the power of the United States was waning, any revolution, wherever it started, could count on the solidarity of most of the world. "Without that solidarity the Cuban revolution would have been smashed." Revolutionaries must expect to fight, but gradually, with every unsuccessful intervention against a revolutionary movement, the policy of intervention would be discredited, and internal changes in the United States would create opposition to such adventures. Thus, revolutionaries could expect to win if they fought, but where the revolution had already taken power, the situation was different. There, coexistence was a necessary strategy to avoid nuclear war. But that strategy did not exclude revolutionary activity elsewhere. In some Latin American countries, where the masses were denied minimal political rights, it was an illusion to talk of the conquest of power by legal and peaceful means. But in other countries, the national stage of the revolution, the program of nationalization supported by the intellectuals as well as the workers and peasants would precede the construction of socialism. The *Pravda* account rendered Castro's sentiments correctly but obscured the support Castro gave to the armed conflict by saying only that the form of revolutionary power depended on the concrete institutions in each country. But although the Soviet report soft-pedaled even what Castro has described as the less likely contingency—an armed revolt when all democratic possibilities had been exhausted—it agreed with his general outlook and ran the account of his speech under the headline "Socialism will triumph."[10]

From later Soviet pronouncements it will emerge that the Soviet faith in new socialist revolutions was genuine, but a motive in trumpeting that confidence was to refute the charge by "Trotskyites, leftists, and dogmatists," the words then used for the Chinese, that coexistence meant abandoning the revolution. A prominent Soviet columnist argued that "peaceful coexistence does not exclude but presupposes revolutionary changes in society. It does not slow down but speeds up the world revolutionary process. It does not conserve the capitalist system but accelerates the dissolution and collapse of imperialism."[11]

The imperialists were on the run, emphasized a Soviet Latin American specialist. A year earlier they had asked no one's permission when they conducted aggression in China, Vietnam, Laos, and the Dominican Republic and organized intervention in Cuba. But now, in view of the growing solidarity of the peoples of Latin America, they were seeking the agreement of the Latin American governments. Cuba could stand up for herself, but the other Latin American peoples needed support.[12] A Chilean reporter stationed in Moscow wrote for a Soviet journal that "the steadfast Cuban people will defend their country and their victories like a lion," but that that risk alone did not deter American aggression. "The countries of the socialist camp will undoubtedly manifest their solidarity with Cuba." Any aggression against Cuba would cause the Latin American volcano to erupt. The imperialists were in a blind alley.[13]

Meanwhile, American diplomacy was being forced to lower its sights. In the negotiations before a conference of the OAS scheduled to take place in Punta del Este, the United States, faced by the opposition of Argentina, Brazil, and Mexico, abandoned its goal of making all the Latin American countries break diplomatic relations with Cuba and now simply sought to suspend Cuba's membership in the OAS.[14]

The U.S. Secretary of State, Rusk, argued for Cuba's exclusion on the ground that the Cuban political system was incompatible with the inter-American system. Dorticós responded that Cuba was, indeed, Marxist-Leninist and that he did not care to conceal that fact. But Cuba did not aspire to export socialism to other countries that would import it voluntarily.[15] *Pravda* explained, quoting the *New York Herald-Tribune,* that Rusk promised the Latin Americans dollars on the condition that Cuba be censured. U.S. policy was bankrupt because Cuba would not capitulate to pressure.[16]

It will be recalled that on 10 January *Pravda* reported among the litany of reassuring statements a single comment that the invasion of Cuba could threaten world peace. Now a statement by a similar committee simply talked about machinations against free Cuba that were doomed to failure.[17] Castro gave an interview to *Pravda* and *Izvestiia* contrasting Cuba's present position with that at the time of the Bay of Pigs. Then the imperialists had planned to establish a counterrevolutionary government on a bridgehead in Cuba. They could not, because the Cuban people were opposed. At that time Cuba had very few planes and even fewer pilots, he said. But since her leaders had guessed the enemy's plans to bomb her airfields, they had dispersed her planes successfully. Now, said Castro, the revolution, "has created a powerful revolutionary armed force that guarantees the defense of the conquests of the revolution against any imperialist efforts."[18]

Castro's Soviet interviewers invited him to repeat his adherence to Marxism-Leninism by asking him about the tasks of the Integrated Revolutionary Organizations (ORI). Castro replied that the basis for a single united revolutionary party was being created and that its members were seriously studying Marxism-Leninism. The imperialists, Castro said, had tried to make out that they were Marxists from the first day of their revolutionary struggle. But that was another lie. The Cuban revolutionaries were like students who took the first lessons in solfeggio. They couldn't call themselves musicians. But they were apt students and learned quickly from experience as well as books. Castro graciously concluded the interview by saying that without Soviet help revolution in a small country like Cuba would have been impossible.[19]

A year earlier in his interview with an Italian journalist Castro had paid tribute to the fighting qualities of the PSP; now there was not a single mention of the role of the Cuban communists in making the revolution. A forgetful reader or one unacquainted with the previous year's interview could easily have believed that there had never been any communists in Cuba but that a band of revolutionaries sympathetic to Marxism but knowing little about it had gradually adopted the faith, led by Castro himself. The Soviet reader was presented with the phenomenon of revolutionaries converting themselves to communism after the national phase of the revolution had succeeded. The role of the communists was unmentioned and the continuing validity or invalidity of the two-stage theory of revolution in colonial countries was ignored. A little later Castro was to remind his listeners once again that during the fighting, communists had hidden under the bed. But even before that Soviet treatment of the question had revealed that the Soviets were prepared, and hoped, to embrace successful revolutionaries who converted themselves and their followers to communism whatever the cost to the morale of extant communist parties.

The Soviet press continued to breathe optimism in the face of the exclusion of Cuba from the OAS at Punta del Este. It is of some importance to present the reasons for this optimism because the Soviet Union was to revive the talk of invasion in the very near future. A commentator in the authoritative *Kommunist* pointed out that countries representing 70 percent of the Latin American population refused to accede to the full demands of the United States. Although the American effort against Cuba, and the struggle against historical change all over the world, was doomed to failure, the United States would continue to try.[20] *Pravda's* Observer stated that despite the superficial diversity of world events, the fundamental direction of the world's social development was now determined by the socialist system. At Punta del Este, Rusk protested that communism was not the wave of the future, but even many bourgeois journalists said that it was. Just as intervention had failed in Russia and China, so would it fail in Cuba.[21] A Soviet correspondent with long service in Latin America explained that the Americans had been defeated at Punta del Este because the more important Latin American states realized that yielding to the United States on Cuba would encourage the former to intervene against them.[22]

On 4 February 1962 a mass meeting took place in Havana, and the Second Declaration of Havana was adopted by a show of hands. It characterized the decision taken at Punta del Este as a Pyrrhic victory for the

United States, and the Alliance for Progress as a fraud. Aggression against Cuba was mentioned almost incidentally; the emphasis was on U.S. attempts to prevent other Latin American countries from following the example of Cuba. The chances for revolution were good. The Declaration returned to Castro's theory of revolution, which had so little room for the proletariat (or its vanguard party). "And while it is true that in America's underdeveloped countries the working class is in general relatively small, there is a social class that, because of the sub-human conditions under which it lives, constitutes a potential force that—led by the workers and the revolutionary intellectuals—has a decisive importance in the struggle for national liberation: the peasantry."[23]

The statement seems grudgingly to give the communists a role. The proletariat will not make the revolution because they are too few, but the workers together with the revolutionary intellectuals will lead the peasants to victory. The two-stage theory of revolution is dismissed out of hand because "in the present historical conditions of Latin America the national bourgeoisie cannot lead the antifeudal and antiimperialist struggle."[24] From the old militant Marxist to the sincere Catholic, "all can and must fight side by side in this broad movement."[25] This is the only mention of Marxists in the Second Declaration of Havana. Nowhere is leadership assigned to them.

The Declaration of Havana also seemed to treat the communist parties, particularly their policy of waiting for the propitious moment, with scorn. The Declaration said that "the duty of every revolutionary is to make revolution. We know that in America and throughout the world the revolution will be victorious. But it is not for revolutionaries to sit in the doorways of their homes and to watch the corpse of imperialism pass by. The role of Job does not behoove a revolutionary."

Who were these revolutionaries who sat passively waiting for imperialism to die? The Declaration did not say, but everybody knew that the communists of Cuba and other Latin American countries had been the target of such accusations and presumably still were.

Technically, the declaration exempted the communists from the charge of passivity since it talked of a coalition that would involve them in political action. By stating that it was an illusion to believe that the dominant classes could be uprooted by legal means, "wherever roads are closed to the peoples, where repression of workers and peasants is fierce," the declaration left room for political action and a peaceful path to power in other countries.

But the declaration insisted that repression was growing and called for increased opposition to meet it. By not listing those countries where legal means might still be effective and by not even discussing them as a group, it clearly implied that armed conflict was the means of revolution and that the leaders of such conflicts would be modeled on Castro. The communists could come along—as they did belatedly in Cuba—or miss the train to victory.

The declaration itself said nothing about the danger of a new attack on Cuba by the United States, and Castro, in his introduction to the reading of the Declaration ridiculed the United States: ". . . We continue to strengthen the defensive capacity of the Fatherland. We continue to temper ourselves daily and are better prepared if the imperialists, blind and deaf, attack us again. They'll get a worse beating than they got at the Bay of Pigs. Let the mercenaries come, or their puppets, or let them come themselves. Because is anyone here afraid of the imperialists? (Cries of "no.") Who is frightened of imperialism? (Cries of "no one.") And when we think about the threats and the maneuvers of the imperialists, what do we do? (Cries: We laugh.) We laugh at the imperialists."[26]

Castro went on to say that all Latin America and all the free peoples of the world would help Cuba, without specifically mentioning the Soviet Union.

The Soviet press carried Castro's speech and the Declaration of Havana in full. The commentaries correctly rendered Castro's contemptuous attitude toward efforts of the United States to overthrow the Cuban revolution and quoted the man in the street as saying that Cuba was not alone, since Khrushchev had again expressed the solidarity of the Soviet Union with the Cuban revolution.[27] *Hoy* summarized a reassuring analysis by the *Pravda* commentator Ermakov that the United States had failed, at Punta del Este, to isolate Cuba diplomatically and economically.[28]

A lengthy analysis of the significance of the Second Declaration of Havana soon appeared in the most authoritative organ of the CPSU.[29] The points of agreement and divergence are instructive. In the Soviet view, the Havana Declaration was a historic document with relevance to all Latin America. Poor social and economic conditions made revolution inevitable in many Latin American countries. The only exit from the blind alley of underdevelopment was in a changed social structure, for which the Havana Declaration called.

United States economic control had facilitated political control but when that was inadequate the United States did not hesitate to employ armed force. Right now, however, the United States was offering some blandishments in the form of aid under the Alliance for Progress. But the United States had made it clear at Punta del Este that such aid was available only to those who joined in its anti-Cuban policy. The Cuban revolution had furnished a great stimulus to the revolution in Latin America. As the situation of the masses had deteriorated and they had stepped up political action, the rulers had lost their grip, thus creating a breach through which the dissatisfaction of the masses could pour. The Havana Declaration was correct in saying that a revolutionary situation existed. The communist parties of Brazil, Colombia, and Ecuador shared this assessment. In an interview with a Cuban journalist, the leader of the Brazilian communists, Luís Carlos Prestes, said that "combustible materials have been accumulated and any spark can ignite the flame of a great conflagration in Brazil."[30]

The Soviet writer followed Castro in saying that the agrarian masses in Latin America were to be led by the proletariat and the advanced intelligentsia. The single passing reference in the declaration to the worker's share in the leadership of the revolution is given a central position in the Soviet account. The declaration mentions "old Marxists" only once, in the company of "honest Catholics." The Soviet account talks of the growing importance of the communist parties of Latin America and their role as leaders of the revolution. The Havana Declaration says that the bourgeoisie cannot lead the revolution. The Soviet version comments that the national bourgeoisie still has a revolutionary potential that could be exploited by the revolutionary classes and that underestimation of that class could do substantial harm to the cause.[31]

The proletariat in Latin America is more numerous and better organized than in Asia and Africa, and every country has a militant Marxist-Leninist party led by experienced leaders. "All these subjective factors in combination with the already existing objective preconditions furnishes the basis for asserting," concluded the Soviet author, "that today Latin America is rapidly being converted into one of the most revolutionary regions of our planet."[32]

The Soviet analysis basically accepted the Cuban prophecy for the future. A wave of anti–U.S. revolutions would engulf Latin America. *Kommunist* assigned a leading role to communists and communist parties, which Castro virtually ignored. But if Cuba was to be the model for other Latin American countries, Castro's imitators had little to fear, and the leaders of the Latin American communist parties had little to hope for. *Kommunist* completely ignored the question of how these nationalist revolutions could become socialist. The emphasis was on the nationalist, anti–U.S. content of the revolution.

Despite these reservations about the role of the communist parties of Latin America, the Soviet article endorsed the Havana Declaration warmly. For a Soviet writer in his first paragraph to hail "the birth of a new historical document of great power," to call it "a manifesto of revolution," and to say that it applied to all Latin America was to give it a ringing endorsement. The Soviet mode of expressing disapproval with allies or fellow communists was clearly established. Views ascribed to "some people" and "some comrades" and "ultraleftists" were attacked in the knowledge that the target and others would know who was meant. This full dress treatment of Cuban plans for revolution in Latin America reflected basic approval. The greater role assigned by the Soviet writer to the communist parties and the national bourgeoisie could either have been meant as advice to Castro to broaden the coalition in countries considered ripe for revolution or as a verbal obeisance to the Latin American communist parties, or both. The choice for the Soviet Union was to associate itself with the nationalist anti–U.S. movements in Latin America or to withhold approval unless Castro followed the Soviet recipe for revolution. For a while the choice was still to enlist Castro as an ally and to accept him as the leader of the Marxist party, which was to become a party of communists.

The wish to confirm the conviction that the tide was running against the United States would have probably been sufficient to mute criticism of Castro. But when this motive was combined with the expectations for a significant improvement of the Soviet strategic military position by the location of missiles in Cuba, the imperative of securing strict Cuban ideological conformity receded. If the Soviet Union had wanted to maximize the chances for U.S. passivity until the missiles had been installed, it might have been more prudent to postpone the call for revolution in Latin America. But if Castro behaved in this case, as he did before and has done since, he probably failed to consult the Soviet Union before issuing his call for revolution. In any case, the Soviet leaders apparently did not believe that the risks of U.S. intervention in Cuba at that time made it too dangerous to put missiles in Cuba. In accordance with such a view of the situation the press kept alive the possibility of a U.S. attack in Cuba as a justification for continued and expanded military support of Cuba but took the position that such support was the best deterrent to an attack.

Red Star wrote that the imperialists, embittered by the failure to break the will of the Cubans, were preparing renewed aggression against Cuba. The socialist camp supported Cuba and warned the aggressors that they could break their necks if they looked for trouble.[33] The article did not indicate whether the United States was planning to attack Cuba directly or through proxies, but the Soviet representative at the United Nations, V. A. Zorin, said that direct intervention in Cuba's affairs had to be reckoned with.[34]

THE SOVIET RATIONALE FOR MISSILES IN CUBA

On 18 February 1962 the Soviet government issued a long formal statement on the Cuban problem. According to a subsequent revelation by Castro, the decision to put missiles into Cuba was taken at "the beginning of 1962."[35] The Soviet statement constitutes the most extensive exposition of the Soviet rationale for putting missiles into Cuba made before the event; it is therefore useful to examine the statement carefully and to provide extensive extracts of its language.

The statement and the editorials in the Soviet press that followed contained a seeming contradiction. While insisting that the United States was on the run and could not prevent Cuba from having whatever social system it chose, it talked about renewed danger to world peace. This seeming contradiction is resolved if the assumption is made that the Soviet leaders decided at this point to place missiles in Cuba. It was necessary to talk about the continued danger of aggression to justify the creation of a Soviet base in Cuba, but the depiction of the United States as in retreat suggested that the locating of missiles with nuclear warheads in Cuba would obviate the necessity for their employment. The statement maintained that in its attempt to isolate Cuba at the Punta del Este meeting, the United States had suffered more harm than Cuba. The United States was still organizing refugees to attack Cuba, and the nations of Latin America had become convinced that they were endangered as long as Cuba was. Therefore, protest against U.S. policy was mounting all over Latin America. Whereas Cuba stood ready to normalize relations with the United States, America was continuing to export counterrevolution. This created a serious danger to world peace. The United States even claimed that Cuba was becoming a Soviet base. In fact, the only foreign base on Cuba's soil was Guantánamo. Then the Soviet statement proceeded to threaten countries that harbored U.S. bases, in the event that the United States threatened Cuba.

By what right and by what law does the U.S. government organize and direct aggression against another country accusing it of having established a social system and a state different from what the United States wanted? If the U.S. government arrogates this right to itself, it is standing on very shaky ground, because it does not, as is well known, possess the military might that would permit it to dictate conditions to other countries. The U.S. political leaders should take into account and not forget that there are other countries possessing no less terrible weapons, standing guard over peace, and prepared to prevent the unloosing of a new war.

It is not necessary to conjecture where and near what states foreign bases are located. The Soviet Union knows their location, as the United States and the whole world does. If the United States threatens Cuba, then let it draw conclusions regarding countries where American military bases are located. Some people in the United States, still relying on the policy of "positions of strength," continue to rattle weapons and threaten other peace-loving states; but this is a stick with two ends. If the United States seizes one end of the stick, then other states can take hold of the other end and employ it against those forces that the United States employs to threaten the Soviet Union and other peace-loving states.

The United States government is mistaken if it believes that its position is in any way exceptional or that it has any right at all to forbid a state with different ideas to be its neighbor. There are not a few states that are neighbors of the Soviet Union that have a different social structure and a different political outlook. But the Soviet Union has never made demands on these states because they have a different social structure. The Soviet Union bases its relationship with all states on the policy of peaceful coexistence. The northern neighbor of the Soviet Union is Finland—a capitalist country—but the Soviet Union has the best good-neighborly relations with her. It could be said that this is a question of a neutral country. Yes, that is so. But the Soviet Union also has neighbors who belong to military blocs headed by the United States and nevertheless it relates to them no less tolerantly on the basis of peaceful coexistence.

Since the Soviet Union once underwent trials like Cuba's, the Soviet statement continued, it has the warmest sympathy for Cuba. If the United States tried to embargo Cuba completely, the Soviet Union and all peace-loving nations would not permit Cuban women and children to die of disease and starvation. "The Republic of Cuba, as the head of the Soviet government, N. S. Khrushchev, has clearly stated, can always count on aid and support from the Soviet people. The well-known warnings of the Soviet government to the enemies of the people of Cuba remain in force even to this very day." The statement concluded with an expression of Soviet confidence that Cuba would be victorious in her just historical struggle.[36]

The warnings of a year and a half earlier were repeated, but the specifics were dropped. Instead of saying that missiles would fly if Cuba was attacked by the United States, the Soviet Union predicted that Cuba, under Soviet protection, would prevail. It is logically possible to interpret this as a diminution of the Soviet pledge, but more likely it meant that the Soviet warnings still in force now deterred the United States, plus a new note: if the United States made claims against Cuba, the Soviet Union could make similar claims against countries allied to the United States. The Soviet Union lived on excellent terms with Finland, a capitalist country, and the United States could follow that example. The Soviet Union even lived on good terms with neighbors who adhered to the American alliance system. The implication was clear. If the United States could not tolerate a Cuba with a different social system, the Soviet Union might have to change its policy "regarding countries where American military bases are located."

On the next day a *Pravda* editorial reiterated the main themes of the statement and carried both accounts from Havana that the Cubans were encouraged by the warning to the United States and reports from New York that some Americans realized that aggression against Cuba could bring retaliation to countries where U.S. bases were located.[37]

A few days later *Pravda* printed Castro's understanding of the Soviet statement, namely, that the United States risked atomic war if they invaded Cuba and that Cuba had "no intention of making any part of its territory available to any government for the erection of military bases."[38]

CASTRO BECOMES THE FIRST CUBAN COMMUNIST

Simultaneously or just after the renewal of the Soviet pledge to protect Cuba against the United States, Castro started to attack sectarianism in the Integrated Revolutionary Organization (ORI). Later, on 26 March, he singled out Escalante by name in a speech on the anniversary of Moncada. Castro contrasted the mistakes of the revolution that had been unavoidable with others that he attributed to Escalante, which he proposed to eradicate immediately.

The renewed pledge for the defense of Cuba, which coincided with the decision to put missiles in Cuba, can be connected with Castro's attack on Escalante. It will be recalled that Escalante had always favored a more rapid radicalization of the Cuban revolution than had the dominant faction of the PSP, headed by Roca. Although Escalante did not prevail, the Soviet press carried his formula as well as Roca's suggesting that Escalante's views had support in Moscow. In a sense Escalante and Castro were closer to each other than either was to Roca. Castro had carried through a more radical agrarian reform than the PSP had recommended, and he and Escalante were more ready to dispense with middle-class support than the PSP thought prudent. But Escalante and Castro differed sharply on who was to lead the Cuban revolution. More than once Escalante had held up the Chinese revolution as an example, emphasizing particularly the success of the Chinese communist party in getting the bourgeoisie to accept a role of passive cooperation. In Cuban terms that meant that Castro would have to follow the lead of the PSP. Castro was silent in the first weeks of the establishment of the Integrated Revolutionary Organization, during which Escalante was consolidating his leadership of the new party. After the decision to place the missiles in Cuba had been made, Castro attacked Escalante. Either Castro did so without consulting the Soviet Union, feeling that its leaders would not interfere with his domestic dispositions while the missiles had yet to be installed, or he came to an agreement with the Soviet Union on Escalante's dismissal. In any case, as we shall see shortly, the Soviet press endorsed Castro's action. In explaining why Escalante had to be dismissed, Castro recalled that earlier there had been a tendency to distrust anyone who was not an old party member. At that time of confusion and vacillation only a 100-percent-reliable person could be appointed to a responsible post. But by the time Castro called the Cuban revolution socialist, that is, 16 April 1961, the masses had become reliable. Subsequently, it was dogmatism and frightful sectarianism to believe that "the only revolutionary, the only comrade who could be trusted, the only one who could be appointed to an important post on a people's farm in a cooperative, in the state administration, or any place, had to be an old Marxist militant." The exclusion of any but old PSP members from leading positions meant that instead of organizing the Integrated Revolutionary Organizations into the embryo of what was to be the United Party of the Socialist Revolution, a tyranny was being organized, a strait jacket.

Castro rather unconvincingly professed not to know whether Escalante, who committed these terrible mistakes, had been appointed or had appointed himself secretary of the ORI. Old communists got all the good jobs and honest revolutionaries who may not have had much book learning or knowledge of Marxism were passed over. Castro singled out a Fidel Pompa of Oriente province who had hidden under the bed while others were fighting. He was rewarded with a high post. All over Cuba, each provincial secretary of the PSP was made the provincial secretary of the ORI, and the same pattern prevailed in lower party organizations. Castro concluded his tirades against the abuses of Escalante by reaffirming his faith in, and adherence to, Marxism-Leninism.[39] By his denunciation of Escalante, Castro demonstrated that his own avowal of Marxism-Leninism had not forced him to yield any authority to old communists. Instead, the PSP had abandoned its own organizational independence for absorption into a new amalgam of which Castro was the boss.

The PSP newspaper, *Hoy*, in commenting approvingly on Castro's talk, said that "there is no breach but greater unity."[40] The Soviet press promptly carried positive accounts of Castro's actions emphasizing that only one leader had fallen victim to the sin of sectarianism and that Castro felt that good Marxist-Leninists should criticize their own mistakes.[41] On 11 April, a very long *Pravda* article gave a considered judgment—of unmixed praise.[42]

Cuba was furnishing the rest of Latin America with a remarkable example of how to win freedom, said *Pravda*—a circumstance that stimulated U.S. preparation of new armed aggression. The Cuban revolution had inscribed a summons to construct socialism on its banners. The unity that was responsible for the victory over Batista was now being forged to defend the revolution against the United States. A Marxist-Leninist party was being created from all the revolutionary parties, constituting "an important step on the path toward a single party based on Marxist-Leninist principles" and also constituting a new stage in the development of the Cuban revolution. Castro's disciplining of Escalante's "dogmatism and sectarianism" was pronounced to be in full conformity with the letter and the spirit of the 1960 statement of the eighty-one communist and workers parties. The introduction of younger cadres into responsible posts was specifically approved. *Comrade* Fidel Castro was referred to as the first secretary of the ORI, and "the well-known warnings of the Soviet government to the enemies of People's Cuba remained in force to this day."[43] No more unequivocal endorsement could have been given.

Meanwhile, the Soviet press continued to assess the dangers of intervention in Cuba and charged the United States with planning to stage an invasion of a Central American country by supposed Castro forces and then using the "invasion" as a pretext for collective action against Cuba.[44] A long and well-informed article in a Soviet foreign affairs journal pointed out that the United States had already paid a heavy political price for its anti-Cuban policy in the form of the splintering of the OAS. The absence of an OAS mandate had restrained Kennedy in his use of military aircraft at the Bay of Pigs, thereby facilitating Castro's victory. The continued pressure of the United States on moderate governments to join in an anti-Cuban policy was polarizing political life in Latin America and creating prospects of civil wars that would create new and larger Cubas or military dictatorships. Direct or indirect U.S. participation could only hold back social revolution temporarily. A professional gambler would not have taken the risks that Rusk had taken in pressing Latin American moderate governments on Cuba. Invasion of Cuba was senseless, yet Washington seemed to be pursuing that policy. Cuba was now too well armed to succumb to a lightning blow, even a heavy one. A war in Cuba would therefore be sufficiently prolonged to set off civil wars all over Latin America, with consequent destruction of U.S. property. Cuba could also count on support from beyond the Western hemisphere: "Are the plans for reconquest of Cuba worth the risk of far greater losses in the rest of Latin America . . . ? Is it worth the risk of hostilities on a much wider scale? Unfortunately, the available evidence indicates that the U.S.A. is about to assume these risks."[45]

The Soviet appraisal seemed to be completely mistaken. According to Cuban refugees in Miami not a single supply boat for the Cuban underground had been able to evade the U.S. authorities and reach Cuba for many months. The U.S. Coast Guard had turned back a ship of Cuban exiles bound for Cuba despite the fact that they had no arms, ammunition, or supplies aboard. The exiles were worried that President Goulart of Brazil had been warmly received in Washington even though he was opposed to Washington's Cuban policy.[46] And *Pravda* noted that while in Washington, Goulart had stuck to his position that Cuba had the right to self-determination.[47]

Moscow's public statements on Cuba continued their inconsistent course, occasionally predicting invasion, as in the article cited above, and then breathing confidence. In a message to Castro on the first anniversary of the Bay of Pigs, Khrushchev addressed Castro as Comrade and expressed confidence that any new imperialist attempts to interfere in Cuban internal affairs would be more shamefully defeated than before.[48] An old time PSP leader visiting Moscow was quoted as saying that Cuba was an example to the rest of Latin America and that guerrilla bands in Guatemala, Venezuela, and Ecuador were becoming more important.[49] It hardly seemed as if the Soviet leaders were afraid that guerrilla activity in Latin America could precipitate an American invasion of Cuba.

The Soviet reader was presented with a generally confident assessment in an article by Blas Roca, now a member of the Secretariat of the National Leadership of the Integrated Revolutionary Organizations of Cuba.[50] Roca discussed the economic difficulties that Cuba was suffering because of the cessation of trade with the United States, Cuba's inexperience, and the heavy but necessary costs of defense. Roca's listing of the defense requirements was interesting, placing the struggle with U.S. espionage agents first, and then the readiness to repel any armed intervention planned by the United States and its lackeys, thus implying that espionage was more likely than invasion.

Roca devoted a great deal of space to the damage done by Escalante. But the national leader, Comrade Castro, was overcoming all these difficulties. He then devoted some attention to the problems of accepting members in the new party. A commisison from the central leadership of the party came to production centers and asked for nominations by the advanced workers. Collaborators with Batista were excluded. The workers nominated by these meetings, whether they had been politically active or not, had a right to enter the party. After they expressed their desire to join, professed their acceptance of the Marxist-Leninist ideology and the program of constructing socialism, and accepted party discipline, they became party members. If old revolutionaries with long service were not nominated at the general workers meetings, the party cells and the committee from the center could submit their names for approval by these meetings.

Castro had attacked Escalante for putting only old PSP members in positions of importance. Now they were dependent on a general meeting of the workers for a transfer of their membership to the new amalgamated party. Roca admitted that the procedure was prolonged but explained that it guaranteed the proper contact with the masses. Not a word was said, of course, about who had nominated Castro or how he had become the head of the Marxist-Leninist party. That was an unmentionable nonevent from the very beginning. Lenin and Stalin had applied for party membership in the normal way and had been admitted. But Castro, the creator of the movement, was self-admitted, like Marx. Presumably *Pravda* readers were familiar with the procedure for the admission of rank and file members: nomination by two party members, a period of trial as a candidate member, etc. It was quite clear from Roca's account that longtime party members in this new Marxist-Leninist party, after Castro's denunciation of Escalante for favoring them, had to be nominated and accepted by the "masses." The Soviet practice had been stood on its head. If the Soviet party leaders found this treatment of old party members obnoxious but felt powerless to affect it, they could have preserved silence. Publishing a detailed account of the admissions procedure by the former head of the PSP constituted an endorsement of Castro's method of managing tried and true Cuban communists.

At this time it would have been awkward for the Soviet Union to protest. Castro had charged, and Roca had echoed the charge, that Escalante's policies had disoriented and angered the masses. The Western press and *Pravda* had reported demonstrations against the regime. The *New York Times* called them hunger demonstrations; *Pravda* explained that a tiny group had made a counterrevolutionary demonstration provoked by supply shortages that grew out of the increase in demand, the imperialist blockade, and the mistakes of the revolutionaries.[51] Although it is not possible to establish precisely when the Soviet Union decided to place missiles in Cuba, it is likely that the decision had already been made.[52] This was hardly the time to argue with Castro about the management of internal Cuban affairs. Simultaneously, ideologists were saying, and perhaps their leaders were believing, "genuine opportunities for the victory of the revolution without world war were growing all over the globe. This was vividly confirmed by the development of the Cuban revolution, which was the first victorious, profoundly popular revolution to grow beyond that into a socialist revolution, to begin in the new third stage of the general crisis of capitalism."[53] Thus the Cuban revolution was not an exceptional case, an anomaly rooted in a special historical situation, but the first of a class of revolutions marking the third and final stage of a general crisis of capitalism. A significant change in the military balance of power in the offing, and the beginning of the final collapse of capitalism—what heady prospects! How niggling to fuss about the difficulties old Cuban communists faced in entering the only Cuban political party! How inappropriate to wonder aloud about how Castro had entered the communist party!

On the contrary, said Blas Roca at the Twenty-eighth National Congress of the Communist Party of Uruguay, "Fidel is the best and ablest Marxist-Leninist in Cuba."[54] Now, said Blas Roca, any country in Latin America, no matter how small or how near to the United States, could destroy imperialism, because socialism was stronger than imperialism. The Cuban revolution had demonstrated that rapid social change was possible. Roca then admitted that the PSP had been faint-hearted during the struggle against Batista and invited the other Latin American communist parties to improve on its experience. Fidel Castro had foreseen that the guerrilla struggle would succeed and had the courage to carry it through. The PSP had not discerned the prospects as clearly and offered help and solidarity to the guerrilla movement only later, which meant it had joined the struggle as a party only tardily and weakly. When the PSP had been organizationally separate, it had claimed a more important role for the proletariat and for itself in the Cuban revolution;

now that it was being absorbed into the Integrated Revolutionary Movement it was eating humbler pie. Roca seemed to be urging his fellow communist leaders in Latin America not to withhold support of guerrilla movements until the very end. Few were to heed his advice and none were to pay the penalty for failing to do so, for nowhere else did guerrillas overthrow a Latin American regime.

The Integrated Revolutionary Movement, Roca said, had created unprecedented unity overcoming the differences between old and new party members, and now everyone was a convinced Marxist-Leninist. The imperialists and some Trotskyites were trying to profit from Comrade Fidel's definition of himself as a Marxist-Leninist. But those who chose to see Fidel's position as alien to Marxism-Leninism were deceiving themselves. All those who gambled that Castro would not remain a convinced Marxist were mistaken, because Castro was the leader of the ORI, and "the best, the ablest, and the most steadfast Marxist-Leninist in Cuba." Roca insisted that a true Marxist-Leninist not only knew theory but also acted in a revolutionary way, as Marx, Lenin, and Fidel did. Even before he had been a Marxist, Roca said, Fidel had acted like one.[55]

Roca was saying that success had given Castro the right to wear the mantle of Marx and Lenin. History had proved that Castro was right all along and the PSP wrong. Roca abandoned the old PSP position that a revolution was only a revolution if the PSP led it. Now the hero who led the revolution to victory was the first Marxist-Leninist in the country. In 1917 the Mensheviks had charged that the Russian Revolution was not really a socialist revolution because Lenin ignored the teachings of Marx (and his own earlier convictions) by establishing a dictatorship of the party of the proletariat-to-be before the bourgeoisie had completed the industrialization of Russia and created a large proletariat. By ripping the revolution untimely from the womb of history, the Bolsheviks had caused a monster to be born. The Mensheviks stuck to their ideological convictions and passed from the stage of history. By surrendering, the leaders of the PSP won a short reprieve. The ideological spoils belong to the victor. The Bolsheviks who had themselves seized the spoils in 1917 only looked foolish when they tried to deny them to Tito and Mao. Tito and Mao threatened Soviet power; Castro bade fair to augment it. Whom did it profit to deny Castro the laurel wreath?

Roca predicted failure for any new attempts to overthrow the Cuban revolution. The counterrevolutionaries were now universally regarded as servitors of a foreign master. An invasion, whether made under OAS cover or openly conducted by the United States, would be defeated. "We are strong enough—heed my words—strong enough to hold them back and give the solidarity of the socialist camp, with the Soviet Union at its head, time to stop the gendarmes of international reaction . . . once and for all in their mad career."

Roca was repeating the formula of the period before the Bay of Pigs invasion. The Cuban mission was to prevent the U.S. government from toppling the Castro regime in a blitzkrieg. During that time, renewed Soviet threats could force the United States to break off the action or to suffer the consequences of a nuclear war. The expectation seemed to be of a Cuban conventional action creating a pause while Soviet power could be brought to bear. As we shall see, Castro very soon changed this scenario to one in which Cuba would participate in a general nuclear war, thereby placing Cuba in a defensive military alliance as a member that joined in a general war when any member of the alliance, including itself, was attacked. Since this change in the picture of the war very likely coincided with the introduction of missiles into Cuba, we may surmise that the old-time communist leader Roca had not yet been informed of it, but that Raúl Castro's trip to Moscow at the beginning of July was to arrange for installation of the missiles.[56] From the Soviet press one could not have guessed that the momentous decision had been taken.

An article in *Red Star* charged that a counterrevolutionary band in Matanzas had shot at Carlos Rafael Rodríguez's car the year before and on direct orders from Washington had planned the assassination of Fidel Castro, Raúl Castro, Che Guevara, Blas Roca, and others. American aircraft continued to violate Cuban airspace, and the Cuban armed forces stood ready to repulse the counterrevolutionary bands.[57] The article represented nothing new in the Soviet appraisal of the Cuban situation and furnished no clue to changes in the military relationship between Cuba and the Soviet Union. Similarly, a reception at the Cuban Embassy in Moscow produced a reiteration of old themes but no clue to the plans for installing missiles. The senior Soviet official present, Frol Kozlov, replying to a statement of Cuban gratitude for support, addressed the Cuban ambassador as Comrade and stated that Cuba was "certainly going along the path of building socialism." He talked of American provocations but made no mention of the possibility of a direct U.S. attack. And at the end of his statement he repeated that the Soviet warning to the enemies of the Cuban Republic remained in force as of that day[58]—again a reiteration of Soviet commitment to the defense of Cuba without any hint that the means for that defense was being altered. It fell to Castro himself to first reflect the change in a public speech on the anniversary of the storming of the Moncada barracks.[59]

CASTRO HINTS THAT THE MISSILES ARE COMING

Castro said that Cuba had to be able to repel a direct attack from the United States. However, consistent with the generally optimistic tone of Cuban (and Soviet) pronouncements of the last year, Castro did not talk of the imminent danger of attack. "To the extent that the imperialists become convinced that the blockade is failing, that the Revolution is resist-ing . . . to the extent that the situation of the imperialists becomes more desperate, the dangers of the direct aggression of Yankee imperialism against our country will again grow."

The danger of invasion by mercenary bands no longer existed because with the weapons Cuba possessed she could sweep them away. But Cuba had to prepare a defense against a direct invasion in the future. That was the only danger still facing the Cuban revolution. "When our Revolution can say that it is in a position to repulse a direct attack, the last danger hanging over it will have disappeared."

Castro could speak precisely as well as eloquently. His formula for defense against the United States had changed materially. Earlier, Cuban security had depended on the Cuban resolve to fight the United States to the last man. Deprived of the prospect of a quick victory, the earlier promises of the Soviet Union to defend Cuba with missiles, which would, it was hoped, be renewed, would have caused the United States to break off the aggression, as she had done at the Bay of Pigs. But when Cuba would be able to repel a direct attack, the last danger to the revolution would have been removed. Cuba would thus become secure on her own rather than through the agency of the Soviet Union. And in the next sen-tence Castro said Cuba had to take such measures because Kennedy had refused to give assurances that he would not attack Cuba.

Castro then explained how Cuba, despite its size, would be in a posi-tion to say "a direct imperialist attack would be shattered against our defenses." Any war would be a world war. As a member of the progres-sive grouping of powers, Cuba would participate in such a war and be defended by the others subjected to attack. Castro's somewhat repetitious formulations, quoted immediately below, left no room for misinterpreta-tion. "It is evident that our country runs the same risks as progressive humanity. Any war that the imperialists unloose against the progressive nations, they would also unloose against us. . . . Progressive humanity, the humanity that fights for Socialism and National Independence and Peace, has the warmongering Yankees as their common enemy."

The imperialists, Castro insisted, needed the threat of war for their profits. The Soviet Union and the socialist camp had made enormous investments to face this danger. Cuba ran the same danger. "And there-fore we must prepare; not only because we know that imperialism threatens us, not only because Mr. Kennedy, who is a stubborn gentle-man, has the fixed idea of attacking our country, which we know, but also because the world lives under the danger of imperialist aggression, because the progressive nations live under the danger of the war that the imperialists threaten."

The internal evidence suggests strongly that Castro was talking about deterring the United States in a situation when missiles with nuclear warheads would be on Cuban soil. Further evidence of a textual nature is to be found in an interview Castro gave Cyrus Sulzberger of the *New York Times* after the missile crisis was over. When asked whether Cuba had a veto power over the use of the missiles, Castro replied, in a language consistent with, and reminiscent of, his 26 July 1962 speech, that circumstances would have made a disagreement impossible. The missiles based in Cuba could not have been employed independently since they would have been used in a general war in which Cuba participated. The accord with Moscow contained the understanding that by agreement between the two parties, the missiles would defend Cuban territory under attack. Had the conflict arisen outside of Cuba—in Berlin, for instance—and general war ensued, the missiles would have been used.[60] In a later interview Castro explained: "We didn't think about retaliation but regarded the missiles as an effective guarantee against a direct attack implying a dangerous risk for the aggressor. That was our point of view. I also think that from a certain point of view the socialist camp was strengthened. We had expected the Soviet Union to take a chance for us, and we had to be willing to do likewise for them."[61]

Castro's speech of July 1962 and the retrospective interviews are consistent. Castro thought he had an effective nuclear deterrent against a direct U.S. attack and "didn't think about retaliation." We do not know if he was told that there were only a few missiles in the Soviet Union with the range to reach the United States. He may simply have been told that the presence of Soviet missiles on Cuban soil would remove any doubts that the United States might have had about the Soviet resolve to employ them. For the Soviet Union, it meant greater military strength and presumably a better chance of gaining political concessions from the United States in places like Berlin. In his speech, Castro emphasized the contribution that Cuba was making to the defense of the whole socialist camp. Cuba was not merely the recipient of Soviet largesse, but a partner in a program of deterrence against Kennedy. Castro's speech made clear that Kennedy would contemplate an invasion of Cuba only when other alternatives had failed, and by that time the measures that Cuba had taken would have removed this last danger to the revolution.

The available information on U.S. understanding of the crisis does not indicate that anyone noted the altered tone of Castro's statement or drew the appropriate conclusion. The Soviet account of the speech avoided the suggestion that a new element would be added to Cuba's defense that would remove the last danger to the Cuban revolution, thus illustrating the efficiency of Soviet press guidance.[62] The speech had been delivered on 26 July in Santiago; the story was filed there the next day and appeared in *Pravda* on 28 July. The short account of a very long speech clearly conveyed that Cuba had become a sort of associate member of the socialist camp and omitted any reference to the novelty of the speech—

the promise that accessions to Cuba's military strength would remove the last danger that hung over the revolution. Whether the selection and emphasis were accomplished in Cuba or in Moscow or in combination, we do not know. What is clear is that the Soviet press avoided hints of dramatic military changes, whereas Castro did not.

Until the end of August the Soviet press continued to reflect this emphasis, pointing to the failures of the Alliance for Progress and the successes of the guerrilla movements, and soft-pedaling the possibility of a U.S. invasion of Cuba by discussing it only briefly as one of many alternatives. An article in *Pravda* by Joseph North, the American communist, illustrates this treatment.[63] He reported that the Cuban revolution had forced the United States to pay attention to the seething revolutionary activity in all Latin America. Three approaches to the problem existed. The more frantic generals, North said, want "to go there and chase them out." Adlai Stevenson wants to make them fall of their own weight when the embargo and other economic and political measures bear fruit, and Kennedy wants to maintain constant pressure. All these approaches have the same object: the destruction of Cuba, and there is hardly a knucklehead in the Congress who does not ape the example of the Roman senator who ended his speeches by crying "Carthage must be destroyed." But all these plans are doomed to failure. The Alliance for Progress is making no progress. The land problem is not being solved. In Venezuela, Ecuador, and Bolivia guerrilla bands are gaining strength, and in Brazil the peasant unions are becoming stronger and more class conscious. North's general tone was that the United States was making a forced retreat while a few extremists talked of armed action. Invasion of Cuba was not specifically mentioned in the article.

Another article on the failures of the Alliance for Progress furnished information on right-wing plots financed by the United States but also said nothing about a possible invasion of Cuba.[64] American training of special mobile forces to put down revolutions all over Latin America was reported a week later in *Pravda*.[65] The impression that the reader would gain from this reportage was that revolutionary activity was popping out all over Latin America. No suggestion of an invasion of Cuba could be read into these reports.

Another commentary on the somber character of the celebrations of the first anniversary of the Alliance for Progress reported that the U.S. program only wanted the most limited and meaningless reform and that Latin Americans now realized that only the antiimperialist struggle could bring liberation from poverty. No mention was made of what the United States might do in its frustration.[66]

In the last ten days of August the U.S. press began to carry reports about extensive military shipments to Cuba from the Soviet Union. During the week of 14–21 August, fifteen Soviet ships, including five passenger vessels, had arrived in Cuba. Although Cuban exiles in Miami asserted that 5,000 East European and Soviet troops had landed on the island in the previous fortnight, administration specialists thought that these were civilian technicians for industry and agriculture with some military advisors to train Cubans in the use of modern weapons. Cuban defenses, they believed, were being improved, and specialized equipment such as radar was being introduced. But a cautionary note was struck. Technicians were formally greeted at Havana, but some ships were unloaded at night under strict security precautions—the usual system for bringing in military equipment.[67]

A few days later a more alarming report was published. Between three to five thousand technicians were said to have arrived—half of them military personnel. The forty-foot crates that housed the equipment indicated that something other than agricultural machines or household goods was inside. Tarpaulins covered the equipment that the trucks carried away. U.S. intelligence circles did not believe that these troops and and equipment would add significantly to the limited offensive power of Cuban forces, who did not possess the means to leave the island. There was no evidence that troops from the Soviet bloc or nuclear warheads had arrived in Cuba.[68]

On 24 August a Cuban exile group shelled beach-front buildings in the Miramar district of Havana from the sea. The U.S. State Department explained that the raid was a spur-of-the-moment action of which the United States had had no prior knowledge. Earlier, unnamed officials had suggested that the Cuban Navy might have shelled the beach front as a provocation to the United States.[69] After a delay of a few days, the Soviet press carried many stories suggesting that the shelling was the prelude to an American invasion of Cuba. A note of crisis replaced the complacent tone of the prior few months. The first *Pravda* account compared the shelling to the aerial bombardment that had preceeded the Bay of Pigs invasion and noted that the U.S. press was again full of reports about the "communist menace" to the Western Hemisphere. The purpose of these reports, said *Pravda,* was to justify the aggression in preparation. The announcement that the high-ranking General Maxwell Taylor was on an "inspection trip" in the Caribbean was regarded as the overture to serious aggravation of the situation in the Caribbean. "All these facts are not just to set a trap. They call for vigilance. The Cuban people are able to stand up for themselves in the event that the imperialists, with a mailed fist, again try to impose their will on the independent republic."[70]

Another account in the same issue of *Pravda,* quoting the *New York Herald-Tribune,* said that the attack on the beach was part of a general plan for an uprising and an open invitation for adventurers to attack Cuba.[71] *Izvestiia's* account excoriated the hypocrisy of the American officials who professed ignorance about the attack and inability to prevent it; but *Izvestiia* said nothing about an invasion.[72]

Red Star in reporting the events added that in recent months U.S. planes flew over Cuba almost daily. Unlike the other Soviet press organs, *Red Star* noted that the "responsible" press no less than the "yellow" journals was calling for no more and no less than military intervention in Cuba. The pretext was the presence of Soviet, North Korean, Chinese, Congolese, Czech, and Algerian troops in Cuba. Does this series of provocations mean that the United States is preparing another defeat for itself like the one it suffered at the Bay of Pigs, asked *Red Star*.[73] Although *Red Star's* tone was a bit more strident than that of *Pravda* or *Izvestiia*, the new danger in Cuba was still cast in terms of the Bay of Pigs invasion.

In its Spanish broadcasts the Soviet radio gave assurances of support, and warned that Cuba could count on powerful friends when the imperialists were hatching plots and aggression against Cuba.[74] A subsequent commentary on Moscow Radio charged that the United States would try once again to get the OAS to call for complete blockade and military intervention against Cuba.[75]

The Cuban and Soviet press carried the argument one step further, with formulations that would accommodate the presence of new weapons on Cuban soil. *Pravda* quoted *Hoy* as saying that the shelling of the Havana shoreline and the inflammatory statements of some American senators were intended "to create the psychological atmosphere required for loosing the direct aggression against Cuba that they had prepared . . . The assertion that any strengthening of the defense of Cuba would constitute a danger for the United States or any other neighboring countries is the height of hypocrisy. Cuba threatened no one. It has had to improve its armed forces in order to defend itself from constant threats of aggression on the part of the United States. Cuba is obliged to take all necessary measures to guarantee its peaceful life and the security of its people and to defend its independence and sovereignty."[76]

The sentiments expressed were unexceptionable. Any state had the right to acquire arms and to defend itself. Hindsight suggests, however, that a campaign to justify the presence of missiles in Cuba had begun.

Almost simultaneously with the campaign in the Soviet press to present the United States as being on the point of reinvading Cuba, President Kennedy was answering questions about Cuba in a press conference. Senator Capehart had called for an invasion of Cuba, charging that Soviet troops, not merely technicians, had been sent to Cuba. Kennedy denied that the United States had information of Soviet troops in Cuba and rejected the advice to invade Cuba. "An action like that which can be very casually suggested could lead to very serious consequences for many people."[77]

Kennedy's restraint was not to survive the information that ballistic missiles had been emplaced in Cuba. In Cuba, for the first time in a year, Blas Roca talked of the danger to the peace of the world because of U.S. plans against Cuba, but he viewed these efforts serenely because he was completely convinced of the victory of the Cuban revolution.[78] The next day an official Soviet communiqué revealed that from 27 August through 2 September a delegation of the leadership of the Integrated Revolutionary Organizations of Cuba had conferred with Khrushchev and other Soviet leaders on a number of international questions. Both the ORI officials named, Comrades Ernesto Guevara and Emilia Aragonés, had been members of the 26th of July Movement component of the new ORI. They discussed Soviet aid to Cuban agriculture and industry. The communiqué also explained that imperialist threats to Cuba had moved that country to request from the USSR new weapons and the appropriate technical specialists to train Cuban personnel. The Cuban Republic had the right to adopt the necessary measures to defend its independence, and all the genuine friends of Cuba had the right to help her in this effort.[79] Now the position that Soviet press accounts had been preparing in recent weeks was officially formulated. Cuba was under threat. She had the right to request and the Soviet Union had the right to send military equipment to Cuba and to provide personnel to train Cubans in its use.

On 29 August, U–2s had photographed eight SAM–2 sites, the SAM–2 being the ground-to-air missile that had downed a U–2 in the Soviet Union on 1 May 1962. This knowledge within the U.S. government and the uproar in the Congress about the Soviet-Cuban military communiqué of 2 September put the Cuban problem on the front pages of American newspapers. Through private channels, Khrushchev gave Kennedy misleading assurances about the nature of the build up in Cuba and simultaneously held out prospects for negotiations at a time most favorable for Kennedy. On 4 September the Soviet ambassador in Washington met the president's brother, Attorney General Robert Kennedy, and transmitted a message for the president that he said he was authorized to deliver only through Robert. It indicated that the Soviet Union would not create trouble for the United States in Berlin or Southeast Asia during the election campaign. When Robert Kennedy pressed him on Cuba, Anatoly Dobrynin was reassuring, saying that his government did not propose to place in the hands of a third party the power to involve the Soviet Union in a thermonuclear war. Dobrynin was technically correct. The control of the missiles remained in Soviet hands, but Dobrynin's message invited the conclusion that the Soviet Union was not installing missiles in Cuba.[80]

Far from being mollified, the president issued a statement on the same day revealing that the Soviet effort to reassure him had backfired, that his suspicions had been aroused but not yet confirmed. He said there was no doubt that the Soviet Union had provided Cuba with a number of anti-aircraft defense missiles, that is, ground-to-air missiles, and about 3,500 Soviet military technicians were either in or en route to Cuba. This number was consistent with the mission of setting up the equipment and training the Cubans in its employment. But, said the presidential statement, there was no evidence of an organized combat force in Cuba or of offensive ground-to-ground missiles "or of other significant offensive capability either in Cuban hands or under Soviet direction and guidance."

Were it to be otherwise, the gravest issues would arise. The Cuban question must be considered as part of the worldwide Communist challenge posed by Communist threats to the peace. It must be dealt with as a part of the larger issue as well as in the context of the special relationships which have long characterized the inter-American system.

It continues to be the policy of the United States that the Castro regime will not be allowed to export its aggressive purposes by force or threat of force. It will be prevented by whatever means may be necessary from taking action against any part of the Western Hemisphere.[81]

The statement was somewhat elliptical. If the promotion of revolution in other Latin American countries was meant by the phrase "to export its aggressive purposes," it was difficult to see how the presence of ground-to-ground missiles in Cuba would further revolution elsewhere. But the warning was clear: if ground-to-ground missiles, or other significant capability for offensive action, were located in Cuba the gravest issue would arise—a threat to peace. The United States would resist the shift in the balance of power represented by the presence of ground-to-ground missiles in Cuba.

At this point the Cuban missile crisis can be said to have begun its final phase. The U.S. president had made clear *what* his country would find unacceptable, but he was no clearer than he had ever been or was to be on *why* it was unacceptable. If the island of Cuba were to contain ground-to-ground missiles or any other significant offensive capability, "the gravest issues would arise." The president was committing himself and his country to do something—what was not said—but the implication was that the action would be appropriate to the threat of offensive weapons on Cuban soil. Why would it be a threat? Offensive weapons on Cuban soil had "to be considered as part of a worldwide challenge posed by the communist threat to peace." The communist threat to peace was presented as self-evident. The communists had designs on the Free World, which defended peace, and a significant shift in the balance of power would furnish an opportunity for the communists to threaten the Free World and, therefore, peace. A corollary of this belief was the conviction that the Castro regime desired "to export its aggressive purposes" and that ground-to-ground missiles on Cuban soil would further such purposes. The connection between ballistic missiles and/or bombers on Cuban soil and a communist regime in Venezuela or Brazil was not specified, but again the missing assumptions had been voiced frequently enough to be easily supplied. Nations with serious internal political and economic problems were prone to join forces with the power grouping that seemed to be in the ascendant, and a significant shift in the military balance of power would make the communist camp seem to be in the ascendant.

The Soviet and Cuban positions shared many of these assumptions, but differed in designating the forces of light and darkness. For the Soviet Union and Cuba the capitalist powers, especially the United States, were the threat to peace, and therefore a shift in the balance of military power in favor of the communist states would help preserve peace. To the Cuban revolutionary leaders and their friends, Cuba was the Island of Freedom, and the replication of Cuba's system elsewhere in Latin America would be a victory of freedom over tyranny. The U.S. and the Soviet-Cuban positions were irreconcilable, and comprehension of the crisis is not furthered by choosing between them. To understand what happened it is better to assume that each side believed what it professed than to assume that one side meant what it had said and the other did not. The two opposing positions had already been well defined and their reiteration alone would not have caused a crisis. The novelty was Kennedy's determination, publicly announced, to prevent the installation of ground-to-ground missiles in Cuba or to cause their removal. The two powers now confronted each other; they would collide unless one retreated.

6. KHRUSHCHEV TAKES THE MISSILES AWAY FROM CUBA

The crisis caused by the installation of ground-to-ground ballistic missiles in Cuba, and President Kennedy's demand that they be removed, was ultimately resolved by the removal of the missiles and a tacit agreement that the United States would not invade Cuba. In the analysis to follow the separate Soviet strategies will be differentiated. The starkness of the alternatives before the Soviet leaders not unexpectedly produced sharply contrasting assessments of the situation and contrary strategies for extrication from the impasse. Counsel is probably divided on most important Soviet decisions, but confirmatory evidence for that assumption is not always available, as in this case. But before embarking on the analysis it might be useful to indicate its limitations. These are best illustrated if we consider briefly the interpretations of U.S. behavior, for which the material is incomparably richer. The literature on American actions in the crisis has concentrated on several crucial questions.

Did Kennedy believe that missiles in Cuba were a troublesome development but that Soviet acquisition of nuclear parity was inevitable in any case? Did he precipitate the crisis in spite of this belief because he thought his domestic opponents could and would impeach him on the basis that he had jeopardized U.S. security?

Did Kennedy believe that the missiles in Cuba threatened U.S. security? His advisors were divided and he himself appears to have modified his position after the event when he emphasized that the appearance of power was as important as its reality. Are the Soviet critics right who said, and presumably still say, that the missiles in Cuba made no difference militarily or politically because Soviet and Cuban intentions were pacific, and, most important, that Kennedy knew this to be the case? Are Kennedy's right-wing critics correct in saying that the missiles gave the Soviet Union a reasonable chance of a successful first strike, especially against the still important air elements of the nuclear force and, most important, that Kennedy knew this to be the case?

Did Kennedy believe that the danger of nuclear war was substantial? His former associates say that he worried a great deal about the possibility of a nuclear war but that he bravely grasped the nettle of danger to pluck the flower of safety. Some critics claim that his fear of nuclear war was within narrow boundaries, that he had absorbed the impact of the revised intelligence estimates, that he knew Khrushchev was a braggart and not a desperate gambler prepared to play Russian roulette. In this version Kennedy emphasized the risks of nuclear war in order to isolate his opponents within the administration and justify the concessions he was prepared to make.

Was Kennedy in control? His former associates and his critics on the right are in agreement that there was a struggle between the Joint Chiefs of Staff and the president's more hawkish advisors on the one side, and the president himself and his more moderate advisors on the other. They disagree on which course was wiser, but agree that counsel was divided. The critics on the left dismiss these differences as irrelevant, arguing that the president was willing to follow his most venturesome advisors in the end and that only Khrushchev's retreat saved the day.

These are not merely rhetorical questions to set the stage for the triumphant revelation of the correct answer. In a sense the answer to each of the questions posed above is yes. Kennedy was reacting to his domestic critics, but he had accepted the cogency of some of their case. He believed that missiles in Cuba threatened American security, but at different times he talked, and very likely felt, differently about the immediacy and directness of the threat. Kennedy worried about the danger of nuclear war, but he also used that worry to cause his opponents within the administration to accept his version of the best course to follow. Kennedy was his own man, but he did accommodate in form and in substance to his opponents within the administration and in the Congress. Different writers have attempted to resolve and will resolve the questions in different ways, but it is as unlikely that we will have an agreed version of the missile crisis as it is that we will have an agreed version of the causes of World War I. The primary duty of the historian is to pose the right questions; his particular answers are of secondary importance. Historians should permit readers to come to different conclusions.

Before proceeding to an account of Soviet and Cuban behavior in the crisis, the major questions and hypotheses will be set forth. The basic assumption is that the Soviet Union and Cuba had not a single goal but several. The Soviet Union and Cuba, considered as entities, had different purposes; different governmental and party groupings in the Soviet Union had different goals or assigned different priorities among common goals. These differing goals sometimes reflected the bureaucratic functions of their sponsors; sometimes their personal preferences. Some groups or individuals had maximal and minimal goals, and they differed on the feasibility and cost of these goals. Thus the ruling group was divided, the subgroups into which it was divided were also divided, and many individuals were of two minds. When success seemed likely, the cluster of compromises that constituted Soviet policy promised enough for each group to keep them all together. When the scheme seemed doomed to failure, the consensus disappeared only to be reformed on a new basis: a program to ward off the greatest dangers and to save some minimal goals. These assumptions about state and group behavior are at least as old as Thucydides, but they are reviewed to put the questions forward while promising only partial answers.

The various assumptions and questions about Soviet behavior in the missile crisis are now set down all together even though some have already been advanced. These will be followed by an account of the crisis and an analysis of Soviet communications during the crisis.

WHY WERE THE MISSILES PUT INTO CUBA?

1. *To improve the Soviet position in the nuclear weapons balance.* Whether the purpose was to defend what was held or to gain what was wanted, it was better to be stronger than weaker. At one time the United States had conducted its policies from "a position of strength." Now the Soviet Union would be able to do the same. Although the Soviet Union could not hope to pursue its goals from a position of exclusive nuclear strength, a contest between two nuclear powers promised a better outcome than a contest between a nuclear and a nonnuclear power. If the United States had been able to establish overseas bases near the Soviet Union with impunity, because it was strong, the Soviet Union now that it was also strong could do the same. Because of its years-long propaganda against American bases, the Soviet Union avoided calling overseas military installations under its control bases, but its claim to equality with the United States in this regard was nevertheless unmistakable. Khrushchev had been trying to draw political checks on a nonexistent or very small account of missiles that could reach the United States. Missiles in Cuba would make the checks good.

2. *To protect Cuba and other progressive regimes.* As the balance of power shifted, the missiles in Cuba being a significant element in the accretion of Soviet power, the costs and risks of U.S. intervention against regimes that were anti-imperialist and moving towards socialism would rise. The natural historical movement of countries from imperialist control to association, and eventually partnership, with socialist countries could proceed shielded by Soviet power. In Soviet language, "the export of counterrevolution would be embargoed."

3. *To deter a direct U.S. attack on Cuba by making Soviet response to such an attack "automatic."* Technically, missiles in Omsk had the same deterrent effect on the United States as missiles in Cuba. But the United States had insisted that missiles in Omaha plus missiles in Europe or Turkey increased the credibility of the deterrent; or in plain language, if American soldiers in Turkey were killed and American weapons in

Turkey were destroyed, it was easier to believe that the United States would strike than if no Americans had been killed and no U.S. military installations destroyed. Following the American model, the Soviet Union gave hostages of blood and treasure to its client. In 1962 the Soviet Union had no choice but to make its own men and weapons hostage, because a significant nuclear capacity depended on their presence nearer to the United States. For a long time the United States had been a prisoner of the same necessity, and it was only beginning to shift its dependence to weapons that could be dispatched to the Soviet Union directly from American soil.

4. *To improve the Soviet position in Europe, particularly in Berlin.* This objective is really part of the first goal but deserves special mention because it figured so largely in American fears and because the Soviet Union never availed itself of the easy opportunity to harass the Western powers in Berlin.

5. *To provide a platform of greater strength and prestige from which to assert leadership over other socialist countries, most notably China.* Ordinary nationalism would explain a desire to keep the Chinese from claiming a share of the leadership of the world communist movement on the ground that the Soviet Union was bungling matters. To this was added the sensitivity to the Chinese charge that the Russians were poor Marxists. Soviet withdrawal of political support to China in 1959 when the USSR adopted a position of neutrality on the Sino-Indian border dispute, and Soviet withdrawal of economic support in the summer of 1960 when the USSR withdrew engineers monitoring technical assistance projects gave the Chinese no further reason to mollify the Soviet Union by following its advice. Presumably a great Soviet victory in Cuba, and resultant gains elsewhere, would force the Chinese to accept Soviet leadership again. The historian of Soviet foreign policy, Adam Ulam, has even speculated that Khrushchev hoped to prevail on the Chinese to surrender their rights to an independent nuclear capacity.

HOW WERE THE MISSILES IN CUBA TO BE USED TO GET WHAT THE SOVIET UNION WANTED?

1. *The United States would have no choice but to accept the missiles in Cuba but would do so only after noisy protests and a crisis.* Soviet employment of its new military strength was to be the mirror of U.S. employment of its military strength when it was preponderant. The Soviet Union had protested bitterly when the United States established or strengthened overseas military bases and had held its ground for a time in the crises that ensued, only to quit and leave the United States in political control of the areas where its military forces had been ensconced (e.g., West Berlin, the Formosa Straits). Now it was the turn of the

United States to attempt to drive the Soviet Union from an established military position with noise and threats. If the Soviet Union stood firm, the sober-minded leaders in the United States would prevail over the hot-heads (as perhaps they had in the Soviet Union). In the end, the United States would have no choice, because neither Cuba nor West Berlin was worth the risk of a nuclear war. What was new was that now the United States was in the same situation the Soviet Union had been in for many years. It either had to accept the opponent's military, economic, and political presence in a country or seek to dislodge him by force, thereby risking the consequences of nuclear war on its own territory. Why should the United States behave any differently than the Soviet Union in analogous circumstances?

The text to follow has been provided by John Foster Dulles in his article in *Life:* "The ability to get to the verge [of war] without getting into war is the necessary art. If you are scared to go to the brink you are lost."[1] The advocates of brinksmanship never envisage the necessity of having to climb down themselves. The art of brinksmanship is to select eminently defensible situations on which to take a stand. Following such a counsel in October 1954 Dulles quickly surrendered the field in Budapest, where the United States could not hope to match the Soviet Union in a contest of local military forces, but he stood firm in the Formosa Straits, where the United States enjoyed strategic and tactical superiority over China. The brinksman can only hold firm as the crisis mounts in danger and intensity, or quit. Negotiation cannot resolve the crisis, it can only seal the opponent's retreat after he has acknowledged defeat. Publicity is the helpmeet of the Soviet brinksmen because some domestic opinion and also allies whose vital interests were not involved put pressure on the United States to compromise.

2. *The United States would soon recognize that it had no choices and would retreat under face-saving formulas to be presented after a summit meeting.* The text for this mode of exploiting strength has been provided by Belisarius, who said that a wise general builds a golden bridge for his enemy to retreat over. Kennedy would be allowed to present the acceptance of missiles in Cuba, and perhaps other Soviet demands, as a victory for peace instead of a humiliating retreat before superior force.

3. *The United States would obdurately resist and would maintain a crisis atmosphere. The crisis would finally issue in a compromise: the Soviet Union would withdraw its missiles and the United States would recognize the Castro regime—the bargaining-counter strategy.* It was possible to be an advocate of the golden bridge strategy and to envisage the necessity of falling back to a strategy of mutual concessions. It was unlikely that brinksmen could entertain the bargaining-counter strategy even as a reserve position. If the United States shrank from the brink and retreated, there was no reason to reward it afterwards. Why surrender

some of the spoils of victory to a defeated enemy? If the Soviet Union shrank from the danger and retreated with its missiles, why should the United States reward the defeated opponent? Brinksmen, committed as they are to the proposition that "it cannot fail," cannot contemplate other alternatives without weakening the belief that the opponent must retreat. The "bargaining-counter strategy" was probably not entertained by the brinksmen before the crisis, but it could have been a fallback strategy after it erupted.

4. *The presence of the missiles in Cuba was to be kept secret until after the U.S. Congressional elections and until the installation had been completed—two events which were expected to be virtually simultaneous.* Keeping the presence of the missiles secret until after the elections supported all three strategies for the political employment of this accession to Soviet military strength. If the brinksmanship strategy was preferred, it was best to confront the United States suddenly with this awesome strength, presumably deriving advantages thereby from shock and surprise. If the golden bridge strategy was preferred, the advantages of shock and surprise were not to be discarded, but Kennedy would find it easier to retreat if the elections were behind him and if his domestic opponents did not have incontrovertible knowledge of the presence of the missiles. However, if it was impossible to prevent the discovery and revelation of the presence of the missiles before the negotiated U.S. retreat, it would be desirable to postpone the discovery or the revelation until after the election.

The Kennedy administration might well be a tacit ally of the USSR in this purpose. It could keep the intelligence material secret; if the information seeped from the intelligence community to the congressional opponents of the president, the president could insist on irrefutable proof. It was presumably in the president's interest to do this, because a postelection concession to the Soviet Union's new strength would entail a smaller domestic cost than a preelection concession. In a preelection crisis where no favorable outcome for the United States could be credibly predicted the domestic political costs for Kennedy would have been higher. It was also in the Soviet interest to preserve the internal political strength of a U.S. president who was willing to accommodate to Soviet political demands and to present the accommodation as a victory for the golden bridge strategy over the brinksmanship strategy. A possible cost of the brinksmanship strategy was the electoral victory in 1962 or 1964 of the American hard-liners.

Premature *discovery* of the presence of the missiles weakened all three alternative strategies. All three strategies would have been further weakened by premature *publicity* about that presence, but only the golden bridge strategy and the bargaining-counter strategy would have suffered fatal damage. All three strategies would have benefited from the postponement of discovery until the missile siting had been accomplished, since shock and surprise would presumably have softened the Americans for defeat, whatever form it was to take. But once the American ruling circles had discovered that the missiles were in place, the timing of the publication of the knowledge would not much affect the brinksmanship strategy, which assumed that all elements in American political life would have to bow to force majeure.

But Kennedy's domestic opponents, in possession of incontrovertible proof of the presence of missiles in Cuba, could force Kennedy to refuse to parley, thus preventing the negotiation of a face-saving retreat or the withdrawal of the missiles in exchange for the recognition of the Cuban regime. As it turned out Kennedy anticipated his domestic opposition, announced the presence of the missiles, and excluded a negotiated retreat or an exchange. After depriving his domestic opponents of their best ammunition by adopting their policy, he then proceeded to negotiate a compromise that became a tacit agreement when Castro vetoed the inspection arrangements that were part of the compromise. It is most unlikely that the Soviet leaders foresaw that events would unfold in this fashion, but the advocates of the golden bridge strategy and the bargaining-counter strategy quite probably realized that a private negotiation after the elections served their purpose best.

The golden bridge builders faced a dilemma. They had to let Kennedy know early on that they were willing to ease his retreat so that he could negotiate without pressures from his domestic opponents in order to retain him as an ally in keeping the presence of the missiles a secret. But dropping hints of readiness to ease Kennedy's retreat risked not only advancing the date of discovery but also alerting Kennedy's opponents to the necessity of forcing the president to deny the intention to make any concessions. The Soviet Union failed to alert Kennedy to the possibility of a negotiated compromise, and his domestic opposition succeeded for a time in having him exclude the option the Soviet Union favored.

5. *Should the Soviet Union interfere with U.S. reconnaissance over Cuba?* In fact Soviet surface-to-air missiles did not interfere with American U-2 reconnaissance until 27 October, after Khrushchev had offered a compromise on minimal terms—the withdrawal of the missiles in exchange for U.S. recognition of Cuba. An important fact in judging Soviet strategy is not available. It is not known if the Soviet forces refrained from shooting down the American U-2 until the crisis was well advanced or whether they were unable to do so until that time. However, the discussion immediately following will proceed on the assumption that the Soviet Union deliberately refrained from shooting down a U-2 until 27 October.

U-2 reconnaissance had been taking place off and on for months, and Soviet interference would have alerted the United States to the possibility that now there was something to hide. Passive concealment measures were effective in hiding just what was being moved to various sites but could hardly be expected to conceal what was being installed. The landscape suffers extensive interference in a quite familiar way. The access roads, launching pads, and storage sites are distinctive, and the pattern for air fields, surface-to-air missile sites, and ballistic missile sites are quite different. After construction, camouflage holds out some hopes for concealment, but during construction only the prevention of reconnaissance provides reliable security.

Discovery had to take place sooner or later, but the possibility of premature publicity would increase with the shooting down of a U–2, doing a disservice to the proponents of the golden bridge strategy and not helping the brinksmen much, either. In recent history, Khrushchev's high hopes for Eisenhower's acquiescence to the Soviet point of view at the Paris summit had foundered because of the U–2 incident. In the view of suspicious Soviet leaders who favored the golden bridge strategy, Americans could have introduced the U–2 aircraft into Cuban airspace to provoke the Soviets into shooting them down, thus acting against their own interests. However, when Khrushchev abandoned all but his minimal objectives, the consensus produced by a policy that promised to satisfy the objectives of all parties disappeared, and the advocates of brinksmanship may have shot down the U–2 to give their policy more time to succeed.

The brinksmen had never considered Kennedy as a tacit ally, but only as an opponent to be frightened into submission; the would-be builders of the golden bridge had already lost him as a partner in their program, thus losing their policies. One can only speculate that some of them moved into the brinksmen camp, but obviously the majority, including Khrushchev, decided to abandon the missiles in return for acceptance by the United States of the Cuban regime. Now there were only two Soviet factions, the brinksmen and the compromisers, and shooting down the U–2 served the interests of the brinksmen only.

HOW DID THE SOVIET LEADERS BEHAVE DURING THE MISSILE CRISIS?

1. *Were Soviet leaders surprised at the discovery of the missiles?* They knew that the missiles would probably be discovered before Khrushchev's planned trip to the United States after the November elections (of which more later); if not, they would have had to be disclosed privately if the golden bridge or the bargaining-counter strategy was to be followed, and probably publicly if the brinksmanship strategy was to be followed.

2. *How did the Soviet leaders respond to Kennedy's treatment of the discovery?* The brinksmen had expected Kennedy to kick and scream a

bit before surrendering. Khrushchev was not yet ready to surrender the hope that Kennedy, having said *a, b,* and *c,* would have to say *z.* The Soviet reply to the Kennedy speech was prompt essentially reiterating the arguments that the Soviet Union had made publicly for many months but soft-pedaling the threat against American positions overseas.

3. *How did the Soviet leaders respond to Kennedy's threat to go beyond the quarantine on Soviet shipping to an attack on Cuba if his conditions were not met?* It is striking that the Soviet Union did not do what it so many times had threatened to do: take measures against U.S. allies on or near its own borders similar to the actions taken against Cuba. The instrumentalities for pressure on West Berlin had been used many times. One explanation is that Khrushchev, who was so convinced that the Kennedy who had broken off the invasion at the Bay of Pigs would be easily intimidated when the Soviet Union was stronger, now swung from one extreme to the other and was afraid to apply the pressures he had threatened in the past. It says something for the relationship of forces within the Politbureau that such measures were never adopted; perhaps the minority faction sought to have its way by taking independent action. Such attempts to force the hand of the first secretary had occurred before, and will be dealt with shortly.

A few remarks about the utility of these questions and propositions about Soviet purposes and behavior are in order. The questions about the Soviets in the missile crisis are much vaguer than questions about the Americans because the data that has stimulated them is so scanty. By contrast, the material for the American side of the crisis, while still incomplete, yields the important questions. The historian can go to work. Future histories, like the already extant accounts, will be based on a more or less commonly accepted body of fact; the interpretations, that is to say, the values of the historians, will differ. Some believe that the preservation of American power justified the risk of nuclear war and that, indeed, only luck saved Kennedy from the risks he incurred through excessive caution. Others believe that to incur a finite risk of a world nuclear war was criminally irresponsible, that no balance-of-power considerations could justify that risk. Such judgments are the stuff of history. The material is not yet at hand for an adequate history of the Soviet side of the crisis; only an essay in history is possible. We do not even know what the right questions are.

More data could make some questions about Soviet motives and behavior irrelevant. If we should learn, for example, that the U-2 was shot down over Cuba by a trigger-happy Soviet commander exceeding his orders, some hypotheses would collapse. If we learned, however, that SAM-2 missiles were not operational until 27 October, we still would not be able to accept or reject the supposition that shooting down the U-2 was the action of only a part of the Soviet ruling group. Guessing, more or less educated, is inescapable in making judgments about some of the more interesting events in human history. In the pages that follow we shall try to separate conjecture, plausible explanations, and well-grounded hypotheses. We shall do this against a background of the beliefs and aims of the Soviet leadership, i.e., the furnishings of their minds on which the material is most abundant. We probably know most of what we will ever know about the beliefs and ambitions of Soviet leaders in 1962. Hypotheses on Soviet behavior during the missile crisis are more or less plausible as they are consistent or inconsistent with our available knowledge of Soviet political beliefs.

THE EVE OF CRISIS

To return to the account of the final phase of the crisis. On 4 September, President Kennedy announced that he would not accept ground-to-ground missiles in Cuba and refused to negotiate about them. Dobrynin arranged an appointment with the president's confidant Theodore C. Sorensen and read him a personal message from Chairman Khrushchev, on which Sorensen took the following notes for the president: "Nothing will be undertaken before the American Congressional elections that could complicate the international situation or aggravate the tension in the relations between our two countries . . . provided there are no actions taken on the other side which would change the situation . . . If the necessity arises for [the Chairman to address the United Nations], this would be possible only in the second half of November. The Chairman does not wish to become involved in your internal political affairs."[2]

This message could be read to mean that the Soviet Union promised to save unpleasant surprises for the United States until after the election, but it could also be read to hint that when Kennedy discovered the presence of the missiles, if he had not already done so, he could discuss them with Khrushchev personally and privately after the election.

Sorensen protested that Soviet arms shipments to Cuba had already caused turmoil in American internal political affairs. Dobrynin promised to report Sorensen's remarks fully to Khrushchev and while neither contradicting nor confirming Sorensen's references to Soviet personnel and equipment in Cuba, repeated several times that they had done nothing new nor extraordinary in Cuba and "he stood by his assurances that all these steps were defensive in nature and did not represent any threat to the security of the United States."[3]

Pravda's reply to Kennedy's statement, which appeared as Dobrynin was talking to Sorensen, encouraged the belief that there were no ground-to-ground missiles in Cuba by repeating that part of Kennedy's statement that said the United States had no indication of the presence of such missiles. It then dealt with Kennedy's charge that peace was in jeopardy by saying that his assertions that Cuba planned to export her aggressive purposes were unproven. The *Pravda* report failed to indicate that Kennedy had linked his warning to the presence in Cuba of ground-to-ground missiles or other equipment with an offensive capability. From the *Pravda* account alone it would have seemed that Kennedy had said that Cuba had no military equipment that could be employed for offensive purposes and that "it follows from the text of President Kennedy's statement . . . that the measures adopted by Cuba has not an aggressive but a defensive character." And yet Kennedy talked in a menacing tone of adopting whatever measures were necessary to foil Cuban actions against any part of the Western Hemisphere.[4]

Red Star was quoted by *Hoy* as saying that the measures Cuba had taken were strictly defensive and that Cuba would not have to fight alone.[5] Some members of the U.S. Congress, like Representative Craig Hosmer, were calling hysterically for immediate action and recommending a blockade of Cuba.[6] The United States was willing to violate international law and to blockade Cuba reported *Pravda* the next day.[7]

The Cubans took Kennedy's warning and the congressional calls for an embargo quite calmly. President Dorticós, in a speech on 8 September, said that he read the news dispatches from the United States with a smile and that these threats did not cost him any sleep. The United States was trying to deprive Cubans of the means to defend themselves. The recent Cuban-Soviet communiqué had furnished the proper answer. Cuba had the right to acquire any means necessary for her defense and had indeed improved her military capacity. The United States was not really afraid of the Cuban weapons but of the example of the Cuban revolution. Although Kennedy had called up 150,000 reservists, the Cubans were unafraid.[8]

Izvestiia reported that right-wing congressmen and senators were calling for the recognition of a Cuban government in exile and for an armed invasion of Cuba. Kennedy's quick response in calling up 150,000 reservists so soon after his press conference statement of 29 August, in which he had said that the United States was not preparing to invade Cuba, shows how heavy the pressure of those desiring new adventures in Cuba was. "The decision of the White House to call up the reserves to active duty shows that the plans for the organization of a new intervention in Cuban affairs have entered the phase of execution."[9]

But Castro took this threat calmly. He said that if Cuba, which was only ninety miles away from the United States was a danger to the United States, then the United States, which was only ninety miles away from Cuba, was a danger to Cuba. Every step that the United States had taken thus far against Cuba had failed. "We don't want them to take the desperate and stupid step of invading us. The story of the shark and the sardine no longer applies. We are not sardines. And let the shark not make a mistake, because this time that mistake could be his last. . . . We have said on other occasions that we don't want imperialism to commit suicide at our expense."[10] Castro expected that when the presence of missiles on Cuban soil become known, the United States would not let itself be destroyed by making war. He was only anticipating slightly the formal Soviet government position of 11 September 1962 on the Cuban crisis in which the theme of a possible world war was prominently revived.

THE TASS 11 SEPTEMBER STATEMENT

The TASS statement of 11 September 1962 differed in several significant ways from the earlier warnings.[11] As it had done after the Bay of Pigs invasion, the Soviet Union now said that it would (not could) employ nuclear weapons if Cuba was attacked. It will be recalled that on several occasions Soviet officials had stated that the earlier warning remained in force, without repeating the content of the warning. In keeping with its low-key handling of the threat to the United States, the Soviet press had not repeated the formulation made by Castro in his 26 July speech of an automatic nuclear response to an attack. Since the Soviet press had minimized the likelihood of a direct U.S. attack on Cuba, it had not been necessary to repeat the words of the warning, but it was pronounced to be still in force. When U.S. reports of Soviet weapons shipments during August heated up the atmosphere, and Kennedy threatened to take strong measures if what he defined as offensive weapons were introduced into Cuba, the Soviet Union repeated the warning but kept from the Soviet public the fact that missiles in Cuba now backed up the threat.

In the second paragraph of the very long statement the United States was accused of provocations that might plunge the world into the catastrophe of a universal world nuclear war. Trouble was being fomented by a propaganda campaign in Congress and in the press for an attack on Cuba and an attack on Soviet ships carrying necessary commodities and food to the Cuban people. At first the Soviet government did not attach special importance to this campaign against peace, believing that the clamor had been raised as part of the contest between Republicans and Democrats before the congressional elections. "During the many years of coexistence with the United States we have become accustomed to this kind of unholy uproar and therefore we did not attribute particular importance to it."

On 15 May 1962 Khrushchev had referred in a speech, which appeared in the Soviet press in a cleaned-up version, to the exchange of threats as a sort of ritualistic muscle-flexing signifying a stand-off rather than as a genuine threat of war. As often happened, his extemporaneous remarks expressed his feelings more cogently, if less elegantly, than formal statements. He argued that the international situation was good even though political struggles that caused higher or lower tension were a constant feature of the scene. Struggle would only cease when the proletariat held power the world over. Yet the situation was good. "They frighten us with war, and we frighten them back, bit by bit. They threaten us with nuclear arms and we tell them. 'Listen, now only fools can do this, because we have them too. . . . So why do foolish things and [try to] frighten us?' This is the situation and this is why we consider the situation to be good."[12]

The balance of terror was not all that terrible, Khrushchev had said in May. Analysis of the 11 September TASS statement reveals that the mood persisted. On 11 September the Soviet Union was "frightening them back bit by bit." Only later was the mood to change.

But now these American provocations could not be ignored, the TASS statement of 11 September continued, because Kennedy had called up 150,000 reserves on the ground that the United States had to have the capacity to respond promptly and effectively to dangers in any part of the world and had linked the call-up to the shipment of arms to Cuba. This request was just a cover-up for the aggressive plans and intentions of the United States. The American imperialists were trying to justify their action by the aggravation of tension. But compared to a year, even two years ago, no special changes could be identified. Therefore, the American purpose was to increase tension. As U.S. congressmen and the press had confessed, it was not Soviet or Cuban action that had upset them but the failure of their economic blockade.

But the statement went on to say that blockade and intervention would fail in Cuba as they had failed in Russia during the first years of the revolution. The supposed basis for the unholy uproar in the United States was the dispatch of weapons and troops. But in fact the United States was frightened of its own shadow because it did not believe in the future of the capitalist system. The Soviet Union could send whatever it pleased to Cuba in its ships, and the United States could keep its nose out of Soviet business.

The 11 September statement first gave the reasons for the shipment of Soviet arms and the dispatch of Soviet military personnel to Cuba, saying that they did not constitute any danger to the United States or to peace, and then sought to create the impression (without actually saying so) that the arms were not nuclear missiles. The Soviet government had supplied Cuba, at her request, with a certain quantity of weapons because she had been threatened. "The arms and military equipment delivered to Cuba are exclusively designated for defensive purposes. . . . Can these means really threaten the United States of America? . . . You have invented this threat yourselves and now you want to persuade others of its existence." If the United States is not preparing to attack Cuba as the president states, the statement went on, "the means of defense that Cuba is acquiring will not be employed, because the necessity for their employment arises only in the event of aggression against Cuba."[13]

At this point the statement departed from what was probably an accurate reflection of Soviet beliefs and sought to mislead the American leadership. One can accept as genuine the Soviet belief that more powerful weapons on Cuban soil meant more reliable deterrence of the United States, but the Soviet leaders knew that the missiles in Cuba were not what these words suggest: "The government of the Soviet Union also authorized TASS to state that the Soviet Union does not have to transfer to any other country, Cuba for example, the means it possesses for the repulsion of aggression, for a retaliatory blow. Our nuclear means are of such powerful explosive force, and the Soviet Union possesses missile vehicles for these nuclear warheads of such power that there is no need to search for places to site them anywhere outside of the Soviet Union."

Technically, a statement that the Soviet Union did not have to place missiles outside the Soviet Union did not necessarily mean that she was not doing so. But the intention was to mislead. The next sentences repeated and expanded the Soviet commitment to use nuclear weapons in the defense of Cuba, but the context is that readiness to employ force obviates the need to do so. "We have said and we repeat that if war is unloosed, if the United States perpetrates an attack on one or another state and that state requests assistance, the Soviet Union has the capacity to render assistance from its own territory to any peace-loving state, not only to Cuba. And let no one doubt that the Soviet Union will render such assistance just as it was ready to render military aid to Egypt in 1956 at the time of the Anglo-French-Israeli aggression in the Suez Canal region."

The statement reemphasized the contrived nature of the war scare by contrasting Marshal Malinovskii's release of servicemen who had completed their term of service with Kennedy's call up of the reserves. Calling up reserves in the nuclear age was a meaningless gesture. "But at a moment when the USA is taking measures to mobilize its armed forces and is preparing aggression against Cuba and other peace-loving states, the Soviet Union would like to draw attention to the fact that now it is impossible for an aggressor to attack Cuba and count on the attack going unpunished. If such an attack is made, it will begin the unloosing of war."

Although the threat expressed in the last sentence quoted was unequivocal, the context and tone were not alarming. The United States was charged with "preparing aggression against Cuba and other peace-loving states." The addition of "other peace-loving states" reduced the acuteness of the crisis. By generalizing U.S. aggressiveness all over the world, the peril from the Cuban crisis was diminished. Before the Bay of Pigs, it will be recalled, the Soviet and Cuban charges that the United States was planning to attack Cuba had been specific and quite accurate, designating the places from which the attack would be mounted, the numbers involved, and the strategy of the attack. Aggression against Cuba was predicted with hardly any qualification; Soviet response to aggression was put forward as a possibility. In September 1962 an American attack on Cuba was flatly described as the first step in a world war, but the likelihood of such an attack was minimized. To paraphrase and somewhat extend Khrushchev's remarks of May in Bulgaria, the United States and the Soviet Union were exchanging threats about nuclear war, but the situation was good.

When as a result of the build-up during the Korean war the United States first acquired the capacity promptly to strike Soviet targets with nuclear weapons, it made no specific commitment to do so. Dulles's threat in January 1954 of massive retaliation at times and places of U.S. choosing was more akin to the Soviet pre–Bay-of-Pigs menace statements than to the 11 September commitment made as the Soviet Union was acquiring the capacity to strike U.S. targets with nuclear weapons on short notice.

The 11 September TASS statement prepared the case for the presence of Soviet nuclear missile sites in Cuba by arguing that what was sauce for the goose was sauce for the gander. The U.S. Navy and merchant marine plied the Mediterranean and used Turkish ports. Why could not the Soviet Union do the same in the Caribbean and in Cuba? "What is pronounced a violation of the norm for one is regarded as normal for the other." Then the statement warned that since nuclear parity existed, it behooved the United States to draw the proper conclusions. The Soviet Union was now militarily as strong as the United States and both had to keep this in mind if peace was to be preserved. It was irresponsible of the United States to try to frighten the Soviet Union. The United States no longer had a monopoly on nuclear weapons. Then the statement reiterated that an attack on Cuba would begin the unloosing of war. ". . . Whoever unlooses war, whoever sows the wind, reaps the whirlwind. The aggressor who digs a pit for his enemy will certainly fall into it himself."[14]

The long statement ended with an appeal to the United States for moderation. If the United States would establish normal diplomatic and commercial relations with Cuba, the necessity for Cuba to strengthen her military capacity would disappear. Instead, the United States was increasing tension by actions such as the mobilization of reserves, which was tantamount to the threat of starting war.

One of the most noteworthy features of the 11 September statement was the omission of the threat so prominent in the 19 February statement to move against U.S. bases contiguous or near the Soviet Union in the same way that the United States was acting against Cuba. The 11 September statement merely said that the populations of the countries that harbored U.S. military bases had to expect heavy blows in the event of a general nuclear war. As a matter of fact, at no time during the crisis did the Soviet Union resume the pressures against U.S. bases that it had employed in the past—specifically against West Berlin. This suggests that as early as 11 September one lever of pressure had been denied the Soviet brinksmen.

Textual examination of the 11 September statement reveals further evidence of divergent Soviet positions. It will be recalled that at the beginning of the statement, the congressional grant of authority to President Kennedy to call up 125,000 reserves had been dismissed as a meaningless gesture in the nuclear age since the course of the war would be determined by the exchange of blows at the very outset. At the end of the statement the call-up of reserves is described, in the traditional prenuclear fashion, as a threat to begin war. If we assume that Soviet notes, like those of other states, are drafted by committees, we can explain this contradiction as a failure to reconcile two divergent positions in the final draft. Since the decisive character of the first phase of a nuclear war was still the subject of public debate in the Soviet Union, the inconsistency in the 11 September statement may simply reflect the division of official Soviet opinion on the subject of the nature of nuclear war. However, it may have reflected a difference of opinion on how dangerous the crisis with the United States might become. The overall tone of the statement was reassuring. The United States could not but realize the facts of life in the nuclear age and could not really contemplate war, despite the bluster and rhetoric of Kennedy's opponents, to whom Kennedy was making some concessions. The characterization of mobilization as the prelude to war may have reflected dissent from the reassuring appraisal of the bulk of the document rather than divergence of opinion on the nature of war.

Examination of the text itself suggests a further question. Did the Soviet leaders or some Soviet leaders always consider one desirable outcome of the crisis to be what the outcome of the crisis in fact was: the acceptance of Castro by the United States and the removal of the missiles by the Soviet Union? Castro had often made the statement that Soviet military aid would be unnecessary if the United States publicly undertook not to invade or support an invasion of Cuba, and the Soviet press and a passage in the statement echoed this. This passage can be simply interpreted as a repetition of the Cuban and the Soviet charge that the United States was completely responsible for the crisis and that the tension would dissipate with U.S. recognition of the Cuban revolution. The simple and obvious explanation may, as is often the case, be the correct one, but the other warrants some examination.

The Soviet statement suggests that the missiles could have been removed from Cuba without publicly revealing that they had ever been there. The Soviet declaration that the USSR had no military requirement to keep missiles in Cuba could be interpreted as an offer to remove them after the United Sates had met Soviet and Cuban political demands, and the suggestion, shortly to be considered in another context, that the negotiation could be deferred until after the congressional elections in November, could be interpreted as an offer to Kennedy to make his concession at a time when he could more easily ignore domestic political opposition. An imaginary reconstruction along the following lines can be offered.

After the November congressional elections, when Kennedy had discovered that Soviet missiles were in Cuba or else the Soviet Union had informed him of their presence, a bargain would have been struck. The United States would restore diplomatic relations with Cuba and give a formal undertaking not to overthrow the Cuban regime or support others in doing so. The missiles would be removed publicly or secretly, depending on what had transpired. The Soviets could claim that they had always taken the position that missiles in Cuba were not necessary for the nuclear balance of power and that their withdrawal was not a concession; they were simply no longer a political necessity now that the United States had accepted the political reality of communism in Cuba. The available evidence permits us neither to embrace this hypothesis nor to reject it completely.

The chief difficulty with this hypothesis is the underlying assumption that the Soviet leaders were trying to serve only a single purpose—the support of the Cuban regime. If multiple purposes are assumed, the idea that the Soviet leaders put the missiles in Cuba to wrest a political concession for their removal is difficult to defend. If we assume multiple purposes, we can also assume that different elements of the Soviet leadership with differing bureaucratic responsibilities were associated with one or another purpose. We can identify the military leaders with a natural interest in multiplying the Soviet first strike nuclear capacity against the United States; the ideological leaders, charged with responsibility for nonruling parties, who wanted to believe and to demonstrate to others that new countries still wanted communism and that Soviet rather than Chinese support was essential to the process; the leaders, charged with responsibility for relations with ruling parties, who perceived a serious threat to the stability of East Germany unless the prestige of West Germany was reduced by a forced concession on the Berlin question, which in turn depended on a dramatic demonstration of enhanced Soviet military power. Only one of these objectives and one of the groups in the political coalition that supported or acquiesced in the missile venture would have been served if the missiles were to be put into Cuba only to be removed.

Speculation on the nature of committee decisions in the Soviet Union does not have to be completely theoretical. Abundant documentation demonstrates that in the first fifteen years of the Soviet regime, divisions within the party were sharp and disputes were conducted with the bitterness and vindictiveness common to struggles for political power. For the period of Stalin's primacy, many clues point to the continuation of the political struggle among factions in altered form, but little documentation is available. After Stalin's death in 1953 public evidence of the struggle behind the scenes again becomes relatively abundant, but it is still too scanty to provide a well-defined picture of the various factions, and the available data is even less able to provide a blow-by-blow account of the factional struggle in a particular case. But the available evidence easily supports the conclusion that the Soviet military felt that Khrushchev's preference for relying on the deterrent capacity of Soviet military forces was misconceived on two grounds: first, that the nuclear force with intercontinental range, the most reliable deterrent against the United States, was growing too slowly; second, that Khrushchev's plan for reducing the air, ground, and naval forces in the European theater was much too radical. It is also clear that the Soviet military were able to thwart Khrushchev's plans for reducing Soviet forces in Europe. But even though many pages of Soviet professional military discussions for this period are available, we do not know to what extent the Soviet military presented a united front to Khrushchev, or whether he was able to play off the European-theater-oriented group against the strategic missile groups. This familiar material has been reviewed to indicate the limits of reasoned speculation about differences within the Soviet ruling groups on the Cuban missile issue.

It is possible that the plan to introduce the missiles into Cuba was adopted over the opposition of the Soviet military or only with their perfunctory approval. If that was indeed the case, then a plan to put the missiles in only to take them out later is possible. This possibility cannot be excluded, but our general information on the power of the Soviet military would argue that they were included in the decision. Granted this assumption, it seems quite unlikely that the Soviet military, or that part of it charged with the responsibility for the nuclear missile forces, would have approved a plan to put missiles into Cuba as a bargaining counter for U.S. recognition of the Cuban regime.

A low confidence has been assigned to the "bargaining-counter" explanation of Soviet purposes in the missile crisis on these general grounds, but it should be noted, nevertheless, that the language of the 11 September Soviet statement is consistent with such an explanation. Khrushchev's subsequent statements that all he had ever wanted was U.S. recognition of Cuba are not useful in resolving the question since however extensive his real goals may have been, it served his purpose after the fact to present them as limited to what he got.

The statement of 11 September echoed the private messages conveyed to the president on 4 September through Robert Kennedy and on 6 September through Sorensen. After some four thousand words devoted to the Cuban question, the German peace treaty was discussed in two paragraphs near the end of the 11 September statement. "It is said that it is difficult for the United States of America to conduct negotiations on the German question now because elections to the American Congress will take place in November of this year. Well, the Soviet Union is prepared to take that into account." Several questions are raised by the abrupt introduction of the German question and the rather unusual public Soviet acceptance of the necessity to adapt to the U.S. electoral process. It is plausible and likely that the Soviet leaders were indicating that they would like to talk about the Berlin question as well as the Cuban question and that they thought the negotiations would be more fruitful after the elections. Whether the Soviet leaders expected Kennedy to yield because missiles in Cuba augmented their nuclear strength or whether they expected him to retreat in Berlin in exchange for the removal of the missiles, they would try to get concessions in as many different areas as possible.

This seems an adequate explanation of the reference to Berlin. But the more unusual expression of solicitude for the awkwardness Kennedy would experience in negotiating during the election campaign raises different kinds of questions. The explanation most frequently offered has been that the Soviet leaders wanted to postpone any American response to, or negotiations about, the missiles in Cuba until their installation had been completed and the ground-to-air installations to defend them against air attack had been put into place. If the Soviet purpose was to negotiate from greater strength—and missiles capable of reaching U.S. targets in Cuba would have represented a very significant accretion to the Soviet capacity to kill Americans—the negotiation would be more promising if the Americans were to be confronted with the missiles completely installed and defended rather than in the process of being installed. This simple and obvious explanation may be complete, but it is worthwhile examining another supplementary explanation.

Kennedy would supposedly have accepted the necessity of making concessions across the board to the Soviet Union and to its clients. But in the preelection campaign he was being forced to yield, at least verbally, to the angry charges of his domestic opponents. After the election he could ignore them at lower cost. Therefore, concealing the nature of the missiles in Cuba would have spared Kennedy the necessity of taking a stronger stand on them than he would have to take after the elections.

Another possibility should be raised, unlikely as it seems to anyone familiar with the American political process; namely, that the Soviets were prepared to remove the missiles secretly if compensated. A well-known precedent of a kind existed. For many years the Soviet Union made no public protest about the U–2 flights. At that time Soviet authorities did not want to advertise their inability to stop these violations of their own territory, and the United States, quite satisfied with the intelligence acquired, was not inclined to jeopardize it by publicizing violations of Soviet sovereignty. Although thousands of Soviet defense personnel charged with radar detection knew of the intrusions into their airspace, the Soviet authorities were under no necessity to defend their weakness in any public forum. For a Soviet official to suppose that any American government could conceal from the general public (1) the presence of ground-to-ground missiles in Cuba; (2) the fact of negotiations about them; and (3) their subsequent discreet removal was to project Soviet experience mechanically onto the American scene.

The U–2 analogy was unserviceable. The officials who knew about the flights were unwilling to embarass the government by broadcasting its secrets, but not because of an overriding attachment to the principles of international law. The same officials, or the same kind of officials, would and apparently did begin to reveal to some Congressmen and to some newspapers information about developments they considered deleterious to the United States in an effort to force the president to take action. Secrecy was easy to maintain in the first case and almost impossible in the second, but it is conceivable that a Soviet official would not have understood this.

This lengthy analysis of the TASS 11 September statement provides speculation—I hope informed speculation—on what purposes Soviet leaders, or particular Soviet leaders, might have had when they put ground-to-ground nuclear missiles into Cuba, but it does not permit confident acceptance of one variant and dismissal of the others. Judgment must remain suspended. The analysis does, however, point to a major oversight in Soviet calculations about how to effect their purposes. There is only a single clue, and it may be a false clue (the contradictory treatment of the significance of the call-up of U.S. reserves), that the Soviet leaders contemplated that the United States might threaten nuclear war as a way out of the crisis. The silence is thundering. In the thousands of words emitted by official Soviet organs, all the changes are rung except one: the United States will threaten nuclear war in order to get the missiles out. The emphasis is on the other side of the coin: the United States cannot and will not attack Cuba because it is not worth the risk of a nuclear war. The Soviets had mesmerized themselves into the belief that events could unfold only in the way they wished.

A book in galleys in mid-August 1962 but with an editorial introduction referring to the 11 September 1962 statement offers evidence that the editors of the Military Publishing House, at least, believed that the United States had been and was being deterred from invading Cuba by Soviet military power. The book argued that Kennedy had not yielded on the night of 18 April 1961 to the advice to expand the scope of the conflict, because of Khrushchev's warnings of July and October 1960. This passage was allowed to remain in the book, suggesting that the editors believed that it retained its validity in mid-September.[15] The Soviet leaders seemed to believe that their warnings had sufficed to stay Kennedy's hand in April 1961, and now that threat had replaced the earlier menace, they had no doubts. Hence their consternation when they had to face what they had not been prepared for, that is, Kennedy's willingness to take actions that he and the Soviet leaders feared might end in nuclear war. Kennedy, too, had paid a heavy price for his complacency before the Bay of Pigs, but the Soviet leaders, like most men, could only learn from their own mistakes.

In fact, the Soviet press imputed complacency to the United States, reporting that Washington circles tried to wave away the serious warning contained in the TASS statement, and at the same time gave the impression that they would continue the policy of aggression toward Cuba. Senator Mike Mansfield could find nothing better to say about the TASS statment than that it was pure propaganda.[16] An editorial in *Pravda* on the same day, after having repeated the warning that the provocations of the U.S. government could lead to the catastrophe of a general nuclear war, dealt with the absurd claim that Cuba represented a threat to American security. "That absurd invention has served the U.S. government as a pretext for the proposal to call a meeting of the foreign ministers of the OAS, at which they expect to involve some Latin American countries in their anti-Cuban provocations." Close readers of the Soviet press who remembered what its pages had said about the effectiveness of the OAS did not have much cause for concern. The source of Soviet self-assurance was revealed in yet another formulation of the changed balance of power, which some American militarists still refused to accept. But it was high time for them to snap out of their unrealistic dreams of military superiority; they lived "in a world where efforts to impose one's will on others by force [could] no longer succeed, because the relationship of forces had long since changed for the worse for the imperialists."[17]

The editorial then repeated the paragraphs in the TASS statement saying that the Soviet Union would not respond in kind with a call-up of its reserves but that the minister of defense had been ordered to bring the armed forces to the highest state of readiness.

The Cuban response to the new Soviet warning was one of relief. Raúl Castro said that now the imperialists would spend a few sleepless nights until Kennedy reconsidered and then convinced the senators and the monopolists. "From now on we will sleep more quietly, without lowering our guard and with eyes open to our duty. For us the problem has been simplified; for them it has gotten many times worse."[18]

On the same day *Pravda* reported that the Cuban people had greeted the TASS statement with joy.[19] But the Soviet press began to carry a few notes of concern about peace. The American government now was described as planning a general offensive in South Vietnam, Berlin, and Korea. Senator Richard B. Russell had raised the question of destroying the Soviet Union and "preventive war" had become almost the official Pentagon policy. The Americans simply did not want to accept one of the lessons of the age, namely, that the Cuban revolution meant that a new social order would inevitably be established in Latin America. The note of alarm had become somewhat shriller. The United States wanted to drag the Latin American nations into a new adventure—intervention against Cuba. "Evidently certain circles across the ocean would like to use only one language in international relations: the language of bombs. The worse their hangover is going to be."

The writer concluded that this policy had no chance of success since the balance of power had shifted in favor of the socialist camp. "In its two years in office the present administration in Washington has had not a few opportunities to convince itself of this. Will they across the ocean be able to grasp this truth at least, now, before it's too late?"[20]

The earlier complacency had been modified. An *Izvestiia* account depicted U.S. congressmen as subservient to the Pentagon and dependent on the golden flood of military expenditures. It advised the hotheads to calm down in their own interests and made no mention of the more sober-minded.[21]

The organ of the Ministry of Defense, *Red Star*, also described Washington as prepared to attack Cuba. In one article, going somewhat beyond the 11 September statement, the U.S. mobilization of 150,000 reserves was regarded as proof that preparations for the attack on Cuba had taken concrete form.[22] Another *Red Star* article said: "The people of Cuba know that they are not alone. The powerful Soviet Union, the socialist countries, and all progressive mankind are at their side. They will never permit the American imperialists to throttle the Cuban revolution by blockade or armed intervention."[23]

The articles in *Red Star* had a somewhat different emphasis from those in *Pravda* and *Izvestiia*, *Red Star* stressing that the crisis could get worse and that the Soviet Union could defend Cuba, *Pravda* and *Izvestiia* urging the wild American warmongers to come to their senses.

On 14 September *Pravda* published a dispatch from Washington describing that city as in the process of choosing between peace and world war. The Soviet correspondent had asked Senator Everett Dirksen whether he realized that military action against Cuba threatened the outbreak of a nuclear war. Dirksen answered that such a danger always existed when both sides had nuclear weapons. The Soviet correspondent then read Dirksen some bellicose statements by Republican senators. Dirksen answered that he did not like strong expressions but something nevertheless had to be done to stop the spread of infection from Cuba. The Soviet reporter concluded: "The immediate future will show whether Washington statesmen will have enough sense and political wisdom to accept the serious warning of the peace-loving country of the Soviets and call to order those raging instigators of war."[24]

A dispatch from Paris reported that the TASS statement had provoked serious thought in both progressive and reactionary circles and that the French foreign office was very disturbed.[25] Raúl Castro's speech mentioning a third world war was reported but the reassuring remarks that the Americans would spend a few sleepless nights before coming to their senses and that the Cubans could stand guard with renewed confidence were dropped.[26] Two TASS reporters filing from Havana reported statements from Cuban organizations saying that they were counting on effective support from the Soviet Union. The categorical Soviet statement and Castro's statements "are effective and genuine contributions to the great cause of the struggle for peace."[27]

The Soviet Committee for the Defense of Peace sent a message to a Cuban committee similarly named saying that "united and determined action by peace-loving peoples can make the aggressive American circles abandon their dangerous policy of provocation and military adventures. . . . In our times it is possible to prevent a worldwide nuclear war and lay a solid base for peace on earth."[28] Although the emphasis was on Soviet deterrence and although the American president was not associated with the dangerous policy of aggressive American circles, the danger of nuclear war was not ignored as it had been in the recent past.

A dispatch from Havana that appeared in the same issue of *Pravda* accentuated the deterrent power of the USSR. A Cuban worker was quoted as saying at a public meeting that this was not the first time Cuba had received help from a country so far away and yet so near. Every time the imperialists threatened Cuba, the mighty voice of the Soviet Union forced even crazy people to reconsider. The year before, when the Cuban worker being interviewed was fighting at the Bay of Pigs, he had heard the Moscow radio statement that had prevented the United States from using its aircraft for direct support of the invasion. Moscow's firm voice has been heard again.[29]

Blas Roca explained that the TASS 11 September statement had created a *new* situation. "The question of the security of Cuba has become inextricably connected with the question of the maintenance of peace in the whole world. Now the imperialists cannot attack our country without taking into account the enormous consequences of such an attack. In these *new* conditions, Cuba, *as never before* feeling the stability of its situation, will continue constructive work for building a socialist society. . . ."[30]

Roca linked the new situation and the new security that Cuba enjoyed to the 11 September statement. He may or may not have known, as Castro knew on 26 July when he explained that "the last danger hanging over the Revolution will have disappeared," that the new element in the situation was the presence of Soviet missiles on Cuban soil.

President Kennedy did not yet have evidence, convincing to him, that missiles had arrived in Cuba. In a public statement he repeated his belief that new shipments to Cuba did not constitute a serious threat to any other part of the Western Hemisphere but that the movement of technical and military personnel was under the most careful surveillance.

However, unilateral military intervention on the part of the United States cannot currently be either required or justified, and it is regrettable that loose talk about such action in this country might give a thin color of legitimacy to the Communist pretense that such a threat exists. But let me make this clear once again: If at any time the Communist build-up in Cuba were to endanger or to interfere with our security in any way . . . or if Cuba . . . should become an offensive military base of significant capacity for the Soviet Union, then this country will do whatever must be done to protect its own security and that of its allies.[31]

Kennedy also reasserted his commitment to the overthrow of the Castro regime by saying that the United States would continue to work with the Cuban refugee leaders. He concluded: "While I recognize that rash talk is cheap, particularly on the part of those who do not have the responsibility, I would hope that the future record will show that the only people talking about a war and invasion at this time are the Communist spokesmen in Moscow and Havana."

TASS charged that Kennedy, after having condemned irresponsible talk about military intervention, made a statement "hardly to be distinguished from the loose talk he had just condemned . . . namely, that the United States will do whatever must be done to protect its security. . . ."[32]

The *Pravda* report from Washington concluded its characterization of Kennedy's statement much as the other press organs had done by saying that it was dangerous to stand with one leg on the ground of realism and the other on the shaky ground of recklessness; but its introductory paragraph suggested that cooler counsels were prevailing. "A number of Kennedy's statements made in yesterday's press conference sounded realistic. Your correspondent, who was almost deafened by the hysterical warlike cries in the Congress, was pleased to note the contrast between the heated atmosphere under the dome of the Capitol and the cool temperature in the State Department auditorium, where the press conference was conducted."[33]

The Minister of Merchant Marine of the USSR in an interview complained about the harassment of Soviet naval vessels by American military aircraft and warned that if U.S. allies submitted to pressure and refused to carry cargo to Cuba in their ships, Soviet ships would do so, to the financial detriment of the capitalists.[34] *Red Star* carried a story about the training of mercenaries in Guatemala, Nicaragua, Panama, the Dominican Republic, and Florida,[35] but made no mention of nuclear war.

Izvestiia reproduced parts of an article by Walter Lippmann. He was described as a supporter of the U.S. anti-Cuban policy who nevertheless looked facts in the face. Stopping ships on the high seas, he wrote, under threat of seizing or sinking them was just as much an act of war against Cuba and the Soviet Union as actually seizing or sinking them. An invasion of Cuba would also be an act of war. The United States could win easily, closing Cuban ports and capturing Havana and other large cities quickly.

But we could not be certain, wrote Lippmann, that we could prevent measures of retaliation against Berlin, Turkey, and Iran. We would be operating on the principle that a possible threat to our security or our interests gives us the right to have recourse to war. We assert that since Cuba is ninety miles away and in the hands of an unfriendly European power, the United States has the right to blockade or occupy that island and that the Soviet Union does not have the same rights to take measures against American military bases in Turkey, Iran, and Pakistan, although they border directly on it. Let us not deceive ourselves, he continued. Our allies will not accept this, and their opinion matters if it comes to war. We could make war on Castro if he attacked us, but we must not do so because of what he might do later. We cannot wage preventive war without establishing preventive war as a lawful means of struggle against our military positions in Berlin, Turkey, Iran, Pakistan, Thailand, etc.[36]

The Soviet statement of 18 February 1962 had also warned that what was sauce for the goose was also sauce for the gander. Lippmann's column was being used to reiterate the warning earlier advanced in Soviet media, namely, that there were steps short of loosing nuclear missiles on U.S. territory that could prevent American interference with Soviet missiles in Cuba.

A further interesting point was made by what *Izvestiia* omitted from its account of Lippmann's article. Lippmann's column had begun with the words: "We have complete knowledge of what goes on in Cuba. We may not know every missile site in the Soviet Union, but unless the cameras are fooling us, we are completely informed about Cuba."[37]

Although most *Izvestiia* readers could not have known that its editors chose to cut out the introduction to Lippmann's argument against a U.S. attack on Cuba, the highest Soviet officials had access to uncensored foreign press materials. In fact, the editor of *Izvestiia*, Aleksei Adzhubei, was Khrushchev's son-in-law. Lippmann was known to be a confidant of presidents, and Khrushchev himself had asked that Lippmann interview

him—an invitation accepted after a considerable delay. A logical interpretation of Lippmann's column was that some influential Americans
knew, through aerial reconnaissance, that Soviet missiles were being
installed in Cuba and had rejected an attack on Cuba because of the vulnerability of U.S. overseas bases to Soviet pressure. In the weeks that followed, Soviet diplomacy seemed to assume that the United States was
prepared to accept the enlargement of Soviet strategic power and negotiate on that basis.

In the United Nations on 21 September Soviet Foreign Minister Andrei
Gromyko made what might be called a moderate speech. Instead of
referring directly to the danger of a third world war, he said that a U.S.
attack on Cuba, still called for by "bellicose American circles," would
have the implications about which the Soviet government warned in its
11 September statement. While noting some of Kennedy's sound appraisals, he pointed out that the president described the United States as at
liberty to mount military attacks against Cuba whenever it deemed them
necessary. This was unacceptable.[38]

In keeping with this stance the Soviet press toned down the shrieks of
alarm. *Izvestiia* reported that the only American response to the Soviet
statement so far had been to seize some sugar in San Juan, Puerto Rico,
that had been purchased from Cuba by the Soviet Union and to have
Stevenson say in the United Nations that Cuba was preparing to attack
the United States, rather than the reverse. But the Americans were keenly
aware that this policy had isolated them. The *New York Times*, according
to *Izvestiia*, wrote that the United States had virtually no support in
Latin America for strong action against Cuba and even less among its
NATO allies. Only West Germany had shown any inclination to heed
American calls to stop carrying freight to Cuba.[39]

The Cubans followed the Soviet lead. Castro made a long speech about
the help the Soviet Union agreed to extend to the Cuban fishing industry
without mentioning U.S. aggression or the necessity to defend Cuban freedom.[40] In reply to speculation in U.S. newspapers that the fishing port
that the Soviet Union would help equip was intended as a submarine
base, the vice-minister of the State Committee of the Council of Ministers of the USSR for Fisheries described it as merely an instance of technical assistance, and the newspaper commented that fear had big eyes.[41]

A few days later, on the second anniversary of the creation of the Committees for the Defense of the Revolution, Castro, like Gromyko, delivered
a moderate speech. He explained that "in the House and the Senate of the
United States there is a veritable competition of irresponsibility to see
who can shout louder, who is more hysterical, who can play the bear to
the Cuban Revolution, influenced in great part by the fact that they have
some elections in November." But they were thereby imperiling peace
and security in the world. Therefore the Cubans kept their guard up.

Gone was the picture of the destruction of the United States, the mad suicide of the imperialists. Castro closed the speech with a quiet statement of confidence in the Soviet Union. "If the imperialists believe that the warnings of the Soviet government are merely words, if the imperialists don't believe and let us hope they do, if the imperialists underestimate the solidarity of the Soviet Union and Cuba; if they are mistaken—and let us hope they are not—if they don't believe, if they don't know, we know how far this solidarity reaches."[42]

The themes were the same. The United States is ignorant and grasping. It threatens the whole world with war. The Soviet Union will defend us. But the tone was confident rather than strident. Only *Red Star* carried letters from Red Army men ready to launch missiles at a moment's notice, and warned that "if the aggressors, taking leave of their senses, undertake a mad adventure, they will get a nuclear missile blow from which they will never recover."[43]

CUBAN CALM ON THE EVE OF THE CRISIS

The Cuban Council of Ministers issued a declaration in which it chided the United States for not taking the Soviet statement of 11 September seriously enough and refused to give any accounting to the United States of how many or what kind of weapons Cuba would acquire for her own defense. The tone was much firmer and more confident than on the eve of the Bay of Pigs, when Castro had exhorted the Cubans to be ready to die to the last man. The Cuban Declaration was given wide coverage in the Soviet press.[44]

The Cubans were now confident of Soviet aid, *Hoy* describing it as "unlimited" with *Pravda* picking up the description.[45] The Cuban president, speaking at the United Nations on 8 October, said that Cuba still held open her offer to the United States to negotiate but did not realistically expect a response. He said that Cuba had the weapons necessary for her defense but would prefer not to use them. An attack on Cuba, he said, could be the beginning of a new world war.[46] Castro, in his speech receiving Dorticós, was to turn "could" into "would."

At the reception for Dorticós on his return from the United Nations, Castro gloried in reviewing the past. Once when the Cuban Revolutionaries were fighting in the Sierra Maestra they had only seven rifles, but now they had many, many arms and powerful ones to boot. When the imperialist indirect aggression failed, they began to entertain ideas of direct aggression. And the Cubans also began to think of other measures. "We have taken the measures that circumstances require to put a bridle on aggression, to stop the hand of the imperialist assassin."

And then Castro contrasted the present situation with that of the Bay of Pigs and expressed a confidence that obviously derived from the presence of missiles on Cuban soil. Aggression against Cuba would not go unpunished, Castro said. "How things have changed . . . how different from those days on the eve of the Bay of Pigs. . . What a different situation from being able to commit aggression with impunity . . . and now. What a difference! That's the reason we have taken the steps we have; that's the reason we have received the arms we have." Castro seemed to be saying that while aggression in April 1961 had only been rebuffed, now the United States would be punished with Cuba's new weapons.

The imperialists could begin an attack, Castro said, but such a beginning would mean their own end. Nobody wants the suicide of imperialism because that would mean a holocaust for humanity. But Cuba would not renounce the "special support" it received from the Soviet Union because it was that support that reined in the imperialists. Stevenson at the United Nations said that if Cuba wants to negotiate with the United States it has to break its ties with the Soviet Union. They want us to break "with the country that has clearly and definitely warned the imperialists that an attack on our Fatherland would mean the beginning of a world conflict . . . [with the country] that runs the risk that its warning implies, that its position implies. . . ."[47]

Pravda carried a faithful summary including the phrase about the risks the Soviet Union ran in defense of Cuba.[48] The *Izvestiia* account of the speech omitted the phrase about the risks run by the Soviet Union.[49] A difference in editorial judgment perhaps, or the difference between the brinksmen who were prepared to be staunch in a crisis and the golden bridge builders who expected an easily arranged compromise. An *Izvestiia* commentary on a *New York Times* story about a possible exchange of weapons in Cuba for concessions to the Soviet Union in Berlin provides another bit of evidence that not all the Soviet leaders had the same goals in positioning missiles in Cuba. On 15 October the *New York Times* carried two stories on Cuba. *Izvestiia* commented extensively on one and ignored the other.

SOVIET CONCERN ABOUT U–2 RECONNAISSANCE AND U.S. FIRMNESS

In the first story, Thomas J. Hamilton reported to the *New York Times* from the United Nations that a prominent Soviet-block official who attended the opening weeks of the General Assembly session had made a suggestion with the full authority of Khrushchev. (The dispatch did not mention that Gromyko had attended the session.) The suggestion was that the Soviet Union was prepared to follow a more moderate course in Cuba if the United States would ease its stand on the West Berlin problem. Several noncommunist delegates had received this message, and one delegate thought that Khrushchev might be offering to refrain from supplying to Cuba weapons that would be used for offensive action against the United States. Other sources told the *New York Times* reporter that Khrushchev had told the Austrian vice-chancellor in September that he would go to New York to attend the General Assembly meetings in the second half of November (i.e., after the elections) if a crisis over Cuba did not arise meanwhile.[50]

In the second story, *New York Times* diplomatic correspondent Max Frankel said that the United States had been conducting close and occasionally provocative surveillance of Cuba without any resistance from the Cuban government. President Kennedy, the account read, had ordered the closest possible observation of Soviet military assistance to Cuba to make certain that it remained defensive. The United States had noted that in recent weeks the Cuban government had been extremely careful to avoid any chance of conflict with the United States.[51] Once again the Soviet leaders could read in the U.S. press that Cuban territory was being photographed, and once again they maintained silence.

Izvestiia carried a polemical piece, rather nastier than usual, ignoring the Frankel story and dealing only with the Berlin element of the Hamilton story. The story, said the *Izvestiia* writer, was more than the usual mud-slinging and lies of the *New York Times*; it was a provocative plot prepared by the American diplomatic authorities. Lincoln White, the State Department spokesman, denied the story, not in contrition but to add fat to the fire of international tension in the USSR and in Western Europe. In the Soviet Union, said *Izvestiia*, the rumors about a Cuba–West Berlin deal have been laughed off. The Soviet Union will never forego its principles no matter what the question is, be it friendship with Cuba or the desire to put an end to the remnants of the war in Europe.

The American talk about firmness, the piece went on, is just a euphemism for recklessness. The United States might find itself the victim of the racket it has raised. "It would not be superfluous to mention that at one time a certain American secretary graphically confirmed this when he made a fatal jump from a window while suffering from a dangerous disturbance of the mind."[52]

The *New York Times* story and the State Department denial were thus indignantly dismissed as provocations. Clarifying Soviet usage of the term *provocation* may contribute to the understanding of this episode in the war of words. The *Izvestiia* account described the *New York Times* story as not merely an invention but a provocation. Originally, in Russian, the term was used primarily in somewhat the same sense that *entrapment* is used in English. A government agent pretending to be a criminal induced someone in a suspect group to commit a crime so that the group could be apprehended. In imperial Russia revolutionary groups, including the Bolsheviks, were thoroughly infiltrated by such agents. When the Bolsheviks came to power they continued the practice.

Now they still continue to suspect the motives of allies. Government-sponsored infiltration into criminal and suspected subversive groups is not unknown in American crime control and politics, but it is perhaps fair to say that the practice is pervasive in the Soviet Union. In Stalin's time police informers numbered in the millions; the number has almost certainly been reduced, but it is perhaps accurate to say that the Soviet government systematically conducts espionage against its own population, and persons in political life operate on that assumption. This partly explains the suspiciousness that has always struck foreigners as a feature of Russian life. This wariness is automatically extended to dealings with foreigners and foreign states. In fact, the unabridged Soviet dictionary defines *provocation* as the encouragement of persons, groups, organizations, and countries to actions that would entail serious, and sometimes disastrous, consequences for them. *Provocation* is the art of instigating an opponent unwittingly to act against his own interests, and in international relations, a war provocateur contrives to put the blame on the enemy for a war his country has secretly initiated. With this understanding of the Soviet usage of the term *provocation,* the purpose of the *Izvestiia* attack on the Hamilton story can be examined.

With a knowledge of U.S. news-gathering practice, we can safely assume that a high communist official, probably a Soviet official and quite possibly Gromyko, told at least two representatives of noncommunist states in Khrushchev's name that the Soviet Union was willing to pursue a more moderate policy in Cuba if the United States was willing to ease its stand on Berlin. One UN delegate offered the thought that Khrushchev might be willing to refrain from providing Cuba with weapons that could be used offensively against the United States. The hint was also dropped that Khrushchev would be willing to come to the United States if a crisis over Cuba did not arise, which could be interpreted to mean that if Kennedy did not reveal the presence of missiles in Cuba, the Soviet Union would not. The Frankel story in the same issue of the *New York Times* revealed, presumably but not necessarily from White House sources, that Kennedy had ordered reconnaissance, which would make the early discovery of the missiles inevitable, if it had not already occurred.

Variant interpretations of the *Izvestiia* reply to one story and the silence of the Soviet press on the other are possible.

1. The only purpose of the hints was to deflect attention from the possibility that there were ground-to-ground missiles in Cuba by suggesting both that the United States could find an easement in Cuba by a concession in Berlin and also that Khrushchev would be prepared to promise not to put ground-to-ground missiles into Cuba, implying that there were none there then.

2. The publication of the hints by the Americans and the further

attention directed toward them by an official denial demonstrated that the Americans, instead of feeling obliged to negotiate with the Soviet Union now that the latter had a stronger position, were rejecting the veiled offer and simultaneously seeking to arouse Castro's suspicions that the Soviet Union was willing to sell him out.

3. Gromyko had dropped the hints circumspectly to make it impossible for the United States to say that it had been directly approached with a deal and had refused; but Gromyko's purpose had been to feel out the ground. It signaled Kennedy that there was a way out of the dilemma in which he found himself. According to the *Izvestiia* version, Kennedy's internal opponents were counseling firmness when they really meant recklessness. When Kennedy discovered the presence of the ground-to-ground missiles, if he had not done so already (one possible interpretation of Frankel's story), it behooved him to keep quiet and negotiate with the Soviet Union. But the Soviet Union would not abandon its friendship with Castro or its position on West Berlin. If Kennedy did not understand this he was suffering from the same kind of dangerous delusions that had brought Secretary James Forrestal to death by his own hand.

4. Gromyko had dropped the hints in order to foil Khrushchev's scheme. Khrushchev planned that after he had privately revealed to the president the presence of the missiles in Cuba, (a) he would invite him to yield on the recognition of Cuba, on the Berlin question, and perhaps on some other political matters because the Soviet Union was now negotiating from a position of greater strength. If the United States failed to retreat for that reason, (b) it would be induced to make the same political concessions in return for the withdrawal of the missiles. By revealing the notion of a "deal" prematurely the United States had been provoked to reject the plan, making variant (b) impossible. According to this variant, it was Khrushchev's internal political enemies who had committed the provocation. Some color of support is lent to this version by the circumstance that Khrushchev's son-in-law Adzhubei was the editor of *Izvestiia*. The artificers of this provocation would have been those for whom the multiplication of Soviet nuclear capacity was the overriding goal.

At this point the reader may well throw up his hands in despair at trying to unravel Soviet diplomacy. Indeed, Soviet suspiciousness, the conviction that adversaries foreign and domestic are duplicitous and that friends can readily turn out to be enemies makes negotiations difficult to initiate and bring to completion. An opponent, approached in confidence to agree on a compromise, can always publicize the approach in order to advertise the weak position of his adversary. Therefore, approaches are made so gingerly that the target often fails to realize he has been made an offer. The skillful and experienced Soviet leader must always be alert to avoid being tricked.

The day before President Kennedy announced that he had received convincing information of the presence of Soviet ground-to-ground missiles in Cuba, *Izvestiia* carried an article on the situation that, although it did not exclude a serious aggravation of the crisis in the future, indicated that there was no immediate danger. The United States had twisted the arms of its Latin American partners at an "unofficial" meeting of the foreign ministers of the OAS, but according to the *New York Times* report, the great majority of the Latin American governments had opposed the idea of a U.S. invasion of Cuba. The Washington meeting had also rejected the proposal that all American states break relations with Cuba, but it did issue some statements about "preventing the activities of international communism."

The United States, realizing that its aggressive plans against Cuba would meet with the hidden and sometimes open opposition of some Latin American governments, had also set in motion a program of subversion supported from abroad. To this end it had quietly arranged to employ the territory of some Central American and Caribbean countries. Under the cover of the formation of a Caribbean NATO, the United States "is organizing intervention in Cuba masked by the participation of the governments of several Central American countries."[53] A severe crisis apparently lay ahead; the Soviet authorities apparently were not yet aware that the United States had discovered the presence of the missiles, or more likely, they believed they had discovered them but chose to maintain silence.

KENNEDY DEMANDS THAT THE MISSILES IN CUBA BE REMOVED

By Monday, 22 October, the American press was aware that urgent conferences were taking place in the White House, and on Monday evening Moscow radio reported press speculations about the secret meetings on Cuba or Berlin.[54] Later that evening in a public speech Kennedy announced that ground-to-ground missiles with a range adequate to reach the southeastern part of the United States had been introduced into Cuba and that additional sites, not yet completed, appeared to be designed to accommodate intermediate-range missiles capable of striking most of the major cities of the Western Hemisphere. He charged that the 11 September TASS statement that the military equipment sent to Cuba was designed exclusively for defensive purposes was false, and he revealed that four days earlier Gromyko had told him that Soviet assistance to Cuba had "pursued solely the purpose of contributing to the defense capabilities of Cuba." That statement was also false, Kennedy charged.

Kennedy combined two arguments, one indubitable and the other regularly rejected by the Soviet Union. The first argument was that the

Soviet Union had introduced the missiles into Cuba under a cloak of secrecy and deception; the second, that "our history, unlike that of the Soviets since the end of World War II, demonstrates that we have no desire to dominate or conquer any other nation or impose our system upon its people." Kennedy announced that it would be U.S. policy "to regard any nuclear missile launched from Cuba against any nation in the Western Hemisphere as an attack by the Soviet Union on the United States, requiring a full retaliatory response." But short of that, Kennedy announced that in order to halt the offensive build-up, no further shipments of offensive military equipment would be permitted, instituting what he called a *quarantine*, preferring it to the term *blockade*, which is recognized in international law as an act of war. He held out the possibility of peace and stable relations between the Soviet Union and the United States if the missiles were withdrawn under the supervision of UN observers. His description of the terms of this stable relationship were very general—a fair and effective disarmament treaty that would eliminate all arms and military bases and a genuinely independent Cuba free to determine its own destiny.

The Soviet and Cuban replies followed the next day. The Cuban reply will be examined first, even though the Soviet reply was available in summary form to Castro when he spoke. The analysis of the Cuban reply is simpler because, unlike the Soviet reply, it does not seem to represent an amalgam of variant views. Having no information that Castro mediated among, or took into account, variant views, the analysis to be presented assumes a monolithic Cuban policy.

THE CUBAN REPLY

A few hours before Kennedy's speech Castro had issued an order of combat alert, which the press explained was employed only in the case of the gravest danger.[55] In his speech,[56] Castro termed the Soviet reply to Kennedy as firm, calm, and exemplary—a real lesson to imperialism. While expressing satisfaction with the Soviet position, the speech focused on what Cuba would do in the face of the American threat. Everything that the Americans had done until now, said Castro, had failed. The latest step was the greatest threat to peace since World War II. Yet Castro hardly gave the impression of a frightened or even a sobered man, since he devoted a good deal of time to reading passages from Kennedy's speech, with frequent interruptions during which he ridiculed and mocked the statements, drawing laughter from the audience and laughing himself.

Tacitly, but unmistakably, Castro accepted Kennedy's charge that Cuba was the first Latin American country to have nuclear weapons on its soil, because he did not reject the charge, as he did almost every other in the passages from Kennedy's speech that he read. Castro made short work of the distinction between offensive and defensive weapons by pointing out that it was the employment of weapons that determined their offensive or defensive character, so that at the Bay of Pigs the Cuban tanks were defensive and the U.S. Sherman tanks were offensive. Although he was probably unfamiliar with their writings, Castro was echoing the position of U.S. writers on nuclear strategy.

He insisted, as he was to continue to do throughout the crisis and afterward, that Cuba would never accept inspection under the UN flag or any other. Cuba was not the Congo. Castro quoted Douglas Dillon as saying in Mexico that the United States was resolutely determined to continue on the course it had taken until the offensive arms in Cuba were either withdrawn or neutralized. "In other words," Castro mocked, "they are resolutely determined to commit suicide." Castro dealt with Cuba's ability to defend herself against a direct attack. "If [they make] a direct attack, we will repel it. I can tell you that. I think that's enough [said]. The people should know it. We have the means to repel a direct attack. Do I have to be any clearer?" The imperialists who try to frighten us with the talk of a nuclear war sound frightened themselves, he continued. They threaten us with being the target of a nuclear attack; we have no choice but to run that risk together with the rest of mankind. But we do have the consolation of knowing that the aggressors in a nuclear war will be exterminated. The imperialists sound scared. How incredible. "The shark is frightened and is asking the other little sardines to devour the ex-sardine, Cuba."

Castro's heavy sarcasm and almost jocular taunting of the United States contrasts sharply with the portentuous tone of Kennedy's speech and the Soviet reply. Castro sounded as calm as he claimed to be. He had already tasted the fear of defeat at the Bay of Pigs—a defeat that would have been the end of his world. For Kennedy and the United States, this was the first time. In October 1962, unlike April 1961, Castro faced the United States possessing or believing he had access to the great equalizer of the age—nuclear weapons. The Soviet Government Statement, as we shall see, failed to directly confront the question: Is an attack on Cuba a *casus belli?* Castro's speech left no room for doubt on that score.

THE SOVIET GOVERNMENT REPLIES TO KENNEDY

The Soviet government issued a reply to Kennedy on the same day as Castro's response. The official Soviet statement was deliberately vague on what would constitute a *casus belli.* Some of its vagueness was deliberate and may well have derived from a desire to negotiate with the United States without taking positions it would be difficult to retreat from and without revealing the Soviet fall-back positions. But part of the vagueness of the Statement must be attributed to the divergent positions it represented. In the Appendix, the Soviet Government Statement and the editorial positions of *Pravda*, *Izvestiia*, and *Red Star* are subjected to a detailed analysis, and what follows immediately below is a précis of that analysis, omitting some of the necessary reservations and qualifications.

The Soviet Government Statement (hereafter referred to as the SGS) is best evaluated by a summary of its main themes, an analysis of the warnings contained therein, and a listing of themes advanced earlier that were now dropped. The SGS briefly reviewed the history of U.S. aggression against Cuba, ridiculed the claim that Cuba represented a threat to U.S. security and drew attention to Cuba's repeated offer to negotiate differences with the United States. Kennedy's announcement of a virtual blockade of Cuba was an unheard-of violation of international law, a violation that threatened world peace because of the Cuban resolve to keep the military equipment required for its defense—a resolution that enjoyed complete Soviet support.

American actions and threats against Cuba had implications for other nations who might well find themselves in Cuba's position if the United States were permitted to play the role of world policeman without being stopped. In the future, the United States could demand the right to interfere with the trade and shipping of any countries whose policies or social structure did not meet with its approval. The United States was intent on strangling Cuba and in doing so had taken the path of unloosing a world nuclear war, a war that would be catastrophic for all mankind, a war no one wanted, including the people of the United States.

The SGS reviewed the proposals it had advanced in the past to reduce international tension, namely, a scheme for complete and general disarmament and a proposal that all troops be withdrawn from foreign territories to their own borders. The United States had ignored these proposals in the past, and now the Soviet Union appealed to all nations to protest the provocative actions of the U.S. government and the blockade in particular. The Soviet delegate to the United Nations had been instructed to put the question of the violation of the UN Charter and the threat to peace on the agenda of the Security Council.

The United States should realize that Soviet nuclear strength now deterred prudent statesmen and that only madmen could pursue a policy from positions of strength and seek to impose their will on others. Without admitting that the weapons in Cuba were ballistic missiles, the Soviet statement rejected the U.S. demand that the military equipment Cuba needed to defend herself be withdrawn from her territory.

Although the Soviet statement referred repeatedly to the danger of a world nuclear war, it was vague on what specific U.S. action would cause such a war. The Soviet government, in its statement, undertook to strike a powerful retaliatory blow against the United States if the United States unloosed war but committed itself never to use its own nuclear weapons "unless aggression had been committed." It neither defined aggression nor revealed whether a U.S. attack on Cuba or a U.S. attack on the Soviet Union or both met the condition for "unloosing war."

The statement repeated what Ambassador Dobrynin had told the president's assistant, Theodore C. Sorensen, at the beginning of September, namely, that the weapons in Cuba were in Soviet hands. Evidently this was meant to reassure U.S. leaders that they did not have to fear the rash employment of these weapons by Castro and, taken together with the promise not to employ Soviet nuclear weapons unless the United States committed an act of aggression, constituted an appeal by the Soviet Union to the United States to exercise restraint. But the import of the message was lost upon those to whom it was addressed since they concentrated on the threat of the statement rather than on its veiled reassurances and offers to negotiate. The most striking omission, which had figured so prominently in the Soviet Government Statement of 19 February, 1962, was the threat to U.S. bases overseas. The Americans failed to note this omission—an omission that deprived the Soviet brinksmen of one of their most important options. On the contrary, the Americans were worried sick about the threat to Berlin since they were unable to devise any satisfactory plans for meeting it.

The SGS represented a retreat from earlier Soviet positions. It did not unequivocally promise to launch nuclear missiles against the United States if Cuba were attacked; it dropped the threat to take action against American installations overseas paralleling U.S. action against Cuba. The absence of such threats made it easier for the United States to maintain unchanged its insistence that the missiles be removed. Mr. Max Frankel has written me that he recalls that Ambasador Thompson felt that the Soviet Government Statement was a backdown because whereas Kennedy had challenged the Russians head on, the latter portrayed the crisis as primarily a quarrel between Kennedy and Castro.

RED STAR'S POSITION

The editorials printed in Red Star and in Izvestiia were much shorter than the statement they accompanied, and the editorial in Pravda was about two-thirds the length. The editorial writers were able to convey their own special position by what parts of that statement they repeated verbatim, by what they dropped, and by what they added. The Red Star editorial, although it did not directly contradict the statement, managed to convey much of what has been described above as the brinksman position. By dropping any references to Cuba's eagerness to negotiate with the United States, any mention of the UN including the Soviet proposal to bring the matter to the Security Council, and by dropping any appeals to other nations to put pressure on the United States, *Red Star* conveyed the essence of the brinksman position: that the Soviet Union need not negotiate. The United States perforce had to accept the new reality of Soviet power which permitted the Soviet Union to maintain weapons and troops abroad.

Whereas the SGS talked about the "catastrophic consequences for all mankind," the *Red Star* editorial dropped the specific allusion to a catastrophe that included the Soviet Union and referred in its last sentence to the readiness of "the mighty Soviet Armed Forces, . . . covered with the glory of victories" to give a rebuff to the aggressors. This difference echoed the polemics of 1954 when Khrushchev, then aligned with the military, forced Malenkov to abandon the formula that in a nuclear war civilization would founder, for the prediction that the capitalists would be destroyed for all time and the socialist countries would survive victorious.

The *Red Star* editorial, which, like the SGS, did not reiterate the threat to U.S. overseas bases contained in the 19 February 1962 Soviet government statement, did refer to the hundreds of U.S. overseas bases, particularly those located in countries "in direct proximity to the Soviet Union." While the *Red Star* editorial did not revive the commitment of a year earlier to strike the United States with nuclear weapons if Cuba were attacked, it went beyond the government position in that regard. The SGS had linked the outbreak of a nuclear war to two contingencies, which it dealt with separately. The first was Kennedy's threat to strike the Soviet Union with nuclear weapons if the United States suffered a nuclear attack launched from the Soviet Union or Cuba. This threat was dismissed as hypocritical since the Soviet Union would not strike without provocation, and, it was intimated, the Soviet Union, not Castro, controlled the nuclear missiles in Cuba. As for the other event that might lead to a U.S. attack, the Soviet government undertook in its statement "to do everything . . . to frustrate the aggressive purposes of the American imperialist circles."

The *Red Star* editorial strengthened the Soviet threat by ignoring Kennedy's warning that a nuclear strike against the United States, wherever it originated, would precipitate a U.S. nuclear strike against the Soviet Union, and by keeping the Soviet warning completely in the context of U.S. actions against Cuba. The government statement discussed the danger of nuclear war in the context of a U.S. nuclear attack on the Soviet Union; *Red Star* threatened retaliation to U.S. aggression against Cuba. Instead of merely promising "to frustrate the aggressive purposes of the American imperialist circles," as the government statement did, *Red Star* also undertook "to smash the aggressor if he dare attempt to accomplish his mad plans."

Each item in the catalogue of differences between the Soviet Government Statement and the *Red Star* editorial could be explained as an editorial vagary or as of little significance, but taken all together they argue for the existence of a separate Soviet military position differing from the combined position of the SGS and the *Pravda* editorial position.

PRAVDA'S POSITION

The *Pravda* editorial devoted a good deal of space to rhetorical excoriation of the United States, with the consequent reduction of specifics, thereby sounding milder than the SGS and of course much milder than *Red Star*. The most striking omission in the *Pravda* editorial is the mention of the presence of Soviet equipment in Cuba. Nor is there any reference, as there is in *Red Star*, to Kennedy's charge that Cuba harbored "offensive" weapons. Having failed to even allude to the presence of ballistic missiles in Cuba, the *Pravda* editorial could drop the statement of Soviet support to Cuba in its resolve to retain the nuclear missiles. By avoiding the mention of missiles in Cuba, the *Pravda* editorial, unlike the SGS or the *Red Star* editorial, suggested that Kennedy's demand for their removal might be met.

The *Pravda* editorial was somewhat weaker in its commitment to Cuba than the official Soviet Government Statement. Whereas the latter committed the USSR to doing everything it could to frustrate aggression against Cuba, *Pravda* talked only of the desire to nip aggression in the bud.

The *Pravda* editorial is noteworthy for its very strong and rather unusual appeal to the United Nations. The statement that people all over the world depended on the United Nations to guard peace very much weakened the claim that the new balance of strategic power had reduced the options of the United States. The League of Nations had earned universal contempt because it was unable to stop Hitler's aggression. Now the United Nations was facing a moment of decision, the *Pravda* editorial said. If it allowed U.S. aggression to go unchecked, it would share the fate of the League of Nations. Thus, other nations, presumably including some allies of the United States, would have to exert pressure on the United States through the United Nations if aggression was to be checked. It is tempting to link such a gloss of the *Pravda* position with the next paragraph in the editorial, which called upon all to look reality soberly in the face. If "atomic maniacs want to gamble with the fate of human civilization," and one has to depend on the allies of the United States to make it stop, perhaps it was realistic to yield. Such a conclusion from the *Pravda* editorial is possible, but not necessary.

IZVESTIIA'S POSITION

Izvestiia went even further than *Pravda* in signaling a Soviet retreat.

Its editorial omitted any reference to Soviet weapons in Cuba, thereby avoiding the necessity of repeating the support of Cuba's resolve to retain them. It dropped the statement that the United States had adopted a posture of combat readiness, and its formulation of Soviet combat readiness was accordingly weaker, implying that the Soviet Union was maintaining its ordinary degree of combat readiness, and failing to link statements of Soviet combat readiness to the resolve to retaliate. Most striking of all was the omission of the warnings that the Soviet Union might be forced to go to war. Vice-President Johnson was quoted as saying that the blockade might lead to a third world war, but Soviet nuclear strikes or retaliation were not threatened. Despite the comparatively large amount of space devoted to hostile U.S. behavior to Cuba, the behavior was described as "tantrums" and "machinations." The gravamen of the *Izvestiia* charge was the illegality of U.S. treatment of Cuba and the illegality of the blockade. This implied that if the United States abandoned the blockade and also its attempts to overthrow the Cuban government, the Soviet government would no longer have need for its missiles in Cuba. Again this is a possible and perhaps even likely interpretation of the *Izvestiia* editorial, but not a necessary conclusion.

The case has been made that the editorials in *Pravda, Izvestiia,* and *Red Star* presented different strategies for the missile crisis and that the SGS represented an amalgam of these views. If the argument is accepted, the circumstances in which these differences were put forward suggest that the differences in strategy were of long standing. The SGS itself was prepared quickly, and the divergent editorials accompanying the statement had to be composed in an even shorter time. Evidently the divergent editorials represented variant views within the government already defined with sufficient precision to permit the composition of distinctive editorials in short order.

It also seems likely from the evidence that Soviet policies were debated by a very small group. Neither the SGS nor any of the three editorials analyzed took direct issue with Kennedy's charge that ballistic missiles were being emplaced in Cuba. *Pravda* and *Izvestiia* avoided the question altogether; the SGS and *Red Star* obscured the issue by confining themselves to the question of whether Soviet weapons in Cuba served a defensive or an offensive purpose. But in a round table discussion on Soviet domestic radio, shortly after the government statement had been issued, Viktor Shragin dismissed Kennedy's charge, without revealing just what it was, explaining that the spy plane photographs had been faked.[57] The most obvious explanation is that the radio commentators did not know that there were Soviet ballistic missiles in Cuba and that in the hectic atmosphere of the crisis no one informed them or else references to the missiles were blue-penciled without any explanation being offered. Perhaps these commentators were still following the older position that had assumed that Kennedy would continue to reject the charge of his domestic critics that Soviet ballistic missiles were being located in Cuba.

It had been Soviet practice since the state was first established to conceal from its own people and from foreigners any evidence of weakness. Most Soviet security measures were directed to that end; Soviet opposition to international inspection in an arms control program derived from the fear that inspection would reveal weakness. When the U–2 flights demonstrated Soviet inability to stop the United States from sending its aircraft across the Soviet Union, the Soviet Union never protested publicly. As soon as they shot down a U–2, they gave the matter maximum publicity because now Khrushchev was displaying strength to his domestic and foreign opponents rather than revealing weakness. Very possibly the Soviet leaders projected their attitudes on to Kennedy and were therefore taken unawares when he publicly confirmed a dramatic shift in power away from the United States.

The events immediately following Kennedy's announcement demonstrated that he had more world support than he himself had anticipated and certainly much more than his Soviet opponents had expected. For years the Soviet press had been chronicling the decline of U.S. control of the OAS. U.S. influence in Latin America had been eroding over the years and was to continue to do so, but on 23 October, one day after Kennedy's announcement, the OAS unanimously supported the U.S. position. Senegal and Guinea, at the request of the United States, denied the airfields at Dakar and Conkary to the Soviet Union for refueling on flights from the Soviet Union to Cuba. In Western Europe the United States was criticized at first by some press organs but soon enjoyed widespread support. The United States was not isolated and, probably as a consequence, Kennedy did not pursue the idea he had briefly entertained of a summit meeting with Khrushchev.[58]

THE KHRUSHCHEV-RUSSELL EXCHANGE OF LETTERS

Bertrand Russell, who had once advocated preventive war against the Soviet Union, had reversed his position, believing now that world peace could only be saved by U.S. concessions, and he accordingly called upon Kennedy to retreat and Khrushchev to wait. Khrushchev seized the opportunity provided by the appeal to call for a summit conference. Private approaches through intermediaries had been made to enlist Great Britain as a broker. Khrushchev's reply to Bertrand Russell, written one day after the publication of the SGS, revealed that wherever Khrushchev may have stood before, he was now at the *Izvestiia* end of the spectrum of Soviet views on what to do about the crisis. Most accounts of the crisis have interpreted this letter as a continuation of an uncompromising Soviet position. In a private letter to Kennedy presumably written shortly before he replied publicly to Bertrand Russell, Khrushchev told

Kennedy that the captains of Soviet vessels bound for Cuba would be instructed not to obey the orders of the U.S. Navy. If Soviet ships were interfered with, "we would then be forced for our part to take the measures we deem necessary and adequate to protect our rights. For this we have all that is necessary."[59]

On one level Khrushchev's letter to Bertrand Russell can be read as an example of Soviet obduracy, continuing the stand on missiles that Khrushchev took in his letter to Kennedy (of which only a few lines are available). But on another level it can be interpreted as a long step toward a retreat from the SGS of 22 October, only two days earlier. Khrushchev's letter to Russell assured him that the Soviet Union would do nothing reckless "nor allow itself to be provoked by the unwarranted actions of the United States." The Soviet Union would do everything in its power to prevent war from being unloosed. Khrushchev took a very hard line on the blockade and pointed out how subversive to international order it would be if the Soviet Union countenanced piracy. "If the U.S. Government crudely flouts and destroys international rights, if it does not follow the voice of reason in its actions, the extremely tense situation could get out of control and could issue in a world war." All states and peoples had to join in preventing a war that would be catastrophic for all mankind. While the Soviet Union would do everything to prevent such a catastrophe, Khrushchev wrote, it had no alternative but to oppose the blockade. The United States should suspend the blockade. "The question of war and peace is so vital that we believe a meeting on the highest level would be useful to discuss all the questions that have arisen and to do everything to remove the danger of unloosing a nuclear war. As long as nuclear missiles have not been launched, there is still a possibility of preventing war. When aggression is unloosed by the Americans, such a meeting would already be impossible and futile."[60]

The last two sentences went a long way in resolving the ambiguity in the SGS about what constituted a *casus belli*. As long as nuclear missiles were not launched, war could be prevented. That could have been interpreted to mean that only an American nuclear strike could precipitate a world war and that the Soviet Union would not "allow itself to be provoked by the unwarranted actions of the United States [below the level of a nuclear strike]. The Soviet commitment to use force to oppose the blockade was compatible with such an interpretation, but as Khrushchev's letter recognized, a confrontation on that level was also quite dangerous. What was striking about the letter was what it failed to say. No commitment to defend Cuba was offered. The statement that Cuba had the right to have whatever weapons she needed for her self-defense was missing. Not even an indirect commitment to go to Cuba's defense if she were attacked was made. The *only* demand was the ending of the blockade; presumably everything else was negotiable.

The text of the letter alone supports such an interpretation. The interpretation is greatly strengthed when the quite disparate reactions of *Pravda* and *Red Star* to the letter are examined. That examination will follow upon a discussion of the blockade and the presentation of an extreme concessionary view in the Soviet press.

The Soviet Union probably expected that its experience in supplying Algeria with weapons would apply to Cuba.[61] During the later stage of that struggle French military forces prevented the introduction into Algerian ports of weapons that the Soviet Union had begun to furnish to the Algerian FLN. Whatever weapons the Algerians received were introduced overland from neighboring countries. On one occasion the French navy tried to stop a shipment of Soviet weapons to one of these countries on the high seas. When the French naval vessel overhauled a merchantman, a Soviet escort submarine surfaced. The French commander had no orders to cover such a contingency, and the arms continued on their way. The chief of Naval Operations, Admiral George Anderson, intimated later that Soviet submarines had been detected and followed, and according to one undocumented account the U.S. Navy harried them mercilessly forcing six submarines to surface on one occasion.[62]

Nevertheless, Kennedy was meeting Khrushchev's appeal in the letter to Russell "to show restraint and stay the execution of its piratical threats." The naval blockade was conducted with the utmost care and no shots were ever fired. The accounts of Kennedy's associates reveal that Secretary of Defense McNamara felt it necessary to supervise the details of the quarantine very closely, much to the dismay and anger of the chief of Naval Operations. According to an undocumented account, American destroyers had already encountered Soviet submarines, unbeknownst to the president and his colleagues.[63]

THE SOVIET DOVE—*LITERATURNAIA GAZETA*

One striking illustration of differences within the Soviet leadership seems to have escaped notice thus far. On the same day that Khrushchev's letter to Bertrand Russell was published, an article appeared that appealed eloquently to both sides to exercise restraint.[64] The message of the article was to put aside the rights and wrongs of the conflict and concentrate on its resolution.

What is going on in the world at this alarming time? Two powerful and sharply differing systems . . . the Soviet Union and the United States oppose each other on our planet. Between them relations are difficult and tense, and given the present level of military technology, pregnant with a terrible and suicidal explosion of worldwide conflict. We put aside the question of why this is happening (we and the Americans understand the causes differently) and turn to the international situation. It unfortunately exists with mutual build-up of deadly forces and with watchful readiness to meet a surprise, "preventive" blow.

It was unusual enough for a Soviet writer to put the two systems on the same plane, but it was even more unusual to call on both to exercise restraint, as the paragraph immediately following upon the preceding one does.

What should be the content of real, statesmanlike wisdom in the political leaders of powers responsible for the fate of the two decisive parts of humanity in such a difficult, heavy-laden moment of world history? Certainly, with every sinew to reduce this danger, carefully to avoid any actions that (like striking steel with a flint) could cause a spark in the international atmosphere, saturated as it is with combustible vapors, and simultaneously to search out opportunities for agreement, to seek mutually acceptable conditions in which the life common to the two different systems of one planet would cease being reminiscent of people trying to get through a minefield without mine detectors.

This evocation of the danger to all humanity is noteworthy not so much for its vividness as for the appeal to statesmen on *both* sides to take steps to end the conflict. The writer then proceeded in the more customary fashion to attack Kennedy's wisdom and his bravery, which was one thing when he was a junior officer in the Pacific and another when it became a "criminal gamble with the lives of millions of people." But he then returned to the theme so unusual for a Soviet writer of the common responsibility of all statesmen for the welfare of humanity. "The politicians from Washington are subjecting the world to an inhumanely severe test. If it is an open road to unloosing a war, its senselessness is monstrous, and the curses of the present generation and all future generations for the murder of millions and for the mutilated fate of their descendants will be the eternal destiny of the country that first raises the nuclear sword."

It should be noted that although the passage starts with a condemnation of Washington, it is not Washington alone that is threatened with the eternal anathema of the world. It is "the country that first raises the nuclear sword." This article went even further than the *Izvestiia* article and Khrushchev's letter to Bertrand Russell in retreating from the position of the SGS. The blockade was not mentioned and the Soviet threat to go to war was dropped; only the overriding necessity of keeping the peace remained. This view became ascendant at the end of the week when the Soviet Union made major concessions to Kennedy's demands. The appearance of this article on 25 October indicates that some Soviet leaders—which ones we do not know—were ready to retreat before they came to believe that an American invasion of Cuba was imminent.

Further documentary evidence that the Soviet leaders were divided on a policy to deal with the missile crisis is to be found in the differential treatment in *Pravda* and *Red Star* of Khrushchev's letter to Bertrand Russell.[65] *Red Star* elected to quote just one phrase from Khrushchev's letter, namely, that the Soviet Union would be obliged to employ means of defense against U.S. piratical actions.[66] *Pravda* paraphrased Khrushchev's phrase that the Soviet Union would do everything in its power to prevent war and quoted verbatim the hopeful statement that as long as missiles had not been launched war could still be averted.[67] By selecting different parts of Khrushchev's letter for quotation the two newspapers gave directly contrary signals. In addition, the *Red Star* editorial charged that "the ruling circles of the United States, having decided to go for broke (*Vesti igru va-bank*), are taking practical measures that could plunge the world into an atomic catastrophe."

It then proceeded to give in great detail an account of American preparations to invade Cuba with regular U.S. troops. The *Pravda* editorial avoided the subject of a possible invasion of Cuba, contenting itself with the remark that any military conflict could plunge the world into a nuclear war. While the *Pravda* editorial said that the Soviet Union was prepared to do its utmost to prevent the start of a war, *Red Star* warned against appeasement: "History teaches that bandits cannot be humored. The policy of appeasing the aggressors has always led to tragic consequences for people."

THE CRISIS RESOLVED

On the same day that the divergent *Red Star* and *Pravda* editorials appeared Kennedy received a private letter from Khrushchev that repeated some of the positions taken in the *Izvestiia* gloss on the SGS and in the *Literary Gazette* article and made concrete what had been only suggested by omission before. The only irreducible Soviet demands were the lifting of the blockade and an American assurance not to participate in an attack on Cuba. The missiles would be destroyed or withdrawn in that event.

The following excerpts are from a compilation of what is available of the letter to Kennedy.[68] They show elements that had already appeared in Soviet press communications.

Elections might seem important in some countries, but they were transient things. "If indeed war should break out, then it would not be in our power to stop it. . . ."

It was obvious that he and Kennedy could not agree on the significance of the missiles in Cuba. Kennedy was mistaken to think of them as offensive missiles. . . . The United States, he went to say, should not be concerned about the missiles in Cuba; they would never be used to attack the United States and were there for defensive purposes only.

You can be calm in this regard that we are of sound mind and understand perfectly well that if we attack you, you will respond the same way. But you too will receive the same that you hurl against us. . . . Only lunatics or suicides, who themselves want to perish and to destroy the whole world before they die, could do this. . . .

This is my proposal, he said. No more weapons to Cuba and those within Cuba withdrawn or destroyed, and you reciprocate by withdrawing your blockade and also agree not to invade Cuba. Don't interfere, he said, in a piratical way with Russian ships.

Khrushchev's private letter to Kennedy outlining what were to become the terms of the settlement of the Cuban missile crisis was sent the same day that the conflicting *Pravda* and *Red Star* editorials appeared. Although it is possible that the editorial writers responded to a version of the letter available to them before it was sent to Kennedy, it is more likely that they were arguing over the desire of some groups within the Soviet leadership to retreat to a bargaining-counter strategy as soon as Kennedy revealed that he would take risks to get the missiles removed from Cuba. An argument raged between the Soviet brinksmen and the bargaining-counter strategists. The golden bridge strategy had disappeared when Kennedy refused to accept the missiles in Cuba. Two circumstances argue that Khrushchev's private letter to Kennedy did not resolve the argument in the Soviet Union. First, another communication followed from the Soviet government that added the removal of U.S. weapons from Turkey to the terms for a settlement outlined by Khrushchev, and second, an American U–2 plane was shot down and several low-flying reconnaissance planes were shot at.

Evidently Khrushchev's strategy in dealing with his internal opponents was to make a quick private settlement with his foreign adversaries and then to confront his domestic opponents with a take-it-or-leave-it choice. It is perhaps for this reason that on 26 October *Red Star* omitted the reference to a summit meeting contained in Khrushchev's letter to Russell, whereas *Pravda* emphasized it. On 27 October a public Soviet note suggested that Soviet missiles would be withdrawn from Cuba if U.S. missiles were withdrawn from Turkey. The chief novelty of the Soviet Government Statement of 19 February 1962, which was not part of the Soviet Government Statement of 23 October 1962 and was only echoed in the *Red Star* editorial of 24 October 1962, now reappeared—the United States and the Soviet Union had equal rights to bases overseas.

On the same day, 27 October, an American U–2 was shot down over Cuba. The *Red Star* editorial of 26 October quoted several times above, had perhaps signaled the event when it said: "An integral part of the preparation for aggressive war is always espionage. It is no secret in the U.S.A. that the ill-famed reconnaissance planes—the U–2—in violation of all the norms of international law, have penetrated Cuban airspace to photograph its defenses and other objectives."[69]

The interpretation of the downing of the U–2 can only be begun because critical facts are unavailable. As pointed out earlier, it is not known whether the Soviet SAM's were first ready only on 27 October or whether they were operational long before, making their employment a departure from earlier practice in Cuba. Since the following interpretation of the event could be radically altered if new facts become available, it will be advanced in only the most general terms.

When the brinksmen realized, either from Khrushchev's response to Russell or from Khrushchev's private letter to Kennedy or from both, that their preferred strategy was to be abandoned for a retreat, they tried to save their policy by what Soviet language would term a provocation— the shooting down of the U–2. In recent Soviet history, the secret police had twice tried to sabotage Khrushchev's policy by taking actions that would hamper negotiations with foreign governments. Professor Frederick C. Barghoorn of Yale University was arrested and held on a trumped-up charge when negotiations for a test-ban moratorium were underway, and only an appeal to Khrushchev by Kennedy secured his release. In 1964 the Soviet police threw acid on a technician from the German Embassy who was visiting Zagorsk. Ostensibly, the purpose was to frustrate Khrushchev's attempt to secure an agreement with West Germany. Although we cannot say that the armed forces in this case tried to frustrate a concession by the Soviet Union on the missiles in Cuba, it was in character for the losers in the Soviet Union to stage a provocation to win a victory for their policy.

The Presidium as a whole overrode the retreat contained in Khrushchev's letter to Kennedy when it specifically proposed that both sides withdraw from overseas bases. It now proposed that the United States withdraw from Turkey if the Soviet Union withdrew from Cuba. This new offer, so disappointing to the American side, arrived simultaneously with the news that a U–2 had been shot down. The Americans speculated that Khrushchev had been overruled, but as events were to prove, he soon recovered control. (It will be recalled that in the party crisis of 1957 Khrushchev's opponents gained what he called "an arithmetic majority" for a while, before he gained the true majority.)

The United States acted as if Khrushchev had made the offer to withdraw the missiles in return for a recognition of Cuba only and accepted such a version of the Soviet offer. Castro frustrated the consummation of that agreement when he refused to allow UN inspection of the removal of the missiles. But Khrushchev and Kennedy were not to be denied. They settled for a tacit agreement that the United States would (1) verify the removal of the missiles by independent reconnaisance; (2) cease attempting to overthrow the Castro regime; and possibly, (3) promise to withdraw the Jupiter missiles in Turkey later. Kennedy was soon to be murdered, Khrushchev driven from power. But they left behind a valuable legacy: nuclear war could be avoided even after a long history of mutual misunderstanding.

 **CONCLUSION**

The chief figures in the events recounted acted according to several theories of how international events could unfold to their advantage and disadvantage: the domino theory, the possibility of spontaneous conversions to communism, the efficacy of intervention against communism, the necessary shift of the political balance of power as the military balance altered, the conviction that nuclear war could only be a disaster for mankind. How the history of these years confirmed, modified, or invalidated these conceptions will be examined first in the light of contemporary beliefs and then in the light of hindsight.

The overturn of the Arbenz regime in Guatemala seemed like a U.S. victory and a Soviet defeat, but only a short time was to pass before it was realized that the United States had lost more than it had gained. John Foster Dulles was convinced that democracy would triumph over communism because democracy rested on a body of just principles, whereas communism embodied evil principles. Therefore, communism bore within it the seeds of its own destruction. The duty of the forces of light was to stop where it could the spread of the forces of darkness. Eisenhower accepted this injunction but sometimes agreed and sometimes disagreed on the prudence of measures to contain communism until it should collapse of itself. He and Dulles disagreed on the wisdom of intervention in Indo-China in 1954 but concurred on intervention in Guatemala in the same year. They were to agree two years later on the wisdom of restraint in Hungary. The differences between Dulles and Eisenhower resembled the differences between Republicans and Democrats. They shared the conception of the threat but differed on the modalities of meeting it. What they both failed to realize was that others had a different hierarchy of values.

For the noncommunist left in Latin America, the primary goal was social reform to be accomplished by a truly independent state. For the United States, the question of Arbenz's ideological orientation was central; for the noncommunist left in Latin America, it was nugatory. Arbenz's overthrow demonstrated to the latter group that the United States was the enemy of reform and of national independence. Castro thus became convinced that Cuba could only become a nation in conflict with the United States, and to achieve true independence for Cuba he was prepared to change the country radically. While unfriendly to, and contemptuous of, their communist countrymen, Castro and the noncommunist left in Latin America perceived the United States as the main obstacle to their ambitions. Hence, Castro was willing first to tolerate the communists and then to fly their banner, after having changed its colors. The noncommunist left, and not only the left, feared most the renewal of North American intervention in their affairs and were able to prevent the employment of the Organization of American States to that end. Prophylactic intervention had removed the danger of Guatemala becoming socialist, but it smoothed the path for Cuba to adopt socialism.

Hence, the tactical Soviet defeat in Guatemala constituted a strategic defeat for the United States. But when Soviet support of nationalist anti-imperialist movements went largely unopposed by the United States, the USSR was not notably successful. Soviet purposes in the Algeria of Ben Bella, the Ghana of Nkrumah, the Egypt of Nasser, the Syria of Kassem, and the Indonesia of Sukarno, on the whole, failed.

If the standards of the time are employed, the conclusion emerges that Castro's conversion to communism could not have been foreseen. Although the Latin American proclivity to adopt the form of new ideologies was generally understood, it hardly seemed likely in 1959 and 1960 that Castro would provoke the United States in its sorest spot by becoming a communist. He had never been one and he did not number them among his associates. The United States and the Soviet Union were agreed that it was out of character and dangerous for Castro to adopt the Soviet political faith. Both failed to realize—what was to become a truism—that the revolutionary left was more radical than the communists. Castro moved Cuba leftward more rapidly than most Cuban communists thought prudent, and in the end they followed him, confirming Castro's conviction that the communists were not true revolutionaries. But Castro's surprising radicalism was not the initial cause for the Soviet shift from conditional, largely verbal, support of Cuba to effective economic and military aid.

The U–2 incident revealed how hollow was Khrushchev's hope that the United States would yield on the major points of dispute, notably on the Berlin question, because it saw the handwriting of history on the wall. After May 1960 the Soviet Union openly joined the opponents of U.S. policy in the Congo, in Cuba, and in Laos—effectively, in the last two instances. If the United States would not yield to the counsels of reason, it would yield to pressure, but to pressure on its flanks, where its exercise was not as dangerous to the Soviet Union as in Berlin.

Soviet economic and military support in the latter part of 1960 reinforced Castro's radical bent, and by February 1961 he had publicly asserted a schema for revolution in Latin America and the world more radical and sanguine than the Soviet conception. And on 16 April, when Cuban exiles invaded Cuba at the Bay of Pigs with U.S. backing, Castro proclaimed the Cuban revolution to be socialist, a characterization promptly reported in the Soviet press.

The American decision to intervene by proxy in Cuba in April 1961 was the lineal descendant of the Guatemalan intervention. Kennedy and Nixon had both promised in the electoral campaign of 1960 that, unlike Guatemala, Cuba would not be allowed to drift toward communism. Tactical errors marked the planning and execution of the enterprise— errors skillfully exploited by Castro. But to concentrate on these mistakes is to obscure the basic American misconception. The United States, as it so often does, operated on the assumption that Latin American politics was all of a piece. It failed to distinguish between a Guatemala where the military were basically anticommunist, where the great majority of the population was outside the political system and as yet unaffected by Arbenz's reforms, and a Cuba in which Castro had replaced a thoroughly discredited regime, had abolished its army, and bore around him the aureole of a Bolívar. The United States failed to realize how readily Cuba could exchange its feeling of impotence for heady faith in its own power, and the former relied on the assessments of emigrés who were eager to believe that their sentiments were shared by the Cubans still on the island.

After a brief period of hesitation Kennedy broke off the Bay of Pigs venture because, being basically prudent, he decided the game was not worth the candle. Kennedy's political history, his failure to denounce Senator McCarthy, his careful movement in winning the presidential nomination and the deliberateness of his support for the civil rights movement bespoke calculated caution. On the other hand, Kennedy highly valued alertness to danger and courage: his first book was *Why England Slept* and his second, *Profiles in Courage*. He had suffered defeats in life but had not been crushed—he had become president of the United States. Khrushchev, schooled in another world, believed Kennedy to be craven and the United States to be in retreat. The mis-understanding between the two leaders lay at the root of the missile crisis, but it is instructive to examine the political expression of these differences—the debate on the balance of power in the world.

Khrushchev had first begun to use Soviet nuclear missile strength on the international scene to influence the conduct of his opponents during the Suez crisis of 1956. By the time of his meeting with President Eisen- hower at Camp David in 1959, the campaign of combined threats and cajolery seemed to be on the point of garnering the fruits of the acces- sion, or more correctly, the imminent accession to Soviet strength of nuclear weapons without running the risk that their employment entailed. But after the fiasco of the U–2 crisis Khrushchev again emphasized the threat of Soviet missiles, now linking them to Cuba. On 9 July 1960 he said that the Soviet Union "figuratively speaking" could support the Cuban people with missiles if the United States began to intervene against Cuba. The novelty of this warning was in its connection with Cuba and not in its nature, for Khrushchev had often spoken of the Soviet capacity to employ nuclear weapons in a particular international crisis without committing himself to do so. The United States paid scant attention to yet another warning; the phrase "figuratively speaking" underlined that it was not a threat to act in a particular contingency. At the end of October of the same year a Cuban journalist obtained a stronger commitment from Khrushchev in an interview published a week later. Now Khrushchev explained that *his* threat would remain symbolic only if the United States did not convert *its* threat into military action. The language was loose, leaving some room for doubt, but now an American attack on Cuba and the Soviet missile capacity were no longer merely juxtaposed but linked.

Khrushchev's menacing statement of 9 July, which in its October version shaded off into a threat, was not taken seriously in the United States because the Soviet position in the Caribbean was considered the analogue of the American position in Berlin. In Berlin, the Soviet Union had preponderant local military strength, which meant that the only credible U.S. response to any of a number of measures the USSR might take to alter the status quo in its favor was a nuclear strike against the Soviet Union. The Americans knew better than anyone else how reluctant they were to contemplate such an alternative, and Kennedy blamed the Eisenhower administration for leaving the country with only the choice of holocaust or humiliation. In the Caribbean, where American military strength was preponderant, the situation was reversed. If the United States directly invaded Cuba, the only credible Soviet option—which Khrushchev scouted in his statements—was to employ nuclear weapons directly against the United States. It seemed no more likely that the Soviet Union would resort to this extreme measure in Cuba than that the United States would have done so in Berlin. What little attention could be diverted to the Soviet statements in the excitement of the close presidential election contest centered on the symmetrical aspect of the Cuba-Berlin calculus—namely, that both sides were strongly inhibited from employing nuclear weapons against each other. It ignored the asymmetrical aspect of the situation, namely, that the United States was planning to take unilateral action against Cuba, and the Soviet Union was not prepared to do the same against Berlin.

The Soviet calculation was different: if the Soviet Union was deterred from action against Berlin by American warnings that were no more specific than Khrushchev's admonitions, the United States should be deterred from directly invading Cuba. Khrushchev was so confident of that reasoning that *during* the Bay of Pigs crisis in April 1961 he dotted some of the i's and crossed some of the t's absent from his July and October 1960 statements. He said: "As for the Soviet Union, let there be no misunderstanding of our position. We will give the Cuban people and their government every assistance necessary to repulse the armed attack on Cuba."

Khrushchev had crossed the important line from saying the Soviet Union *could* help Cuba to saying that the Soviet Union *would* help Cuba, even though he did not commit his government to the prompt and automatic use of nuclear weapons in Cuba's defense. Khrushchev now felt that the United States had already been deterred by Soviet missile nuclear power and he regarded the emplacement of missiles in Cuba as only an augmentation of that power. For him, missiles in Cuba consolidated an established position; for Kennedy it was a new departure.

Khrushchev immediately leaped to the political opportunities offered by what he believed to be a mutual acceptance of a new balance of power and expected, with Castro, that the Cuban revolution, now on the path to socialism, could be replicated in Latin America and elsewhere in the world. Now socialist revolutions were not confined in space to the peripheries of the Soviet Union and China or in time to the aftermath of world wars, in which war weariness made the imperialists half-hearted, as they had been in 1918–21 in their intervention against the newly established Soviet state, or passive, as they had been in China and Eastern Europe after World War II. The Soviet Union had become a reliable shield for nationalist movements, that is, wars of national liberation that now might rapidly proceed to the socialist stage as they had not after World War I.

Therefore, Khrushchev accepted Castro's unorthodox Marxism without demur. The conversion of this charismatic national leader to socialism, bringing his country along with him, could accomplish the transition from the bourgeois to the socialist stage of the revolution. By contrast, Khrushchev and the keepers of Soviet ideological purity bitterly opposed the Chinese revisions of Marxism. The Chinese theory, like Castro's, emphasized the crucial role of the peasantry but, unlike Castro, insisted on the leadership of the communist party from the beginning of the process. Both views were new departures, and according to some, even heretical, but Soviet acceptance of the one and rejection of the other was not theoretically based. While Castro promised to act as a surrogate revolution-maker for the Soviet Union, China proposed to act, although in fact she did not, as a rival in bringing new countries to socialism. In 1958 China rejected the Soviet proposal to put military installations on her territory; Castro accepted with alacrity in 1962.

In terms of contemporary assumptions, the United States failed to note the extension of Soviet pretensions. It missed the significant change in the nature of the Soviet nuclear guarantee made during the Bay of Pigs invasion in April 1961. It missed the indirect assertion of the Soviet right to overseas bases in the statement of 18 February 1962, which denied the exclusivity of American rights to overseas bases and drew attention to the vulnerability of those bases if the United States threatened Cuba. Either the statement publicly reflected the still-secret decision to put missiles into Cuba or it was a last test of American acquiescence to the changed state of affairs. In either case, U.S. silence must have been reassuring. If anyone in the Kennedy administration had read Castro's speech of 25 July 1962, its meaning might have been apprehended. But once Kennedy had abandoned his plans to intervene in Cuba, U.S. attention was directed to thwarting Cuban revolutionary activity abroad by means of the Alliance for Progress and counterinsurgency measures, and little attention was paid to developments within Cuba. It was already "lost" to socialism.

The American lapses can be most readily explained by the revised estimates about relative Soviet and U.S. military strength. After the review of the missile gap data conducted during the spring and summer of 1961, the United States became complacent in its conviction that the Soviet Union possessed only exiguous intercontinental forces. This, and the virtual acceptance of inferiority by Khrushchev, notably at the Twenty-Second Congress of the CPSU, led the United States to believe what it desperately wanted to believe, namely, that it would be many years before the Soviet Union could achieve parity in the capacity to hit U.S. targets with nuclear weapons. American confidence was justified if the issue was limited to intercontinental nuclear missiles. But no serious attention was devoted to the possibility that the Soviet Union could extend the reach of its nuclear strength by using Cuba as a base for its medium and intermediate range missiles much as the United States had employed overseas bases to improve the efficiency of its strategic aircraft. Kennedy could not imagine that Khrushchev was at least as eager to alter the strategic balance as he himself was to maintain it.

The mistake of the USSR was to believe that the United States had accepted the political consequences of augmented Soviet military strength and that, therefore, Kennedy would yield where Eisenhower had not. The American failure to follow up the indirect intervention of the Bay of Pigs with a full-scale invasion and the U.S. retreat in Laos confirmed the Soviet leaders in their mistaken hopes. In retrospect, the Soviet leaders can be faulted for not realizing how much the reassessment of the balance of forces had restored the confidence of the Kennedy administration. Soviet failure to realize that the new euphoria of the Americans was not compatible with their own was rooted in the obligatory optimism of the Marxian view of history. It was easy to believe what the Republicans had charged: the Democrats had invented the missile gap as a stick to beat the Republicans with. The Democrats therefore had no basis for an access of buoyant optimism. The Soviet leaders did not know that Kennedy was silent in the face of the expanding Soviet verbal commitment to Cuba because he was unaware of it; as the Russian proverb enjoins, silence was taken to mean consent.

Here was the source of the Soviet mistakes that were to follow. The leaders of the USSR thought that U.S. reconnaissance had detected their missiles in Cuba but maintained silence until after the congressional elections in an effort to reduce the political costs of the reverse. Thus far, no evidence has come to light that the scheme to put missiles in Cuba was opposed before its execution. At any rate, the effective majority assumed that the venture would come off without a hitch. When Kennedy demanded the removal of the missiles, established a quarantine, and threatened further measures, Khrushchev, like Kennedy at the Bay of Pigs, realized that he had been deceived by his own hopes and decided to cut his losses. His domestic opponents argued that the Americans were bluffing and would yield in the end if the Soviet Union stood its ground. A careful reading of the Soviet response to Kennedy's disclosure and his demands and a careful reading of the editorial comment on the response would have promptly revealed, as the preceding pages have sought to demonstrate, the division in Soviet counsels. But this does not constitute a valid criticism of the American conduct of the crisis if only because the analysis took longer than the crisis. In any case, the division in the Soviet Union became unmistakable only a few days later when Khrushchev's letter signaled retreat while a Presidium communication made U.S. withdrawal of its missiles from Turkey a condition of that retreat. But once the Soviet Union retired its complacent belief that the United States had already accepted the presence of the missiles, the two parties began to negotiate on the substance of the matter, ceasing to act on putative judgments of the other's intentions. They quickly found common ground, having in each case to overcome the opposition of internal hardliners.

Although each party to the dispute claimed that the outcome was a victory for itself and a defeat for the adversary, it was neither one nor the other. The result demonstrated what had already been theoretically apprehended. Both sides were too fearful of the consequences of nuclear war to run an appreciable risk of its outbreak. Within both countries, men differed on what risks and what outcomes were acceptable before the preponderant majority on both sides reached compromise.

But in one sense the missile crisis was a Soviet reverse, for the outcome disappointed the great expectations the Soviet leaders had entertained that once the United States had publicly accepted the dramatic evidence of greatly increased Soviet capacity to destroy American cities, Kennedy would retreat across the board. The United States had only to yield, and tacitly at that, what it had already abandoned—its ambition to do away with Castro. But Castro won the prize he had sought so long—an effective, though informal, guarantee of Cuban independence.

Now that more than a decade has passed, the principles upon which men acted can be reevaluated. The domino theory should be ready for retirement. Had the United States let events take their course in Guatemala, not much would have been lost, and great costs would have been avoided. At the very worst Guatemala might have become a socialist state, but its prospects would have been much dimmer than Cuba's since it was much less developed economically and politically than Cuba—and the latter is hardly a lodestone for the continent. If Castro had been left to his own devices in 1960 and 1961 he might well have shuttled between Soviet and American cliency as Nasser and Sadat have done. The Soviet Union seems to have learned that the conversion to communism of poor and exposed states entails burdensome economic costs and has therefore not encouraged rapid movement leftward in states led by radical anti–U.S. nationalists. In Chile, for example, the communist party tried and failed to moderate the radicalism that eventually caused the downfall of the Allende regime.

But the United States has not yet ceased to act on the domino theory. While Kissinger does not believe, as Dulles did, that the major communist states will collapse because of their inherent weakness, he has intervened in the internal affairs of states that he thought might go communist. Although American subversion in Chile was moderate by comparison with its actions in Cuba, intervention obscured the valuable political lesson of the Chilean events, namely, that intemperate radicalism would have foundered of its own weight in Chile and perhaps elsewhere. It is only proper to equate American intervention in Chile with Soviet intervention in Czechoslovakia if it is assumed that both systems are equally vulnerable to the consequences of deviance.

The Soviet and American leaders shared the belief, before and after the missile crisis, that the world political balance of power would automatically adjust to changes in the military balance of power. But in fact nuclear weapons have deprived that asumption of much of its validity. Now that two states possess extensive nuclear strength, even large differences in that power are not automatically reflected in differential political power. The mining of the Haiphong harbor and the bombing of North Vietnam that preceded the withdrawal of U.S. forces from Vietnam were far in excess of any measures that the United States took against Cuba, and yet in the interim, the Soviet Union had vastly improved its relative nuclear position. This single example suffices to illustrate how simplistic is the postulation of a direct relationship between military and political power. That is not to say that there is no longer *any* relationship between military and political power. The traditional conceptions are still valid in the relationships between nuclear and nonnuclear powers and between nonnuclear powers. For the nuclear powers, changes in military capacity below the strategic nuclear level still shape events. One need only note the alteration of Soviet behavior in the Eastern Mediterranean when the USSR established a military presence there.

But the overriding conclusion that emerges from an examination of Soviet–U.S. relations in the last thirty years is that each has harmed the other remarkably little; the most grievous wounds have been self-inflicted. Exaggerated fears or misplaced confidence have produced a veritable catalogue of disasters. Neither Kennedy nor Khrushchev desired the crisis of October 1962; they frightened each other and the rest of the world perhaps needlessly.

> They have mouths and speak not;
> Eyes have they, and see not.
> They have ears, and hear not.

 **APPENDIX 1**

THEMATIC ANALYSIS OF THE SOVIET GOVERNMENT STATEMENT OF 23 OCTOBER 1962 AND OF SOVIET PRESS EDITORIALS ON THE STATEMENT

In this analysis, the Soviet Government Statement (SGS) of 23 October 1962 is compared with three editorials on the same subject that appeared simultaneously. The SGS and the editorials on it are rearranged according to their main themes to facilitate comparison. Thus the reader can readily see how particular themes were modified and which themes appeared only in some of the materials analyzed. The SGS and the editorials follow, in Appendix 2. Particular Russian terms and phrases have been rendered into English consistently throughout to avoid the pitfall of analyzing differences in translation rather than differences in the texts. The material in the SGS and the editorials have been grouped under the following four headings: U.S. behavior characterized; What a war would mean for the United States and the world; What the Soviet Union and Cuba have already done and are now doing; What the Soviet Union and Cuba could and might do. Some excerpts from the SGS appear under two headings, since different parts of the same passage fall under two rubrics. The materials from the SGS are closely paraphrased or quoted verbatim; segments quoted verbatim are preceded by a □.

THEMATIC ANALYSIS OF SOVIET GOVERNMENT STATEMENT, 23 OCTOBER 1962

I. U.S. behavior characterized
   A. U.S. intentions toward Cuba
   1. □ The imperialist circles in the United States are trying to dictate to Cuba what policy to pursue, what system to establish in its own homeland, and what weapons to maintain for its defense.
   2. The United States does not want to negotiate with Cuba, although Cuba has frequently asserted her desire to do so.
       □ The Cubans wish to secure their homeland and their independence against the threats emanating from the United States. The government of Cuba appeals to reason and conscience and calls upon the United States to refrain from making claims on the independence of Cuba and to establish normal relations with the Cuban state. Doesn't the official Cuban government announcement of its

aspiration to regulate all disputed questions by negotiations with the United States government ring true?

Only recently in a speech to the session of the UN General Assembly, the president of the Republic of Cuba, O. Dorticós, reiterated that Cuba "had always expressed her readiness to conduct negotiations through the normal diplomatic channels or by any other means in order to discuss the differences between the United States and Cuba." Now the president of the United States implies that these Cuban government statements are somehow inadequate. But that is the way to justify any aggressive action, any adventure.

3. The United States wants to destroy the Cuban regime.

   a) □ The statement of the president of the United States shows that American imperialist circles will stop at nothing in their efforts to stifle a sovereign state that is a member of the United Nations.

   b) □ The United States has stopped at nothing, not even organization of the armed intervention in Cuba of April 1961, to deprive the Cuban people of the freedom and independence it had won and once again to subject it to the domination of the American monopolies and to make Cuba an American puppet.

B. U.S. charges against Cuba

   1. The United States claims that little Cuba is a threat to its security. No one believes that.

      a) □ The president is trying to justify these unprecedented aggressive measures with the argument that Cuba is supposedly the source of a threat to the national security of the United States.

      b) □ The United States government accuses Cuba of creating a so-called threat to the security of the United States. But who believes that Cuba can threaten the United States? If the size, resources, and armaments of both countries are considered, no statesman in his right mind could see in Cuba a threat to the United States or to any other country. It is hypocrisy, at the very least, to say that little Cuba can imperil the security of the United States.

C. U.S. actions against Cuba

   1. The United States invaded Cuba in April 1961 and continues provocations against her.

      a) □ The United States government has stopped at nothing, not even the organization of the armed intervention in Cuba of April 1961, to deprive the Cuban people of the freedom and independence it had won. . . .

      b) □ The subjection of the Cuban Republic from the first days of its existence to constant threats and provocations on the part of the United States has necessitated Soviet help in improving the defenses of Cuba.

   2. The United States has reinforced Guantánamo and put its forces in a state of combat readiness, and conducts reconnaissance.

   a) □ . . . The landing of new troops on the American Guantánamo
       base, situated on Cuban territory, has begun, and United States
       Armed Forces are being placed in a state of combat readiness.
   b) □ An order had also been issued for constant and close sur-
       veillance of Cuba.
  3. A virtual blockade has been imposed on Cuba in violation of inter-
     national law.
   a) □ Last night, on 22 October, the president of the United States
       of America, [John F.] Kennedy, announced that he had ordered
       the United States Navy to intercept all ships bound for Cuba, to
       subject them to inspection, and not to permit the passage of
       ships with weapons that in the judgment of the American au-
       thorities, were offensive in character. An order had also been
       issued for constant and close surveillance of Cuba. Thus, the
       United States government has virtually imposed a naval block-
       ade on the Republic of Cuba.
   b) □ The imposition by the United States of a virtual blockade of
       the shores of Cuba is a provocative step and an unprecedented
       violation of international law and a challenge to all peace-loving
       peoples.
           Obviously, if the United States today tries to prohibit other
       countries from trading with Cuba and from using their ships
       to transport goods and cargoes to Cuba, tomorrow the American
       ruling circles could demand the adoption of similar measures
       against any other state whose policy or social structure does not
       suit the ruling circles of the United States.
           The United States government arrogates to itself the right to
       demand that states account to it on how they organize their
       defense and report what their ships are carrying on the high
       seas.
 D. U.S. demands on Cuba
  1. The United States demands that the equipment needed for the
     defense of Cuba be removed.
   a) □ The United States demands that the military equipment
       Cuba needs for her defense be removed from her territory—a
       course to which no state that values its independence could, of
       course, agree.
 E. The wider implications of U.S. behavior
  1. The United States is playing the role of world policeman instead of
     accepting the Soviet proposal for the liquidation of all foreign
     bases.
   a) □ The Soviet Union maintains that all foreign troops should
       be withdrawn from the territory of other states and brought
       back within their own national frontiers. If the United States
       is genuinely concerned to strengthen friendly relations with
       [other] states and is trying to secure lasting peace in the whole
       world, as President Kennedy asserted in his speech of 22 Octo-
       ber, it would have accepted the Soviet proposal to withdraw its

troops and military equipment and to dismantle its military bases situated on foreign territory in various parts of the world.

However, the United States, which has its armed forces and armaments scattered all over the world, stubbornly refuses to accept this proposal. The United States employs them to intervene in the internal affairs of other states and to accomplish its aggressive purposes. It is American imperialism that has adopted the role of international policeman.

2. The United States threatens the Soviet Union with a nuclear attack.

a) ☐ The representatives of the United States constantly boast that American aircraft can attack the Soviet Union at any time, can drop bombs on peaceful cities and villages, can strike heavy blows. Not a day passes without the statesmen, military leaders, and the press of the United States uttering threats that American submarines, plying many seas and oceans with Polaris missiles aboard, can bring an atomic blow down upon the Soviet Union and other peace-loving states. In the light of these facts there is a particularly false ring to President Kennedy's words that the government of the United States is guided by the interests of peace in its presumptuous demands that Cuba be deprived of the means of defense.

b) ☐ The president of the United States said in his statement that if even one nuclear bomb fell on the territory of the United States, the United States would strike a retaliatory blow.

3. The United States is undermining international law and endangering the existence of the United Nations.

a) ☐ Brazenly flouting the international norms for the conduct of states and the principles of the UN Charter, the United States has arrogated to itself the right—and has so announced—to attack the ships of other states on the high seas, i.e., to engage in piracy.

b) ☐ According to the UN Charter all countries, large and small, have the right to order their affairs in their own way and to adopt the measures they deem necessary to guarantee their security and to repulse aggressors against their freedom and independence. To ignore this is to undermine the very basis of the existence of the United Nations, to introduce the laws of the jungle into international life, and to engender conflicts and wars without end.

II. What a war would mean for the United States and the world

A. The United States has created the danger of a world nuclear war

1. ☐ To that end [stifling Cuba] they are ready to push the world to the abyss of a military catastrophe. The peoples of all countries must clearly realize that in embarking on such an adventure, the United States of America is taking a step toward unloosing a world nuclear war.

2. ☐ The insolent actions of U.S. imperialism could lead to catastrophic consequences for all mankind that no people, including the people of the United States, want.

III. What the Soviet Union and Cuba have already done and are now doing
   A. Appeals
      1. ☐ The Soviet government has repeatedly drawn the attention of the governments of all countries and of world public opinion to the serious danger to the cause of peace represented by the policy pursued by the United States toward the Republic of Cuba.
      2. ☐ It is the Soviet Union that has advanced and established a program of universal and complete disarmament whose realization would open up genuine prospects for the establishment of a peace without wars and weapons. These proposals have gained growing support in the world; they have captured the imagination of people; they have become the rallying cry of the times. If until now the cause of disarmament has not made any headway, the fault lies with the United States and its NATO allies. They are afraid of disarmament, not wanting to part with the big stick with which they try to dictate their will to other countries.
      3. ☐ The Soviet Union maintains that all foreign troops should be withdrawn from the territory of other states and brought back within their own national frontiers.
      4. ☐ The peace-loving states cannot but protest against the piratical operations against ships bound for Cuban shores announced by the president of the United States and against the institution of controls over the ships of sovereign states on the high seas.
      5. ☐ The Soviet Union appeals to all governments and peoples to raise their voices in protest against the aggressive actions of the United States of America against Cuba and other states, to condemn these actions firmly, and to bar the way to the unloosing of nuclear war by the United States government.
      6. ☐ The government of Cuba appeals to reason and conscience and calls upon the United States to refrain from making claims on the independence of Cuba and to establish normal relations with the Cuban state.
   B. Soviet military aid to Cuba
      1. ☐ With regard to the Soviet Union's aid to Cuba: this aid is exclusively for the purpose of contributing to the defensive capacity of Cuba. As the joint Soviet-Cuban communiqué of 3 September of this year on the visit to the Soviet Union of a Cuban delegation composed of E. Guevara and E. Aragonés indicated, the Soviet government responded to the request of the Cuban government to help Cuba with arms. The communiqué states that these arms and military equipment are exclusively designated for the purposes of defense. The governments of both countries still firmly adhere to that position.
   C. The deterrent force of Soviet military might
      1. ☐ The leaders of the United States must at last realize that times have now changed completely. Only madmen can now rely on a policy "from positions of strength" and believe that that policy will be at all successful and permit them to impose their order on other states. If once the United States could regard itself as the very

greatest military power, now there is no basis at all for such a view. There is another force in the world, no less powerful, which maintains that people should order their own affairs as they wish. Now as never before statesmen must be cool and prudent and not countenance the brandishing of weapons.

The Soviet government attests once again that all the weapons in its possession serve, and will serve, the purposes of defense against aggressors. In existing international circumstances the presence of powerful weapons, including nuclear missiles, in the Soviet Union is acknowledged by all peoples of the world as the decisive means to deter the aggressive forces of imperialism from unloosing a world war of annihiliation. The Soviet Union will continue even in the future to discharge this mission with complete firmness and consistency.

D. Soviet combat readiness
    1. ☐ The Soviet government is taking all the necessary steps so that our country is not taken unawares and is in a position to give a fitting answer to the aggressor.

IV. What the Soviet Union and Cuba could and might do
  A. Excluded measure—the withdrawal of missiles from Cuba
    1. ☐ The United States demands that the military equipment Cuba needs for her self-defense be removed from her territory—a course to which no state that values its independence could, of course, agree.
  B. UN action
    1. ☐ In view of the seriousness of the situation that the United States government has created over Cuba, the Soviet government has instructed its representative in the United Nations to raise the question of the immediate convocation of the Security Council to consider the [following] question: "The violation of the Charter of the United Nations and the threat to peace by the United States of America."
  C. Soviet commitment to defend Cuba and the peace
    1. ☐ The Soviet government will do everything it can to frustrate the aggressive purposes of the imperialist circles of the United States and to defend and to consolidate peace on earth.
    (From its context, following upon a description of the appeal to the United Nations and preceding a statement of combat readiness, the commitment comprised political and military measures.)
  D. Admonition to the United States that it is responsible for the fate of the world
    1. ☐ In this anxious hour the Soviet government considers itself duty bound to earnestly caution the government of the United States and to warn it that, in carrying out the measures announced by President Kennedy, it is recklessly playing with fire and assuming a grave responsibility for the fate of the world.
  E. Warning to retaliate against a nuclear blow
    1. ☐ The president of the United States said in his statement that if

even one nuclear bomb fell on the territory of the United States, the United States would strike a retaliatory blow. Such an assertion is shot through with hypocrisy since the Soviet Union has already repeatedly stated that not a single nuclear bomb will fall either on the United States or on any other country unless aggression has been committed. The nuclear weapons made by the Soviet people are in the hands of the people and will never be employed for purposes of aggression.

But if the aggressors unloose war, the Soviet Union will strike a most powerful retaliatory blow.

This summary and thematic rearrangement of the Soviet Government Statement is largely self-explanatory. One feature, however, requires comment—the equivocal commitment to use nuclear weapons to defend Cuba against an attack from the United States. In IV E1 the Soviet Union undertook to strike a powerful retaliatory blow against the United States if the United States unloosed war. Whether the action triggering the execution of the Soviet commitment was war against Cuba or a nuclear blow against the Soviet Union was not made clear. "Retaliatory blow" (*otvetnyi udar*) had been a stock phrase in Soviet writing about nuclear strategy since the middle fifties. The term was employed to mean a blow in answer to a blow of the same kind, a nuclear strike; this was the common usage. The drafters of the statement could have written: "But if the aggressors unloose a nuclear strike on the Soviet Union, the Soviet Union will deal a most powerful retaliatory blow." Similarly, in the sentence just cited, the Soviet Union committed itself never to use a nuclear bomb "unless aggression has been committed." The drafters could have written "unless the Soviet Union has been hit by a nuclear bomb." Thus the statement avoided limiting a Soviet retaliatory strike to the situation when it was responding to a nuclear strike. It was not a no-first-use-of-nuclear-weapons statement. On the other hand, the statement did not say, as it had a year and a half earlier, that the Soviet Union would use nuclear weapons if the United States invaded Cuba. The ambiguity was deliberate.

It will be noted that in paragraph IV E1 the United States is reminded of what Dobrynin had told Sorensen and Robert Kennedy in early September, that the nuclear weapons in Cuba were in Soviet hands, a circumstance that militated against the interpretation that a U.S. attack on Cuba meant a Soviet nuclear strike. Presumably U.S. uncertainty and anxiety would be heightened if the United States thought that Castro controlled the weapons. It appears, however, that the Soviet Union was communicating oversubtly, for the accounts of the missile crisis do not note that the Kennedy Executive Committee noticed this hint.

Another element of ambiguity in the statement was the context of the Soviet warning, namely, Kennedy's warning that the United States would respond to a nuclear strike wherever it came from with a strike on the Soviet Union. The context does not relieve the studied ambiguity of the words, but it shifts attention from Cuba to a U.S.–USSR nuclear exchange. The Soviet commitment to strike a nuclear retaliatory blow is made in the context of an American strike whose likelihood is reduced by the explanation that Kennedy's statement was shot through with hypocrisy. Kennedy, according to the explanation, was threatening a retaliatory blow only if the Soviet Union struck first, and the Soviet Union would not let even a single nuclear bomb fly "unless aggression had been committed." Since aggression is not defined, the Soviet statement is ambiguous.

In another part of the statement the commitment is reiterated, but it is still ambiguous. "The Soviet Union will do everything it can to frustrate the aggressive purposes of the imperialist circles of the United States and to defend and to consolidate peace on earth" (IV C1). This sentence does not reveal at what point in the execution of America's aggressive purposes the Soviet Union would move to frustrate them, and it commits the Soviet Union to do everything it can. From the context of this sentence, both military and political aid could be meant, and no links are made between particular U.S. action and particular Soviet actions.

The statement could have read, "The Soviet Union will do everything it can, including a nuclear strike if necessary, to defend Cuba's freedom." The conclusion that the ambiguity of the actual warning was studied is inescapable. Missing from the specific threats that the Soviet Union could have made was the warning to U.S. bases overseas that figured so prominently in the Soviet government statement of 19 February 1962.

The editorials printed in *Izvestiia* and *Red Star* were much shorter than the Soviet Government Statement they accompanied. The editorial in *Pravda* was about two-thirds as long. The editorial writers conveyed their on views by the parts of the statement they chose to repeat verbatim or paraphrase, by what they dropped, and perhaps most significantly by what they added. The thematic analysis of the editorials, which follows immediately below, will suggest that the *Red Star* editorial was closest to what has been termed the brinksman strategy; the *Izvestiia* editorial closest to the golden bridge strategy; *Pravda* fell between but was closer to the second than to the first.

THEMATIC ANALYSIS OF "WE ARE ON THE ALERT,"
RED STAR (KRASNAIA ZVEZDA), 24 OCTOBER 1962

I. U.S. behavior characterized
  A. U.S. intentions toward Cuba
    1. □ Assuming the role of world policeman, American imperialism is trying to dictate to Cuba how to live, what [political] system to have, and what weapons to acquire, for her defense.
      (Substantially the same as the SGS.)
    2. The United States does not want to negotiate with Cuba, although Cuba has frequently asserted her desire to do so.
      (Not mentioned.)
    3. The United States wants to destroy the Cuban regime.
      a) □ . . . Everybody knows that from the day the independent Republic of Cuba was born, the American predators, who wanted to make Cuba their colony and puppet, bared their teeth at her. It is they who organized and prepared the invasion of Cuba by mercenaries. It is they who constantly arrange armed

provocations on Cuban soil. It is they who are trying to strangle Cuba with famine.

(Same purport as the SGS, but the reference to Cuba's membership in the United Nations has been omitted.)

B. U.S. charges against Cuba

1. The United States claims that little Cuba is a threat to its security. No one believes that.

   a) ☐ How can officials in Washington have the effrontery to complain about the dangers supposedly threatening their country from Cuba?

   (Same purport as the SGS.)

   b) ☐ Washington is trying to justify these actions in vain by reference to the threat to the security of the United States . . . on the part of Cuba. That kind of reference is false and hypocritical through and through.

   (Same purport as the SGS.)

C. U.S. actions against Cuba

1. The United States invaded Cuba in April 1961 and continues provocations against her.

   a) ☐ It is they [the United States] who organized and prepared the invasion of Cuba by mercenaries.

   (Substantially the same as the SGS.)

   b) ☐ It is they [the United States] who constantly arrange armed provocations on Cuban soil.

   (Substantially the same as the SGS.)

2. The United States has reinforced Guantánamo and put its forces in a state of combat readiness, and conducts reconnaissance.

   a) ☐ New units are being landed on the American Guantánamo base, situated on Cuban territory. The United States Armed Forces are being placed in a state of combat readiness.

   (Virtually identical with the SGS.)

   b) (The statement's reference to U.S. reconnaissance of Cuba has been omitted.)

3. A virtual blockade has been imposed on Cuba in violation of international law.

   a) ☐ The president of the United States, Kennedy, has announced that he has given the order to intercept all ships going to Cuba, to subject them to inspection, and not to permit the passage of ships with weapons which in the opinion of the American authorities, are offensive in character. In other words, the United States has virtually imposed a naval blockade on Cuba and arrogates to itself the right to attack ships of other countries on the high seas, that is, to engage in piracy.

   (Virtually identical with the SGS.)

   b) ☐ The new piratical actions of the United States imperialists cannot be regarded as anything but a crude provocational step, an unheard of violation of international law, and a challenge to all peace-loving peoples.

   (Virtually identical with the SGS.)

4. The United States is about to attack Cuba.
   a) □ It is they [the United States] who are now sending dozens of ships into the Caribbean and preparing a new attack on the island of freedom, as the American press openly asserts.
   (Not mentioned in the SGS.)
D. U.S. demands on Cuba
   1. The United States demands that the equipment needed for the defense of Cuba be removed.
   a) □ Washington's demand to remove Soviet military equipment from Cuba is the height of effrontery.
   (Substantially the same as the SGS.)
E. The wider implications of U.S. behavior
   1. The United States is playing the role of world policeman instead of accepting the Soviet proposal for the liquidation of all foreign bases.
   a) □ Assuming the role of world policeman, American imperialism is trying to dictate to Cuba how to live. . . .
   b) □ The United States maintains its weapons and troops on hundreds of American military bases scattered all over the world, and in particular, even in those countries that are in direct proximity to the Soviet Union. The United States is not willing to withdraw its troops from other countries and eliminate its military bases there as the Soviet Union has proposed.
   (Same purport as the SGS.)
   2. The United States threatens the Soviet Union with a nuclear attack.
   (Not mentioned.)
   3. The United States is undermining international law and endangering the existence of the United Nations.
   a) □ The new piratical actions of the United States imperialists cannot be regarded as anything but a crude provocational step, an unheard of violation of international law, and a challenge to all peace-loving peoples.
   (Same purport as the SGS.)
   b) (Here *Red Star* omits the paragraph on the United Nations as it does throughout.)
II. What a war would mean for the United States and the world
   A. The United States has created the danger of a world nuclear war
   1. □ . . . The honest people of the whole globe will brand with infamy the brazen aggressors, who recklessly play with fire and push the world to the brink of catastrophe.
   2. □ Whoever unlooses a new war will inevitably be himself consumed in its flames.
   (The *Red Star* implication in the sentence quoted as II A1 that the United States will be the loser in a nuclear exchange is absent from the statement. The implication is made explicit in the reference to Soviet victory appearing in III D2.)
III. What the Soviet Union and Cuba have already done and are now doing
   A. Appeals

1. (Not mentioned.)
2. (Not mentioned.)
3. (Not mentioned.)
4. (Not mentioned.)
5. (Not mentioned.)
6. (Not mentioned.)
B. Soviet military aid to Cuba
   1. ☐ With regard to the aid that the Soviet Union renders to the Republic of Cuba: everybody knows that it is designated exclusively for purposes of defense.

      (Same purport as the statement.)
C. The deterrent force of Soviet military might
   1. ☐ The government of the United States must realize that the times of unpunished imperialistic brigandage have long since passed. Cuba is not alone today. At her side are powerful forces capable of curbing any aggressor. Whoever unlooses a new war will inevitably be himself consumed in its flames.

      (Same purport as the statement, but greater brevity lends more force to the *Red Star* formulation.)
D. Soviet combat readiness
   1. ☐ The Soviet government is taking all the necessary steps so that our country is not taken unawares and is in a position to give a fitting answer to the aggressor.

      (Identical with the statement.)
   2. ☐ Together with all the Soviet peoples, the fighting men of our army and navy warmly approve the new measures, adopted by the Council of Ministers of the USSR, to strengthen the security of our country. The Soviet fighting men in the same ranks as their brothers-in-arms—the fighting men of the socialist commonwealth —vigilantly stand guard over the peace and security of the peoples.

      (Not mentioned in the SGS.)
   3. ☐ The Soviet fighting men are redoubling their vigilance and combat readiness, not sparing any efforts to strengthen the defensive might of our Motherland.

      (Not mentioned in the SGS.)
   4. We will not be taken unawares! Covered with the glory of victories, the mighty Soviet Armed Forces are ready to give a rebuff to any aggressor.

      (The reference to victory is absent from the SGS.)
IV. What the Soviet Union and Cuba could and might do
  A. Excluded measure—the withdrawal of missiles from Cuba
   1. ☐ Washington's demand to remove Soviet military equipment from Cuba is the height of effrontery.

      (Same purport as the SGS.)
  B. UN action
     (Not mentioned.)
  C, D, and E, *Soviet commitment to defend Cuba and the peace, Admonition to the United States that it is responsible for the fate of the*

world, and *Warning to retaliate against a nuclear blow* are combined in the following:

    1. ☐ The statement of the Soviet government published today contains a stern warning to the American aggressors. The government of the United States must realize that the times of unpunished imperialistic brigandage have long since passed. Cuba is not alone today. At her side are powerful forces capable of curbing any aggressor. Whoever unlooses a new war will inevitably be himself consumed in its flames.

    We want peace. But we have never feared, and do not fear, threats. We realize that the aggressive actions of the United States constitute a serious danger to the peace of the whole world. And we will do everything to prevent this danger and to smash the aggressor if he dare attempt to accomplish his mad plans.

F. Hint of action against U.S. overseas bases and an indication that military aid to Cuba will be continued

    1. ☐ The United States is not willing to withdraw its troops from other countries and eliminate its military bases there as the Soviet Union has proposed.

        a) ☐ The United States maintains its weapons and troops on hundreds of American military bases all over the world, and in particular, even in those countries that are in direct proximity to the Soviet Union. The United States is not willing to withdraw its troops from other countries and eliminate its military bases there as the Soviet Union has proposed. How then do they have the right to oppose the aid the Soviet Union renders Cuba in strengthening her defense!

        (Does not appear in SGS. The reference to bases in the statement [III A3] is general and does not assert an equal right, as does the above.)

The differences between the *Red Star editorial* "We Are on the Alert" and the Soviet Government Statement of 22 October emerge upon a comparison of the themes of the two pieces. Several themes in the statement are absent from the *Red Star* editorial.

1. (I A2) Cuban willingness to negotiate with the United States.
2. (I E3) Violation of the UN Charter.
3. (II 2) The catastrophe to mankind is not desired by anybody, including the American people.
4. (III A) The appeals to the peace-loving peoples to join in protest and the rehearsal of past Soviet peace initiatives.
5. (IV B) The Soviet decision to ask the UN Security Council to adopt a resolution condemning the United States.

These suggest some of the elements of the brinksman position. There is nothing for Cuba to negotiate about; hence, the references to Cuba's willingness to resolve the crisis and dispense with Soviet military aid in return for U.S. recognition and guarantees have been dropped. There is nothing the Soviet Union need negotiate, so the United Nations has no role to play. In fact, the United

Nations is not even mentioned in passing in the *Red Star* editorial. The lengthy appeals to others to join in the condemnation of, and protests to, the United States are absent. For the brinksman, it is Soviet might that will force the United States to accept the new reality of Soviet power that now permits the Soviet Union to have weapons and troops abroad. Appeals to others to put pressure on the United States imply that Soviet strength alone is inadequate.

The *Red Star* editorial also drops the phrase about "catastrophic consequences for all mankind," which nobody, including the American people, wants. This omission is not in itself of great significance since the charge that the United States is pushing the world to the brink of catastrophe amounts to much the same thing. However, the omission echoes the polemics of 1954 when Khrushchev, then aligned with the armed forces, compelled Malenkov to abandon the formula that in a nuclear war, civilization would founder.

Furthermore, in another place, the *Red Star* editorial, in contrast to the prediction of "catastrophic consequences for all mankind," implies that a Soviet victory is possible. "Covered with the glory of victories the powerful Soviet Armed Forces is ready to give a rebuff to any aggressor" (III D4).

The themes that appear in the *Red Star* article but that do not appear in the statement are also useful in limning the outlines of the brinksman position.

Red Star said that the United States was preparing a new attack on the island of freedom; (I C4g) the Soviet Government Statement did not say so. Two divergent interpretations are possible. The first is that by pointing to the imminence of U.S. aggression, to which the Soviet Union would have to respond, a veiled plea is being made for Soviet concessions to avoid facing the two undesirable alternatives of going to war or accepting a great blow to Soviet prestige. The second is that by referring to the U.S. intention to invade Cuba, the circumstances that would impel the Soviet Union to strike a nuclear blow are made a little more concrete. The Soviet government statement used the ambiguous phrases "unless aggression has been committed" (IV E1) and "if the aggressors unloose war" (IV E1). The second interpretation is preferred to the first as being more in harmony with the overall tone of the *Red Star* editorial and particularly with the *Red Star* version of the warning to the United States.

In the Soviet Government Statement a warning of war appears twice, the first time (IV E1) in the context of Kennedy's threat to retaliate to a Soviet nuclear strike, the second time (IV C1) in the context of a description of the actions that the United States had taken against Cuba. In the second context the warning in the SGS was considerably weaker, namely, "The Soviet Government will do everything it can to frustrate the aggressive purposes of the imperialist circles of the United States." The *Red Star* editorial amalgamated the two warnings in a way that made the commitment to Cuba much stronger (IV C,D,E). After having said that Cuba was not alone but had a powerful ally able to restrain any aggressor, the warning, "Whoever unlooses a new war, will inevitably be himself consumed in the flames," was issued. Instead of promising to frustrate the aggressive purposes of the American imperialist circles, *Red Star* promised to "do everything to prevent this danger and to smash the aggressor if he dare attempt to accomplish his mad plans."

Two textual differences and also the context make *Red Star* stronger than the statement. *Red Star* is specific about crushing the aggressor. The SGS only talks about unspecific measures to frustrate the aggressive purposes of imperialist circles. The second textual difference is the Soviet Government Statement's use of the phrase "imperialist circles" (IV C1), implying that the sober-minded statesmen and the firebrands were at odds. The *Red Star* use of the blunt term "aggressor" (IV C,D, E1) denied that a war faction and a peace faction existed in the United States; the phrase "aggressive" or "imperialist circles" is routinely used in Soviet political language to convey this idea. Rejecting the notion that the U.S. government was divided in its purposes eliminated the option of appealing to the "softs" in the United States. The aggressor would be frightened into yielding.

The contextual difference is the most important because it makes the warning in the *Red Star* editorial stronger than that in the SGS. By ignoring Kennedy's warning that a nuclear strike against the United States, wherever it originated, would precipitate a U.S. nuclear strike against the Soviet Union, and keeping the warning completely in the context of U.S. actions against Cuba, the *Red Star* editorial conveys the message that the Soviet warning to go to war is linked to U.S. actions against Cuba. The SGS diminishes the force of the warning by introducing another set of circumstances.

Lastly, the *Red Star* editorial goes farther than the Soviet Government Statement in reviving the "What's-sauce-for-the-goose-is-sauce-for-the-gander" argument as it applied to overseas bases. The official Soviet Government Statement dealt with overseas bases in the most general way (III A3), repeating the proposal that all nations return their troops to their own territory from abroad. The *Red Star* editorial (IV F1) said that the Soviet Union would continue its activities in Cuba, since the United States had not agreed to withdraw from its hundreds of bases all over the world. The *Red Star* editorial did not mention but did not contradict the long-standing Soviet position that the Soviet Union was prepared for both superpowers to return all their troops to their national boundaries. It did assert that the United States had no right to oppose Soviet help to Cuba.

The *Red Star* editorial, unlike the SGS, echoed but did not convey the full force of the 19 February 1962 threat to U.S. overseas bases when it referred to bases "in particular, even in those countries that are in direct proximity to the Soviet Union."

Each item in the catalogue of differences between the SGS and the *Red Star* editorial could be explained as an editorial vagary or as of little significance. Taken together, however, they argue for the existence of a separate Soviet military position differing from the combined position of the Soviet Government Statement and the *Pravda* position to which we now turn.

THEMATIC ANALYSIS OF "FRUSTRATE THE CRIMINAL SCHEMES OF THE ENEMIES OF PEACE," *PRAVDA*, 24 OCTOBER 1962

I. U.S. behavior characterized
   A. U.S. intentions toward Cuba
      1. (The charge in the SGS that the United States was trying to dictate Cuban policy and determine what weapons it should have is not repeated.)

2. The United States does not want to negotiate with Cuba, although Cuba has frequently asserted her desire to do so.

☐ The Cubans only want to secure their homeland against the threats emanating from the imperialists of the United States. The Cuban government calls on Washington to establish normal relations and to settle disputed questions by negotiations.

(Same purport as the SGS.)

3. The events of the Bay of Pigs outraged the whole world and proved that the United States wanted to destroy the Cuban regime—as it still does.

☐ American imperialism, assuming the role of world policeman, has been weaving its nets of provocation around the Cuban Republic for quite a long time now. The events of the Bay of Pigs are still fresh in memory. The attacks of the American mercenaries who perpetrated arbitrary acts on the high seas and conducted piratical raids on the peaceful cities and villages of Cuba have aroused the indignation of the whole world. At that time the American ruling clique tried to hide behind false statements of their noninvolvement in these actions. But now the cards are at last on the table. It is obvious to the whole world that the present actions are the logical culmination of the criminal plan inherited by the Kennedy government from Eisenhower's administration and carried out by order of the Pentagon.

(Same purport as the SGS.)

B. U.S. charges against Cuba

1. The United States claims that little Cuba is a threat to its security. No one believes that.

☐ President Kennedy could think of nothing better in his address than to make accusations against Cuba, refuted long ago, that she supposedly threatens the security of the United States. But the whole world knows that revolutionary Cuba, a nation that has chosen the path of freedom and the path of the construction of a new society does not, and because of the nature of her social structure, cannot threaten anyone.

(The same purport as the SGS, but more general.)

C. U.S. actions against Cuba

1. The United States invaded Cuba in April 1961 and continues provocations against her.

 a) ☐ American imperialism, assuming the role of world policeman, has been weaving its nets of provocation around the Cuban Republic for quite a long time now.

(More general than the SGS.)

2. ☐ Concentrating its fleet in the Caribbean, the American government . . . has placed its armed forces in a state of combat readiness.

(Virtually identical with the SGS on combat readiness, but the reinforcement of the Guantánamo base and the reference to reconnaissance of Cuba have been dropped.)

3. A blockade has been imposed on Cuba in violation of international law.

     a) ☐ . . . The American government in the person of President Kennedy, with unexampled effrontery, has announced its intention to impose a naval blockade against the Republic of Cuba. . . .

         (Almost identical with the SGS, but the characterization of the blockade as virtual has been dropped.)

     b) *The measures adopted by the American ruling circles are a flagrant violation of the elementary norms of international law and of all international custom.*

         (Virtually identical with the SGS.)

D. U.S. demands on Cuba

   1. (No mention of U.S. demands that equipment needed for the defense of Cuba be removed.)

E. The wider implications of U.S. behavior

   1. The United States is playing the role of world policeman.

     a) ☐ American imperialism, assuming the role of world policeman, has been weaving its nets of provocation. . . .

         (Same purport as the SGS, but the reference to the Soviet proposal for mutual liquidation of foreign bases has been dropped.)

   2. The United States threatens the Soviet Union with a nuclear attack

     a) ☐ The American ruling circles are playing with fire in threatening war against the Soviet Union. They cynically declare that they are ready to rain down atomic and hydrogen bombs on the heads of hundreds of millions of people. . . .

         (Much more general than the SGS; Kennedy's declaration that any nuclear bomb dropped on the United States would bring retaliation against the Soviet Union has been dropped.)

   3. The United States is undermining international law and endangering the existence of the United Nations.

     a) ☐ *The measures adopted by the American ruling circles are a flagrant violation of the elementary norms of international law and of all international custom. They are incompatible with the principles of the UN Charter. They are a challenge to all peace-loving nations. Such actions are an open revival of piracy and international brigandage, which mankind hoped had been ended forever with the conviction in Nuremberg and Tokyo of major war criminals responsible for unloosing the Second World War and for crimes against peace and humanity.*

         (Same purport as the SGS.)

     b) ☐ In the situation that has arisen a special responsibility rests on the United Nations. It was created after World War II to stand guard over the peace. The peoples have placed their hopes in it, hopes which, unfortunately, have not always been justified. At the present decisive moment the United Nations is confronted with a new, most serious test. The question is whether it fulfills the mission that the peoples have laid upon it and thereby justifies its real purpose or whether the fate of the League of Nations and the universal contempt of the peoples await it. There is no third way.

(More emphasis on the necessity of pressure on the United States—through the agency of the United Nations, of American allies, and of the Third World—than in the SGS.)

II. What a war would mean for the United States and the world
  A. The United States has created the danger of a world nuclear war
    1. □ The American imperialists have adopted unprecedented, aggressive measures, confronting the world with the threat of global nuclear war.

(Same purport as the SGS.)

    2. □ The actions of the American militarists represent crude blackmail capable of bringing catastrophic consequences to all mankind.

(Substantially the same as the SGS, but the phrase about the outcome being unwanted by the American people has been dropped.)

    3. □ In the aggression against Cuba, the peoples of other countries see an attempt on their own rights and freedoms, on peace and security in the whole world.

(Same purport as the SGS.)

    4. □ Dark clouds have gathered over the world. In these grim days we must look reality soberly in the face. The atomic maniacs want to gamble with the fate of human civilization.

(Same purport as II A2 of the SGS.)

III. What the Soviet Union and Cuba have already done and are now doing
  A. Appeals
    1. (Not mentioned.)
    2. (Not mentioned.)
    3. (Not mentioned.)
    4. (Not mentioned.)
    5. *a*) □ *A wave of angry protests against the fanatical actions of the American militarists is rolling over the whole world.*
      b) □ An appeal to defend Cuba against aggression is being heard on all continents and in hundreds of languages.
      c) □ The peoples cannot remain indifferent to the events in the Caribbean. *Energetic actions, united efforts, and a common will can stay the hand raised by the American aggressors against peace. In the face of the reckless adventure of the United States government, the peoples demand: stop this dangerous playing with fire; curb the American aggressors!*
    6. (Not mentioned.)
  B. Soviet military aid to Cuba
    1. (Not mentioned. This means that the characterization of the weapons as defensive also disappears.)

C. The deterrent force of Soviet military might
   1. □ However, the times have passed when pirates could act with impunity. . . . The Soviet Union, the socialist countries, and the peace-loving nations have enough strength and the means *to put a strait jacket on the aggressors.*
      (Much shorter than the SGS. The statement that the Soviet Union is no less powerful than the United States has been dropped. In contrast to *Red Star*, there is no denial of fear, no promise to crush the aggressor, and no recollections of past victories in the recital of Soviet strength.)
D. Soviet combat readiness
   1. (Not mentioned.)
IV. What the Soviet Union and Cuba could and might do
   A. Excluded measure—the withdrawal of missiles from Cuba
      (The necessity for excluding the withdrawal of missiles from Cuba does not even arise because Soviet equipment in Cuba has not been mentioned; nor does the *Pravda* editorial refer to Kennedy's charge that "offensive" weapons were located in Cuba.)
   B. UN action
      (See I IE 3b of analysis of *Pravda* editorial.)
   C. Soviet commitment to defend Cuba and the peace
      1. □ Let the authors of the criminal plans not delude themselves. The socialist countries are as one in their efforts to nip any aggression in the very bud. We have powerful forces and an inflexible will to defend peace.
         (A statement of capability rather than of intent when compared with the SGS and hence a weaker commitment to frustrate U.S. plans.)
   D. Admonition to the United States that it is responsible for the fate of the world
      1. See I E2*a* of analysis of *Pravda* editorial.
         (Same purport as the SGS.)
   E. Warning to retaliate against a nuclear blow
      1. □ The American ruling circles are playing with fire in threatening war against the Soviet Union. They cynically declare that they are ready to rain down atomic and hydrogen bombs on the heads of hundreds of millions of people and to destroy what human civilization has taken centuries to create.
         However, the times have passed when pirates could act with impunity. *"If the aggressors unloose war,"* the statement of the Soviet government published today says, *"the Soviet Union will strike a most powerful retaliatory blow."* The statement of the Soviet government is a stern warning to those who are losing their reason.
         (Same purport as the SGS.)
      2. □ *The imperialist aggressors should remember that if they try to kindle the flames of world war, they will inevitably be incinerated in its fire.*

Several themes in the Soviet Government Statement are absent or substantially modified in the *Pravda* editorial.

1. (I A1) The Soviet government charge that the United States has arrogated to itself the right to tell Cuba what its policy should be and what weapons it should have for its own defense is absent.
2. (I A3a) Instead of the charge that the United States wants to stifle Cuba (I A3), *Pravda* makes the weaker charge that the United States has been weaving provocative nets around Cuba (I A3).
3. (I D1a) The U.S. demand that the military equipment required for Cuban defense be removed is missing in *Pravda*.
4. The *Pravda* editorial, instead of repeating the appeals in the SGS (III A 1–6), rolls them all up into a more general appeal (III A5). In so doing, the specific demand for the end to the blockade is lost.
5. (III B1) The Soviet role in supplying weapons for Cuba's defense is not mentioned, obviating the necessity for insisting that the weapons are intended for defensive purposes.
6. (III C1) The *Pravda* editorial, like the SGS and unlike *Red Star*, contains no hints either of crushing the aggressor or of victory but is exclusively deterrent in content. The *Pravda* editorial puts much less emphasis on the decline of U.S. power and the increase in Soviet power.
7. (III D1) The *Pravda* editorial has no call for military readiness.
8. (IV A) There is no need to exclude the measure of withdrawing the missiles since they are never mentioned even by implication.
9. (IV C1) The commitment to defend Cuba is weaker. It is an effort to nip aggression in the bud rather than a promise to do everything the Soviet government can to frustrate the criminal schemes of the American imperialist circles.
10. (IV E1) The warning to strike a nuclear blow at the United States is linked to an even more loosely defined American action than that in the SGS. The *Pravda* editorial talks of American threats to rain bombs and American readiness to destroy what it took centuries for human civilization to build, whereas the SGS tied the Soviet use of nuclear weapons to the commission of aggression by the United States.
11. (I E3b) The *Pravda* editorial contains one theme in much stronger form than it appears in the SGS, namely, the very high reliance placed on the role of the United Nations in the saving of peace.

This listing of the differences between the *Pravda* editorial and the Soviet government position reveals a stand on the Cuban crisis that can be distinguished from the Soviet Government Statement and, of course, from the *Red Star* editorial. The disaster to human civilization, i.e., the mutual destructiveness of war, is emphasized somewhat more in *Pravda*. Soviet weapons in Cuba are not mentioned; thus, the *Pravda* editorial does not commit the Soviet Union to keeping them in Cuba. Although the blockade is condemned, a specific demand for its end is not made. In fact, much of the wordage of the *Pravda* editorial is rhetorical excoriation of the United States in general terms, with the consequence that specific demands are reduced in number. The commitment to defend Cuba is somewhat but perhaps not significantly weaker than the official government position. The very strong appeal to the United Nations and the rather unusual statement that people all over the world depend on the United Nations to guard peace very much weakens the claim that the new balance of forces represented by Soviet strength has reduced the options of the United

States. The League of Nations earned the universal contempt of the peoples because it was unable to stop Hitler's aggression. Now, says *Pravda*, the United Nations faces its decisive moment. Will it share the fate of the League of Nations (by permitting U.S. aggression to go unchecked) or will it fulfill its mission? In other words, nations not allied with the Soviet Union, some of them presumably allies of the United States, have to oppose the United States if aggression is to be checked. When the *Pravda* passage on the United Nations is read with such a gloss, the next paragraph, with the admonition to look reality soberly in the face, falls into place. If "maniacs want to gamble with the fate of human civilization" and no one seems able to stop them, then perhaps it is realistic to yield. This is not the necessary conclusion from the *Pravda* editorial, but it is a possible conclusion. The *Izvestiia* editorial represented even further movement toward a compromise solution.

THEMATIC ANALYSIS OF "THINK IT OVER, MR. PRESIDENT," *IZVESTIIA*, 24 OCTOBER 1962

I. U.S. behavior characterized
  A. U.S. intentions toward Cuba
    1. ☐ They try to arrogate to themselves the "right" to determine a question that is in the jurisdiction of Cuba itself—the question of its security and defense.
        (Virtually the same as the SGS.)
    2. ☐ Rarely has any power resorted to methods so monstrous, treacherous, and aggressive in its relations with a neighboring country as has the United States in relation to Cuba today. It is well-known that Cuba is a peace-loving country.
        (Implies but does not assert, as the SGS does, that Cuba wants to negotiate.)
    3., ☐ In an effort to restore the overturned despotic regime on the island, the United States has worked out a plan that comes down to strangling Cuba economically.
        (Same purport as the SGS.)
  B. U.S. charges against Cuba
    1. The United States claims that little Cuba is a threat to its security. No one believes that.
        ☐ The U.S. Navy has been ordered to impose a virtual blockade on Cuba on the pretext that Cuba supposedly threatens the United States and even the whole Western Hemisphere. . . . And now the president of the United States, Kennedy, is not ashamed to give currency to a crude lie and falsehood that Cuba has suddenly become a "threat to the Western Hemisphere."
        (Same purport as the SGS.)
  C. U.S. actions against Cuba
    1. ☐ No, it is American aircraft that are flying over the territory of the Cuban Republic.
        (The specific indication that the purpose of the flights is reconnaissance is missing.)

2. □ . . . The American militarists have a base for aggressive operations on Cuban soil.

(The reinforcement of Guantánamo and the combat readiness of the U.S. armed forces has been omitted.)

3. □ The U.S. Navy has been ordered to impose a virtual blockade on Cuba. . . .

□ The actions of medieval pirates pale before the brigandage of the U.S. Navy on the high seas. Raising piracy to the level of state policy, the ruling figures of the United States have announced their intention to attack ships plying Cuban waters.

(Substantially the same as the SGS, but wordier.)

4. □ Fanning an anti-Cuban psychosis and bringing up the worn-out bugaboo of the "communist menace," Washington sought to pass over to direct aggression. At the end of September the U.S. Congress adopted a joint resolution authorizing in advance the adventure in preparation against Cuba.

(Not in the SGS.)

D. U.S. demands on Cuba

1. (No mention of U.S. demands that equipment needed for the defense of Cuba be removed.)

E. The wider implications of U.S. behavior

1. □ Showing complete disregard for the generally accepted norms of international intercourse, the ruling circles of the United States appear in the uniform of the world policeman and shake a club threateningly at the Cuban people.

2. (There is no mention of the United States threatening the Soviet Union with a nuclear attack. As in the *Pravda* editorial, the reference to the Soviet proposal for mutual withdrawal from overseas bases has been dropped, but *Izvestiia*, like *Red Star*, makes no reference to the United Nations.)

II. What a war would mean for the United States and the world

A. The United States has created the danger of a world nuclear war

1. □ It can be recalled that a few days ago, for example, none other than the Vice-President of the United States, Lyndon Johnson, spoke in New Mexico. In his words, a blockade of Cuba could lead to a third world war. Thus, is the United States of America consciously bringing matters to a world nuclear war?!

(Although the danger of a nuclear war is as clearly assessed as in the SGS, the phrase "the catastrophic consequences for all mankind" has been omitted.)

III. What the Soviet Union and Cuba have already done and are now doing

A. Appeals

1. (Not mentioned.)

2. (Not mentioned.)

3. (Not mentioned.)

4. □ The fervent sympathies of all the people on the globe who value the cause of freedom and independence are on the side of the freedom-loving people of Cuba.

5. (Not mentioned.)
6. (Not mentioned.)

B. Soviet military aid to Cuba

1. ☐ As a sovereign, independent state, Cuba has had, and has, the full right to take the necessary measures to safeguard its security and defense in the face of the intensified aggression of American imperialism. The Soviet Union, loyal to its international obligations, has extended the hand of friendly aid to the heroic Cuban people in the building and development of the economy of Cuba and in the the elevation of its culture and in the strengthening of its defense.

(A weaker commitment than the SGS to the defense of Cuba in that it avoids a direct reference to Soviet weapons in Cuba.)

C. The deterrent force of Soviet military might

1. ☐ The adventuristic circles across the ocean are evidently so blinded by hatred for the Cuban republic that they forget in what century they are living and with what dangerous combustible material they are recklessly playing.

☐ At the present time American imperialism is opposed by the mighty camp of the socialist countries who possess everything necessary to curb any aggressor, and it is opposed by the great front of the peoples.

(More general than the SGS and weaker in that weapons are not specifically mentioned.)

D. Soviet combat readiness

1. ☐ The Soviet government, as always, will do everything necessary so that no machinations of the imperialist aggressive forces take the Soviet Union unawares, and so that the defense of our country is in a condition of constant combat readiness.

("As always," which does not appear in the SGS, suggests that no special measures are being taken.)

IV. What the Soviet Union and Cuba could and might do

A. Excluded measure—the withdrawal of missiles from Cuba

1. (Not mentioned. As in *Pravda*, the necessity for excluding this measure does not arise, for nowhere is there any mention of Soviet equipment in Cuba or any reference to Kennedy's charge that there were "offensive" weapons in Cuba.)

B. UN action

(Not mentioned.)

C. Soviet commitment to defend Cuba and the peace

1. ☐ As regards the Soviet Union and the Soviet people, no tantrums of the imperialist aggressors will prevent us in the future from discharging our great international duty to support and help nations defending their freedom and independence. The Soviet people respond to the ravings of the American imperialists by closing ranks more closely around our own Communist Party and the Soviet government.

(Much weaker than the SGS. "Aggressive purposes" have become "tantrums" (*metanie*). The undertaking to "do everything it can to frustrate" has become "no tantrums . . . will prevent us . . . from fulfilling our great international duty.")

D. Admonition to the United States that it is responsible for the fate of the world

   1. □ As a consequence of the weakening of their imperialistic positions in the world at large and in Latin America in particular, the ruling circles of the United States, like a reckless gambler who has gone too far, have now decided on a new, desperate step that is evidence neither of sound judgment, of self-control, or of concern for the destiny of the United States itself.

   (Somewhat weaker than the SGS since the "fate of the world" is not mentioned.)

E. Warning to retaliate against a nuclear blow

   1. (Not mentioned.)

The following themes in the Soviet Government Statement are not mentioned in the *Izvestiia* editorial.

1. The United States is in a position of combat readiness. (I C2*a*) ·
2. The U.S. demand that military equipment necessary for Cuba's defense be withdrawn. (I D)
3. The United States arrogates to itself the right to interfere with the trade and shipping of countries of whose policies or social structure it disapproves. (I C3*b*)
4. No references to the United Nations or appeals for its action. (IV B1 and passim)
5. Appeals to the United States for far reaching disarmament measures, particularly mutual withdrawal from military installations in foreign countries, and appeals to other countries to join in protest and putting pressure on the United States. (III A, 1, 2, 3, 5, and 6)
6. Support of Cuba's resolve to keep Soviet weapons.
7. Warning to retaliate to a nuclear blow.

A reference in the *Izvestiia* editorial that does not appear in the Soviet Government Statement is that to the joint resolution of Congress authorizing in advance the U.S. plan for direct aggression against Cuba. (I C4)

The most striking feature of the *Izvestiia* editorial is the omission of the Soviet warning that it will retaliate in kind if the United States commits aggression or unlooses war. Consequently, the formula on Soviet combat readiness is considerably weaker, implying that the present state of combat readiness is the ordinary state; *Izvestiia* omits the reference to retaliation, thus slighting the possibility of the opponent's action, and downgrades the actions of the opponent by calling them machinations. As in *Pravda*, support of the Cuban resolve to keep the weapons described as "offensive" by Kennedy is missing—an omission that can be interpreted as a willingness to give up the missiles in Cuba. Khrushchev's failure to reiterate Soviet support of the Cuban resolve to keep the missiles in his reply to Bertrand Russell's telegram given the same day as the *Izvestiia* editorial reinforces this interpretation. The *Izvestiia* editorial, like Khrushchev's reply to Russell, focuses on the illegality of the blockade and on

American illegal treatment of Cuba, which suggests that the authors of these documents were willing to withdraw the missiles if the blockade were abandoned and if the United States either recognized the government of Cuba or undertook to abandon its attempts to overthrow it. This is a possible and perhaps even a likely interpretation of the textual evidence, but not a necessary conclusion.

A puzzling element in the *Izvestiia* editorial is the absence of reference to the United Nations and of appeals to others to put pressure on the United States. A possible explanation is that the Soviet government statement and the *Pravda* editorial occupied a medial position between the standpat *Red Star* position and the retreat of the *Izvestiia* position. The Soviet Government Statement and the *Pravda* editorial clung to the hope that world pressure could save some elements of the Soviet position. *Izvestiia* and *Red Star* both omitted appeals to the United Nations and to other nations to put pressure on the United States, although for contrary reasons. *Red Star* felt they were unnecessary and would signal weakness; *Izvestiia* wanted to resolve the crisis by meeting Kennedy's demands.

APPENDIX 2

SOVIET GOVERNMENT STATEMENT OF 23 OCTOBER 1962

Last night, on 22 October, the president of the United States of America, [John F.] Kennedy, announced that he had ordered the United States Navy to intercept all ships bound for Cuba, to subject them to inspection, and not to permit the passage of ships with weapons that, in the judgment of the American authorities, were offensive in character. An order had also been issued for constant and close surveillance of Cuba. Thus, the United States government has virtually imposed a naval blockade on the Republic of Cuba. Simultaneously, the landing of new troops on the American Guantánamo base, situated on Cuban territory, has begun, and United States Armed Forces are being placed in a state of combat readiness.

The president is trying to justify these unprecedented aggressive measures with the argument that Cuba is supposedly the source of a threat to the national security of the United States.

The Soviet government has repeatedly drawn the attention of the governments of all countries and of world public opinion to the serious danger to the cause of peace represented by the policy pursued by the United States toward the Republic of Cuba. The statement of the president of the United States shows that American imperialist circles will stop at nothing in their efforts to stifle a sovereign state that is a member of the United Nations. To that end they are ready to push the world to the abyss of a military catastrophe. The peoples of all countries must clearly realize that in embarking on such an adventure, the United States of America is taking a step toward unloosing a world nuclear war. Brazenly flouting the international norms for the conduct of states and the principles of the UN Charter, the United States has arrogated to itself the right—and has so announced—to attack the ships of other states on the high seas, i.e., to engage in piracy.

The imperialist circles in the United States are trying to dictate to Cuba what policy to pursue, what system to establish in its own homeland, and what weapons to maintain for its defense. But who gave the United States the right to assume the role of ruler of the destinies of other countries and peoples? Why must the Cubans conduct the domestic affairs of their state not as they see fit but as the United States prefers? Cuba belongs to the Cuban people and only it can be master of its fate.

According to the UN Charter all countries, large and small, have the right to order their affairs in their own way and to adopt the measures they deem necessary to guarantee their security and to repulse aggressors against their freedom and independence. To ignore this is to undermine the very basis of the existence of the United Nations, to introduce the laws of the jungle into international life, and to engender conflicts and wars without end.

In this anxious hour the Soviet government considers itself duty bound to earnestly caution the government of the United States and to warn it that, in carrying out the measures announced by President Kennedy, it is recklessly playing with fire and assuming a grave responsibility for the fate of the world.

The leaders of the United States must at last realize that times have now changed completely. Only madmen can now rely on a policy "from positions of strength" and believe that that policy will be at all successful and permit them to impose their order on other states. If once the United States could regard itself as the very greatest military power, now there is no basis at all for such a view. There is another force in the world, no less powerful, which maintains that people should order their own affairs as they wish. Now as never before statesmen must be cool and prudent and not countenance the brandishing of weapons.

The Soviet Government attests once again that all the weapons in its possession serve, and will serve, the purposes of defense against aggressors. In existing international circumstances the presence of powerful weapons, including nuclear missiles, in the Soviet Union is acknowledged by all the peoples of the world as the decisive means to deter the aggressive forces of imperialism from unloosing a world war of annihilation. The Soviet Union will continue even in the future to discharge this mission with complete firmness and consistency.

The president of the United States said in his statement that if even one nuclear bomb fell on the territory of the United States, the United States would strike a retaliatory blow. Such an assertion is shot through with hypocrisy since the Soviet Union has already repeatedly stated that not a single nuclear bomb will fall either on the United States or on any other country unless aggression has been committed. The nuclear weapons made by the Soviet people are in the hands of the people and will never be employed for purposes of aggression.

But if the aggressors unloose war, the Soviet Union will strike a most powerful retaliatory blow.

The Soviet Union has always been true to the principles of the UN Charter. It has consistently pursued, and pursues, a policy directed to maintaining and strengthening peace. The whole world knows what enormous efforts the Soviet Union has exerted to relax international tension, to eliminate sources of conflicts and disputes among states, and to put into practice the principles of the peaceful coexistence of states with different social structures. It is the Soviet

Union that has advanced and established a program of universal and complete disarmament whose realization would open up genuine prospects for the establishment of a peace without wars and weapons. These proposals have gained growing support in the world; they have captured the imagination of people; they have become the rallying cry of the times. If until now the cause of disarmament has not made any headway, the fault lies with the United States and its NATO allies. They are afraid of disarmament, not wanting to part with the big stick with which they try to dictate their will to other countries.

The United States government accuses Cuba of creating a so-called threat to the security of the United States. But who believes that Cuba can threaten the United States? If the size, resources, and armaments of both countries are considered, no statesman in his right mind could see in Cuba a threat to the United States or to any other country. It is hypocrisy, at the very least, to say that little Cuba can imperil the security of the United States.

The Cubans wish to secure their homeland and their independence against the threats emanating from the United States. The government of Cuba appeals to reason and conscience and calls upon the United States to refrain from making claims on the independence of Cuba and to establish normal relations with the Cuban state. Doesn't the official Cuban government announcement of its aspiration to regulate all disputed questions by negotiations with the United States government ring true?

Only recently in a speech to the session of the UN General Assembly, the president of the Republic of Cuba, O. Dorticós, reiterated that Cuba "had always expressed her readiness to conduct negotiations through the normal diplomatic channels or by any other means in order to discuss the differences between the United States and Cuba." Now the president of the United States implies that these Cuban government statements are somehow inadequate. But that is the way to justify any aggressive action, any adventure.

With regard to the Soviet Union's aid to Cuba: this aid is exclusively for the purpose of contributing to the defensive capacity of Cuba. As the joint Soviet-Cuban communiqué of 3 September of this year on the visit to the Soviet Union of a Cuban delegation composed of E. Guevara and E. Aragonés indicated, the Soviet government responded to the request of the Cuban government to help Cuba with arms. The communiqué states that these arms and military equipment are exclusively designated for the purposes of defense. The governments of both countries still firmly adhere to that position.

The subjection of the Cuban Republic from the first days of its existence to constant threats and provocations on the part of the United States has necessitated Soviet help in improving the defenses of Cuba. The United States has stopped at nothing, not even the organization of the armed intervention in Cuba of April 1961, to deprive the Cuban people of the freedom and independence it had won and once again to subject it to the domination of the American monopolies and to make Cuba an American puppet.

The United States demands that the military equipment Cuba needs for her self-defense be removed from her territory—a course to which no state that values its independence could, of course, agree.

The Soviet Union maintains that all foreign troops should be withdrawn from the territory of other states and brought back within their own national frontiers. If the United States is genuinely concerned to strengthen friendly relations with [other] states and is trying to secure lasting peace in the whole world, as President Kennedy asserted in his speech of 22 October, it would have accepted the Soviet proposal to withdraw its troops and military equipment and to dismantle its military bases situated on foreign territory in various parts of the world.

However, the United States, which has its armed forces and armaments scattered all over the world, stubbornly refuses to accept this proposal. The United States employs them to intervene in the internal affairs of other states and to the role of international policeman. The representatives of the United States constantly boast that American aircraft can attack the Soviet Union at any time, can drop bombs on peaceful cities and villages, can strike heavy blows. Not a day passes without the statesmen, military leaders, and the press of the United States uttering threats that American submarines, plying many seas and oceans with Polaris missiles aboard, can bring an atomic blow down upon the Soviet Union and other peace-loving states. In the light of these facts there is a particularly false ring to President Kennedy's words that the government of the United States is guided by the interests of peace in its presumptuous demands that Cuba be deprived of the means of defense.

The peace-loving states cannot but protest against the piratical operations against ships bound for Cuban shores announced by the president of the United States and against the institution of controls over the ships of sovereign states on the high seas. We know that American statesmen like to talk about their devotion to the principles of international law and to expatiate on the necessity for the rule of law in the world. But in reality they evidently believe that laws are not written for the United States, but for other states. The imposition by the United States of a virtual blockade of the shores of Cuba is a provocative step and an unprecedented violation of international law and a challenge to all peace-loving peoples.

Obviously, if the United States today tries to prohibit other countries from trading with Cuba and from using their ships to transport goods and cargoes to Cuba, tomorrow the American ruling circles could demand the adoption of similar measures against any other state whose policy or social structure does not suit the ruling circles of the United States.

The United States government arrogates to itself the right to demand that states account to it on how they organize their defense and report what their ships are carrying on the high seas.

The Soviet Government firmly repudiates such claims. The insolent actions of U.S. imperialism could lead to catastrophic consequences for all mankind that no people, including the people of the United States, want.

In view of the seriousness of the situation that the United States government has created over Cuba, the Soviet government has instructed its representative in the United Nations to raise the question of the immediate convocation of the Security Council to consider the [following] question: "The violation of the Charter of the United Nations and the threat to peace by the United States of

America."

The Soviet Union appeals to all governments and peoples to raise their voices in protest against the aggressive actions of the United States of America against Cuba and other states, to condemn these actions firmly, and to bar the way to the unloosing of nuclear war by the United States government.

The Soviet government will do everything it can to frustrate the aggressive purposes of the imperialist circles of the United States and to defend and to consolidate peace on earth.

The Soviet government expresses its firm belief that the Soviet people will increase their efforts to work still further to strengthen the economic and defensive might of the Soviet Motherland. The Soviet government is taking all the necessary steps so that our country is not taken unawares and is in a position to give a fitting answer to the aggressor.

"WE ARE ON THE ALERT," *RED STAR (KRASNAIA ZVEZDA)*, 24 OCTOBER 1962

The world is alarmed and disturbed by the new criminal adventure of the imperialists of the United States of America who have adopted unprecedented, aggressive measures against heroic Cuba. All the Soviet people, the peoples of the other socialist countries, the honest people of the whole globe will brand with infamy the brazen aggressors, who recklessly play with fire and push the world to the brink of catastrophe.

Assuming the role of world policeman, American imperialism is trying to dictate to Cuba how to live, what [political] system to have, and what weapons to acquire for her defense. The president of the United States, Kennedy, has announced that he has given the order to intercept all ships going to Cuba, to subject them to inspection, and not to permit the passage of ships with weapons that, in the opinion of the American authorities, are offensive in character. In other words, the United States has virtually imposed a naval blockade on Cuba and arrogates to itself the right to attack ships of other countries on the high seas, that is, to engage in piracy. New units are being landed on the American Guantánamo base, situated on Cuban territory. The United States Armed Forces are being placed in a state of combat readiness.

The new piratical actions of the United States imperialists cannot be regarded as anything but a crude provocational step, an unheard of violation of international law, and a challenge to all peace-loving peoples. Washington is trying to justify these actions in vain by reference to the threat to the security of the United States . . .° on the part of Cuba. That kind of reference [to a threat] is false and hypocritical through and through. Cuba cannot and never has threatened the United States. Besides, everybody knows that from the day the independent Republic of Cuba was born, the American predators, who wanted to make Cuba their colony and puppet, bared their teeth at her. It is they who organized and prepared the invasion of Cuba by mercenaries. It is they who constantly arrange armed provocations on Cuban soil. It is they who who are trying to strangle Cuba with famine. It is they who are now sending dozens of ships into the Caribbean and preparing a new attack on the island of freedom, as the American press openly asserts. How can officials in Washington

° Ellipsis in original.

have the effrontery to complain about the dangers supposedly threatening their country from Cuba?

In reality it is Cuba that wants to secure her domain from the encroachments of the United States. It is time that Washington understood that it's not its business to give Cuba advice about what is best for Cuba to do. Cuba belongs to the Cuban people! And they know very well how to order their internal affairs. Cuba is fighting for a just cause—she is defending her freedom and independence.

With regard to the aid that the Soviet Union renders to the Republic of Cuba: everybody knows that it is designated exclusively for purposes of defense. Washington's demand to remove Soviet military equipment from Cuba is the height of effrontery. The United States maintains its weapons and troops on hundreds of American military bases scattered all over the world, and in particular, even in those countries that are in direct proximity to the Soviet Union. The United States is not willing to withdraw its troops from other countries and eliminate its military bases there as the Soviet Union has proposed. How then do they have the right to oppose the aid the Soviet Union renders Cuba in strengthening her defense!

The statement of the Soviet government published today contains a stern warning to the American aggressors. The government of the United States must realize that the times of unpunished imperialistic brigandage have long since passed. Cuba is not alone today. At her side are powerful forces capable of curbing any aggressor. Whoever unlooses a new war will inevitably be himself consumed in its flames.

We want peace. But we never have feared, and do not fear, threats. We realize that the aggressive actions of the United States constitute a serious danger to the peace of the whole world. And we will do everything to prevent this danger and to smash the aggressor if he dare attempt to accomplish his mad plans.

The Soviet government in its statement expressed the firm belief that the Soviet people would increase their efforts at work still further to strengthen the economic and defensive might of the Soviet Motherland. The Soviet government is taking all the necessary steps so that our country is not taken unawares and is in a position to give a fitting answer to the aggressor.

Together with all the Soviet peoples, the fighting men of our army and navy warmly approve the new measures, adopted by the Council of Ministers of the USSR,* to strengthen the security of our country. The Soviet fighting men in the same ranks as their brothers-in-arms—the fighting men of the socialist commonwealth—vigilantly stand guard over the peace and security of the peoples.

The Soviet fighting men are redoubling their vigilance and combat readiness, not sparing any efforts to strengthen the defensive might of our Motherland.

We will not be taken unawares! Covered with the glory of victories, the mighty Soviet Armed Forces are ready to give a rebuff to any aggressor.

* On 23 October 1962 the Soviet government ordered the minister of defense to defer the release of the older classes from the Strategic Missile Forces, the Air Defense Forces, and the Submarine Forces; to cancel all leaves; and to raise the combat readiness and vigilance of all forces (*Pravda*, 24 October 1962).

"FRUSTRATE THE CRIMINAL SCHEMES OF ENEMIES OF PEACE," *PRAVDA,* 24 OCTOBER 1962

Alarming news has spread throughout the whole world. The American imperialists have adopted unprecedented, aggressive measures, confronting the world with the threat of global nuclear war. Concentrating its fleet in the Caribbean, the American government in the person of President Kennedy, with unexampled effrontery, has announced its intention to impose a naval blockade against the Republic of Cuba and has placed its armed forces in a state of combat readiness.

American imperialism, assuming the role of world policeman, has been weaving its nets of provocation around the Cuban Republic for quite a long time now. The events of the Bay of Pigs are still fresh in memory. The attacks of the American mercenaries· who perpetrated arbitrary acts on the high seas and conducted piratical raids on the peaceful cities and villages of Cuba have aroused the indignation of the whole world. At that time the American ruling clique tried to hide behind false statements of their noninvolvement in these actions. But now the cards are at last on the table. It is obvious to the whole world that the present actions are the logical culmination of the criminal plan inherited by the Kennedy government from Eisenhower's administration and carried out by order of the Pentagon.

The measures adopted by the American ruling circles are a flagrant violation of the elementary norms of international law and of all international custom. They are incompatible with the principles of the UN Charter. They are a challenge to all peace-loving nations. Such actions are an open revival of piracy and international brigandage, which mankind hoped had been ended forever with the conviction in Nuremberg and Tokyo of the major war criminals responsible for unloosing the Second World War and for crimes against peace and humanity.

In embarking on this new adventure the American ruling circles are acting like craven predators. They know that the peace-loving peoples will brand them with infamy, and therefore they lie and squirm. President Kennedy's speech on radio and television from the first to the last word was shot through with lies and hypocrisy. It was like a highwayman's prayer before taking to the high road.

President Kennedy could think of nothing better in his address than to make accusations against Cuba, refuted long ago, that she supposedly threatens the security of the United States. But the whole world knows that revolutionary Cuba, a nation that has chosen the path of freedom and the path of the construction of a new society does not, and because of the nature of her new social structure, cannot threaten anyone. The Cubans only want to secure their homeland against the threats emanating from the imperialists of the United States. The Cuban government calls on Washington to establish normal relations and to settle disputed questions by negotiations.

The American ruling circles see that the ideas of national independence and social justice kindled by the Cuban revolution in the Western Hemisphere find understanding and support in the hearts of the peoples of Latin America. They fear the inexorable march of history. They are becoming convinced that they cannot cope even in their own country with the social problems engendered by the internal contradictions of capitalism. The position taken by the United States government is evidence not of strength but of the doom of the system of capitalist exploitation.

The actions of the American militarists represent crude blackmail capable of bringing catastrophic consequences to all mankind. The American ruling circles are playing with fire in threatening war against the Soviet Union. They cynically declare that they are ready to rain down atomic and hydrogen bombs on the heads of hundreds of millions of people and to destroy what human civilization has taken centuries to create.

the aggressors unloose war," the statement of the Soviet government published today says, "the Soviet Union will strike a most powerful retaliatory blow." The Statement of the Soviet Government is a stern warning to those who are losing their reason. The Soviet Union, the socialist countries, and the peace-loving nations have enough strength and the means to put a strait jacket on the aggressors.

Many thousands of meetings are taking place all over the Soviet land. The working people of the Soviet Union are angrily protesting against the reckless actions of the American maniacs. The Soviet people are united in their support of the peace-loving policy of the Communist Party and of their beloved government. They are unanimous in their readiness to still further increase their efforts at work to strengthen the economic and defensive might of their Motherland.

The Soviet Union and the socialist countries in all their actions on the international scene have firmly stood, and stand, on positions of peace. The socialist countries are for settling all disputed questions not by military means but at the negotiation table on a mutually acceptable basis.

But our people has a good memory. We remember the crafty methods of the aggressors who unloosed the Second World War and we will not let ourselves be taken unawares. We are building the shining house of communism for ourselves and for our children and will not let anyone destroy the peace. The Soviet Armed Forces armed with the most up-to-date and the best military equipment in the world stand guard over peaceful labor.

A wave of angry protests against the fanatical actions of the American militarists is rolling over the whole world. The mighty socialist camp and all the peace-loving nations of the globe are on the side of revolutionary Cuba. Let the authors of the criminal plans not delude themselves. The socialist countries are as one in their efforts to nip any aggression in the very bud. We have powerful forces and an inflexible will to defend peace.

An appeal to defend Cuba against aggression is being heard on all continents and in hundreds of languages. In a short time revolutionary Cuba has won the sympathy, respect, and love of the millions of laboring masses who are fighting for democracy and progress. In the aggression against Cuba, the peoples of other countries see an attempt on their own rights and freedoms, on peace and security in the whole world. The peoples cannot remain indifferent to the events in the Caribbean. Energetic actions, united efforts, and a common *will can stay the hand raised by the American aggressors against peace. In the face of the reckless adventure of the United States government, the peoples demand: stop this dangerous playing with fire; curb the American aggressors! The imperialist aggressors should remember that if they try to kindle the flames of world war, they will inevitably be incinerated in its fire.*

In the situation that has arisen a special responsibility rests on the United Nations. It was created after World War II to stand guard over the peace. The peoples have placed their hopes in it, hopes which, unfortunately, have not always been justified. At the present decisive moment the United Nations is confronted with a new, most serious test. The question is whether it fulfills the mission that the peoples have laid upon it and thereby justifies its real purpose or whether the fate of the League of Nations and the universal contempt of the peoples await it. There is no third way.

Dark clouds have gathered over the world. In these grim days we must look reality soberly in the face. The atomic maniacs want to gamble with the fate of human civilization. The peoples warn them. It will not work! The criminal schemes of the enemies of peace must be thwarted. The peoples have a single will—to defend and strengthen peace on earth!

"THINK IT OVER, MR. PRESIDENT," *IZVESTIIA,* 24 OCTOBER 1962

The ruling circles of the United States have resorted to an act of international brigandage unprecedented in peacetime, that is, aggressive measures against Cuba—a sovereign independent state whose people at the cost of a painful struggle have overthrown the yoke of imperialist slavery. The U.S. Navy has been ordered to impose a virtual blockade on Cuba on the pretext that Cuba supposedly threatens the United States and even the whole Western Hemisphere.

In plotting these aggressive actions the imperialists never hesitated to advance any reasons for them no matter how absurd they would have appeared to world public opinion. And now the president of the United States, Kennedy, is not ashamed to give currency to a crude lie and falsehood that Cuba has suddenly become a "threat to the Western Hemisphere."

But what has happened? Are Cuban aircraft really violating the airspace of the United States and flying over its territory? No, it is American aircraft that are flying over the territory of the Cuban Republic. Is a Cuban military base on American territory? No, the American militarists have a base for aggressive operations on Cuban soil.

Here is only a short calendar of Washington's aggressive acts against revolutionary Cuba:

In an effort to restore the overturned despotic regime on the island, the United States has worked out a plan that comes down to strangling Cuba economically.

As these aggressive actions collapsed, Washington openly began to prepare direct armed intervention against the Cuban Republic. In April 1961, on the Pentagon's orders, armed intervention at the Bay of Pigs was unloosed. Everyone remembers the stunning fiasco that put an end to Wasihngton's adventure.

But as subsequent events showed, the American imperialists learned no lessons from this. The United States not only did not put aside its aggressive policy toward Cuba but on the contrary began in defiance of common sense to feverishly fan the flames of new provocations. To this end at the beginning of 1962 a meeting of the Ministers of Foreign Affairs of the member states of the Organization of American States was convoked at Punta del Este (Uruguay). It was conceived as a sort of court of judgment over revolutionary Cuba and a preamble to new acts of aggression against her.

Fanning an anti-Cuban psychosis and bringing up the worn-out bugaboo of the "communist menace," Washington sought to pass over to direct aggression. At the end of September the U.S. Congress adopted a joint resolution authorizing in advance the adventure in preparation against Cuba.

Rarely has any power resorted to methods so monstrous, treacherous, and aggressive in its relations with a neighboring country as has the United States in relation to Cuba today. It is well known that Cuba is a peace-loving country.

As a sovereign, independent state Cuba has had, and has, the full right to take the necessary measures to safeguard its security and defense in the face of the intensified aggression of American imperialism. The Soviet Union, loyal to its international° obligations, has extended the hand of friendly aid to the heroic Cuban people in the building and development of the economy of Cuba and in the elevation of its culture and in the strengthening of its defense.

The fervent sympathies of all the people on the globe who value the cause of freedom and independence are on the side of the freedom-loving people of Cuba.

Showing complete disregard for the generally accepted norms of international intercourse, the ruling circles of the United States appear in the uniform of the world policeman and shake a club threateningly at the Cuban people. They try to arrogate to themselves the "right" to determine a question that is in the jurisdiction of Cuba itself—the question of its security and defense.

The adventuristic circles across the ocean are evidently so blinded by hatred for the Cuban Republic that they forget in what century they are living and with what dangerous combustible material they are recklessly playing. It can be recalled that a few days ago, for example, none other than the Vice-President of the United States, Lyndon Johnson, spoke in New Mexico. In his words, a blockade of Cuba could lead to a third world war. Thus, is the United States of America consciously bringing matters to a world nuclear war?!

The actions of medieval pirates pale before the brigandage of the U.S. Navy on the high seas. Raising piracy to the level of state policy, the ruling figures of the United States have announced their intention to attack ships plying Cuban waters.

As a consequence of the weakening of their imperialistic positions in the world at large and in Latin America in particular, the ruling circles of the United States, like a reckless gambler who has gone too far, have now decided on a new, desperate step that is evidence neither of sound judgment, of self-control, or of concern for the destiny of the United States itself.

° In Soviet usage, *internatsional'nyi* the term employed above, refers to relations between Soviet republics or peoples and socialist states. *Mezhdunarodny,* also translated as "international," refers to the relations between any states.

The peoples of the Soviet Union know from their own bitter experience what a blockade of the imperialist powers is. However, the military campaigns of the imperialist beasts of prey against the young Soviet republic failed shamefully. At the present time American imperialism is opposed by the mighty camp of the socialist countries who possess everything necessary to curb any aggressor, and it is opposed by the great front of the peoples.

As regards the Soviet Union and the Soviet people, no tantrums of the imperialist aggressors will prevent us in the future from discharging our great international† duty to support and help nations defending their freedom and independence. The Soviet people respond to the ravings of the American imperialists by closing ranks more closely around our own Communist Party and the Soviet government. The Soviet people will work with even greater energy for the welfare of its Motherland and for the welfare of general peace and security.

The Soviet government, as always, will do everything necessary so that no machinations of the imperialist aggressive force take the Soviet Union unawares, and so that the defense of our country is in a condition of constant combat readiness.

APPENDIX 3

LETTER FROM N. KHRUSHCHEV TO HIS EXCELLENCY
JOHN KENNEDY, PRESIDENT OF THE UNITED STATES OF
AMERICA, 26 OCTOBER 1962

Dear Mr. President,

I have received your letter of October 25. From your letter I sense that you have some understanding of the existing situation and a consciousness of responsibility. This I value.

Now we have already publicly exchanged our appraisals of the Cuban events and each of us has set forth his explanation and understanding of these events. Therefore I hardly think it likely that continued exchange of views at this distance, even in private letters, could add to what each side has already told the other.

I think that you understand me correctly if you are genuinely concerned about the blessings of peace. Everyone needs peace; the capitalists if they have not taken leave of their senses and even more so the Communists who have the capacity to value not only their own lives but above all the lives of the people. In general, we Communists are opposed to all wars between states and we have defended the cause of peace since we appeared on the scene. We have always viewed war as a calamity; not as a game nor as a means to attain particular goals and above all not as a goal in itself. Our goals are clear and the means to attain them is work. War is our enemy and a calamity for all people.

That is how we, the Soviet people and other peoples, understand the questions of war and peace. In any case I can say this to you firmly on behalf of the peoples of the socialist countries and also of all the progressive people who want peace, happiness and friendship among peoples.

† In the sense of among socialist states.

I see, Mr. President, that you, too, are not without feelings of concern for the fate of the world and not without comprehension of, and a correct evaluation of, the nature of contemporary war and everything that it brings in its train. What will war avail you? You threaten us with war. But surely, you know that, at the very least, you will get back what you send us and you will suffer the very same consequences. And that should be clear to us as trusted and responsible people, invested with power. Whether or not elections are due in some country, we should not succumb to irrationality and petty passions. These are all transient matters and should war indeed break out, we could not deter or stop it because that is the logic of war. I have been in two wars and know that war only ends when it has rolled through cities and villages, sowing death and destruction everywhere.

I assure you in the name of the Soviet government and the Soviet people that your conclusions about offensive weapons in Cuba are without any foundation. From what you have written me it is obvious that we have different judgments on this score, or, rather, that we evaluate some military means differently. And as a matter of fact the very same types of weapons can be appraised differently.

As a military man, I hope you understand me. Let's take an ordinary gun, for example. What kind of weapon is it, offensive or defensive? A gun is a means of defense if it is positioned to defend a border or a fortified region. But if artillery is concentrated and the necessary number of troops are attached, these guns become means of offense because they have prepared and cleared the way for infantry to attack. It is the same with nuclear missiles of all types.

You are mistaken if you believe that some of our [military] means in Cuba are offensive. However, let's not quarrel about that now. Apparently I cannot convince you of that. But I say this to you: Mr. President, as a military man you should understand that missiles alone, even a vast number of varying ranges and power cannot mount an offensive. These missiles are means of destruction and devastation. It is impossible to mount an offensive with missiles even if they are 100 megaton nuclear missiles because only people, i.e., troops, can mount an offensive. Failing people, any means, no matter how powerful, cannot be a means of offense.

How, therefore, is it possible to come to the completely incorrect interpretation that you have reached, namely that, as you say, some of the [military] means in Cuba are offensive. All the means to be found there are, I assure you, defensive in character and are in Cuba exclusively for the purposes of defense and we sent them to Cuba at the request of the Cuban government. But you still say that they are means for offense.

But Mr. President do you really believe that Cuba could attack the United States and that even we and Cuba together could attack you from Cuban territory? Do you really think so? How can that be? We don't understand it. Has something novel emerged in military strategy, to think that an offensive could be mounted this way? That's just what I'm saying: to mount an offensive but not to destroy; it is barbarians and people who have taken leave of their senses who destroy.

You have no cause to think that, I believe. You may regard us with distrust but at any rate you can rest assured that we are of sound mind and understand very well that if we fall upon you, you will respond the same way. But you too will get exactly what you throw at us. I think you understand that, too. Our conversation in Vienna gives me the right to talk like this.

It shows that we are normal people, are of sound judgement and evaluate the situation correctly. How then can we permit the misdeeds that you charge us with? Only madmen or suicides who want to kill themselves before they destroy the whole world could do this. But we want to live and we by no means want to destroy your country. We want something quite different: to compete with your country in peaceful pursuits. We argue with you; we differ on ideological questions. But in our conception of the world, ideological questions and economic problems should not be resolved by warfare but in peaceful emulation or, as it would be put in capitalist society, in competition. We have assumed and do assume that the peaceful coexistence of the two different socio-political systems, as they actually exist in the world, is necessary as is lasting peace. This is our view of the principles to which we adhere.

You have just announced measures of piracy like those employed in the middle ages when they attacked ships plying the high seas and you call this a "quarantine" of Cuba. Our ships will, very likely, soon reach the zone patroled by your navy. I assure you that these vessels now bound for Cuba are carrying the most innocent peaceful cargo. Do you really think that all we are interested in is to ship so-called offensive weapons, atomic and hydrogen bombs? Although, perhaps, your military people imagine that it is some special type of weapon I assure you that it is the most ordinary peaceful product.

Therefore, Mr. President, let us show good judgement. I assure you that there are no weapons of any kind on the ships bound for Cuba. The weapons necessary for the defense of Cuba are already there. I wouldn't say no weapons at all were shipped. No, there were such shipments. But now Cuba has long since received the means necessary for defense.

I don't know if you can understand and believe me. But I would like for you to believe in yourself and to agree that one cannot give the reins to passions; they must be mastered. And what course are things taking now? You know yourself that if you stop the ships, it's piracy. Now we and the whole world are outraged, as you would be, if we did this to your ships. Such actions cannot be evaluated any other way, because lawlessness cannot be condoned. If it [lawlessness] is permitted then there will be neither peace nor peaceful coexistence. Then we will be compelled to take the necessary defensive measures to protect our interests in accordance with international law. Why do it? What will it all lead to?

Let us normalize relations. We have received the appeal of the Acting Secretary-General of the UN, U Tant with his proposal. I have already answered him. In essence his proposal is that our side not deliver any weapons to Cuba during the period of negotiations—and we are ready to engage in such negotiations—and the other side will not commit acts of piracy against our ships on the high seas. I think it is a sensible proposal. It would be a way out of the situation that has arisen and it would give the peoples an opportunity to draw a peaceful breath.

You ask what provoked the delivery of weapons to Cuba? You have talked about this to our Minister of Foreign Affairs. I will tell you frankly, Mr. President, what provoked it.

We were much grieved—I talked about it in Vienna—that there was a landing, that Cuba was attacked with many Cuban casualties.

You yourself told me then it was a mistake. I respected that explanation. You repeated it to me several times noting that not everybody holding high office acknowledged his own mistakes as you did. I value such frankness. For my part I told you that we have no less courage, that we had also acknowledged the mistakes committed in the history of our state, and not only acknowledged them but sharply condemned them.

If you are really concerned about peace and about the welfare of your people as is your duty as President, then I, as Chairman of the Council of Ministers, am concerned about my people. Moreover, we should jointly be concerned to preserve general peace because if war broke out in present circumstances, it would not only be a war between the Soviet Union and the USA, who as a matter of fact have no claims against each other, but a terrible, destructive world war.

Why did we decide to render such military and economic assistance to Cuba? The answer is that we did this purely for humanitarian reasons. When our people made its revolution Russia was still a backward country. Then we were attacked. We were the object of the attack of many countries. The USA participated in this adventure.* This has been documented by the participants in the aggression against our country. General Graves who then commanded the American expeditionary corps has written a whole book about it. Graves called it "America's Siberian Adventure."

We know how difficult it is to make a revolution and how difficult it is to put a country on a new basis. We have genuine sympathy for Cuba and the Cuban people. But we don't interfere in the questions of their internal structure or their affairs. The Soviet Union wants to help the Cubans to build their life the way they want to and we want others not to interfere.

You have said that the United States is not preparing an invasion. But you have also affirmed your sympathy with the Cuban counterrevolutionary emigrés, and your support, present and future, in the execution of their plans against the incumbent Cuban government. Nor is it a secret that the threat of armed attack and aggression has always, and still does, hang over Cuba. The only reason we responded to the request of the Cuban government was to help them to strengthen the defensive capacity of their country.

If the President and the government of the United States gave assurances that the USA itself would not participate in an attack on Cuba and would restrain others from such actions, if you recalled your Navy—everything would change very quickly. I do not speak for Fidel Castro, but I think that he and the government of Cuba very likely would demobilize and recall the people to peaceful pursuits. Then the question of weapons would disappear because weapons are a burden for any people when there is no threat. Then the

---

* *Adventure* in Russian means an unprincipled, risky enterprise undertaken without an appraisal of the true state of affairs.

destruction of the weapons that you term offensive, and even the destruction of all other weapons would become an entirely different question.

In the name of the Soviet government I spoke in the United Nations to propose the dissolution of all armies and the destruction of all weapons. How then can I now insist on these weapons?

Weapons bring only tragedy. Their acquisition damages the economy and when employed they destroy people on both sides. Therefore only a madman can believe that weapons are the chief thing in the life of society. No, they are an enforced waste of human energy and, what is more, are for the destruction of man himself. In the final analysis if people are not wise they will collide like blind moles and then mutual destruction will have begun.

Let us show statesmen-like wisdom. I propose: we for our part declare that our ships bound for Cuba carry no weapons. You declare that the United States will not invade Cuba with its troops and will not support any other forces planning to invade Cuba. Then the necessity for the presence of our military specialists in Cuba will disappear.

Mr. President, I appeal to you to weigh carefully where the aggressive acts of piracy that you have announced the USA intends to commit in international waters might lead. You know yourself that no sane minded person could accept it or recognize your right to behave like this.

If this is your first step in starting a war, obviously we cannot but accept your challenge. If you have not lost your self-control and sensibly conceive what this might lead to, then, Mr. President, we both should not pull on the ends of the rope in which you have tied the knot of war, because the more the two of us pull, the tighter the knot will be tied. And a moment may come when the knot will be tied so tight that not even he who tied it will have the strength to untie it and then it will be necessary to cut the knot. And what that will mean is not for me to explain to you, because you yourself understand perfectly how terrible are the forces that our countries command.

Consequently, if there is no intention to tighten that knot, and thereby to doom the world to the catastrophe of thermonuclear war, then let us not only relax the forces pulling on the ends of the rope, let us take measures to untie that knot. We are ready for this.

We welcome all the forces that stand for peace. Therefore I thanked Mr. Bertrand Russell who displayed alarm and concern for the fate of the world and I responded eagerly to the appeal of the Acting Secretary General of the UN, U Tant.

That Mr. President is my idea of how—if you agree—to put an end to the present crisis that distresses all the peoples.

This idea is dictated by the sincere desire to defuse the situation and eliminate the threat of war. Respectfully,

N. KHRUSHCHEV

26 October 1962

ANALYSIS OF N. S. KHRUSHCHEV'S LETTER TO
JOHN F. KENNEDY OF 26 OCTOBER 1962

This letter was not employed in the preparation of the text of this book. The full text illuminates Khrushchev's understanding of the nature of nuclear war and better explains why he thought the United States would accept the installation of nuclear weapons in Cuba. It is gratifying, but not surprising, that the letter is compatible with the thesis and the supporting arguments of this book. Page references which follow indicate the earlier appearance in the text of the main themes either in Khrushchev's own statements or in other Soviet materials. If enough information is available to compose an account of events and purposes in some detail, new information should fill out, not alter, the picture.

The letter was apparently written in haste; no editor seems to have smoothed out clumsy passages and excised repetitions. The ideas are familiar. Despite, or perhaps because of, the letter's personal tone and loose construction, what Khrushchev hoped to get from, and his disappointment in, the missile venture come across more clearly than elsewhere.

The lines devoted to the nature of nuclear warfare constitute perhaps his clearest rejection of nuclear warfare as a political act. He argues that a bilateral nuclear exchange in which ground forces could not follow up the strikes to occupy territory and to impose a political settlement, would not be war. It would be barbarism. Thus he again rejects nuclear war as an instrument of policy, but assumes that changes in the balance of military forces have political utility.

In addition to deterring a central war between Moscow and Washington, nuclear weapons had deterred an invasion of Cuba. The Soviet press had claimed that Khrushchev's October 1960 statement on Soviet nuclear capacity and its relevance to the defense of Cuba had scotched Eisenhower's plans for an invasion of Cuba on the eve of the presidential elections (pp. 102, 105). During the Bay of Pigs invasion Khrushchev warned that he would give Cuba all necessary assistance and that a continuation of the American action could lead to world war (p. 130). Kennedy's repeated acknowledgement in Vienna that the Bay of Pigs invasion had been a mistake, confirmed Khrushchev in his belief that fears about the consequences of nuclear war had stopped Kennedy from trying to rescue the Bay of Pigs operation by expanding its scope. But subsequently Kennedy continued to support Cuban counterrevolutionaries, causing the Soviet Union to repeat its pledge to protect Cuba in its 18 February 1962 (p. 168) and its 11 September 1962 (p. 196) statements. That was why the Soviet Union had dispatched nuclear missiles to Cuba, wrote Khrushchev. Khrushchev seemed to have believed that the stronger the Soviet Union was and the more visible its power, the more likely that its public commitment to defend Cuba would be efficacious. Just as Kennedy had planned for only one contingency in the Bay of Pigs operation—success, Khrushchev gave no thought to the possibility that his scheme might miscarry.

Hence Khrushchev's alarm and rapid retreat when Kennedy insisted that he withdraw his missiles. Khrushchev's letter made only a single condition for negotiations—that the United States not interfere with the free passage of Soviet ships in international waters. If, then, the United States promised not to invade Cuba and not to support counterrevolutionaries in an invasion, not only nuclear but all Soviet weapons could be withdrawn from Cuba. If Kennedy would give formal assurances, not merely assert, that the United States would not invade Cuba, the Soviet Union would take the missiles away. The missiles had been installed to compel the United States to drop its plans to overthrow Castro, and Khrushchev had probably thought they would remain. Now he was willing to withdraw them in exchange for a promise. Once before Khrushchev had incorrectly predicted the behavior of an American president after a face-to-face meeting. The meeting with Eisenhower at Camp David in 1959 was followed by the U-2 crisis in May 1960; the October 1962 missile crisis followed the Vienna meeting in June 1961.

Khrushchev's letter, as far as it goes, tells the truth as he saw it. Surely, he wanted to use Soviet military power to save the Cuban revolution, and he did not want to, or expect to, fight to do so. And, optimistic as he was, he hoped to build other political gains on success in Cuba. But a letter that recognized the failure of his hopes was not the place to recall them.

 **NOTES**

1. THE GUATEMALAN CRISIS

1. The most accessible short statement on this period is to be found in Ronald M. Schneider, *Communism in Guatemala, 1944–1955* (New York: Frederick Praeger, 1959), chaps. 1 and 2.

2. Juan José Arévalo, *The Shark and the Sardines* (New York: Lyle Stuart, 1961).

3. Ibid., p. 123.

4. Speech of Juan José Arévalo, 27 September 1947, as quoted in Ildegar Perez-Segnini, "Lo inexplicado en el caso Guatemala," *Humanismo* (Mexico City), March 1955, p. 40.

5. Luis Cardoza y Aragon, *La Revolución Guatemalteca* (Montevideo: Editiones Pueblos Unidos, 1956), p. 155.

6. Guatemalan Transcripts, Manuscript Room, Library of Congress, Washington, D.C. Microfilm is cited by roll number, photostats by box and document number.

7. The Guatemalan Transcripts in the Library of Congress contain some Guatemalan state documents and the files of the Guatemalan Labor Party and its high officials. The categories and the handwritten labels on the manila folders indicate that they were selected to make the case that communist infiltration was widespread, and indeed, some of the documents appear in the published records of congressional investigating committees. Given these principles of selection, the absence of any predictions that the bourgeois phase of the revolution would be quickly concluded and that the socialist phase would soon follow is significant.

8. "Nuestra América," *Humanismo*, March 1953, pp. 74–76; ibid., August 1953, pp. 58–63; Vicente Sáenz, "El fraude del anticomunismo," *Humanismo*, December 1953, pp. 27–28.

9. Gregorio Selser, *El Guatemalazo* (Buenos Aires: Ediciones Iguazu, 1961), pp. 55, 71.

10. "It must be borne in mind that the communists always operate in terms of small minorities who gain positions of power." John Foster Dulles's 25 May 1954 statement on Guatemala, *New York Times*, 26 May 1954.

11. U.S. Department of State, *Intervention of International Communism in Guatemala* (Washington, D.C., August 1954), pp. 66–67, 83–85. The memorandum was dated as revised in May 1954.

12. *New York Times*, 20 May 1954.

13. S. Gonionsky, "U.S. Colonial Oppression in Latin America," *New Times* (Moscow), 20 February 1954, pp. 16–17.

14. S. Gonionskii, "Opposition to the Dictates of the U.S.A. is Growing in Latin America," *Kommunist*, 1954, no. 6, pp. 85–96.

15. S. Vorobyov, "Defeat in Caracas," *New Times*, 3 April 1954, p. 12.

16. Osvaldo Peralva, *O. Retrato* (Belo Horizonte: Editora Itatiaia Limitada, 1960), p. 26.

17. M. V. Danilevich, *Polozhenie i bor'ba rabochego klassa stran Latinskoi Ameriki* [The situation and struggle of the Latin American working class] (Moscow: Izd. Akad Nauk SSSR, 1953), pp. 53–54; signed to the press, 6 June.

18. V. Ermolaev, S. Semenov, and A. Sivolobov, "Serious Mistakes in a Book about the Workers' Movement in Latin America," *Kommunist*, 1954, no. 7, pp. 120–27.

19. O. Kuusinen, "On the Slogan of Freedom and on American Conduct," *Pravda*, 10 May 1954. Kuusinen had been secretary of the Executive Committee of the Comintern from 1921 to 1939.

20. Sidney Gruson, "Useless Weapons and Duds Sent Guatemala by Reds, Officers Say," *New York Times*, 9 July 1954.

21. Ibid.

22. Guatemalan Transcripts, Box 72, nos. 90030 and 90032.

23. Paul P. Kennedy, "U.S. Envoy Called from Guatemala," *New York Times*, 19 April 1954.

24. *New York Times*, 18 May 1954.

25. Ibid., 24 May 1954.

26. Ibid., 25 May 1954.

27. Ibid., 26 May 1954.

28. Ibid., 28 May 1954.

29. Ibid., 1 June 1954.

30. Ibid., 9 June 1954.

31. Ibid., 16 June 1954.

32. Ibid., 22 October 1960. Kennedy-Nixon television debate, text of 21 October 1960.

33. V. Chichkov, "The Republic of Guatemala and U.S. Imperialism," *Kommunist*, 1954, no. 10, p. 106.

34. Y. Bochkaryov, "The Crime against Guatemala," *New Times*, 3 July 1954, pp. 8–10.

35. M. Grechev, *Imperialisticheskaia ekspansiia SShA v stranakh Latinskoi Ameriki posle vtoroi mirovoi voiny* [Imperialist expansion of the United States in countries of Latin America after World War II] (Moscow: Izd. Akademiia Nauk, 1954). Prepared for the press, 9 December 1954, p. 237.

36. S. A. Gonionskii, *Latinskaia Amerika i SShA 1939–1959: Ocherki istorii diplomaticheskikh otnoshenii* [Latin America and the U.S.A.: an outline of the history of diplomatic relations, 1939–1959] (Moscow: Izd. Instituta Mezhdunarodnykh otnoshenii, 1960), p. 310.

37. Grechev, "Imperialist Expansion of the United States," p. 237.

38. Bochkaryov, "The Crime against Guatemala," p. 10.

39. Guillermo Toriello, *La batalla de Guatemala* (Santiago de Chile: Editorial Universitaria, 1955), pp. 65–66, 125.

40. Julio Castello, *Así cayó la democracia en Guatemala* (Havana: Ediciones Faro, 1961), p. 146. The introduction states that *La Calle*, a Havana newspaper, had published the same account serially in mid-1955.

2. THE CUBAN REVOLUTION: THE BEGINNINGS AND THE FIRST YEAR

1. "Conclusiones del Pleno del Comité Nacional del Partido Socialista Popular, realizado en los días 25 al 28 de Mayo de 1959," *Noticias de Hoy*, 7 June 1959.

2. Blas Roca, "Report to the Eighth National Congress of the Popular Socialist Party of Cuba," in *The Cuban Revolution* (New York: New Century Publishers, 1961), p. 8.

3. *Respuestas* (illegal organ of the PSP), 7 December 1956, as quoted in L. Yu. Slezkin, *Istoriia Kubinskoi Respubliki* [The history of the Cuban republic] (Moscow: Nauka, 1966), p. 331.

4. Hugh Thomas, *Cuba: The Pursuit of Freedom* (New York: Harper & Row, 1971), pp. 803–4, and Enrique Meneses, *Fidel Castro* (New York: Taplinger Publishing Co., 1960), p. 32. Both say that Castro's father was a soldier in the Spanish army fighting the Cuban rebels. Meneses knew Castro when he was in the Sierra Maestra. The very thorough and reliable Rolando E. Bonachea and Nelson P. Valdés, in *Revolutionary Struggle, 1947–1958*, Vol. 1 of *The Selected Works of Fidel Castro* (Cambridge, Mass.: M.I.T. Press, 1972), p. 3, describe Fidel Castro's father, Angel, simply as an immigrant in the 1890s.

5. Thomas, *Cuba*, p. 804.

6. Ignacio Reyes, "La Experiencia Guatemalteca y la revolución Cubana," *Hoy Domingo* [Sunday magazine of *Hoy*], 3 January 1960, pp. 6–7 (*Noticias de Hoy* became *Hoy* on 1 January 1960).

7. Thomas, *Cuba*, pp. 909–18, is particularly good on this point.

8. *Respuestas*, 7 and 14 December 1956, as quoted in Slezkin, *Istoriia*, pp. 331–33.

9. Ibid.

10. *Carta del Comité Nacional del Partido Socialista Popular al Movimiento 26 de Julio*, Havana, June 1957. Theodore Draper, *Castroism: Theory and Practice* (New York: Frederick Praeger, 1965), pp. 29–30; Boris Goldenberg, *Kommunismus in Lateinamerika* (Stuttgart: W. Kohlhammer, 1971), p. 312; and Fausto Maso, "Cuando los comunistas atacaban a Fidel Castro," *Bohemia Libre*, 7 July 1963, pp. 20, 21, 46, have extensive extracts from the letter.

11. Juan Marinello to Herbert Matthews, 17 March 1957, as quoted in Draper, *Castroism*, p. 30.

12. Aníbal Escalante, *Fundamentos*, August 1959, p. 12, as quoted in Draper, *Castroism*, p. 31.

13. *Carta Seminal*, 12 March 1958, as quoted in Slezkin, *Istoriia*, p. 336.

14. Draper, *Castroism*, p. 31, uses evidence of Escalante's opposition to Castro in 1959, 1961, and 1964 to argue that Escalante had been opposed to Castro in 1958. In the absence of documentation from party files in 1958, the issue cannot be conclusively resolved.

15. "Stop the Bloodletting in Cuba," *Pravda*, 14 February 1958.

16. M. Ruiz, "The People's Struggle in Cuba," ibid., 22 February 1958.

17. "Joint Statement of the Communist Party of Argentina and the People's Socialist Party of Cuba," ibid., 1 March 1958.

18. Thomas, *Cuba*, p. 810.

19. *New York Times*, 1 April 1958.

20. Private interview.

21. *New York Times*, 3 April 1958.

22. Bonachea and Valdés, *Revolutionary Struggle*, p. 106.

23. Fulgencio Batista, *Cuba Betrayed* (New York: Vantage Press, 1962), p. 42 and passim.

24. Goldenberg, *Kommunismus in Lateinamerika*, p. 310.

25. Claude Julien, *La Révolution Cubaine* (Paris: R. Julliard, 1961), p. 82; Yves Guilbert, *Castro l'infidèle* (Paris: Table Ronde, 1961), p. 81.

26. Thomas, *Cuba*, pp. 618 ff.

27. K. M. Obyden, *Kuba v bor'be za svobodu i nezavisimost'* [Cuba in the struggle for freedom and independence] (Moscow: Gos. izd. politicheskoi literatury, 1959), p. 55. Delivered to the printer 4 November 1959; in galleys 1 December 1959.

28. Sacha Volman, "El General Batista y la revolución comunista," *Combate* 1 no. 1 (1958) (San José, Costa Rica): 45–48. Rómulo Betancourt and Haya de la Torre were two of the editors and Norman Thomas, Robert Alexander, and José Figueres were among the contributors.

29. David D. Burks, *Cuba under Castro*, Headline Series, The Foreign Policy Association, no. 165 (New York, 29 June 1964), p. 10. Burks gives no source for this statement, but his work is most reliable and cogent throughout.

30. Thomas, *Cuba*, pp. 988–92.

31. Obyden, *Kuba*, pp. 59–69; Vasilii Chichkov, *Zaria nad Kuboi: Zapiski zhurnalista* [Dawn over Cuba: a journalist's notes] (Moscow: IMO, 1961), pp. 58–62; in galleys 2 March 1960; Slezkin, *Istoriia*, pp. 336–40.

32. Julien, *La Révolution Cubaine*, p. 82 ff; Jacques Arnault, *Cuba et le Marxisme* (Paris: Editions Sociales, 1963), p. 84.

33. Jules Dubois, *Fidel Castro: Rebel-Liberator or Dictator?* (New York: Bobbs-Merrill, 1959), p. 264; Fidel Castro, *La Revolución Cubana*, ed. Gregorio Selser (Buenos Aires: Editorial Palestra, 1960), p. 150.

34. Julien, *La Révolution Cubaine*, p. 82; the letter is dated 5 June 1958.

35. See above, p. 32.

36. *Noticias de Hoy*, 11 January 1959, for the Rodríguez account, and Thomas,

Cuba, p. 996–1007; for *Caracas Unity Manifesto of the Sierra Maestra*, see Bonachea and Valdés, *Revolutionary Struggle*, pp. 386–89.

37. Roca, *The Cuban Revolution*, p. 38.

38. "Intervista con Castro," *L'Unità*, 1 February 1961. Miss Vivienne Ascher kindly provided a translation from the Italian.

39. *Documentos del XI Congreso Nacional, realizado en Noviembre de 1958, Santiago 1959*, p. 29, as quoted in Goldenberg, *Kommunismus in Lateinamerika*, p. 313.

40. Rodney Arismendi, *La Lucha por la Paz, la Independencia Nacional, la Democracia y el Bienestar del Pueblo Uruguayo* (Montevideo: Comisión Nacional de Propaganda del Partido Comunista, 1958), p. 10. The text of the report given by the first secretary of the Central Committee at the Congress of the Uruguayan Party of 15–17 August 1958; the same text was published in the Soviet Union as *XVII S"ezd kommunisticheskoi partii Urugvaia* [Seventeenth Congress of the communist party of Uruguay] (Moscow: Gos. izd-vo politeratury, 1959), p. 10.

41. "Khrushchev's answer to the questions of the Brazilian journalist Murilo Marroquiin de Souza," *Mezhdunarodnaia zhizn'* [International affairs], 1958, no. 11, p. 5.

42. Draper, *Castroism*, p. 31.

43. "Tesis [of the PSP] sobre la situación actual," *Noticias de Hoy*, 11 January 1959.

44. Ibid.

45. Pedro Reyes, "Some Aspects of the Liberation Movement in Latin America," *World Marxist Review*, 1959, no. 1, pp. 34–40. The same text appears in the Russian edition of the magazine, entitled *Problemy mira i sotsializma* [Problems of peace and socialism], 1959, no. 1, pp. 36–42.

46. *Noticias de Hoy*, 11 January 1959.

47. "Note from K. Voroshilov to Manuelo Urrutia, 10 January 1959," *Pravda*, 11 January 1959.

48. *Noticias de Hoy*, 16 January 1959.

49. "El derracomiento de la tiranía y las tareas inmediatas," Comité Nacional del Partido Socialista Popular, Juan Marinello, President, Blas Roca, Secretary General, 5 January 1959, ibid., 7 January 1959.

50. *Noticias de Hoy*, 15 January 1959.

51. Ibid., 16 January 1959.

52. Blas Roca, "Unidad para detener a los ingerencistas y Aplastar a todos los conspiradores," ibid., 18 January 1959; "Carta a los trabajadores," ibid., 24 January 1959.

53. *Noticias de Hoy*, 20 January 1959.

54. Blas Roca, "La Tarea Fundamental es Hoy Defender la Revolución y Hacerla Avanzar," in *29 Articulos sobre la Revolución Cubana* ([Havana, 1960]), pp. 11–13.

55. Blas Roca in *Noticias de Hoy*, 1 February 1959, reporting on the meeting of the enlarged national committee of the PSP.

56. Chichkov, *Zaria*, p. 42.

57. Ibid., pp. 40, 103, and 104.

58. Editorial, "Cuba Free," *New Times*, no. 2 (January 1959), p. 2.

59. Achille Finzi, "Les perspectives de la révolution cubaine," *Cahiers du Communisme* 35, nos. 1–2 (1959): 94–96.

60. Juan Marinello, "The Great Victory of the Cuban People" in *Latinskaia Amerika v proshlom i nastoiashchem* [Latin America past and present] (Moscow: Izd. sotsial'no, ekomicheskoi literatury, 1969), p. 156. Actually the two organizations mentioned by Marinello, BRAC (El Buro Represivo de Actividades Communistas) and SIM (Servicio de Inteligencia Militar), were abolished on 18 February 1959 according to Eescuelas de Instrucción Revolucionaria del PCC, *Cronologia de la Revolución II, 1959–1965* (Havana, 1965), p. 20 (hereinafter cited as *Cronologia II*). Apparently Marinello failed to update parts of his article, which was dated March 1959.

61. Carlos Rafael Rodríguez, "El peor camino," *Noticias de Hoy*, 31 January 1959.

62. Juan Marinello, chairman of the People's Socialist Party of Cuba, "Chto proizoshlo na Kube" [What has happened in Cuba], *Ogonek*, 22 March 1959, pp. 17–19.

63. *Noticias de Hoy*, 17 March 1959.
64. Gustavo Mujica, "Entrevista con Nikita Jruschov," ibid., 24 March 1959. The interview took place 28 February 1959.
65. Lazaro Peña, "Los sindicatos y las tareas de la revolución," ibid., 28 March 1959.
66. Text of Castro's television interview, ibid., 3 April 1959.
67. Blas Roca, "Nuevas Campañas y amenazas contra Cuba," ibid., 2 April 1959.
68. Blas Rok [sic], "Narodnaia revoliutsiia na Kube i perspektivy ee dal'neishego razvitiia" [The people's revolution in Cuba and the outlook for its further development], *Partiinaia zhizn'* [Party life], 1959, no. 6, pp. 68–74.
69. V. Levin, "The Maneuvers of the Protectors of Tyranny," *Pravda*, 1 April 1959.
70. A. Kalinin, "Cuba at a New Stage," ibid., 12 May 1959.
71. *New York Times*, 21 April 1959, quoting press conference of 20 April 1959.
72. *Noticias de Hoy*, 21 April 1959.
73. *Revolución*, 25 April 1959.
74. *New York Times*, 21 April 1959.
75. Television interview with Blas Roca, *Noticias de Hoy*, 6 May 1959.
76. Ibid., 8 May 1959.
77. Thomas, *Cuba*, p. 1212.
78. *Revolución*, 28 April 1959, p. 13.
79. Castro interview in flight over Cuba, ibid., 29 April 1959. Raúl Castro also criticized the invaders of Panama in his 1 May 1959 speech (ibid., 2 May, 1959). According to an author who was then an intimate of Castro's, Castro later had the Caribbean exiles arrested on the ground that they wanted to involve Cuba in conflicts with the United States (Teresa Casuso, *Cuba and Castro* [New York, 1961]), p. 164.
80. "El Pleno del Comité Nacional del PSP," *Noticias de Hoy*, 9 October 1959.
81. "Discurso de Aníbal Escalante en Pekin," ibid., 21 October 1959.
82. "El Pleno del Comité Nacional del PSP," ibid., 9 October 1959.
83. M. Kremnyov, "In Cuba," *New Times*, no. 22 (May 1959), pp. 13–15.
84. For Castro's speech in Montevideo, see *Revolución*, 4 May 1959.
85. Editorial, "Estamos con la Unidad por la Base," ibid., 4 May 1959.
86. Speech of Raúl Castro on 1 May, ibid., 2 May 1959.
87. Interviews cited in Thomas, *Cuba*, p. 1212, and in Edward Gonzalez, *The Cuban Revolution and the Soviet Union, 1959–1960* (Ph.D. diss., University of California at Los Angeles, 1966), p. 375–76—an exhaustive and indispensable monograph.
88. "Respuesta a Blas Roca," *Revolución*, 8 May 1959.
89. A contemporary observer writers: "On various occasions I saw Carlos Franqui, then editor of *Revolución*, show Castro the final copy for the paper before it went to print. Castro ordered any changes he wanted made . . . it seems logical to assume that the attacks on the communists by *Revolución* reflected Castro's political position" (Rufo López-Fresquet, *My 14 Months with Castro* [Cleveland: World Publishing Co., 1966], p. 147).
90. "Conjura divisionista," *Revolución*, 16 May 1959.
91. Castro television interview of 21 May, ibid., 22 May 1959.
92. "Declaraciones del PSP," *Noticias de Hoy*, 23 May 1959.
93. *Noticias de Hoy*, 26 May 1959.
94. See Roca, p. 43, above.
95. "Conclusiones del Pleno del Comité Nacional del Partido Socialista Popular, realizado en los días 25 al 28 de Mayo 1959," *Noticias de Hoy*, 7 June 1959.
96. See earlier statements on pp. 41 and 42, above.
97. Jacinto Torras, "Las Causas de su Crisis y lo que Cuba debe hacer," *Noticias de Hoy*, 16 April 1959.
98. "The Development of International Relations and the Struggle for Peace," *Kommunist*, 1959, no. 11, p. 86.
99. See above, p. 40.
100. "Las relaciones entre Cuba y la URSS," *Noticias de Hoy*, 2 July 1959. Gonzalez argues that these articles advocating the Soviet purchase of Cuban sugar were

signals to the USSR; it seems that they were meant instead to put pressure on Castro, for as Khrushchev had said, it was up to the Cubans.

101. Thomas, *Cuba*, pp. 1222–26.

102. Testimony of Major Pedro Díaz Lanz, 14 July 1959, in "Communist Threat to the United States through the Caribbean," *Hearings before the Senate subcommittee to Investigate the Administration of the Internal Security Act and other Internal Security Laws of the Committee on the Judiciary, 86th Cong., 1st sess., pt. 2* (Washington, D.C.: GPO, 1959).

103. *New York Times*, 28 June 1959.

104. Ibid., 4 July 1959.

105. Castro television interview, *Noticias de Hoy*, 4 July 1959.

106. *Noticias de Hoy*, 24 July 1959.

107. Castro press conference, ibid., 29 July 1959.

108. TASS report, ibid., 30 July 1959; I have not been able to find this report in the Soviet press.

109. "Declaraciones del Partido Socialista Popular Dominicano," ibid., 31 July 1959.

110. Gonzalez, *The Cuban Revolution*, p. 462; *Noticias de Hoy*, 30 October 1959; Thomas, *Cuba*, p. 1267.

111. Blas Roca, "Discurso en el 34 Aniversario [of the PSP]," *Noticias de Hoy*, 18 August 1959.

112. Luis Martin, reporting from Peking, "Podemos comprar mucha azúcar de Cuba mediante trato directo," ibid., 2 October 1959.

113. Blas Roca, "Los Varios Partidos en China," ibid., 6 October 1959; "Informa Blas Roca ante el Pleno del Comité Nacional del Partido Socialista Popular," ibid., 7 October 1959.

114. Thomas, *Cuba*, p. 1243.

115. Ibid., pp. 1245–46.

116. Juan Marinello, "Doctrina y Acción," *Noticias de Hoy*, 24 October 1959; Roca's speech, ibid., 8 November 1959.

117. L. Kamynin, "South American Spring," *Izvestiia*, 3 November 1959.

118. V. Levin, "Cuba, Vigilant and United," *Pravda*, 11 November 1959.

119. Chichkov, *Zaria*, pp. 111–12.

120. Joseph North, *Kubinskaia revoliutsiia* [Cuba's revolution] (Moscow: Izd. inostrannoi literatury, 1960), foreword by K. M. Obyden, pp. 10–13 (English title, carried on the title page: *I Saw the People's Victory*).

121. Roca's speech, *Noticias de Hoy*, 8 November 1959.

122. November 3 and 17, as cited in Thomas, *Cuba*, p. 1252, note 53.

123. Pazos interview as cited in Gonzalez, *The Cuban Revolution*, pp. 550–58.

124. See below, chap. 3, n. 11.

125. *Noticias de Hoy*, 22 December 1959.

126. Aníbal Escalante, executive secretary of the Popular Socialist Party of Cuba, "The Today and the Tomorrow of the Cuban People," *Pravda*, 4 December 1959. One can presume that communist politicians abroad search out resolutions of the party taken in their absence as diligently as U.S. politicians in a similar situation obtain public opinion polls.

127. Emphasis supplied.

128. A. Alekseev, "Cuba Strides Forward," *Izvestiia*, 8 December 1959.

129. *Hoy Domingo* [Sunday magazine of *Hoy*], 17 January 1960, p. 5; text of Khrushchev's interview with the editor of the *Mexico City Clarion*.

130. "Nuestra opinión," *Noticias de Hoy*, 27 December 1959.

3. CUBA AND THE SOVIET UNION EMBRACE

1. "Intervista con Castro," *L'Unità*, 1 February 1961.

2. John Newhouse, *Cold Dawn: The Story of SALT* (New York: Holt, Rinehart & Winston, 1973), p. 56.

3. M. A. Seleznev, *Gosudarstvo, revoliutsiia, diktatura proleteriata* [The state, the

revolution, the dictatorship of the proletariat] (Moscow: Vysshaia partiinaia shkola pri TsK KPSS, 1960), p. 69.

4. Ibid., p. 59.

5. Iu. Eliutin, "Reactionary Intrigues in Cuba," *Mirovaia Ekonomika i Mezhdunarodnye Otnosheniia* [World economy and international relations], 1960, no. 1, p. 108 (hereafter cited *MEIMO*).

6. Trinidad Martillo, "The Evolution of the Interamerican System," *Mezhdunarodnaia zhizn'* [International affairs], 1960, no. 1, p. 86.

7. V. Chichkov, "Glorious Anniversary of Revolutionary Cuba," *Pravda*, 6 January 1960.

8. "The World Last Month, January 1960," *Izvestiia*, 31 January 1960.

9. *New York Times*, 31 January 1960.

10. Ibid., 1 February 1960.

11. Mikoian later revealed that the Cubans had invited him to visit Cuba when he was in Mexico (in December 1959) and that the Soviet government in the person of Khrushchev had granted him permission to do so. But he does not say when permission was granted. See Mikoian's toast in "Reception in the Embassy of the Republic of Cuba," *Pravda*, 15 November 1960.

12. "Alocución del PSP," *Hoy*, 1 January 1960.

13. Ignacio Reyes, "La Experiencia Guatemalteca y la revolución Cubana," *Hoy Domingo* [Sunday Magazine of *Hoy*], 3 January 1960, pp. 6–7.

14. Blas Roca, *Los Fundamentos del Socialismo en Cuba*, New ed., in *Hoy Domingo Edición Extraordinaria*, 3 January 1960, pp. 41, 52, 56.

15. "Nuestra opinión," *Hoy*, 27 January 1960.

16. Aníbal Escalante television interview of 9 January 1960, *Hoy*, 14 January 1960.

17. Aníbal Escalante, *Un año de Revolución*, a pamphlet issued by the Comisión de Educacion y Propaganda del Comité Municipal de la Habana del Partido Socialista Popular, 20 January 1960, pp. 12, 15, 17.

18. "Speech of A. I. Mikoian," *Pravda*, 7 February 1960.

19. "Nuestra opinión," *Hoy*, 7 January 1960.

20. Escalante television interview, *Hoy*, 14 January 1960.

21. "Nuestra opinión," *Hoy*, 27 January 1960.

22. *Hoy*, 5 February 1960.

23. "Entrevista al gobernante soviético realizada por Violeta Casal para Radio Rebelde," ibid., 10 February 1960.

24. Juan Marinello television interview, ibid., 12 February 1960.

25. *Pravda*, 15 February 1960.

26. Mikoian press conference, *Hoy*, 14 February 1960. The passages cited here and in the next few paragraphs do not appear in "A. I. Mikoian's Press Conference in Havana," *Pravda*, 16 February 1960.

27. *Hoy*, 14 February 1960. The awkwardness of the language may be due to a poor Spanish translation of Mikoian's remarks or may reflect the garbled syntax of a statesman under pressure at a press conference.

28. Castro television interview, *Hoy*, 20 February 1960; "El Convenio Cubano-Soviético," ibid., 19 February 1960.

29. *New York Times*, 18 February 1960; Reston column, ibid., 20 and 23 February and 1 March 1960.

30. "Summary of the Report of Blas Roca to the Plenum of the PSP," *Hoy*, 1 March 1960; Blas Roca, general secretary of the Popular Socialist Party of Cuba, "The Cuban People in the Struggle for Freedom and Independence," abbreviated text of a report to the Plenum of the National Committee of the People's Socialist Party of Cuba, 29 February–3 March 1960, *Kommunist*, 1960, no. 7, pp. 77–89.

31. "Report of Aníbal Escalante to the Plenum of the PSP, 29 February 1960," *Hoy*, 2 March 1960.

32. "Resolución del Pleno del Comité Nacional del PSP sobre la situacion actual, el desarrollo nacional y la defensa de la patria y la Revolución," ibid., 16 March 1960.

33. "Eisenhower Tells of Role in Cuba," press conference at Cincinnati, June 12,

1961, *New York Times,* 13 June 1961, gives March 17 as the date Eisenhower accepted the C.I.A. proposal to conduct a revolution to overthrow Castro. The plans at that time had been in the discussion stage for almost a year, according to C.I.A. Director for Plans Richard Bissell. See Hugh Thomas, *Cuba: The Pursuit of Freedom* (New York: Harper & Row, 1971), p. 1271.

34. "Resolución del Pleno del Comité Nacional del PSP . . . ," *Hoy,* 16 March 1960.

35. V. Borovskii, "In the Land of Miranda and Bolivar," *Pravda,* 14 March 1960.

36. V. Borovskii, "The Cuban People Won't Be Frightened," ibid., 24 April 1960.

37. B. Ponomarev, "For New Victories of the Forces of Peace and Socialism," ibid., 1 May 1960.

38. "Slogans of the CC of the CPSU of 1 May 1960," ibid., 10 April 1960.

39. Blas Roca, "El programa del Partido y la Revolución Cubana," *Hoy,* 13 March 1960.

40. *New York Times,* 19 March 1960.

41. Ibid., 24, 26, 27, and 29 March 1960.

42. Ibid., 9 April 1960, for Herter's press conference of 8 April 1960.

43. Ibid., 14, 15, 19, 20, and 21 April 1960.

44. "Comunicado Conjunto," *Hoy,* 8 May 1960; *Pravda,* 13 May 1960.

45. "The USSR and Cuba," *New Times,* 16 May 1961, p. 10.

46. Raúl Castro, *Las Fuerzas Armadas y Las Milicias en la Defensa de la Patria.* A 15 May radio-television presentation printed in *Universidad Popular Segundo Ciclo Defensa de Cuba* ([Havana], July 1960), p. 28.

47. "N. S. Khrushchev's Press Conference in Paris, 18 May 1960," *Pravda,* 19 May 1960.

48. *New York Times,* 19 May 1960.

49. Castro's speech to the Congress of Construction Workers, *Hoy,* 29 May 1960.

50. Carlos Rafael Rodríguez, "Lecciones en un discurso," *Hoy,* 2 June 1960.

51. Ernesto Guevara, "Political Sovereignty and Economic Independence," *MEIMO,* 1960, no. 6, pp. 59–67.

52. Juan Marinello, "Signification et portée de la révolution cubaine," *Democratie nouvelle* 14, no. 6 (1960): 67.

53. A. Kalinin, "Cuba: A Year of Liberation, a Year of Agrarian Reform," *MEIMO,* 1960, no. 7, pp. 58–69.

54. Ibid., p. 69.

55. "Current Problems of World Politics: International Review, January–June 1960," ibid., p. 28. The review six months earlier had nothing to say about Latin America.

56. *New York Times,* 3 July 1960.

57. "Nuestra opinión, la guerra económica y la respuesta cubana," *Hoy,* 6 July 1960.

58. "Nuestra opinión, Asi actúan los patriotas," ibid., 7 July 1960.

59. *Hoy,* 7 July 1960.

60. *Revolución,* 9 July 1960.

61. Aníbal Escalante, "Patria y antipatria," *Hoy,* 8 July 1960.

62. *Hoy,* 4 June 1960.

63. Ibid., 8 June 1960. As far as I know, the Soviet press did not carry this account of the interview.

64. *Revolución,* 16 July 1960.

65. "Cuba puede vender azúcar a otros mercados aparte del de los Estados Unidos," *Hoy,* 9 July 1960, reporting from Paris.

66. Manuel Díaz Martínez, "Entrevista con Nuñez Jiménez," *Hoy,* 16 July 1960. A fuller and slightly different account of the interview than in the 9 July issue.

67. *New York Times,* 7 July 1960.

68. Ibid., 9 July 1960.

69. V. Borovskii, "The Cuban People Will Not Yield," *Pravda,* 9 July 1960. The same text is to be found in *Hoy* and *Revolución* for 9 July 1960.

70. R. K. Karanjia and Ramesh Sanghvi, *Castro: Storm over Latin America* (Bombay: Perennial Press, 1961), p. 66. This account is more extensive than the newspaper accounts.

71. "Speech by Comrade N. S. Khrushchev to the All-Russian Teachers' Congress," *Pravda*, 10 July 1960.

72. *Hoy*, 10 July 1960.

73. Hedrick Smith, "The Intolerable Andrei Sakharov," *New York Times Magazine*, 4 November 1973.

74. *New York Times*, 10 July 1960.

75. Ibid., 13 July 1960, carries the TASS version of the Khrushchev press conference of 12 July.

76. "Discurso del Presidente Dorticós," *Hoy*, 12 July 1960. The text of the Soviet note was read by Dorticós in this speech, given 10 July.

77. "El mundo se vuelve contra EE.UU. dijo el Dr. Fidel Castro," *Hoy*, 12 July 1960.

78. *Hoy*, 10 July 1960.

79. Raúl Valdes Vivo, "La Union Soviética fiel a si Misma," ibid., 13 July 1960.

80. *Revolución*, 12 July 1960.

81. Ibid., 16 July 1960.

82. Ibid.

83. Editorial, "Una verdad que no podrá ser desvirtuada," *Hoy*, 19 July 1960. Emphasis supplied.

84. *Cronología II*, p. 47; text of Guevara's statement at the rally in front of the Presidential Palace 10 July 1960, *Hoy*, 12 July 1962.

85. Castro's 19 July television speech, *Hoy*, 20 July 1960.

86. "Far-reaching Optimism," *Izvestiia*, 12 July 1960.

87. "Sincere Thanks," ibid., 13 July 1960.

88. "Noose Destroyed," ibid., 15 July 1960.

89. V. Borovskii, "The Mightiest Power in the World is on Cuba's Side," *Pravda* 12 July 1960.

90. "There's No Going Back," ibid.

91. "N. S. Khrushchev's Press Conference for Soviet and Foreign Journalists," ibid., 13 July 1960.

92. V, Konstantinov, "Lay Down the Big Stick, Uncle Sam!" *Krasnaia zvezda*, 14 July 1960.

93. N. Chigir, *Krasnaia zvezda*, 15 July 1960. Neither *Pravda* nor *Isvestiia* carried this TASS report.

94. "The Latin American Nightmare of Washington," *Izvestiia*, 17 July 1960.

95. Nuñez Jiménez on television, *Hoy*, 17 July 1960, pp. 7, 8.

96. D. Dinichenko, "In Tribute to the Past," *Izvestiia*, 16 July 1960.

97. I. G. Lemus, "Raúl Castro," *World Student News* (Prague) 19, no. 9 (1960): 3.

98. "Television interview with Raúl Castro," *Hoy*, 6 August 1960.

99. "The Octopus of Monopoly will not Strangle Cuba!" Communiqué on the Meeting of the Chairman of the Council of Ministers of the USSR, N. S. Khrushchev, with the Minister of the Revolutionary Armed Forces of the Republic of Cuba, Raúl Castro (*Izvestiia*, 22 July 1960).

100. "Comunicado Conjunto de Cuba y la U.R.S.S.," *Revolución*, 21 July 1960.

101. "N. Khrushchev to His Excellency Mr. Fidel Castro Ruiz, Prime Minister of the Republic of Cuba, 25 July 1960," *Pravda*, 26 July 1960; "La causa de Cuba es la de A. Latina," *Hoy*, 28 July 1960.

102. "The U.S.A. is the Gendarme of Latin America," *Izvestiia*, 22 July 1960.

103. Prof. G. Tunkin, "A Myth [the Monroe Doctrine] Dispelled," *Pravda*, 24 July 1960.

104. "The Cuban Revolution Will Not Retreat," ibid., 30 July 1960.

105. "The Help of the USSR Assures the Future of Cuba," ibid., 31 July 1960.

106. "Nuestra opinión. El significado de la relaciones de Cuba y los países socialistas," *Hoy*, 30 July 1960.

107. *New York Times*, 8 August 1960.
108. Ibid., 10 August 1960.
109. *Hoy*, 5 August 1960; *Revolución*, 4 August 1960.
110. "Raúl Castro: The Aggressors Will Be Rebuffed," *Pravda*, 6 August 1960.
111. "Fidel Castro: The Cuban Revolution Will Live," ibid., 10 August 1960.
112. *New York Times*, 11 August 1960.
113. Ibid., 15 August 1960.
114. Ibid., 22 August 1960.
115. Ibid., 24 August 1960.
116. "Informe de Blas Roca ante la VIII Asamblea Nacional del Partido Socialista Popular," *Hoy*, 21 August 1960, Sunday Supplement, p. 13; "Defend and Develop the Cuban Revolution. The Report of Comrade Blas Roca to the VIIIth Congress of the People's Socialist Party of Cuba," *Pravda*, 19 August 1960.
117. "Informe de Blas Roca . . . ," p. 12.
118. Ibid., p. 13.
119. Ibid., pp. 16–17, 27.
120. Aníbal Escalante, "Report on the Party Program," *Hoy*, 19 August 1960.
121. "VIII Asamblea Nacional del Partido Socialista Popular. Conclusiones de Blas Roca sobre los puntos II, III, y IV del orden del dia," *Hoy*, 28 August 1960.
122. E.g., "Herter Outdoes Himself," *Izvestiia*, 26 August 1960; "A Forced Measure," *Pravda*, 27 August 1960; L. Kamynin, "The Sufferings of the Elderly Herter," *Izvestiia*, 28 August 1960; Vl. Zhukov and V. Levin, "International Review," *Pravda*, 29 August 1960; "Statement by the Minister of Foreign Affairs of the USSR, A. A. Gromyko, on the Address of the Secretary of State, C. Herter," ibid., 31 August 1960; "Cuba Has Emerged Victorious," ibid., 2 September 1960.
123. This account is drawn from Catherine Hoskyns, *The Congo since Independence, January 1960–December 1961* (London: Oxford University Press, 1965).
124. "La voz de Cuba" [Castro's speech], *Hoy*, 3 September 1960; *Revolución*, 3 September 1960.
125. "The Cuban People Give a Rebuff," *Pravda*, 8 September 1960.
126. *Revolución*, 19 September 1960.
127. "Statement by the Minister of Foreign Affairs of the USSR, A. A. Gromyko, on the address of Secretary of State C. Herter," *Pravda*, 31 August 1960.
128. "Speech by N. S. Khrushchev in the General Debate of the Fifteenth UN General Assembly," 23 September 1960, Supplement to *New Times*, no. 40 (September 1960), p. 6.
129. Maurice Halperin, *The Rise and Decline of Fidel Castro: An Essay in Contemporary History* (Berkeley and Los Angeles: University of California Press, 1972), p. 81.
130. Castro television appearance, *Hoy*, 16 October 1960; *Revolución*, 17 October 1960.
131. "Address of Fidel Castro," *Pravda*, 18 October 1960.
132. Moscow Home Service, 12 October 1960; *BBC Summary of World Broadcasts*, 13 October 1960; *Revolución*, 12 October 1960.
133. *New York Times*, 8, 21, and 22 October 1960.
134. Vl. Zhukov, "The Provocateurs are Playing with Fire," *Pravda*, 21 October 1960; a full translation appears in *Hoy*, 22 October 1960.
135. "Cuba Threatened by Invasion," *Izvestiia*, 23 October 1960.
136. *BBC Summary of World Broadcasts*, 29 October 1960; Anatolii Belobrov commentary on Moscow Home Service, 27 October; Erik Alekseev commentary on Moscow Home Service, 28 October 1960.
137. "Un comentario: Vigilancia y Unidad!" *Hoy*, 23 October 1960.
138. Valdés, "Entrevista de Jruschov con un grupo de periodistas cubanos," ibid., 23 October 1960.
139. V. Borovskii, "Cuba Will Not Go Down on Its Knees," *Pravda*, 23 October 1960; L. Kamynin, "Cuba Will Not Be Intimidated," *Izvestiia*, 23 October 1960; V. Maevskii, "International Review," *Pravda*, 24 October 1960; "Angry Protest, Firm Resolve," *Izvestiia*, 25 October 1960; Jacobo Arbenz, "Cuba's Example Is an Inspira-

tion," *Pravda*, 26 October 1960; "The Aggressors Are Playing with Fire," *Izvestiia*, 26 October 1960.

140. "Talk between N. S. Khrushchev and Cuban Journalists on 22 October 1960," *Pravda*, 30 October 1960; *Revolución*, 28 October 1960; "Text of N. S. Khrushchev's Interview with Cuban Journalists on 22 October 1960," Moscow, TASS, radioteletype in English to Europe, 29 October 1960, 14:02 GMT, *Daily Report, Foreign Radio Broadcasts, Foreign Broadcasts Information Service* (Washington, D.C.), 31 October 1960, pp. BB 1–6. The TASS translation is cited. My own translation is added in brackets when it is somewhat clearer or expresses a different shade of meaning.

141. *New York Times*, 29 October 1960.

142. "Miente y se engaña el imperialism yanqui," *Revolución*, 31 October 1960.

143. "Pese al 'N.Y. Times' los cohetes serían poco simbólicos," *Hoy*, 30 October 1960.

144. *Hoy*, 30 October 1960.

145. *BBC Summary of World Broadcasts*, 1 November 1960; Alexander Druzhinin commentary, Moscow Home Service, 30 October 1960.

146. L. Kamynin, "Guantánamo—the Staging Ground for Aggression," *Izvestiia*, 30 October 1960.

147. *New York Times*, 2 November 1960.

148. *Hoy*, 2 November 1960; *New York Times*, 3 November 1960.

149. "La Revolución no será puesta de rodillas," *Revolución*, 2 November 1960.

150. *Hoy*, 1 November 1960.

151. V. Borovskii, "Cuba: We Will Defend the Revolution," *Pravda*, 6 November 1960; ellipsis in original.

152. Blas Roca, "La URSS es el escudo de la soberanía de los pueblos frente al imperialismo," *Hoy*, 13 November 1960.

153. "No vinimos a Moscú a hablar de fútbol," *Revolución*, 8 November 1960.

154. Castro 8 November speech, *Revolución*, 9 November 1960; *Hoy*, 9 November 1960.

155. "The Revolution Goes Forward. An Address by F. Castro," *Pravda*, 12 November 1960.

156. "In an Atmosphere of Warm Friendship. Reception in the Embassy of the Republic of Cuba," *Izvestiia*, 16 November 1960.

157. "Expulsa la CTC a David Salvador por traición a la clase trabajadora," *Revolución*, 7 November 1960; *New York Times*, 8 November 1960; Fritz René Allemann, *Fidel Castro: Die Revolution der Bärte* (Hamburg: Rütten & Loening, 1961), p. 120.

158. "Si hay agresión los cohetes soviéticos no serán símbolos," *Revolución*, 7 November 1960.

159. Speech of José María de la Aguilera, *Hoy*, 8 November 1960.

160. Blas Roca, "Eighth National Congress of the Popular Socialist Party of Cuba," *World Marxist Review* 3, no. 11 (1960): 40.

161. *Revolución*, 8 November 1960.

162. "Un Comentario: El 'Times' engaña al pueblo americano," *Hoy*, 22 November 1960.

163. Ibid.

164. *Revolución*, 19 November 1960 (the story was filed from Moscow on 18 November 1960).

165. Ibid.

166. *New York Times*, 27 November 1960 (dateline Havana, 25 November 1960).

167. Allemann, *Fidel Castro*, p. 127.

168. Ibid.

169. "Report of the Minister of Foreign Affairs of the USSR, Deputy A. A. Gromyko, to the Sixth Session of the Supreme Soviet of the USSR," *Sovetskaia Rossiia*, 24 December 1960.

170. "Soviet-Cuban Communiqué," *Pravda*, 20 December 1960.

171. *Le Monde*, 21 December 1960.

172. This account is based on Arthur J. Dommen, *Conflict in Laos: The Politics of Neutralization*, rev. ed. (New York: Praeger Publishers, 1971); Paul F. Langer and

Joseph J. Zasloff, *North Vietnam and the Pathet Lao: Partners in the Struggle for Laos* (Cambridge: Harvard University Press, 1970); Charles A. Stevenson, *The End of Nowhere: American Policy toward Laos since 1954* (Boston: Beacon Press, 1972); Hugh Toye, *Laos: Buffer State or Battle Ground?* (New York: Oxford University Press, 1968).

173. "Cuba Is Fighting, Cuba Will Win," *Pravda,* 11 December 1960.

174. *Hoy,* 11 December 1960.

175. "Aggression by the Back Door," commentary by the diplomatic correspondent of *Izvestiia, Izvestiia,* 20 November 1960; L. Kamynin, "The Guns Advance," ibid.; V. Borovskii, "Storm Clouds over the Caribbean," *Pravda,* 19 November 1960; V. Borovskii, "Aggressors without Masks," ibid., 20 November 1960; V. Borovskii, I. Alfer'ev, F. Litoshko, and B. Strel'nikov, "The Provocateurs Betray Themselves," ibid., 21 November 1960.

176. "Aggressors without Masks," *Pravda* and *Krasnaia zvezda,* 1 December 1960.

177. Capt. V. Polianskii, "The Torch of Freedom Will Not Be Extinguished," *Krasnaia zvezda,* 3 December 1960. This article seems to have been based on Soviet or Cuban intelligence materials, since much of the detail had not appeared in the U.S. press.

178. Castro's New Year's Eve midnight speech, *Revolución,* 2 January 1961.

179. "For the Happiness and Prosperity of the People of Cuba. Speech of Comrade N. S. Khrushchev," *Pravda,* 3 January 1961.

180. Ibid.

181. Castro speech, *Revolución,* 3 January 1961. Apparently Castro made this demand for the reduction of the embassy staff on the spur of the moment. A member of the U.S. Embassy in Cuba told me that on hearing this demand, he called up the Foreign Office to learn whether the embassy was to be restricted to eleven persons in all or eleven State Department officials. The demand was news to the Foreign Office.

182. D. Goriunov and G. Osheverov, "The People Are on the *Qui Vive,*" *Izvestiia,* 5 January 1961.

183. "Who Thirsts for Storms in the Caribbean," ibid., 7 January 1961; Observer, "The Provocateurs Receive a Rebuff," *Pravda,* 6 January 1961.

184. "Guevara Reports on Trade Talks with Bloc," Foreign Broadcast Information Service, p. g8, 9 January 1961, speech of 7 January 1961.

185. Castro's speech of 13 January 1961, *Revolución,* 14 January 1961.

186. D. Kraminov, "International Review," *Pravda,* 10 January 1961.

187. Juan Marinello, "The Second Anniversary of the Cuban Revolution," *Kommunist,* 1961, no. 1, pp. 96–103; Aníbal Escalante, "Defend and Develop the Revolution Further," *Partiinaia zhizn'* [Party life], 1961, no. 1, pp. 64–69.

188. Marinello, "The Second Anniversary of the Cuban Revolution," p. 97.

189. Escalante, "Defend and Develop the Revolution Further," p. 64.

190. Marinello, "The Second Anniversary of the Cuban Revolution," pp. 97–98.

191. Escalante, "Defend and Develop the Revolution Further," p. 65.

192. Ibid., p. 67.

4. CUBA COMES TO SOCIALISM

1. Fidel Castro, "Las trincheras se llenaron de hombres pero seguió la producción," *Hoy,* 21 January 1961.

2. Che Guevara, "El peligro no ha pasado del todo," *Revolución,* 23 January 1961.

3. Ibid.

4. Blas Roca, "Lo que determina y condiciona la actual situación de Cuba, son los éxitos alcanzados por la Revolución. Informe de Blas Roca en el pleno del Comité Nacional del PSP el 25 de Enero de 1961," pp. 7–12. A pamphlet (Havana: Impr. Nacional de Cuba, n.d.) in the Library of Congress, call no. F1788.C233.

5. Ibid., p. 38.

6. Ibid., pp. 7–12.

7. Ibid., p. 38.

8. Arminio Savioli, "Intervista con Castro," *L'Unità,* 1 February 1961, is the most

complete text and citations are from it; "Successful Cooperation. Two Interviews with Fidel Castro," *Pravda*, 2 February 1961.

9. The Soviet version of the interview was not nearly as uncompromising on this point: ". . . The privileged circles can no longer participate in revolutions, much less lead them. The forces on whom the historical task of revolution is placed in Latin America are the industrial and agricultural proletariat, the peasants, the petite bourgeoisie, especially the intelligentsia. I don't deny that particular strata of the national bourgeoisie can support some revolutionary actions partially or for a particular period."

10. *Hoy* for 1 February 1961, the date on which the interview would have appeared, is missing from the Library of Congress microfilm holding of that newspaper and is unavailable anywhere else to my knowledge. But not even a single reference appears in the weeks that followed this important interview.

11. *Arminio Savioli*, "Intervista con Castro."

12. See Luigi Roberto Einaudi, *Marxism in Latin America: From Aprismo to Fidelismo* (Ph.D. diss., Harvard University, 1967), for a convincing demonstration that Castro's generation in Latin America had abandoned the hope of making changes with the United States and believed they had to be made against the United States.

13. Arminio Savioli, "Intervista con Castro," p. 28.

14. "Fidel dijo," *Revolución*, 13 February 1961.

15. "Entrevista con Fidel Castro," *Revolución*, 1 February 1961; see also "Successful Cooperation. Two Interviews with F. Castro," *Pravda*, 2 February 1961 for the Russian version of this and for Arminio Savioli's interview. The above citation is from the Spanish.

16. "Brasil y Mexico no actúan contra Cuba, declaró Fidel," *Revolución*, 16 February 1961.

17. *New York Times*, 25 February 1961.

18. Arminio Savioli, "Intervista con Castro."

19. "Entrevista con Fidel Castro," *Revolución*, 1 February 1961.

20. *Revolución*, 20 February 1961.

21. "An Appeal for Peace and Cooperation. Cuban Note to the Countries of Latin America," *Pravda*, 2 March 1961; "The Fire of the Ideal of Freedom Cannot Be Quenched," *Izvestiia*, 2 March 1961.

22. V. Stepanov, "Cuba Fights and Builds," *Pravda*, 3 March 1961.

23. "Anunció Fidel en el acto de La Coubre," *Revolución*, 6 March 1961.

24. *Revolución*, 2 March 1961; "The Schemes against Cuba Meet with a Rebuff," *Pravda*, 4 March 1961; "Intrigues Continue," *Krasnaia zvezda*, 11 March 1961; *Revolución*, 12 March 1961.

25. "Zona Rebelde," *Revolución*, 15 March 1961.

26. "Jugando a la guerra local puede el imperialismo hallar su destrucción," *Revolución*, 26 March 1961.

27. "The Flame of Revolutionary Struggle Burns," *Pravda*, 27 March 1961.

28. "Dijo Che en Santa Clara," *Revolución*, 29 March 1961; "Ernesto Guevara: We Are United as Never Before," *Pravda*, 31 March 1961.

29. "Anti-Cuban Concoction," *Pravda*, 6 April 1961; *Revolución*, 6 April 1961, quoting Joseph Newman in the *New York Herald Tribune*.

30. *New York Times*, 4 April 1961, p. 14.

31. Ibid., 7 April 1961.

32. "A Rebuff to the Provocateurs," *Pravda*, 7 April 1961.

33. "The Intrigues of the Counterrevolutionaries and Their Protectors," ibid., 10 April 1961.

34. Robert Taber, "Cuba será vencedora," *Revolución*, 14 April 1961.

35. Rodney Arismendi, "Latin America Comes to the Forefront," *Kommunist*, 1961, no. 5, pp. 69–86.

36. Ibid., p. 71.

37. Ibid., pp. 70–71.

38. Ibid.

39. Ibid., p. 78.

40. Contemporary Marxists use the term "stratum" (*sloi* in Russian) to describe a social grouping that does not fit into the traditional class categories.

41. Arismendi, "Latin America Comes to the Forefront," p. 84.

42. Ibid., p. 85.

43. Ibid., p. 72.

44. See above, p. 124.

45. "Viva nuestra revolución socialista: Texto del discurso de Fidel," *Revolución*, 17 April 1961.

46. "Foul Attack. Address of Fidel Castro," *Pravda*, 18 April 1961, and repeated in *Krasnaia zvezda* on 19 April (dateline Havana, 17 April).

47. "Stop Provocation against Cuba" is the heading under which the TASS story, dated New York, 16 April, appears (*Pravda*, 17 April 1961).

48. *New York Times*, 18 April 1961.

49. David Wise and Thomas B. Ross, *The Invisible Government* (New York: Random House, 1964), pp. 69–70.

50. "USSR Government Statement in Connection with Armed Invasion of Cuba," *Pravda* and *Izvestiia*, 19 April 1961; *Current Digest of the Soviet Press*, 17 May 1961, pp. 3, 4 (hereafter cited as *CDSP*).

51. *CDSP*, 17 May 1961, p. 5.

52. Ibid.

53. "President Kennedy's Statement to Premier Khrushchev," *New York Times*, 19 April 1961.

54. N. Karev, "Caught Red-Handed," *Izvestiia*, 20 April 1961 (dateline New York, 19 April).

55. "Nuestra opinión: La advertencia de la URSS," *Hoy*, 19 April 1961.

I know of no such statement by an America spokesman. Probably a dispatch from Moscow of 17 April, which appeared in the *New York Times* of 18 April, was meant. Seymour Topping, who has been described by *Hoy* in the past as an official apologist, said that Western experts in Moscow believed that the Soviet reaction would be confined to strong diplomatic representations, that Khrushchev had backed off somewhat from his implied threat of rocket intervention of 22 October, and that Soviet conventional military intervention in Cuba would face severe logistical constraints.

56. Ibid.

57. " 'Powerful Support," Statement by the Cuban Ambassador, Faure Chomón," *Pravda*, 19 April 1961; "Elogia Chomón la gran ayuda de la URSS," *Hoy*, 19 April 1961.

58. "Un Comentario: Cuba defiende su Revolución Socialista," *Hoy*, 28 April 1961.

59. Ibid., 25 April 1961; *Pravda*, 25 April 1961.

60. "Message [April 22] from N. S. Khrushchev, Chairman of the USSR Council of Ministers, to U.S. President J. Kennedy," *Pravda* and *Izvestiia*, 23 April 1961; *CDSP*, 17 May 1961, pp. 7–9.

61. "The Aggressors Have Not Left Off," *Pravda*, 26 April 1961; Observer, "The White House and the Buzzard of American Imperialism," ibid., 28 April 1961; Observer, "On a Dangerous Line," ibid., 30 April 1961.

62. *New York Times*, 27 April 1961.

63. "Premier Chou En-Lai's Message of Support to Premier Fidel Castro," New China News Agency, in English, 19 April 1961, *Survey of the China Mainland Press*, 27 April 1961.

64. New China News Agency broadcast, 19 April 1961, of Jen-min Jih-Pao editorial the same day, *Survey of the China Mainland Press*, 23 April 1961.

65. "The People Will Win" (dateline Peking, 21 April), *Pravda*, 26 April 1961.

66. Roger Hilsman, *To Move a Nation: The Politics of Foreign Policy in the Administration of John F. Kennedy* (New York: Doubleday & Co., 1967), p. 130.

67. Theodore C. Sorensen, *Kennedy* (New York: Bantam Books, 1966), p. 726.

68. B. Ponomarev, "On the National Democratic State," *Kommunist*, 1961, no. 8, pp. 33–48.

69. Ibid., p. 40.

70. Ibid., p. 45.

71. Ibid., p. 47.
72. "Great Victories in the Cause of Peace. A Speech by Fidel Castro," *Pravda*, 28 July 1961.
73. *Hoy*, 2 May 1961.
74. "Speech by Comrade N. S. Khrushchev at Erevan, 6 May 1961," *CDSP*, 31 May 1961, p. 7.
75. Aníbal Escalante, "El Desarrollo de la Revolución y el Papel de las Fuerzas Revolucionarias," *Hoy*, 9 May 1961.
76. Che Guevara, "Le podemos decir: Aquí está nuestra revolución," *Hoy*, 10 May 1961; speech delivered 8 May 1961.
77. "Cuba Called Base for Latin Revolt," *New York Times*, 15 Jun 1961.
78. *New York Times*, 4 July 1961.
79. "In Honor of the Cuban National Holiday," *Pravda*, 27 July 1961.
80. "Latins Press U.S. for Cuba Accord," *New York Times*, 15 August 1961.
81. "Dillon Rules out U.S. Aid to Cuba," ibid., 18 August 1961.
82. Richard N. Goodwin, "Annals of Politics: A Footnote," *New Yorker*, 25 May 1968, pp. 93–114.
83. Ibid., p. 104.
84. Ibid., p. 110.
85. "Comunicado de la Conferencia de los Partidos Comunistas y Obreros de Guatemala, El Salvador, Honduras, Nicaragua y Costa Rica," *Hoy*, 24 August 1961.
86. "For a Better Future for the People of Central America," *Pravda*, 26 August 1961.
87. Thomas E. Skidmore, *Politics in Brazil, 1930–1964: An Experiment in Democracy* (New York: Oxford University Press, 1967), p. 199. The subsequent account is drawn from this excellent study.
88. Ibid., p. 213.
89. "Events in Brazil," *Pravda*, 28 August 1961; V. Tkachenko, "Familiar Methods of American Gendarmes," *Izvestiia*, 30 August 1961; V. Levin, "The Situation in Brazil," *Pravda*, 30 August 1961; "The Situation in Brazil," ibid., 4 September 1961; V. Levin, "The Worries and Hopes of Brazil," ibid., 7 September 1961; "Brazil Will Conduct an Independent Course," ibid., 13 September 1961.
90. "Victory of the Brazilian People," *Pravda*, 17 September 1961.
91. "Regime of Cubans at Miami Barred," *New York Times*, 8 October 1961.
92. "U.S. Consulting Latins on Castro," ibid., 12 October 1961.
93. "Cuba Accuses U.S. of Invasion Plot," ibid., 10 October 1961; "Cuba Tells UN U.S. Still Plots," ibid., 11 October 1961.
94. "Replies of N. S. Khrushchev to the Questions of *New York Times* Columnist Cyrus Sulzberger," *Pravda*, 10 September 1961.
95. "Declaraciónes de Jruschov," *Hoy*, 10 September 1961, omits these statements from its account of the interview and *Revolución* seems to have ignored the interview altogether.
96. "Heartfelt Greeting to the Delegates of Heroic Cuba," and "Speech of L. I. Brezhnev at the Kremlin," both in *Pravda*, 12 September 1961.
97. "Speech of O. Dorticós," ibid., 21 September 1961.
98. "Joint Soviet-Cuban Communiqué," *Izvestiia*, 22 September 1961.
99. V. Korionov, "The Greatest Contemporary Force," *Kommunist*, 1961, no. 14, p. 44.
100. Blas Roca, "How the Unity of the Revolutionary Forces of Cuba Was Created," *Politicheskoe samoobrazovanie* [Political self-education] 5, no. 12 (1961): 55–60.
101. Ibid., p. 59.
102. Ibid., p. 60.
103. Ibid., p. 58.
104. See above, p. 144.
105. "Comparecencia de Fidel en la 'Universidad Popular,' 1 December 1961," *Hoy*, 2 December 1961.

106. The late Ambassador Llewellyn Thompson, serving in Moscow at this time, recalled in conversation that top Soviet leaders told him more than once that Castro made them feel young again.

107. Tad Szulc, "Castro's Embrace of Marxism Embarrassing Red Onlookers," *New York Times*, 8 December 1961.

108. "The Cuban People Confidently Build a New Life. Fidel Castro's Speech," *Pravda*, 5 December 1961.

109. A. I. Kalinin, "The Working Class and the Cuban Revolution," in *Rabochee dvizheniie v kapitalisticheskikh stranakh (1959–1961)* [The workers' movement in capitalist countries, 1959–1961] (Moscow: Gosudarstvennoe Izdatel'stvo Politicheskoi Literatury, 1961), p. 218.

110. M. Danilevich, *Rabochii klass v osvoboditel'nom dvizhenii narodov Latinskoi Ameriki* [The working class in the liberationist movement of the people of Latin America] (Moscow: Gosudarstvennoe Izdatel'stvo Politicheskoi Literatury, 1962), p. 348. The manuscript was in galleys 19 April 1962.

5. KHRUSHCHEV BRINGS MISSILES TO CUBA

1. Arnold L. Horelick and Myron Rush, *Strategic Power and Soviet Foreign Policy* (Chicago: University of Chicago Press, 1966), is the indispensable guide to the subject of the nuclear balance and its political employment in the sixties.

2. I have eschewed jargon like "assured destruction" and have chosen to talk of "millions of corpses" in the belief that the political leaders thought in terms of the latter rather than the former.

3. Robert F. Kennedy, *Thirteen Days: A Memoir of the Cuban Missile Crisis* (New York: W. W. Norton, 1969), p. 67.

4. N. Khrushchev and L. Brezhnev, "To Doctor Fidel Castro Ruiz, Doctor Osvaldo Dorticós Torrado, 31 December 1961," *Pravda*, 1 January 1962.

5. "Glorious Anniversary of the Cuban Revolution," *Pravda*, 3 January 1962.

6. S. Gonionskii, "The Style of Washington's Diplomacy," *Mezhdunarodnaia zhizn'* [International affairs], 1962, no. 1, p. 90.

7. Juan Arcocha, "Cuba: Three Years of Revolution," *Mezhdunarodnaia zhizn'* [International affairs], 1962, no. 1, pp. 88–91.

8. V. Gavrilin, "The Beacon of Freedom," *Krasnaia zvezda*, 25 January 1962.

9. "Hands Off Free Cuba. A statement of the Presidium of the Soviet Committee for Solidarity with the Countries of Asia and Africa," *Pravda*, 10 January 1962.

10. "Charla de Fidel con Periodistas de la OIP," *Hoy*, 18 January 1962; "F. Castro: Socialism Will Triumph," *Pravda*, 20 January 1962.

11. N. Inozemtsev, "Peaceful Coexistence—the Most Important Contemporary Question," *Pravda*, 17 January 1962.

12. V. Borovskii, "Cuba Is Able to Stand Up for Herself," ibid., 24 January 1962.

13. Salvador Marini, "The Conspiracy against Cuba," *Za rubezhom* [Abroad], 20 January 1962, pp. 4, 5.

14. *New York Times*, 24 January 1962.

15. Ibid., 26 January 1962.

16. V. Levin, "Maneuvers Behind the Scenes at Punta del Este," *Pravda*, 17 January 1962.

17. "Telegram from the Soviet Committee for the Defense of Peace to the Participants in the Conference of the Peoples of America in Havana," ibid., 27 January 1962.

18. "Interview of Fidel Castro with the Newspapers *Pravda* and *Izvestiia*," *Izvestiia*, 30 January 1962; "Entrevista de Fidel a Directores de 'Pravda' e 'Izvestia,'" *Hoy*, 30 January 1962.

19. Ibid.

20. N. Shishlin, "International Review. The Plans of the Enemies of Peace Are Doomed to Failure," *Kommunist*, 1962, no. 3, p. 114.

21. Observer, "The Prisoner of Worn Out Dogmas. On the Speech of the U.S. Secretary of State, Dean Rusk, at Punta del Este," *Pravda*, 2 February 1962.

22. V. Borovskii, "The Lessons of Punta del Este," ibid., 3 February 1962.

23. *2a Asamblea General del Pueblo de Cuba Declaración de la Habana*, pp. 28–29; pamphlet published in Havana, 4 February.

24. Ibid., p. 29.

25. Ibid., p. 30.

26. Ibid., pp. 7, 8.

27. V. Borovskii, "The Voice of Revolutionary Cuba," *Pravda*, 5 February 1962; N. S. Khrushchev, "Letter to the Second General National Assembly of the People of Cuba and to the Prime Minister of the Republic of Cuba, Dr. Fidel Castro, 3 February 1962," *Pravda*, 5 February 1962; Editorial, "Cuba's Cause Will Triumph," ibid., 6 February 1962; "A Report from Revolution Square," *Izvestiia*, 6 February 1962; V. Borovskii, "The Defense of Cuba is Our First Obligation," *Pravda*, 8 February 1962.

28. "Comenta 'Pravda' Ultimos acontecimientos mundiales," *Hoy*, 6 February 1962.

29. K. Tarasaov, "The Havana Declaration: A Summons to the Struggle against Imperialism," *Kommunist*, 1962, no. 4, pp. 80–89.

30. Ibid., p. 87.

31. Ibid., p. 88.

32. Ibid., p. 89.

33. Capt. V. Pustov and Lt. Col. A. Leont'ev, "New Intrigues of Cuba's Enemies," *Krasnaia zvezda*, 9 February 1962.

34. "Discurso de Valerian Zorin en las Naciones Unidas," *Hoy*, 9 February 1962; "Put an End to American Interference in Cuban Affairs," *Pravda*, 16 February 1962.

35. "Conversation with Fidel Castro," *Oui*, January 1975, p. 158.

36. "Statement of the Soviet Government," *Pravda*, 19 February 1962.

37. Editorial, "All the Peace-loving Peoples of the World Are on Cuba's Side," *Pravda*, 20 February 1962; V. Borovskii, "The Soviet Union is with us, say the Cubans," ibid.; B. Strel'nikov, "A Serious Warning," ibid.

38. "Statement of the Cuban Revolutionary Government" (signed by Castro), *Pravda*, 26 February 1962.

39. "Informe textual de Fidel Castro sobre las ORI," *Hoy*, 27 March 1962.

40. Ibid.

41. "We Will Not Make One Step Backwards, Only Forward. Fidel Castro's Speech," *Pravda*, 29 March 1962; "F. Castro: Only Forward," *Krasnaia zvezda*, 29 March 1962.

42. "The Unity of Forces of the Cuban Revolution," *Pravda*, 11 April 1962.

43. Italics supplied. This is the first time, to my knowledge, that Castro is called "Comrade" in the Soviet press.

44. Vitaly Levin, "Tension in the Caribbean," *New Times*, 4 April 1962, pp. 13–15.

45. Tancredo Mondragon, "Madness in Punta del Este" *Mezhdunarodnaia zhizn'* [International affairs], 1962, no. 5, p. 29.

46. "Cuban Exiles Fear U.S. Shifts Views," *New York Times*, 29 April 1962.

47. "Goulart: Brazil Pursues an Independent Policy," *Pravda*, 6 April 1962.

48. "Message from N. S. Khrushchev to Comrade Fidel Castro, Prime Minister of the Republic of Cuba," ibid., 19 April 1962.

49. "Cuba Has Worked Well for the Cause of Freedom," ibid.

50. Blas Roca, Member of the Secretariat of the National Leadership of the Integrated Revolutionary Organizations of Cuba, "The Significance of the Construction of a Marxist-Leninist Party in Cuba," ibid., 13 June 1962.

51. "Display of Force Staged in Cuba in Reply to Food Demonstration," *New York Times*, 17 June 1962; "The People of Cuba Rebuff the Intrigues of the Enemies of the Revolution," *Pravda*, 18 June 1962.

52. Castro said later that the decision was taken at "the beginning of 1962." See "Conversation with Fidel Castro," *Oui*, January 1975, p. 158.

53. T. Timofeev, "The Working Class is the Leading Force of the Revolutionary Transformation of the World," *Pravda*, 20 June 1962.

54. "Palabras de Blas Roca en el XVIII Congreso del PCU," *Hoy*, 3 July 1962.

55. Ibid.
56. "Califica Raúl Castro como vital la ayuda de la URSS," *Hoy*, 6 July 1962.
57. V. Gavrilin, "Friends Are Coming Closer Together," *Krasnaia zvezda*, 26 July 1962.
58. "The Peoples of the USSR and Cuba Are Forever Together," *Pravda*, 27 July 1962.
59. "Fidel en el noveno aniversario del 26–27," *Hoy*, 27 July 1962.
60. C. L. Sulzberger, *An Age of Mediocrity: Memoirs and Diaries, 1963–1972* (New York: Macmillan Co., 1972), pp. 128–29.
61. "Conversation with Fidel Castro," *Oui*, January 1975, p. 158.
62. V. Borovskii, "Cuba Will Not Retreat," *Pravda*, 28 July 1962.
63. Joseph North, "The U.S.A. 'Discovers' Latin America," ibid., 1 August 1962.
64. L. Kamynin, "The Celebration Is Called Off; Slavery Remains," *Izvestiia*, 3 August 1962.
65. V. Levin, "The 'Big Stick' Once More," *Pravda*, 10 August 1962.
66. V. Levin, "To a Funereal Knell," ibid., 22 August 1962.
67. "Fifteen Soviet Vessels Carry Aid to Cuba," *New York Times*, 21 August 1962.
68. "Russians Step Up Flow of Arms Aid to Castro Regime," ibid., 25 August 1962.
69. "Havana Suburb Is Shelled in Sea Raid by Exile Group," ibid., 26 August 1962.
70. V. Levin, "The Trail Leads to Washington," *Pravda*, 27 August 1962.
71. S. Vishnevskii, "The Pirates Go on a Rampage in Florida," ibid., 28 August 1962.
72. S. Kondrashov, "The Pirates Again," *Izvestiia*, 28 August 1962.
73. Iu. Dymov, "Hands Off Cuba," *Krasnaia zvezda*, 28 August 1962.
74. "Advierte Radio Moscú a los imperialistas norteamericanos: NO TOCAR A CUBA!" *Hoy*, 28 August 1962.
75. "Denuncia Radio Moscú plan de Washington para utilizar a la OEA en un ataque a Cuba," ibid., 29 August 1962.
76. "The Defeat of the Aggressors Is Inevitable. An article in *Noticias de Hoy*," *Pravda*, 30 August 1962.
77. "Transcript of the President's News Conference on Domestic and Foreign Matters," *New York Times*, 30 August 1962.
78. Speech by Blas Roca at the beginning of the term in the people's schools of Havana, 1 September 1962. Radio Broadcast. Typescript of monitoring is in my possession.
79. "Fraternal Aid to Revolutionary Cuba, on the Visit to the USSR of the Delegation of the National Leadership of the Integrated Revolutionary Organization of Cuba," *Pravda*, 3 September 1962.
80. Elie Abel, *The Missile Crisis* (New York: Bantam Books, 1966), p. 8. Robert Kennedy's own account has Dobrynin categorically stating that no ground-to-ground missiles would be placed in Cuba (Kennedy, *Thirteen Days*, p. 25).
81. *New York Times*, 5 September 1962.

6. KHRUSHCHEV TAKES THE MISSILES AWAY FROM CUBA

1. Roscoe Drummond and Gaston Coblentz, *Duel at the Brink* (Garden City, N.Y.: Doubleday & Co., 1960), p. 69.
2. Theodore C. Sorensen, *Kennedy* (New York: Bantam Books, 1966), p. 752. Ellipses in original.
3. Ibid., p. 753.
4. "Statement by President Kennedy," *Pravda*, 6 September 1962.
5. "Los que planean nueva agresión deben saber: Cuba está alerta!" *Hoy*, 8 September 1962.
6. "The U.S. Is Fanning an Anti-Cuban Campaign," *Pravda*, 7 September 1962.
7. S. Vishnievskii, "Anti-Cuban Hysteria Is Rampant in the U.S.A.," ibid., 8 September 1962.

8. "Para el miedo estan cerrados las fronteras de Cuba!" *Revolución,* 8 September 1962.

9. Iu. Barsukov, "The Maniacs Rave," *Izvestiia,* 9 September 1962.

10. "Fidel en la Clausura del III Congreso de educación," *Hoy,* 11 September 1962.

11. "TASS Statement of 11 September 1962," *Pravda,* 12 September 1962.

12. Remarks made in Maritsa, Bulgaria, as quoted in Horelick and Rush, *Strategic Power and Soviet Foreign Policy,* p. 106.

13. "TASS Statement of 11 September 1962," *Pravda,* 12 September 1962.

14. Ibid.

15. V. Gavrilin, *Soldaty ostrova svobody* [Soldiers of the island of freedom] (Moscow: Voennoe izdatel'stvo, 1962), pp. 78, 79; in galleys 18 August 1962.

16. "A Serious Warning—Foreign Responses to the TASS Statement," *Pravda,* 12 September 1962.

17. "A Warning to the Aggressors," ibid., 13 September 1962.

18. "La advertencia soviética mantendrá a los imperialistas insomnes varios dias: Raúl," *Hoy,* 13 September 1962.

19. "Heartfelt Thanks," *Pravda,* 13 September 1962.

20. "The Peoples of the World Condemn the Aggressive Designs of the U.S.A. against Cuba," ibid.

21. N. Karev, "Confound the Schemes of the Aggressors! An Unholy Uproar in the Capitol," *Izvestiia,* 13 September 1962.

22. "The Aggressor Will Come a Cropper," *Krasnaia zvezda,* 13 September 1962.

23. "Cuba is Ready to Give a Rebuff," ibid.

24. S. Vishnevskii, "Hot War Hysteria," *Pravda,* 14 September 1962.

25. "Firmness and Love of Peace," ibid.

26. "Be on the Alert," ibid. Havana dispatch of 13 September.

27. TASS correspondents M. Buzivskii and A. Ivannikov, "Fatherland or Death. We Will Win," *Krasnaia zevzda,* 14 September 1962; by the same authors, "Concern for the Fate of Mankind," *Pravda,* 14 September 1962. The texts are almost identical.

28. "The Soviet Committee for the Defense of Peace to the Cuban National Committee of the Movement in Defense of Peace and the Sovereignty of Peoples," *Pravda,* 15 September 1962.

29. T. Gaidar, "The Firm Tread of the Patriots of Cuba," ibid.

30. Ibid. Italics supplied.

31. Statement by President Kennedy on Cuba, 13 September 1962, in David L. Larson, *The 'Cuban Crisis' of 1962: Selected Documents and Chronology* (Boston: Houghton Mifflin, 1963), pp. 16, 17.

32. "Kennedy's Statement," *Izvestiia,* 15 September 1962.

33. S. Vishnevskii, "Common Sense and Recklessness," *Pravda,* 15 September 1962.

34. "The Ships Are Not Changing Course, Says the Minister of the Merchant Marine of the USSR, V. G. Bakaev," *Krasnaia zvezda,* 15 September 1962.

35. "Hornets' Nests of Aggression," ibid., 16 September 1962.

36. " 'Let Us Not Deceive Ourselves': Lippmann on the Provocative Plans of the U.S.A. against Cuba," *Izvestiia,* 20 September 1962.

37. Walter Lippmann, "Cuba: Watchful Waiting," *New York Herald-Tribune,* 17 September 1962.

38. *New York Times,* 22 September 1962.

39. N. Drachinskii and S. Kondrashov, "The Encouragement of Piracy," *Izvestiia,* 25 September 1962.

40. Fidel Castro, "La Unión Soviética es un gran ejemplo del desarrollo que puede alcanzar la industria pesquera en pocos años," *Hoy,* 26 September 1962.

41. "Instead of Fish, an Apparition of Bombs. The American Hullabaloo about the Soviet-Cuban Convention," *Izvestiia,* 28 September 1962.

42. "Discurso de Fidel en II Aniversario de los CDR," *Hoy,* 29 September 1962.

43. "We Are with You, Cuba: A Review of Letters," *Krasnaia zvezda,* 29 September 1962.

44. "Declaración del Consejo de Ministros sobre la Resolución yanqui," *Hoy,* 30

September 1962; "The Cuban People Will Not Break," *Pravda*, 2 October 1962; "Cuba Is Ready To Repel the Aggressors," *Izvestiia*, 2 October 1962; "The Cuban People Will Not Break," *Krasnaia zvezda*, 2 October 1962.

45. "Cuba Is at Her Battle Post," *Pravda*, 8 October 1962.

46. "Cuba Fights for Peace, Freedom, and Independence against Aggression. The Speech of Osvaldo Dorticós at the Session of the UN General Assembly, 8 October 1962," ibid., 11 October 1962.

47. "Discurso de Fidel en el Recibimiento a Dorticós," *Hoy*, 10 October 1962.

48. "Cuba Is Together with Those Who Defend Peace and Freedom," *Pravda*, 12 October 1962, TASS dispatch, dateline Havana, 11 October 1962.

49. "Cuba Will Not Be Deflected from the Path She Has Chosen," *Izvestiia*, 13 October 1962. The *Izvestiia* account is described as filed by its special correspondent from Havana on 12 October. Both accounts use precisely the same Russian equivalents to render verbatim passages from the speech. Normally, two translators would not achieve such identity of diction. Hence we can conclude that both stories were composed from the same Russian text.

50. "Khrushchev Offers a Deal on Cuba and Berlin Crises," *New York Times*, 15 October 1962.

51. "Castro Adopts a Cautious Policy," ibid.

52. N. Polianov, "The Anatomy of a Forged Document," *Izvestiia*, 18 October 1962.

53. M. Baturin, "A Caribbean NATO," ibid., 21 October 1962.

54. Moscow TASS, in Russian, to Europe, 10:52 GMT, 22 October 1962, *Foreign Broadcast Information Service, USSR* (Washington, D.C.), 22 October 1962, BB1.

55. "Order de alarme del combate," *Hoy*, 23 October 1962.

56. "Comparecencia del doctor Fidel Castro . . . ," ibid., 24 October 1962.

57. Moscow Domestic Service, in Russian, 19:30 GMT, 23 October 1962, *Foreign Broadcast Information Service, USSR*, 24 October 1962, pp. BB18–25.

58. Robert F. Kennedy, *Thirteen Days: A Memoir of the Cuban Missile Crisis* (New York: W. W. Norton, 1969), p. 66.

59. Ibid., p. 58. Robert Kennedy does not give the date of Khrushchev's letter but says it was received on 23 October.

60. "N. S. Khrushchev's Answer to Bertrand Russell," *Pravda*, 25 October 1962. The letter was dated 24 October.

61. This account represents a departure from the practice I have followed throughout, i.e., to avoid citing information that cannot be documented. It was supplied by a French source.

62. Elie Abel, *The Missile Crisis* (New York: Bantam Books, 1966), pp. 135–36.

63. Graham T. Allison, *Essence of Decision: Explaining the Cuban Missile Crisis* (Boston: Little Brown & Co., 1971), p. 138.

64. S. S. Smirnov, "Cuba—Yes; War—No," *Literaturnaia gazeta* [The literary gazette], 25 October 1962.

65. See Roman Kolkowicz, *Conflicts in Soviet Party–Military Relations, 1962–1963*, RAND Corporation Memorandum RM 3760 (Santa Monica, Calif., August 1963), pp. 10–15, for the earliest treatment of Soviet internal differences on the missile crisis.

66. Observer, "Cuba Is Not Alone," *Krasnaia zvezda*, 26 October 1962.

67. Editorial, "Reason Must Triumph!" *Pravda*, 26 October 1962.

68. The full text of Khrushchev's letter to Kennedy has not been published. Graham T. Allison, *Essence of Decision*, pp. 221–22, has compiled what is available in the public record. All the matter in the text is from his compilation, with original excerpts in quotation marks.

69. "Cuba Is Not Alone," *Krasnaia zvezda*, 26 October 1962.

 **INDEX**

Dillon, Douglas, 96, 138, 217
Directorio Revolucionario, 128, 142
Dirksen, Senator Everett, 205
Dobrynin, Anatoly, 181, 193, 219
Dominican Republic, 41, 43, 48, 74; suspected Cuban invasion of, 47
Dorticós, Osvaldo, 81, 89, 91, 104–5, 141–42, 161; speech of, 194; speech of, at U.N., 210–11
Draper, Theodore, 35
Dubcek, Alexander, 48
Dudman, Richard, 114
Dulles, John Foster, 1, 8, 9, 12–13, 15–17, 20, 58, 188, 198
Duvalier, François, 26

Eastern Europe, 62
East Germany, 59, 77, 84
Ecuador, 165
Egypt, 12, 57–58, 109–10, 197
Eisenhower, Dwight D.: on communist regimes in Latin America, 10; on intervention in Indochina, 8–9, 20; on Guatemalan crisis, 17; on Castro's conversion to communism, 47, 57, 64; on missile gap, 56; and Camp David summit, 60; and U–2 fiasco, 76–77; reduces sugar quota, 79; response of, to Khrushchev's 9 July 1960 missile statement, 85–86, 95–96; on Guantánamo base, 104
El Mundo, 47
El Salvador, 7
Ermakov (Pravda commentator), 164
Escalante, Aníbal: and rivalry with Roca and Rodríguez, 29, 35–36, 49; on radicalization of Castro, 43, 65; trip to China of, 52–54, 66–67; and PSP plenum (March 1960), 71–73; on reduction of U.S. sugar quota, 80; at Eighth Party Congress of PSP, 96–97; assessment of Cuban revolution by, 116–17; dismissal of, 169–70, 172–73
Escambray, 125

Falangism, 4, 122
Florida, 64
Force Publique, 98–99
Formosa Straits crisis. See Taiwan Straits crisis
Forrestal, Secretary James, 212, 214
Fortuny, José Manuel, 5, 19

France: in Indochina, 8, 9, 56; invasion of Egypt (1956) by, 57–58, 84, 197; in Algeria, 225
Franco, Francisco, 19
Frankel, Max, 108–9, 212–14, 219
Franqui, Carlos, 103–5
French communists, on Cuban revolution, 39
Frondizi, Arturo, 94
Fundamentos, 35

Geneva agreement of 1954, 111–12, 135
German peace treaty, 202
Germany, 2, 5, 59, 60, 151, 154, 157, 229. See also West Germany
Goldenberg, Boris, 31
Golden bridge strategy, 188–91, 228
Goodwin, Richard N., 138–39, 141
Goulart, João, 140, 171
Granma (ship), 45
Great Britain: sales of aircraft to Cuba by, 50; invasion of Egypt (1956) by, 57–58, 84, 197; rivalry of, with Germany, 157; in missile crisis, 223
Gromyko, Andrei, 100–101, 110, 135, 208, 211–15
Gruson, Sydney, 15
Guantánamo, 104–5, 167
Guatemala: revolution of 1944–45 in, 3–4; as base for U.S. invasion of Cuba, 114, 126
Guatemalan agrarian reform, 4, 5, 11
Guatemalan Army, 15, 16, 18, 49
Guatemalan communists, 9, 18, 19, 24
Guatemalan Labor Party (PGT), 5, 9, 15
Guatemalan land reform, 4, 5, 11
Guevara, Ernesto "Che": on Cuban revolution, 38–39; on industrialization, 79; on Khrushchev's 9 July 1960 missile statement, 89; on San José Conference, 100; visit to Moscow of, 105, 109–10; and interview with M. Tatu, 110; on possible U.S. invasion, 113–14; on break in relations with United States, 115–16; conversation of, with R. Goodwin, 138–39, 141; and Soviet-Cuban military communiqué, 181
Guinea, 223
Gutiérrez, Victor Manuel, 5

Haiti, 41
Hamilton, Thomas J., 211–13

Library of Congress Cataloging in Publication Data
Dinerstein, Herbert Samuel, 1919–
    The making of a missile crisis.
    Includes index.
    1. Cuban Missile Crisis, Oct. 1962.   2. Russia—Foreign relations—Cuba.   3. Cuba—Foreign relations—Russia.   I. Title.
    E841.D45   972.91'064   75–36943
    ISBN 0–8018–1788–9 (hardcover)
    ISBN 0–8018–2146–0 (paperback)